KT-568-446

INSIGHT ⊙ GUIDES

ESTONIA, LATVIA & LITHUANIA

C800651225

◉ Walking Eye App

YOUR FREE DESTINATION CONTENT AND EBOOK AVAILABLE THROUGH THE WALKING EYE APP

Your guide now includes a free eBook and destination content for your chosen destination, all for the same great price as before. Simply download the Walking Eye App from the App Store or Google Play to access your free eBook and destination content.

HOW THE WALKING EYE APP WORKS

Through the Walking Eye App, you can purchase a range of eBooks and destination content. However, when you buy this book, you can download the corresponding eBook and destination content for free. Just see below in the grey panels where to find your free content and then scan the QR code at the bottom of this page.

Destinations: Download your corresponding essential destination content from here, featuring recommended sights and attractions, restaurants, hotels and an A–Z of practical information, all for free. Other destinations are available for purchase.

Ships: Interested in ship reviews? Find independent reviews of river and ocean ships in this section, all available for purchase.

eBooks: You can download your free accompanying digital version of this guide here. You will also find a whole range of other eBooks, all available for purchase.

Free access to travel-related blog articles about different destinations, updated on a daily basis.

HOW THE DESTINATION CONTENT WORKS

Each destination includes a short introduction, an A–Z of practical information and recommended points of interest, split into 4 different categories:
- Highlights
- Accommodation
- Eating out
- What to do

You can view the location of every point of interest and save it by adding it to your Favourites. In the 'Around Me' section you can view all the points of interest within 5km.

HOW THE EBOOKS WORK

The eBooks are provided in EPUB file format. Please note that you will need an eBook reader installed on your device to open the file. Many devices come with this as standard, but you may still need to install one manually from Google Play.

The eBook content is identical to the content in the printed guide.

HOW TO DOWNLOAD THE WALKING EYE APP

1. Download the Walking Eye App from the App Store or Google Play.
2. Open the app and select the scanning function from the main menu.
3. Scan the QR code on this page – you will then be asked a security question to verify ownership of the book.
4. Once this has been verified, you will see your eBook and destination content in the purchased ebook and destination sections, where you will be able to download them.

Other destination apps and eBooks are available for purchase separately or are free with the purchase of the Insight Guide book.

CONTENTS

Travel tips

TRANSPORT

A-Z

LANGUAGE

FURTHER READING

Maps

LEGEND

Insight on
Photo story

THE BEST OF ESTONIA, LATVIA & LITHUANIA: TOP ATTRACTIONS

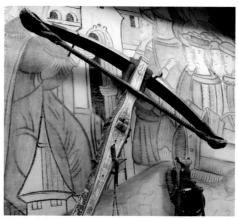

△ **Tallinn Old Town**. This is as pretty as Old Towns get, with cobbled streets, a harmonious square and attractive buildings such as The Three Sisters. Like the other two capitals, Tallinn is a Unesco World Heritage Site. See page 115.

△ **Museum of the History of Rīga and Navigation**. The best historical museum in the Baltics, it explains the Latvian capital's rich past acquired by the Hansa merchants, with paintings, furniture and decorative arts. See page 212.

▽ **Palmse Manor**. One of the finest restored manors around, the house and grounds show the luxurious lifestyle of the Baltic German nobles who bought it in 1873. There is an orangery with exotic plants, too. See page 171.

△ **The Curonian Spit**. This magnificent 98km (60-mile) spit is a dazzling white sandy hill alongside the Lithuanian coast. "One must see it to give pleasure to one's soul," wrote Alexander von Humboldt. See page 330.

△ **Gauja National Park**. This is the place to go for outdoor activities, from bobsleighing to canoeing, horse riding to bungee-jumping. It's a favourite of Latvians, who, like all Baltic people, love the outdoor life. See page 251.

◁ **Art Nouveau, Rīga**. Latvia's capital is known for its Art Nouveau, which flourished here at the turn of the 20th century. Among its architects was Mikhail Eisenstein, father of the great filmmaker. See page 219.

△ **Saaremaa**. The largest of Estonia's many islands is a real rural retreat, with a marina, meteorite craters and the castle at Kuressaare, the only complete medieval fortress in the Baltics. See page 160.

▷ **Saunas**. Don't visit without trying a sauna. Traditionally, these lie at the heart of country homes, but today can be found in hotels and locations throughout the three countries. See page 64.

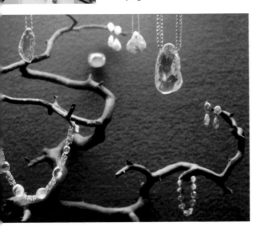

▽ **Trakai**. Built just outside Vilnius in the 14th century by Grand Duke Vytautas, this imposing brick Gothic castle, beautifully set on a lake, embodies Lithuania's glorious past. See page 295.

△ **Amber Museum, Palanga**. This extraordinary fossil of pine resin is a feature of the Baltic coast, where it made many fortunes. The museum in Palanga, Lithuania, is the place to find out all about it. See page 329.

THE BEST OF ESTONIA, LATVIA & LITHUANIA: EDITOR'S CHOICE

On the beach at Palanga.

FAMILY ATTRACTIONS

Open-air museums. All three countries have open-air museums where traditional buildings have been brought together. Here, costumed blacksmiths, potters and other craftspeople show their skills. See pages 132, 220 and 305.

Estonian Puppet Theatre. A popular local attraction, and although shows are in Estonian, they are not hard to follow. There is also a high-tech museum of puppet history, and theatres in Rīga and Kaunas, too.

Zoos. Zoos in Tallinn, Rīga and Kaunas have large animal collections, and with children's playgrounds they are orientated towards families. See page 220.

Horse riding. The quiet lanes and forest tracks are ideal for hacking, and there are stables throughout the three countries. See page 77.

Druskininkai. Adventure park, snow park, water park, cycling paths and wonderful forests – Druskininkai has all a child could wish for. See page 75.

In costume at Tallinn's open-air museum.

BEST BEACHES

Pärnu. Estonia's "summer capital" buzzes with beach parties and barbecues to make the most of the white nights. See page 149.

Jūrmala. This string of small towns lies just outside Rīga, attracting a holiday crowd. The name in Latvian simply means "seaside". See page 223.

Ventspils. This prosperous small town on Latvia's coast has a fine beach, an outdoor museum of old fishing boats and a narrow-gauge railway. See page 232.

Palanga. This Lithuanian settlement of fishermen and amber-gatherers is now a popular resort. See page 329.

Nida. The main resort of Lithuania's Curonian Spit has sandy beaches and several museums, including the summer home of Thomas Mann. See page 332.

BIRD-WATCHING

Matsalu National Park. The flatlands of Matsalu Bay in Estonia attract waders, terns and white-tailed eagles. See page 154.

Vilsandi National Park. Covering 150 islets off the coast of Estonia, this is a hatching ground for many European species. See page 163.

Pape Nature Park. This is the best place to see migrating birds in Latvia.

See page 234.

Engure Lake and Nature Reserve. Around 50,000 birds a year visit Latvia's 18km (12-mile) long lake, which has a floating ornithological station. See page 245.

Nemunas Delta Regional Park (Lithuania). Base of the Vente Horn ornithological ringing station, Nemunas is notable for its migratory birds. See page 333.

Sighting a snow bunting in Estonia.

PILGRIM SIGHTS

Pühajärv Oak. The biggest and oldest oak in Estonia is said to possess magical powers. See page 142.

Occupation Museum, Rīga. The museum depicts life under the Soviets, with a railway wagon to show how, from 1941 to 1949, 15,000 were deported from Rīga to Siberia and elsewhere. See page 208.

The Virgin of Aglona. This venerated Byzantine figure is the object of Latvia's largest annual pilgrimage. See page 240.

Madonna of the Gates of Dawn. Lithuanians and Poles come every year to pray before Vilnius' most venerated icon. See page 287.

Museum of the Holocaust, Vilnius. This tells the story of the thousands of Jews in "the Jerusalem of Lithuania" who were forced into ghettos, then sent to their deaths. See page 289.

The Ninth Fort, Kaunas. A haunting memorial to the 30,000 Jews who were shot in the 19th-century fort that became the burial ground for the victims of Kaunus' ghetto. See page 304.

Hill of Crosses, Šiauliai. A remarkable symbol of the resilience and faith of the Lithuanians, this hill has collected thousands of crosses, brought here by ordinary people. See page 337.

The Hill of Crosses at Šiauliai, Lithuania.

KUMU Art Museum, Tallinn.

ART GALLERIES AND MUSEUMS

Kumu, Tallinn. This multi-functional maze of copper, limestone and glass is the highlight of the Art Museum of Estonia. See page 129.

Mark Rothko Art Centre, Daugavpils. Explore the life of the famous expressionist and admire paintings donated by his family, as well as works by other contemporary Latvian artists. See page 239.

Užupis Gallery, Vilnius. Contemporary exhibitions are held here

at the heart of the arty, breakaway republic of Užupis. See page 286.

National Art Gallery, Vilnius. The gallery includes a collection of folk art. Its changing exhibitions are worth a look. See page 293.

The MK Čiurlionis Art Museum, Kaunas. Some 360 works by Lithuania's best-known artist-composer, with the chance to hear some of his work in the "listening hall". See page 303.

Looking across the rooftops of old Tallinn, Estonia.

On the beach at Jūrmala, Latvia.

Aukštaitija, Lithuania.

A rural Estonian setting.

THE BALTIC STATES

Estonia, Latvia and Lithuania, each with its own strong individual identity and rich culture, are lands of vibrant capitals, exquisite architecture, pristine beaches and unspoilt rural landscapes.

Festivals are a part of Baltic life.

The term "Baltic States" groups together three small neighbouring northern European countries that have shared histories, similar geographies, different languages and quite separate identities. Lying between Scandinavia in the north and Poland in the south, with Russia looking on from the east, they are arranged from north to south in helpful alphabetical order – Estonia, Latvia and Lithuania, the order they appear in this guide. Their combined total area of 175,000 sq km (67,500 sq miles) makes them smaller than Austria and about the size of Oklahoma.

Travelling between the three is relatively simple by road, on the Via Baltica, but north–south transport has yet to be developed: there is no direct rail link between the capital cities of Estonia and Latvia, 300km (186 miles; passengers need to switch trains at Valga) apart, and it takes about 40 hours to travel from Warsaw to Tallinn, though a new "Rail Baltica" project is under way.

FAIRYTALE OLD TOWNS

Many visitors will head for the capitals to see the extraordinarily attractive and well-preserved Old Towns that have won each of them a place on the Unesco World Heritage list. They have distinct flavours: Estonia's fairytale Tallinn with cobblestones, Lutheran church spires and any excuse for a song; Latvia's busy Rīga on the Daugava, largest of the capitals (pop. 704,000), with guild halls, an impressive Gothic

Birch forest in eastern Latvia.

cathedral and a great market in former Zeppelin hangars; and Lithuania's Baroque Vilnius, where there is an emphasis on art and a background of Catholic shrines. Beautiful to look at and easily assimilated, with cultural attractions and some good bars and restaurants, it is not surprising that they have become popular short-break destinations. Vilnius was European Capital of Culture in 2009, Tallinn in 2011 and Rīga in 2014.

The summer holiday resorts of Pärnu (Estonia), Jūrmala (Latvia) and Palanga (Lithuania) have been popular since the 19th century, and you will still hear Russian spoken on their promenades, as sea-starved neighbours return for a traditional break. Backed by dunes and pine woods, the blond sands of the islands and coasts are washed by the safe, shallow Baltic Sea.

MANORS AND MYTHS

A longer break might take in more than one capital, or a second city: Tartu, the university town of Estonia, ancient Cēsis in Latvia, or Kaunas, the former capital of Lithuania, all rich in culture and traditions. Castles and manor houses will also tempt people out of town: the handsomely restored Palmse Manor in Estonia; Rundāle Palace in Latvia, built by Bartolomeo Rastrelli, architect of St Petersburg's Winter Palace; or the beautifully situated island castle of Trakai in Lithuania. Most towns have a civic gallery or museum that will tell you about the life of the area. All three

Žemaitija lakes, Lithuania.

countries maintain the kind of pride in their past that newly re-established nations so often feel the need for. Myths and legends, stories of local heroes and bold defenders of freedom lurk in every ruin and monument. Sometimes the ghastly events of the 20th century, which wrenched the countries in all directions, don't seem far away.

FROM E-CAPITAL TO RURAL RETREAT

Life in the capitals is much like life in any modern city, and highly wired Tallinn, where Skype was invented and where the world's first paperless parliament was introduced, is in advance of most.

But the urban dwellers feel a need to escape to the countryside, and most weekends see an exodus to friends or relations who have a patch of land and some space. Here is peace and quiet, in some quite untouched places, in woodland and forest inhabited by elk and boar, in meadows and marshes where many birds gather, and by countless lakes and rivers.

In Lithuania shrines sprout from roadsides, and each country has its open-air rural museums where you can see how life was lived before the Industrial Revolution, when houses and churches were hewn with axes and the Baltic serfs had to live under their foreign masters. Attendants are dressed in traditional costumes, which are worn on any of the many festive occasions that have kept the nations singing and dancing through hard times.

Painted doorway, Tallinn.

People remain deeply attached to their rural roots, and visiting the countryside or staying on a farm is most certainly the best way to enter the local soul. Here are plots of land, carefully tended for local use, with flowers planted alongside vegetables and fruit, and perhaps some chicken and fowl for the pot.

LONG SUMMER DAYS

The seasons are pronounced, and life follows them closely. Winters are deep and dark, so when days lengthen and the sun shines, people are more than ready to get outdoors. Children have a full three months' holiday in summer, and there are myriad attractions and activities on offer in the widespread national parks, from canoeing and horse riding to archery, and even kiiking, a hair-raising swing invented by an Estonian. Beach parties make the most of light evenings, with barbecues, DJs and occasional skinny dipping.

Whether in the city or down on the farm, don't leave without experiencing a sauna, one of the Baltic States' great institutions.

Singers at a cultural festival in Estonia.

THE BALTIC PEOPLES

In terms of history and geography, these countries have much in common – and yet each retains a strong national characteristic in its approach to life.

The people of the three Baltic nations are as different from each other as the Poles are from the Norwegians, or the Irish from the Dutch, but one characteristic that showed itself immediately after independence, in common with all newly emergent or re-emergent states, was a tendency for self-absorption, accompanied by a constant need to discuss their plight. In part, this is a general complaint of small countries, but, more importantly, it was the result of the systematic, and partially successful, attempt by the Soviet Union to exterminate them, leaving many with a strong sense of doubt as to their own worth, and to the worth of their countries on the world stage.

If repression had been any harsher, Estonians, Latvians and Lithuanians might have met the same fate as the Ingrians, Kalmuks, Tatars and other small nations who got in Stalin's way. As it was, the debasement of the language and national culture through Russification and Sovietisation left a deep-rooted scar on the collective psyche.

NEW-FOUND CONFIDENCE

But as the Baltic States began to make a name for themselves, winning and staging the Eurovision Song Contest (a dubious honour, but certainly a way of becoming noticed), gaining medals at the Olympics, joining NATO and the EU, adopting the euro and sending forces to Afghanistan, the endless soul-searching diminished.

Having a shared recent past has done little to diminish national differences. For instance, Lithuanians remain stereotypically the most outgoing people from the three countries, and are perhaps the most nationalistic. A memory of the Grand Duchy that ran from the Baltic to

Young girl in traditional dress.

In the first decade after independence all three countries suffered a decline in population, taking their numbers back to where they were before the intense Russification of the 1970s.

the Black Sea still exerts a profound influence over people. Sometimes the result is attractive: national self-confidence gives Lithuanians a zeal to succeed and regain their rightful place among what they consider to be Europe's "real" countries. The desire not to be outstripped economically by Poland, their historical partner and sometime coloniser, is deep.

"The world may not know much about us, but it should," is a deeply ingrained attitude – though anyone who follows basketball will know its stars well. This "think big" *Weltanschauung* meshes neatly with a continuing fixation with the USA, the Promised Land to which many tens of thousands of Lithuanians have emigrated over the past 100 years. Despite its distance, the USA remains a dominant cultural influence: televised NBA basketball games attract an avid following, while the American ambassador's comings and goings are front-

A military parade, Rīga.

page news. Conversely, Lithuanians tend to be remarkably uninterested in their neighbours. Few could name the prime ministers of major neighbours such as Poland, Sweden or Belarus. The idea, therefore, that economic or political self-interest should lead to a close engagement with such countries is regarded with amused indifference, or, in the case of Poland, with suspicion and defensiveness.

Lithuanians like talking about Baltic co-operation, but they are generally much less enthusiastic about following it up in practice. Despite close linguistic ties with their Baltic cousins, the Latvians, Lithuanians treat their northern neighbours rather as Americans treat Canadians: benignly and with sweeping ignorance.

Contacts between Estonians and Lithuanians, when they happen, seem to be the warmest, with the austere Nordic character of the former complementing the exuberance of the latter. But all three Baltic republics share a certain shrewd scepticism in their humour.

SOLID STOCK

The stereotype goes that the Latvian national character lies somewhere in between the reserved Estonians and the outgoing Lithuanians, but this really doesn't begin to do them justice. The German, Protestant influence, as in Estonia, results in a solid, reliable work ethic that has largely survived the effects of Soviet Communism. Slow starters, Latvians initially lagged behind their Baltic neighbours in economic reform, but soon easily overtook Lithuania in attracting investment from abroad, and on several scores were doing even better than Estonia, the unquestioned star performer. But when the downturn struck, they were hardest hit.

Latvians' roots are traditionally in the countryside – something apparent in everything from folk art to the national cuisine. But while the Latvians treasure their rustic roots, they have also taken to their new way of life with aplomb. Most work hard in their determination to make a better life for themselves, and it is perfectly common for young people to hold down a demanding full-time job, study for a higher degree, attend language lessons and go to the gym, while still maintaining a full social life. Latvians' good nature is sometimes said to be their undoing. Whereas the Estonians maintained a stony inner resistance to Russification, this process advanced far further in Latvia: mixed marriages were more frequent, and national consciousness seemed the weakest in the Baltics when the independence struggle began in the late 1980s. Whereas Lithuanians make up 80 percent of the population of their country, Latvians are in a bare majority (just under 60 percent at the last count) in theirs – which adds a bitter edge to the question of naturalising the hundreds of thousands of post-war settlers, many of whom have taken up their entitlement for Latvian citizenship.

Not to be forgotten among the Latvians are the Livs, a handful of descendants of the original

Today there are around 5,000 Jews in Vilnius. Until World War II there were some 100,000, making up nearly half the population of the city, which was described as the Centre of Jewry in Europe. Over 200,000 Lithuanian Jews were murdered in the Holocaust.

coastal tribe, who like the Estonians speak a Finno-Ugric language. Latvians have a special respect for this almost extinct race and its mystical link with the past.

LINGUISTIC DIFFERENCES

The difference between Estonians and their Baltic neighbours – and indeed most of Europe – is well illustrated by the language. Whereas Latvian and Lithuanian have some elements in common, Estonian, with its unfamiliar vocabulary, chirruping intonation, ultra-complex grammar and distinctive word order, is as impenetrable to most European ears as Hungarian or Finnish. This is not surprising: Estonians, like these two nations, are members of the Finno-Ugric ethnic family, whose origins lie deep in the marshes of Siberia. Despite substantial influences from their Swedish, Danish, German and Russian rulers over the past six centuries, Estonians prize their bloodline – sometimes comically: "War is an Indo-European phenomenon," one visitor was startled to hear. "It's because of your settlement pattern: you live in villages, while we prefer solitary forest clearings."

Equally incongruously, the Estonians' Finno-Ugric near neighbours, the Finns, are regarded rather disparagingly, frequently referred to as "elk". Of course, there have long been close ties between the two countries. During Soviet times Estonians could not be prevented from tuning in to Finnish television, and Finland's helping hand in the early days of independence was invaluable. But the long-standing tradition of boatloads of Finns turning up in Tallinn for a weekend of heavy drinking is as strong as ever, and for many Estonians, this is the image they have of their neighbours. Estonians have had many years to brood on the misfortune that has soured their history. Just as Lithuanians like to tell you that their country is at

the geographical centre of Europe, that their language is archaic and their folk art extraordinary, and just as Latvians will point out that in the pre-war years of their first independence they were one of Europe's great dairy exporters, so Estonians relish any chance to explain that their country was, before the war, more prosperous than Finland.

LOOKING TO SCANDINAVIA

Estonia has its face set squarely towards Helsinki and Stockholm. The majority of young,

Dining alfresco on a summer evening in Vilnius.

economically active Estonians have visited one or both of these cities. Unlike Lithuanians or Latvians, whose emigrations are far more dispersed – Ireland is an especially popular destination in recent years – in other hemispheres, one of the most active Estonian diasporas lies just across the Baltic Sea, in Sweden. Estonians are only too aware of the importance of their Scandinavian neighbours: indeed, many Estonians would be glad to shed their "Baltic" tag altogether and are more likely to describe themselves as being Scandinavian.

However, even if Estonia does consider itself the "least" Baltic of the three states, no Estonian would deny that their country is historically inextricable from both Latvia and

Lithuania. Estonia sometimes chooses to see itself as more Scandinavian simply to differentiate itself from its southern neighbours. It is not a rational attitude to geopolitics that distinguishes the Estonian national character, but rather its degree of reserve, which is in stark contrast to the other Baltic States. Staying for more than a few days in Vilnius, for example, a foreigner is likely to be invited into a Lithuanian household, stuffed with food, offered presents, taken on guided tours, introduced to family, friends and pets, and generally made

But, as with so much else in the Baltics, old habits are changing, especially with the young and more widely travelled generation. Public displays of affection were once disdainfully regarded as a "Russian thing", but young Estonians increasingly kiss each other on the cheeks or hug by way of greeting each other and generally behave like most other Europeans in public settings.

Despite their differences, Estonians, Latvians and Lithuanians are united by a love of nature and the outdoors. Admittedly, they enjoy it in dif-

Tourists are well-catered for in the Baltic capitals.

to feel at home. In Latvia the visitor will find hospitality, too, though the atmosphere will be more relaxed and not quite so intense. Invited to a house, you will not escape without sampling home produce, some of which may be pressed on you to take away.

SHOWING AFFECTION

Estonians, however, have mastered the art of being impeccably polite without being friendly, and an invitation to an Estonian home is rare. Friendship, an Estonian may tell you, is for life, and it would not be right for a new acquaintance to be invited into their home when they know that sooner or later he or she will go away.

Though the idea that real friendship is like a precious cordial which should only be offered to one's nearest and dearest can be off-putting to foreigners, Estonians are not unfriendly: once the friendship is actually made, it is solid and lasting.

ferent ways. Lithuanians will drive their car to a beauty spot and blast their surroundings with pop music, whereas Latvians will organise barbecues or swimming parties. Estonians tend to regard such habits with horror, going to great lengths to find a truly solitary spot where they can sit in silence.

THE RUSSIANS

Relationships with the largest minority are not always easy on a political level, and equality laws are on the agenda.

Russian-speakers make up substantial communities in Estonia and Latvia. Currently, ethnic Russians make up 24 percent of Estonia's population. In Latvia, which brought in similar laws, ethnic Russians make up around 27 percent of the population – about 40 percent of Rīga, and just over half of Daugavpils – and more than half have Latvian citizenship.

Relations between Balts and Russians can be seen on two levels. On a personal level, as friends and neighbours, they tend to get along fine. Russians are, on the whole, easygoing and cause few problems in the countries that are their homes. Politically, matters are easily stirred. History is a cause of great contention. Russia continues to portray Stalin as the countries' saviour. The Baltic States see him as their destroyer. Both sides are capable of seeing themselves as the oppressed.

WAVES OF IMMIGRATION

Small communities of Russians had lived in the area since the early Middle Ages, when some Baltic tribes paid tribute to Russian princes. After the conquest by Peter the Great, these were joined by Russian soldiers, merchants and officials. At the end of the 19th century a major influx of Russian workers began. This was interrupted by World War I and the Russian Revolution, which drove considerable numbers of White Russian refugees to the Baltics. Before 1940, Rīga was the greatest Russian émigré centre after Paris.

When Stalin occupied the Baltic States in June 1940, these émigrés were among the first to suffer from the secret police. Newspapers and cultural centres were closed and churches converted for secular purposes. In 1944–5 the reconquest of the Baltics by the Soviet Union (or the liberation, as Russia today would have it) began a process of Russian immigration that drastically altered the region's demography. The majority of Russians now living in the Baltic area are immigrants from the Soviet period.

A QUESTION OF CITIZENSHIP

Lithuania, with far fewer Russians (14 percent of Vilnius, 21 percent of Klaipėda) granted citizenship to all of its residents during the early 1990s, but the Latvian and Estonian governments decided that its "non-citizens" would not be allowed such automatic rights. Once the European Union spotlight fell on the Baltic States, however, all three governments had to deal with the minority issue.

Tensions today remain, particularly after Russia annexed Crimea in 2014 and has continued to support Ukrainian separatists in the Eastern Ukraine. None of the countries have ministers with responsi-

Tallinn's Nevsky Cathedral.

bilities for minorities, and it was only in 2009 that the first law dealing with discrimination – The Equal Treatment Act – came into force in Estonia, where a progressive programme of naturalisation has been backed up by the creation of a large, state-funded Russian cultural centre in Tallinn. Meanwhile, public administration employees, such as nurses, police and prison officials, are required to have a minimum level of Estonian-language ability and, with the exception of Narva, which has a high Russian population, all public administration is in Estonian. Ethnic Russians must pass a citizenship test, which includes a language test. In Latvia and Estonia 60 percent of all classes must be held in Latvian and Estonian.

Charles XII of Sweden crossing the Düna in 1701.

DECISIVE DATES

Peter the Great.

6000 BC
Finno-Ugric peoples from southeast Europe reach Estonia.

2500 BC
Indo-European culture merges with indigenous population in Latvia and Lithuania. Kurs, Semigallians, Letgallians, Sels and Finno-Ugric Livs settle.

9th–10th centuries
Vikings establish trade routes to Byzantium via the River Daugava.

CHRISTIAN CRUSADERS

1201
German crusaders establish a bishopric in Liv settlement at Rīga, which becomes capital of Livonia (Terra Mariana), part of the Holy Roman Empire.

1219
Danes take Tallinn.

1230
Mindaugas unites the Grand Duchy of Lithuania. He adopts Christianity and is crowned king (1253).

1236
Latvian and Lithuanian forces defeat crusaders at Saulė.

1282
Rīga joins Hanseatic League; Tallinn joins three years later.

1316
Lithuanian expansion begins.

1346
Danes sell Duchy of Estonia to the Teutonic Order.

1386
Duke Jogaila and Queen Jadwiga marry, uniting Poland and Lithuania until 1795.

1410
Joint Polish-Lithuanian forces defeat the Teutonic Knights in the Battle of Grunwald/Tannenberg/Žalgiris.

1520s
The Reformation establishes Lutheranism in Latvia and Estonia.

SHIFTING POWERS

1558–83
Livonian Wars. Northern Estonia comes under Swedish rule, southern Estonia under Polish. Polish duchies established in Kurzeme (Courland) and Pārdaugava in Latvia. German bishop of Piltene (Latvia) and Oesel (Saaremaa Island) sells land to Denmark.

1579
Vilnius University founded.

1600–29
Polish-Swedish War leaves Estonia and northern Latvia in

Swedish hands; southern Latvia and Lithuania in Poland's.

1694
St Peter's steeple, Rīga, the "tallest in the world", is completed.

1700–21
Great Northern War between Charles XII of Sweden and Peter the Great results in Russian victory. Russia occupies Estonia and Latvia.

1712
Martha Skavronska, a peasant from Latvia, marries Peter the Great and is later crowned Anna, Empress of Russia.

1795
Lithuania becomes part of the Russian Empire. Lithuania Minor (modern-day Klaipėda and Kaliningrad) falls to Prussia.

NATIONAL AWAKENING

1812
Napoleon marches through Lithuania en route to Moscow, raising hopes of freedom from Russia.

1860–85
The era of National Awakening. Abolition of serfdom and new educational opportunities lead to literary and artistic flowering.

1885
An era of intense Russification begins following unsuccessful uprisings against Russia; local languages displaced.

1905
The first socialist revolution demands independence.

German troops in Latvia, 1917.

Manors are burnt and hundreds of citizens executed.

1914–18
World War I. War is waged on three fronts, between Germans and White and Red Russians. Bolsheviks seize power in bloodless coup in Estonia, but are unable to maintain control. Germany occupies Latvia and Lithuania.

FIRST INDEPENDENCE
1918
Republics declared in Estonia and Latvia. German Army moves in, and power briefly returns to German aristocracy. Soviets move in, but with some Allied help are fought back.

1920
Independence in Estonia, Latvia, and Lithuania. Poland, also newly independent, seizes Vilnius.

1923
Lithuania reclaims Klaipėda.

1939
Hitler–Stalin Pact puts the Baltic States under the Soviet sphere of influence; Soviet soldiers arrive. Baltic Germans are ordered back to Germany.

1940–41
Red Army terror rages. Thousands are deported or shot.

1941–4
German occupation of Baltics. Concentration camps are set up. Almost the entire Jewish population is exterminated.

1944
The Soviets reoccupy the Baltics and turn them into Soviet republics. Mass reprisals and deportations to Siberia.

1953
Death of Stalin.

THE END OF OCCUPATION
1988
Opposition parties established.

1989
A 690km (430-mile) human chain, from Tallinn to Vilnius, links up in protest in the "Singing Revolution".

1991
Soviet intervention. Independence restored.

1993
Pope John Paul II pays a visit to Lithuania's Hill of Crosses.

1994
Last Russian troops depart. Tallinn–Helsinki ferry, Estonia, sinks with loss of 852 lives.

2003
Rolandas Paksas, president of Lithuania, is impeached.

2004
All three countries become members of NATO and the European Union.

2008
"Baltic tiger" boom ends.

2011
Estonia joins the Eurozone. Tallinn is the European Capital of Culture.

2014
Russia's annexation of Crimea and military intervention in eastern Ukraine makes relations between Moscow and Baltic States tense. Latvia swaps national currency for euro. Riga is the European Capital of Culture.

2015
Lithuania joins the Eurozone.

2017
NATO deploys troops in Estonia, Latvia and Lithuania as part of their strategic Enhanced Forward Presence deterrence posture.

2018
Estonia, Latvia and Lithuania celebrate their centenary of gaining independence.

2022
Kaunas to be the European Capital of Culture.

Estonia has led the way into the Eurozone.

Vladimir I of Kiev, also known as
Vladimir Svyatoslavich the Great.

СТЫЙ РАВНО
АПЛЬНЫЙ
КНАЗЬ
ВЛАДИМІРЪ

A SHARED HISTORY

Before independence, Estonia and Latvia had lived under occupation for the best part of eight centuries, while Lithuania flourished in a union with Poland.

One of the most perplexing problems facing the Paris peace conference in 1919 was what to do about the Baltic provinces of tsarist Russia, which the Bolsheviks, not without a fight, had consented to let go. Lithuania had once ruled the largest empire in Europe. It was somewhat overwhelmed by Poland before both were swallowed, almost but not quite whole, by Russia in the 18th century. Estonia and what was put forward to the peace conference as an independent state which called itself Latvia were, by any historical or political criteria, equally elusive.

Nevertheless, three independent states were internationally recognised under these names, although first the Bolsheviks and then Stalin made it plain that it was not a situation that could be tolerated for ever.

Their independence was sentenced to death by the Nazi–Soviet Pact just before World War II. The pact implied that Poland and the Baltic States would be parcelled out between the two, but it was overtaken by events with Hitler's invasion of the Soviet Union.

The three Baltic States were incorporated into the Soviet Union in 1940 and at the end of the war they were reconquered, and though there were some minor concessions to autonomy, they became virtual Russian provinces once again.

RUSSIA'S GRAND DESIGNS

Few peoples were ground finer in the Soviet mill than in Estonia, Latvia and Lithuania. They occupied a special place in Soviet strategy, an updated version of Peter the Great's "window to the West", which began with the founding of St Petersburg but envisaged expansion southwards to maximise Russia's access to the Baltic, often referred to as the "Northern Mediterranean".

Teutonic Knights.

Russia had initially been held to ransom by German Baltics who controlled the Estonian and Latvian ports, and Peter the Great was determined that it would never happen again, a view with which the later Soviet regime totally concurred.

Lithuania was regarded in exactly the same light, and it was agents of the tsar, long before any thought of Soviet Man, who vowed to obliterate all signs of national Baltic identities. The Russification of the Baltic provinces in the 19th century was so successful that when the matter of their independence came up at the Paris peace conference one question asked was sublimely naive: "Who are these people and whence did they come?" For three nations buried so deep in the history of others that their identities were long presumed to have been lost, they have surprisingly robust tales to tell.

THREE LANGUAGES

The countries also have common bonds. With their backs to the Baltic Sea, they have been hemmed in by the great powers of Sweden, Denmark, Germany and Russia, who have all interfered in their affairs for 800 years. In fact, the peoples of the three countries come from two distinct groups, neither Slavic like the Russians nor Teutonic like the Germans. In the north there

sacred oaks and thunderous gods. Some of the earliest Christian teaching came from Orthodox traders from the east. The trade routes were well established, up the River Daugava and down the Dnieper to the Black Sea. Amber was the singular commodity the Balts possessed, and others wanted it. This gem, made of fossilised pine resin, made its way to ancient Egypt and Greece.

Among those taking this trade route were the Vikings, and it was their leader, Vladimir I, who first united the Slavic Russians and made a

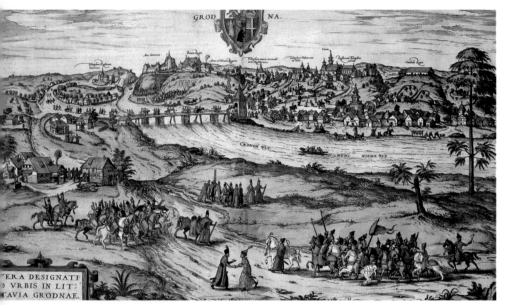

A 16th-century map of Grodna or Grodno, Lithuania.

were the Finno-Ugric tribes of Estonia and the Livs of Latvia, of whom only a handful remain.

Latvia was otherwise peopled by Letts, who, like Lithuanians, were Indo-European Balts whose language has some similarities with Sanskrit. For instance, the words for "god", "day" and "son" in Lithuanian are *dievas*, *diena* and *sunus* and *devas*, *dina* and *sunu* in Sanskrit. In Estonian, which has similarities with Hungarian, those words are *jumal*, *poeg* and *päev*. But it was a long time before the languages, with their extended alphabets and complex word endings, were written down.

RELIGION FOLLOWS TRADE

Baltic peoples also took longer than the rest of Europe to embrace Christianity, preferring their

capital on the Dnieper at Kiev. When the Scandinavians settled down on the Baltic coast, they did so in Estonia: *Taani Linn* (Tallinn) is Estonian for Danish town. By then the real conquering force of the Baltics was beginning to dig in. The German crusaders appeared in 1201 in Rīga, where they installed a bishopric for Albrecht of Bremen. From there, they set down roots of a ruling class in all three countries that lasted into the 20th century.

This elite arrived in religious orders, which fought among themselves as much as they fought against those who opposed them. There were the ministers of the archbishop, the burghers of the city and the Knights of the Sword, who became Knights of the Livonian Order.

The Latin Mare Balticum is known as the West Sea by Estonians and the East Sea by Scandinavians and Germans. English-, Lithuanian-, Latvian- and Romance-language-speakers call it the Baltic Sea.

The country of Livonia that they created put the different peoples of Latvia and Estonia under the same authority and established a healthy and lucrative environment for the Hanseatic League's merchants, the powerful German trading confederation that followed in their wake.

Lithuania, however, was not so easily brought to heel, and it frequently joined forces with the Kuronian and Semigallian Letts in clashes with the German knights. By the middle of the 13th century the Lithuanian tribes had been unified under Mindaugas, who briefly adopted Christianity so that the Pope, in 1252, could crown him king. When the German knights opposed him, he reverted to his pagan beliefs, and stood his ground against the knights. In 1325 the Lithuanian ruler Gediminas allied himself to the Poles, who had similar problems with the Teutonic Knights.

This union also gave Poland invaluable access to the sea. At its height the duchy was one of Europe's largest countries, stretching from the Baltic to the Black Sea. Gediminas' grandson married the Polish queen and the two houses were united for the next 400 years.

JESUIT BUILDERS

Poland brought a strong Catholic influence to Lithuania, and the Jesuits arrived to build their schools and fancy Baroque churches, while the Reformation whipped through the Germanic northern Baltic lands in a trice, converting everyone overnight. In the brief period when half of Latvia became a Polish principality, everyone converted back to Catholicism. The Balts had little say in this matter as in everything else. Compulsory church attendance made them indifferent as to how the service was conducted. The local inhabitants were denied virtually every privilege and for centuries were not permitted to build houses of stone nor live within the city walls. Membership of the greater guilds was

forbidden; even semi-skilled workers, such as millers and weavers, were brought in from abroad. The ruling society was impenetrable. In Estonia and Latvia the German descendants of the knights ruled; in Lithuania there was a rigid aristocracy of Poles. This survived even the break-up of Livonia by the Swedes during the mid-16th century.

The Swedish period is sometimes looked on as an enlightened one, in spite of wars against Poland, then Russia. But there was more talk than action. In Tallinn in 1601 Charles IX

Silver ruble, dated to 1714.

demanded peasant children be sent to school and learn a trade. "We further want them to be allowed, without hindrance, to have themselves put to use as they like, because to keep children as slaves is not done in Christendom and has been discontinued there for many years." Despite noble intentions, however, his words fell on deaf ears.

SERFS EXCHANGED FOR DOGS

Further upheaval followed in the 18th century. When Charles XI threatened to take away more than 80 percent of the domains occupied by the descendants of the Teutonic Knights, these German Balts called him a "peasant king" and turned to their other enemy for help. Russia was soon in charge and thereafter took control of Lithuania as well.

In 1764 Catherine the Great visited Estonia and Latvia and found serfs still being sold or exchanged for horses or dogs, and fugitives branded and even mutilated. Little became of her demands for change. In 1771 public auctions of serfs became illegal, but there are records of auctions for years afterwards, while in Lithuania a noble who killed a serf faced only a fine. The barons remained powerful, making laws and practising their *droit de seigneur*.

Serfdom was not finally abolished until the middle of the 19th century.

NATIONALIST IDEALS

In the 18th century the idea of nationhood was fomented by teachers such as Johann Gottfried Herder, but it wasn't until the 19th century and the Romantic movements, with towering poets and intellects such as Polish Adam Mickiewicz, that the idea really started gaining ground. There was much lost time to catch up on. The more enlightened German landlords did their

A painting of the conscription of Estonians into the Russian Army in the 19th century.

⊘ IMPOSSIBLE DECISIONS

One recent event confirms the impossible choices people had to make at the start of World War II. In Lihula in Estonia a former dissident who had become mayor allowed a statue of a soldier in German (Nazi) uniform to be erected. Though disagreeing with Nazi ideology, many veterans see the Germans as delaying Stalin's return and providing a breather in which to try to re-establish independence as well as allowing people to escape abroad. Many of this dwindling band of "freedom fighters" spent years in Soviet labour camps and argue that if Soviet army monuments can remain, the Germans should have one, too. The mayor was told to take it down.

best to make amends, starting schools and themselves learning the local languages perhaps for the first time. Tartu University, near the Latvian border, was the intellectual force behind the National Awakening in both Estonia and Latvia. However, Lithuania suffered a setback with the closing of its university in 1832, followed by a ban on printing Lithuanian books, which was a punishment for uprisings against the tsar. Paradoxically, throughout the Baltics there was as much Russification towards the end of the century as there was national fervour.

THE PEASANTS REVOLT

Discontent with the unenlightened tsars broke out into the Russian Revolution of 1905. This peasants' revolt was a horrifically violent time that affected all the Baltic States, where many were delighted to torch the grand palaces, manors and other buildings of the ruling class. The destruction sparked was the start of a savage century. The two world wars were particularly fiercely fought.

The Red Army, retreating before the German advance, scorched its way homewards at the end of World War I, leaving the land in ruins. Again ravaged by the two sides in World War II, only a few dozen people crawled from the rub-

There are strong feelings about the Red Latvian Riflemen statue in Rīga. Some see the riflemen as part of the Soviet oppression, others as patriotic fighters against Germany, while some Russians view them as foreign mercenaries.

were sent home, first through land reforms, and in the end by Hitler who, under his pact with Stalin, ordered them out. There was great hard-

Hitler leads German troops in the occupation of Klaipėda (Memel), Lithuania, on 23 March 1939.

ble of major ports such as Klaipėda, Ventspils and Narva. Vilnius, the Jerusalem of Lithuania, witnessed the wholesale extermination of the 50,000 Jewish population.

The final injustice was the permanent imposition of Soviet rule and Stalinist terror. Anyone a visitor meets today in the Baltics is likely to have a relation who was sent to Siberia or shot.

FLOWERING BETWEEN THE WARS

The period between the two world wars saw the extraordinary flowering of three quite separate cultures, each coming into its own as a nation state. From 1918 to 1939 the land belonged to the people of the Baltics for the first time for more than seven centuries. The German Balts

ship to overcome, but the economies, based on agriculture, grew to match those in the West. Political life was not all roses, but at least it was their own.

This golden age of political autonomy was an era that the Balts looked back to for 50 years thereafter. Only in the late 1980s did they turn away from the past and start to build a new future for themselves.

The struggle for independence during this period cost many lives, but secured for Estonia, Latvia and Lithuania the freedom of self-determination and a future over which they were to have control.

For the three nations' individual histories, see the relevant country chapters.

LIFE TODAY

Having battled to overcome the recession and joined the Eurozone, the Baltic Tigers are gearing up to roar once again.

On 13 January 2009 around 10,000 angry Latvians gathered before parliament in Rīga. For the first time since ejecting the Russians nearly 20 years earlier, there were riots and windows were shattered, a shocking thing in a country whose people are not known for their aggression. But the government of Ivars Godmanis was under pressure, and there were tales of corruption. Three days later, Lithuanians were out on the streets of Vilnius, though their government, not long in power, had an easier ride, while Estonians took their cuts stoically and, having had a budget surplus for 18 years, it passed all economic tests to join the Eurozone in 2011.

It was never going to be too easy for the people of the three small Baltic countries to find wealth as well as health and happiness in the modern world, and the recession of 2008 came as a bitter blow after the "Baltic tiger" had come roaring out into the full light of Europe. While preparing to join the Eurozone on 1 January 2011, GDPs fell like stones and unemployment soared. The worst hit by the crisis was Latvia. A year after it had the fastest-growing economy in Europe, it was forced to take on a $7.5 billion-dollar loan from the International Monetary Fund.

However, all three governments undertook drastic measures to straighten things out by implementing expenditure cuts and increasing revenues. As a result, the Baltic States' economies swiftly rebounded and since 2011 have seen robust growth rates (exceeding two percent in 2014), among the highest in the EU. Moreover, wages have steadily increased while unemployment has fallen. The fact is that the three countries had invested their hopes in the European Union. The vote to become members of the EU in 2004 had an enormous effect on

Keeping an eye on share prices.

national pride. It was final proof that they had surfaced from the great crushing boulder of the Soviet Union into the light of the democratic West. Personal self-confidence and self-esteem were restored.

FREE PRESS AND CIVIC PRIDE

In order to accede to the EU, the countries had been made to demonstrate that they were both socially and economically fit. The intervening decade had been far from easy. They were years characterised by divisive political infighting, institutionalised corruption, rampant crime, high prices and appalling wages, all of which contributed to a sense of malaise. Now, a generation after independence, the most pressing remaining social problems have largely been addressed. The mafia and other crooks, always in the vanguard of capitalism's advance, are generally under control, and those who have spent their lives involved in crime and corruption are simply starting to die out. The press is free. There are fewer political parties, and those that remain are more clearly defined.

In many different areas hard work has paid off. A civic pride has revitalised old buildings, constructed new ones and kept the streets clean and litter-free, making a necessarily dignified backdrop to progress. Many people have more than one job – not always paid legally – and will often tell you how busy they are. Despite this new-found dynamism, there is a pleasantly relaxed rhythm about day-to-day life.

With super-fast broadband and an unequalled e-government platform, Estonia prides itself at being at the cutting edge of technology, and it is certainly one of the most wired countries in the world, while Lithuania has embarked on an "ambitious vision" to become a world high-tech service hub by 2020.

At a concert in Vilnius.

⊘ THE RUSSIAN THREAT

The annexation of Crimea by a resurgent Russia and the subsequent war in eastern Ukraine in 2014 stirred up bad memories in the Baltic countries that yet again felt threatened by its powerful neighbour. Relations with Moscow soured as its officials made inflammatory statements and warned that the same conditions (large Russian communities "oppressed" and "discriminated against" by local authorities), which triggered Russian intervention in Ukraine, also exist in the three Baltic republics. Several border incidents, including the capture of a Estonian border guard, followed, causing further deterioration in the mutual relations and a temporary deployment of NATO troops in the Baltic states. In 2017, NATO troops deployed there permanently as part of NATO Enhanced Presence.

The situation's previous worst point was in 2007 when a statue of a Soviet soldier was removed from a war memorial in the centre of Tallinn, triggering protests and the arrest of some 1,300 Russians living in Estonia. Russia unleashed a concerted three-week cyberattack on its neighbour in retribution, paralysing government, banking, media and the Estonian embassy from Russia websites. At its height it also froze Estonia's banks, credit cards and mobile network.

Thanks to the digital ID card, Estonians have access to around 4,000 online services allowing them to check their bank accounts or medical records, set up a business or just pay for parking.

HEALTH AND EDUCATION

Despite huge advances made since independence, there is still need for improvement, particularly in the basic services of education, healthcare and transport. The public healthcare systems in the main work well. Hygiene is strict, and there are no problems with medical supplies. Scandinavians book into Estonia for cosmetic surgery, and all three countries offer inexpensive medical tourism. Although often underfunded, the education system is good and the literacy rate is high. Many teachers from school right through to university tenaciously cling on to traditional pedagogy, which gives children a sound schooling in maths, literacy and science. In many ways Balts are better educated than some of their Western counterparts. In a 2015 OECD PISA test, the world's yardstick used for assessing the quality of education around the world, Estonia placed at an excellent 3rd position, while Latvia and Lithuania were classified as 32nd and 37th places respectively.

The majority of people are fluent in two languages, and a great many are proficient in three. Most Estonians and Latvians are fluent in Russian, a language spoken by some 250 million people. After years of going out of fashion, it is being taken up again by the young. English is taught in almost every school, beginning at an early age, and there are few young people who are not reasonably fluent. Many older people increasingly choose to study German, French, Spanish and other European languages, either for work or pleasure.

All three countries have a minimum wage, and a statutory 28 days holiday a year. Many foreign companies have set up in the Baltics, taking advantage of the highly educated workforce and helping to create a modernised and efficient working culture. Estonia had pioneered the introduction of a flat tax to get the economy off the ground, and the other countries followed suit. After accession to the EU, the rate was lowered to encourage business. Of the three countries, Estonia has the lowest unemployment, while its debt levels are among the lowest in Europe.

FOLLOWING THE SEASONS

Capitalism has not, on the whole, made people particularly greedy. Few people are overly materialistic. While people cherish comfort and certainly enjoy material wealth, most retain a strong sense of what's really important in life, such as family, friends and the need to spend time communing with nature. The changing seasons are

Encapsulating the old and new.

very much a part of the rhythm of their lives, from the arrival of storks in the spring, when ice melts can lead to floods, to the celebration of midsummer, the most important event in the calendar. The berry- and mushroom-picking of early autumn are followed by hunkering down of winter, when skis, skates and sledges provide mobility and fun for several months.

Many town dwellers head for the country at weekends, arriving back with baskets full of provisions. Some have bought the allotment plots provided by factories and companies during Soviet times, and many city blocks have cellars in which to store produce. These rural connections are important, as country fare can help city dwellers through hard times.

POPULATION

The average life expectancy has risen to around 76.9 in Estonia, 75 in Lithuania and 74.7 in Latvia, and this is forecast to rise further. Obesity is notable by its absence in all three Baltic countries, perhaps due to the fact that eating habits remain by and large healthy. Many Balts lead an active life. Saunas are regularly taken, and if you are invited to have one, especially in the countryside, it's an offer worth accepting. However, alcoholism is still serious, despite government legislation to try to tackle the problem, such as

A newly built kindergarten.

banning the sale of alcohol in shops after 10pm in Latvia and some parts of Estonia. Among society's poorest members, there is still a widespread culture of consuming cheap, potent and sometimes lethal home-made alcohol.

There is also concern about the decrease in populations. Public figures have urged procreation as a matter of patriotic duty, as figures in all three countries since 1991 have shown a gradual decline, with a drift away from rural populations. All in all, the region's population dropped from around 8 million in 1992 to slightly over 6 million today. Unemployment has risen as a result of the recession. It has been a driving force behind sex trafficking, particularly in Latvia and Lithuania, from where women are sent

to work in the UK, Scandinavia and elsewhere. The countries also provide other EU countries with cheap labour.

HOME LIFE

A burgeoning middle class has built homes, taking out mortgages and loans. A mass programme of re-privatising state-owned homes in the years following independence gave them a good start. Property prices were incredibly cheap throughout the 1990s and there were strict state regulations in relation to the purchase of property by foreigners. If you could prove familial ownership of a property prior to the Soviet occupation, you could reclaim the property. Many people who didn't have any claim took advantage of the relatively cheap prices to take on a mortgage.

Property prices in the capital cities have, however, rocketed, thanks in no small part to EU membership and the willingness of some foreigners to pay anything asked. However, prices are still very low in the provinces and in smaller towns. The mortgage market is steadily growing year on year, especially among young people who want to live independently of their families. The average cost of renting and a mortgage are roughly the same. Many families are increasingly choosing to build larger, more spacious houses in the countryside, from where they then commute to the cities.

You can clearly tell when a new home is nearly complete – oak wreaths are displayed when a building is "topped out". There is little or

---

⊘ DEMOCRATIC REPUBLICS

The Baltic republics are all parliamentary democracies with a president as the head of state, and the elected governments are led by prime ministers.

The president of Estonia is called the Riigivanem (state elder). The parliament, the Riigikogu, is responsible for all national legislative matters. In Latvia, a 100-member parliament, the Saeima, elects government personnel, including the prime minister. In Lithuania, the Seimas has 141 seats, of which 71 members are elected by popular vote and 70 by proportional representation. The prime minister is appointed by the president on the approval of parliament. Elections are held every four years.

Since independence, Lithuania has become the country with one of the highest suicide rates in the world. This is largely a rural phenomenon.

no inheritance tax, a huge incentive for parents to pass on their wealth to the next generation.

TELEVISION AND SEX

At home, television is a staple entertainment, and there are a number of public and private

pronouncement on Twitter: "I proudly announce I am gay ... Good luck all of you! " thus becoming the first top-ranking politician in the Baltics to come out publicly. Baltic Pride is an annual gay pride parade organised each year in a different Baltic capital. Nevertheless, to avoid any problems, it is generally advisable for same sex couples to refrain from public displays of affection.

Lithuania, the most conservative of the three countries, is loosening its Catholic ties. While Tallinn and Rīga have a widespread reputation for their wild nightlife, Vilnius isn't far behind.

The Baltic States have a highly educated populace.

channels on a regional as well as a local basis; Estonia has five free digital TV channels. Schedules are a mixture of home-grown programmes and US and Russian imports. Reality TV shows are popular and there was a national scandal when a young couple had sex on one such Lithuanian programme. The man involved proudly proclaimed that he did it "for Lithuania", while the woman was so vilified in the media for her actions that she moved abroad.

Equality of the sexes still has a way to go in this predominantly male culture. Homosexuality is something that is often declared only behind firmly closed doors, but attitudes are changing fast. In November 2014, the Latvian foreign minister, Edgars Rinkēvičs, made the

Estonia and Latvia are generally liberal in relation to sex.

LOOKING BACK

As time moves on, a nostalgia for the Soviet era gnaws at a few folk. Grūtas Park (www.grutoparkas.lt), the Soviet "theme park" in Lithuania, has attracted world attention, and Lenin memorabilia has become collectable. Some say that people have short memories, others that it is a sign of no longer being ashamed of having been "Soviet". Some miss the fact that people had more time, that friendships were more treasured in that atmosphere of mistrust. Others like to talk about that "crazy" time with those who understand.

Bernt Notke's Dance of Death
(detail; 1463) in Tallinn's
Niguliste Church Museum.

THE CHURCH AND RELIGION

The variety of Christian and Jewish beliefs practised has helped define the architecture of the three countries, and major restoration programmes have uncovered superb examples of decorative Baroque and striking Gothic.

Throughout the Baltics, religion often sets the defining architectural style of a place, from simple wooden Lutheran churches in the north to lavish Baroque masterpieces in the south. Their restoration has been a major part of independence and has helped the Old Towns of the three capitals become Unesco World Heritage Sites.

Ever at the mercy of changing spheres of influence, the Baltics have amassed a collection of churches with an extraordinary variety of styles. Their history has also left the countries with some two dozen differing belief codes and has created such a tolerance towards other people and their religions that there are Lutherans who regularly attend Catholic Mass and Catholics who sing in Orthodox choirs. In Tallinn, for example, Methodists and Seventh Day Adventists both share the same church.

ORTHODOX BEGINNING

With the help of Greek Orthodox Russian merchants, the first teachings of Christ were voiced here in the 11th and 12th centuries, but Christianity did not arrive in full force until the early 13th century when the German crusaders subjugated Estonia and Latvia. This belated start meant that the early European ecclesiastic style, Romanesque, was on the decline. Only St George's in Rīga and the remains of Ikšķile church on an island on the River Daugava give a glimmer of that expiring style. Church architecture in the Baltics begins with Gothic.

In Estonia the earliest stone churches, built of limestone and dating from the end of the 13th century, are on the islands. These were simple Gothic buildings without towers, and were used for protection. On Saaremaa the churches at

Decorative detail on St Catherine's Church in Karja, Estonia.

Kaarma and Valjala have interesting murals and the one at Karja has beautiful sculptures.

Lithuania converted to Christianity nearly two centuries after its Baltic neighbours, in 1387. Although nothing remains of Vilnius' first church, it must have echoed the red-brick building of the castle. When St Anne's and the Bernardine monastery were built in the 15th century, its bricks would not have looked as out of place as they do today.

The Reformation took hold almost immediately after Martin Luther published his thesis in 1520 and its first centres were Tallinn and Rīga, where sacred paintings began to be destroyed. There is a strong painterly tradition in Baltic churches, and many churches had decorated walls and ceilings.

These were mostly done by Balts, and only the "easel" paintings were produced by foreigners.

In Tallinn, the late 15th-century Baltic painter Bernt Notke, who produced the high altar of Aarhus Cathedral, Denmark, and Lübeck cathedral's great cross, was responsible for the folding altar at the Holy Spirit Church (1483), which has more paintings than any other in the Baltics. He also produced the macabre *Dance of Death* painting now in the Niguliste Museum and Concert Hall. In the middle of the 16th century the newly formed Duchy of Courland sought to

A synagogue in Vilnius.

secure its power base by ordering the building of 70 new Lutheran churches.

CATHOLIC BAROQUE

Catholics sought refuge in the Polish territories of southern and eastern Latvia and Lithuania where the Jesuits began to build their sumptuous churches. Many of Vilnius' 40 Catholic churches are in the highly decorative Baroque style. The first, begun in 1604, was dedicated to Lithuania's patron saint, Casimir. Among the finest is the Church of Sts Peter and Paul, supposedly built on the pagan temple to the goddess Milda. Its Italian sculptors adorned it with more than 2,000 white stucco figures. The churches, which typically feature a twin-towered

facade, show Hispanic influence. In the Latgale region of Latvia both St Peter's in Daugavpils and the huge, isolated church at Aglona, which attracts pilgrims from all over eastern Europe on the Feast of the Assumption, are in this style.

Catholics were not the only refugees. A split in the Russian Church in the 17th century brought an influx of Old Believers to the Baltics and elsewhere (see box). They belong to the *bezpopovci* (without ministers) faction: during Russia's great repressions against the Church all trustworthy bishops were eliminated and it was impossible to ordain new priests. Today the world's largest Old Believers congregation, numbering some 5,000, is in the gold-domed Grebenschikova temple in the Moscow district of Rīga, which is the largest landowner in the city. The church's walls are lined with stunning icons depicting only the saints' faces, and services are led by someone from the congregation, elected teachers *(nastavniki)* of the church.

WOODEN CHURCHES

Though they tend not to last as long, there are still a number of wooden churches throughout the three countries, mostly in Lithuania. The oldest examples date from the middle of the 18th century. The Ethnographic Museum near Rīga has a typical example. Its figurative carvings and round log walls were all hewn with nothing more refined than an axe. It has a special fancy seat for the local German landlord and the front pews were more elaborately made for German workers; the native peasants were obliged to sit at the back – and were put in the stocks if they failed to attend services.

⊘ OLD BELIEVERS OF LAKE PEIPSI

Some of the Old Believers who fled persecution under successive Russian rulers settled beside Lake Peipsi in Estonia in the late 17th century. Here, just south of Mustvee, a shore-side road connects the villages of Raja, Kükita, Tiheda and Kasepää, where four functioning Old Believers churches can be seen. Houses are two-storeyed, with towers and wooden balconies, and contain icons. Gavrila Frolov (1854–1930) was a well-known icon painter from Raja, and there is an Old Believers Museum, with icons, at Kolkja. In Estonia there are around 15,000 Old Believers in 11 congregations, and they receive state support for preserving their culture.

Because the Lutheran churches in Estonia and Latvia served the interests of the overlords, the Herrnhuters, or United Brethren Church, gained many followers during the 18th and 19th centuries. Services were conducted in farmers' houses or specially built prayer halls, and it became known as "the people's church", with an emphasis on education and religious enlightenment. The United Brethren's activities diminished during the middle of the 19th century as pressure was put on them by both the Lutheran Church and the tsar, who won some conversions

The Pilgrim Route of John Paul II links 16 religious sites across Lithuania, including those visited by the Pope in 1993.

Towards the end of the 19th century the first Baptist churches appeared in Estonia and Latvia, and around the beginning of the 20th century Seventh Day Adventists and other Protestant sects arrived. After World War I and the break with Russia the countries formed independent

Statue of Pope John Paul II, Kaunas, Lithuania.

to Orthodoxy after promising support to farmers against the demands of German land barons. After Poland failed to gain independence in the 1863 uprising, the tsarist government also came down heavily on Old Believers, whom it looked on as renegades, and Catholics, whom it thought were a threat to the empire.

A huge building programme brought a crop of onion-domed churches, including the Orthodox cathedrals of the Holy Theophany of Our Lord in Rīga (1844) and the Alexander Nevsky in Tallinn (1900). Many can be seen, abandoned, throughout the countryside today. There are still a few practising Orthodox Latvian and Estonian churches, though commercial links with Moscow have been severed.

Evangelical Lutheran Churches, while all the Catholic Churches came under the direct subordination of the Pope.

DEMISE OF THE SYNAGOGUES

Jewish populations were well established in the Baltic region, which was one of the world's largest Yiddish language centres. Vilnius, the "Jerusalem of Lithuania", had 98 synagogues, some of them elaborate wooden buildings, and there were synagogues in nearly every town in the countryside, where small businesses were often Jewish-run. Almost the entire population was deported or killed during the Nazi occupation: around 55,000 died in Vilnius. Though some of the synagogue

> *After independence smart-suited evangelists arrived in the Baltics with a zeal to match the early Crusaders.*

buildings around the countries remain, it is hard to identify them. One or two have reopened in the capitals and the one in Rīga has been beautifully restored. Optimistic plans to rebuild the Great Synagogue in Vilnius have been mooted.

Kuremäe Convent is the only functioning Russian Orthodox nunnery in Estonia.

THE CHURCH UNDERGROUND

During the Soviet years, all Church properties and holdings were nationalised and many churches became concert halls or museums. St Casimir's in Vilnius was turned into a Museum of Atheism, and Rīga's Orthodox cathedral became a planetarium. Those who attended church found their careers threatened, and their children were banned from higher education.

Local authorities in the Baltic countries were more lenient and liberal compared with the Soviet heartland. There were many more working churches in Rīga than in Leningrad (St Petersburg). Because it was easier to register a church and educate children in the Baltics,

many Baptists, Adventists, Pentecostals and other believers emigrated here from Russia, the Ukraine and elsewhere.

The Roman Catholic Seminary in Rīga educated all new priests from the Soviet Union, except for Lithuania. Other institutions survived, such as the only Orthodox nunnery in the Soviet Union, at Kuremäe in Estonia. Many priests, evangelists and activists were imprisoned for their work. Estonia lost more than two-thirds of its clergy in the early Soviet years.

Some churches were most successful in organising their opposition. A group of Catholic priests regularly published the underground *Chronicles of the Lithuanian Catholic Church*, which informed the world about repression and human-rights violations. The people, too, remained resilient. The Hill of Crosses, just north of Šiauliai on the Kaunas–Rīga highway, was bulldozed by the Soviets three times, but each time the crosses were rebuilt. Encouraged by the late Pope John Paul II's visit in 1993, a Franciscan monastery has been built beside it.

CHANGING CONGREGATIONS

Today the Baltics are still centres of religion, with a bishop's chair for the German Evangelical Lutheran church in Rīga, and Vilnius re-established as one of Catholicism's citadels in Europe. People have returned to the church but things have changed. The Lutheran and other Protestant congregations have fallen in the intervening years. By contrast, the Catholic Church has held its flock.

Everywhere there are still signs of the religious mix. In Trakai and Vilnius are two *kenessas*, prayer houses of the Karaites, a surviving Jewish sect of Tatars who arrived in the 14th century at the behest of Grand Duke Vytautas. There are Muslims and Mormons, Uniats and *dievturi*, pagan Latvians whose churches are holy places built around sacred oaks.

Not all the ecclesiastic splendours are on the beaten track. The wonderful Pažaislis monastery should be sought out near Kaunas. One of Rīga's architectural secrets is hidden behind the Academy of Sciences: the 1822 Church of Jesus, the Lutheran bishop's seat, is a wooden octagonal building in the Empire style. The largest wooden church in the country, it measures 27 metres (90ft) wide and has eight Ionic columns supporting elliptical domes.

🔍 TIMBER BUILDINGS

Combining craftsmanship with folk art, the wooden buildings of the Baltics are all highly individual, exuding character and style.

Wood is the natural building material of the Baltics. Spruce, pine and oak are the main materials used in buildings that have survived from as far back as the 16th century. Some were constructed on foundations of alder logs, with oak shingle roofs and pine floorboards 30cm (12in) wide. The oldest existing wooden buildings tend to be churches. None of the elaborate synagogues of Lithuania survive, but the country has 265 wooden churches and its roadside shrines are an art in themselves. It is intriguing to think that the very trees that have always brought out the pagan in Balts should be doing duty supporting so many faiths.

FARMSTEADS AND VILLAS

The best places to see wooden folk architecture is in the larger of the open-air ethnographic museums, just outside Tallinn, Rīga and Kaunas. Here, farmhouses, barns, saunas, windmills and workshops can all be seen in one place.

Traditional farmsteads were built to share with livestock and dry storage, and the comfort of their hearths was enhanced with smoking meat or fish. Few large farmsteads have survived. In the 19th century, with the drift towards the cities, timber suburbs grew up and though many of these are now dilapidated, they are full of character. Rīga's Moscow district, for example, is attracting a young, arty crowd. Across the river is Pārdaugava, a suburb of delightful wooden buildings that are increasingly sought after. In its citation of Rīga as a World Heritage Site, Unesco made particular mention of the city's "19th-century architecture in wood".

Timber houses in other suburbs, such as Kalamaja in Tallinn, are also beginning to be fully appreciated and the restorer's crafts have been revived, often with help and expertise from Scandinavia.

With the 19th-century railways came the burgeoning of resorts. Grand villas grew beside the sea in places such as Pärnu and Narva-Jõesuu in Estonia, Jūrmala and Liepāja in Latvia and Palanga and Druskininkai in Lithuania. Chisel and saw added finesse that axes could not match, with fancy finials, balustrades, duckboards, verandas, balconies, towers and turrets, all prettily painted. Among the best-known architects-in-wood was the multi-talented artist Stanisław Witkiewicz (1851–1915), inventor of the Zakopane style, whose flights of fancy decorated the villas of Palanga. Railway stations, such as the one in Haapsalu that now houses a railway museum, were architectural gems.

When the 20th century arrived, prospering cities continued to use wood as a building material. The eclectic European revival styles – classicism, Gothic,

Art Nouveau in Jurmala, Latvia.

Baroque – could all be replicated in timber. Among the masters of the craft was Alexander Vladovski, whose handiwork can be seen in Tallinn's Art Nouveau, a movement that had a strong folkloric, back-to-nature element that suited wooden buildings.

THATCHED ROOFS

Many buildings suffered from neglect in Soviet times. Thatched roofs were replaced with corrugated iron, and the rot set in. But renovation in recent years has shown just how attractive these buildings can be, and there is a great enthusiasm to see them restored. Thatch is coming back – and few villages are more picturesque than Altja, on the coast east of Tallinn, where trees and reeds combine in the most harmonious country style.

CULTURE

The contemporary arts scene may sometimes poke fun at the past, but it's the rich cultural inheritance of the Baltic States that makes music and literature so forceful today.

Bertolt Brecht wrote: "Unhappy the land that needs heroes." Yet the Baltic states could hardly have political and cultural subjugation without consolation from folklore and literature. Heroes from old legends embodying the national fate, and those from painting, poetry and music, offered freedom and a refuge. Theatre, opera and ballet performances were packed, and writers exploited subsidies to keep national pride and independent thought alive. They fostered a climate for independence that was brought to the surface in the 1980s by rock music, which united classical composers, politicians and people in a mass gesture of defiance, which is why prime ministers can join the stage with bands today.

A WAVE OF NEW EXPERIENCE

Artists no longer need national myths to sustain them. The freedom to travel west as well as east led to a tidal wave of influences, and those best able to handle this have often been those old enough to have experienced two very different cultural worlds. Artists struggle to balance aesthetic aspirations with the need to stay financially afloat, to secure grants, find agents to promote their work and, in theatre and film, forge co-productions with foreign participation.

Culture, happily, is not for the few. Theatres, festivals, exhibitions and concerts are well attended, and governments have realised that small countries need strong cultural initiatives to earn respect in the wider world. Baltic writers, painters, musicians, sculptors, composers and philosophers have, historically, been prime movers in public life. Being a musicologist was no bar to Vytautas Landsbergis becoming president of the newly independent Lithuania, nor was a background as a novelist anything but an asset

Tonu Kaljuste leading the Estonian Philharmonic Chamber Choir and the Tallinn Chamber Orchestra.

when Lennart Meri became Estonia's first postwar president. The former Latvian president Vaira Vīķe-Freiberga is well known as a folklorist and literature specialist, a psychologist and linguist.

ROOTS OF LITERATURE

Intellectuals and artists have nurtured the idea of independent nationhood since it emerged in the early 19th century, when the three languages began to be recorded in written form. The freedom to write and to express a national sentiment in this manner arrived in a burst of romantic novels and epic verses from which the modern culture took off. Latvian Andrējs Pumpurs told in *Lāčplēsis* the tale of the bear-slayer drowned in the River Daugava, who, on returning to life, will ensure the eternal freedom of his people. Friedrich Reinhold Kreutzwald fathered the national Estonian epic, *Kalevipoeg*, which ends with the hero trapped in hell but vowing to rise again and build a new Estonia.

Despite a tsarist ban on printed Baltic languages, the lyrics to *Pavarasario balsai* (*Voices of Spring*, 1885), by a Lithuanian priest, perfectly encapsulated national striving and romantic sentiment. Indeed, priests, doctors and professors played a large part in establishing the region's

When the Russians closed Vilnius University, between 1832 and 1905, many culturally active Lithuanians moved to Rīga, while Tartu educated Balts of all origins. Students of the 1850s included Latvian Krišjānis Barons, who collated the Latvian folk songs called *dainas*, and Krišjānis Valdemārs and Juris Alunāns, who founded Latvian theatre. Much Latvian effort went into overcoming perceived German colonial condescension. Budding Estonian culture was less confrontational, and many Germans teaching and studying in Tartu were fascinated with

Monument to the Estonian poet Kristjan Jaak Peterson.

written cultures, first in German, then later in Estonian, Latvian and Lithuanian. The Baltic peoples could boast early of high-quality European centres of learning and a fertile intellectual ambience. In Lithuania, the Jesuits created Vilnius University in 1579, and in 1632 the Swedes established a university in Tartu, southern Estonia.

Rīga, meanwhile, acquired a cosmopolitan cultural importance. The East Prussian-born Johann Gottfried Herder (1744–1803), author of the idea of folklore, was a popular young preacher at its Dom cathedral, while from 1837–8, Wagner managed the German Opera and Drama Theatre. Today, you can see the delightful Art Nouveau residence where the philosopher Isaiah Berlin (1909–97) was born.

⊘ MUSIC AT THE TOP

Musical accomplishments are generally accepted in the Baltic States – even among the highest offices in the land.

At the 2008 Punk Song Festival in Rakvere, Estonia's President Toomas Hendrik Ilves got on stage to sing the Sex Pistols' *Anarchy in the UK* – he knew all the words. Later that year Latvian Prime Minister Ivars Giodmanis took over Roger Taylor's famous Queen drum kit to play *All Right Now* at the Queen + Paul Rodgers concert in Rīga.

In Lithuania a former Prime Minister Andrius Kubilius is a classical music fan, and his wife, Rasa, is a violinist with the Lithuanian National Symphony Orchestra.

the native language and themes. But for young Estonians the birth of their nation was above all romantic. As Kristjan Jaak Peterson (1801–22), a poet and Tartu graduate living in Rīga, declared:

Why should not my country's tongue
Soaring through the gale of song
Rising to the heights of heaven
Find its own eternity?

Peterson's question has remained relevant to the present day. The Baltic languages are no longer oppressed, but the populations are declining, while the post-war émigré communi-

Estonian author Jaan Kross.

ties abroad that have striven to keep those languages alive are dwindling.

Literature led the emerging 19th-century arts, with the novel of social realism, to the fore. In Lithuania, Jonas Biliūnas described peasant life under his own name; more familiar are three assumed names, Julija Žemaite, Juozas Vaižgantas and Antanas Vienuolis. In Estonia, novelist Eduard Vilde and playwright August Kitzberg ploughed a similar furrow, while the Brothers Kaudzīte wrote the first Latvian novel, *The Times of the Land Surveyors* (1879).

EXILED GENIUS

Then suddenly, from Latvia, emerged a world-class talent, Jānis Pliekšāns (1865–1929), who

assumed the pseudonym of Rainis. A complex, multifaceted figure, he was a lyrical poet, drama-tist, translator (of *Faust*) and political activist. He wrote his best plays in Switzerland, where he fled after his involvement in the 1905 Revolution. *Fire and Night* (1905) is a dramatic statement of the Latvian spirit; *The Sons of Jacob* (1919), based on his own experience, deals with the conflict between art and politics. Jānis Tilbergs' portrait of Rainis in the State Musuem of Art conveys his authority as a national elder and the personal loneliness voiced in his poetry. Modern Latvian literature still rotates around this giant figure, while his wife, Aspazija (1868–1943), a roman-tic poet and feminist, is also revered. Both are remembered in a museum in their Jūrmala home.

Latvian literature, always influenced by folk traditions and rustic life, was given a lyrical quality by the terse, philosophical *daina*. The plays of Rūdolfs Blaumanis (1863–1908) also set a high artistic standard. His folk comedy *The Days of the Tailor* in *Silmači* (1902) is still staged in the open air every midsummer.

Affected by his German education and familiar-ity with the German poets, Jānis Poruks (1871–1911) introduced introspection, melancholy and dreams to Latvian poetry and prose. Kārlis Skalbe (1879–1945) was dubbed the Latvian Hans Christian Andersen for his allegorical tales; he was also an exquisite poet and short-story teller.

Other notable poets include the symbol-ist Fricis Bārda (1880–1919), Anna Brigadere (1861–1933) and Aleksandrs Čaks (1901–50), whose Imagist style burst forth with Latvia's 1918 independence and brushed the realities of urban life in Rīga with lyrical excitement.

Lithuanian literature did not develop such early power and variety, which may explain its greater openness to European influences. The literary group Four Winds, formed by Kazys Binkis (1893–1932), was devoted to Futurism; others imitated German Expressionism. Vincas Krėvė-Mickevičius (1882–1954) was a great prose writer and drama-tist whose work continued in exile. Having briefly been foreign minister, he fled in 1940, and his epic *The Sons of Heaven and Earth* was never finished.

The Young Estonia Movement, devoted to rais-ing Estonian literary standards to a European level, flourished in the decade after 1905. The traveller Friedebert Tuglas (1886–1971) brought the world to Estonian readers through his romantic, exotic

> *Vytautas Landsbergis, Lithuania's independence prime minister and a musicologist, was involved with the Fluxus Movement in the 1960s – an art movement that was joined by Yoko Ono – though he opposed the smashing of pianos.*

stories. A.H. Tammsaare (1878–1940), author of the epic *Truth and Justice*, was influenced by Dostoevsky, Knut Hamsun and George Bernard Shaw. He has been called the greatest Estonian prose writer of the 20th century. Find out more about the modest lifestyle of this retiring, reflective man at the tumbledown villa in Kadriorg, Tallinn, where he once lived. A more radical experimental literary group, Siuru, nurtured the poets Jaan Oks (1884–1918) and Marie Under (1883–1977). Under, who spent the Soviet period in exile, is one of Estonia's most highly regarded poets, along with Betty Alver, whose poetry is generally darker, and whose husband was deported to Siberia.

VISUAL ARTS

Foreign influences and rural life stimulated the visual arts and music in the Baltic region. National Romanticism, imported from St Petersburg in the 1900s, ousted academic painting and influenced architecture, taking over from Art Nouveau. When that dreamy style became exhausted, new schools of national painting took over. The Baltic National Romantic style incorporates folk heroes and legends, with echoes of Munch, Beardsley, Klimt, Boecklin and Bakst.

In this vein, over Latvia's Vilhelms Purvītis (1872–1945) and Estonia's Konrad Mägi towers the Lithuanian mystical painter and musician Mikalojus Konstantinas Čiurlionis (1875–1911), a Baltic William Blake. In thin, richly coloured pastels and tempera, he created symbolic landscapes suggesting a mystical universe, with motifs from Lithuanian folklore. He conceived many of his paintings as linked musical movements or as cycles of life and death, day and night. They are extraordinary, pantheistic, poetic distillations of human life. Čiurlionis' own nature was rich and varied. He travelled widely, wrote for newspapers and almost single-handedly founded the nation's cultural life before dying at the age of 36. His pictures can be seen, and his music heard, at his own museum in Kaunas.

After Čiurlionis, Lithuanian painting, in the hands of the Kaunas-based Ars Group, grew into a satisfyingly complex art of landscape and portraiture, well informed on European developments and characterised by a rich, dark palette. Emerald green, dark pink, mauve and a touch of yellow evolved into national colours, and a persistent motif was the inclusion of folkloric wooden figures and toys.

The first Estonian school was realist, shaped by Russian and German artistic influence. Impressionism came late, and is best seen in

Nikolai Petrovich Bogdanov-Belsky's work.

the works of Ants Laikmaa, Alexsander Vardi and Kondrad Mägi. Mägi co-founded the Pallas Art School in Tartu, which produced the highly individual painter Eduard Wiiralt (1898–1954), best known for his graphics, and Jaan Koort, whose deer sculpture stands at the foot of Toompea on Tallinn's Nunne Street. By the end of the 19th century, there was a strong interest in national romanticism and quasi-mythological themes, as in the symbolist-influenced works of Kristjan Raud, who illustrated *Kalevipoeg*. Ado Vabbe is the greatest Estonian Modernist of the early 20th century, while noteworthy Cubists include Karin Luts and Karl Pärsimägi. Any Baltic visitor interested in painting should head for Latvia, where Vilhelms Purvītis, Jānis Rozentāls

(1866–1917) and Jānis Valters (1869–1932) combined European Impressionist, Fauvist and German Expressionist tendencies with their own distinctive approach to landscape and portraiture. Their influence extended to Lithuania and to future generations of Baltic artists.

Purvītis, founder of the Rīga Art Academy, depicted the Latvian landscape, but most of his work was burnt in Jelgava during the war; Valters, who studied in Germany, painted landscapes tinged by subjective mood and represented in stark Fauvist colours; Rozentāls' work

To a modern ear, the symphonic work often recalls the music of Bruckner, Mahler and Sibelius, but Čiurlionis was a distinct talent in his own right. He later reworked folk songs, wrote choral pieces and organised the nation's musical life in Vilnius.

From the First National Awakening, all the Baltic cultures developed strong traditions in choral singing. The first operas were written on national themes in the early 20th century, establishing opera as a popular but conservative genre. Baltic symphonic music evolved from the St Petersburg Conservatoire, echoing the

Going to Church (detail) by Janis Rozentāls.

peaks with his portraiture. Generally, the Latvian portrait tradition is outstanding. Rozentāls' depiction of his mother and a painting of opera singer Pāvils Gruzdna by Voldemārs Zeltiņš (1879–1905), using Purvītis' pale Latvian colours, lead into the highly coloured avant-garde movement. Artists such as Oto Skulme, Leo Svemps and Jānis Tīdemanis bring this rich period to life.

NOTABLE COMPOSERS

Čiurlionis contributed to modern Lithuanian culture not only through painting, but through music. An intensely active year at the Leipzig Conservatoire produced works still recorded today, including the String Quartet in C minor and the first Lithuanian symphonic composition, *In the Forest*.

⊘ NEW CULTURAL SPACES

The 21st century has brought new art houses to the three countries. In 2006 the Estonian Art Museum Kumu, designed by the Finnish architect Pekka Vapaavuori, opened in Kadriorg Park, Tallinn, and the 1,800-seat Concert Hall opened in 2009. The National Art Gallery in Vilnius, Lithuania, reopened in 2009 after complete reconstruction. Latvia's plans to build a new concert hall on a dam on the River Daugava in Rīga, for which a foundation stone was laid in 2010 (to be erected by 2030), and a Museum of Contemporary Art designed by Rem Koolhaas in a former power plant in Rīga's port is scheduled to be inaugurated by late 2021, while the new national library opened in 2014.

memory of Tchaikovsky and Rimsky-Korsakov. Outstanding composers of the era included Latvia's Emīls Dārziņš, best known for his *Melancholy Waltz*, and Estonia's Artur Kapp.

Latvians consider Alfrēds Kalniņš a musical father-figure for his varied work, both romantic and choral. His son Jānis also became a composer, later well known in Canada as John Kalniņš.

In all the arts, there was strong Scandinavian influence between the wars. An equally strong sense of alienation was felt from the Russian soul, the so-called "Asiatic principle". In the applied arts, the Balts excelled in graphic work, textiles, book publishing and illustration.

POST-WAR WRITING

All the Baltic cultures reach out to the larger world through theatre, frequently devoting half their repertoire to world classics, with many adaptations also from prose. A strong tradition of open-air performances, with real animals on stage, persists in Latvia, alongside rather verbose poetic theatre. After the war, alien ideology and the expulsion of several key figures cramped the development of the arts. Latvians Anšlavs Eglītis, Zenta Mauriņa and Mārtiņš Zīverts, Lithuanians Antanas Vaiculaitis and Kreve, and Estonian Marie Under continued the best pre-war traditions of theatre, prose and poetry abroad. But many writers died during the war or shortly after.

A literature of suffering and displacement, recounting the mass deportations to Siberia, emerged only in the 1980s, though in 1946, *The Forest of Gods*, by Balys Sruoga, recounted the experience of Lithuanian intellectuals in a German camp with irony and humour. The Estonian Jaan Kross (1920–2007), who was imprisoned by the Nazis, spent nine years in Russian labour camps, and his novels and short stories provide poignant accounts of his country's history and of the awful compromises faced by a repeatedly occupied population.

SOVIET AVANT-GARDE

A new creative generation emerged during the Khrushchev thaw, ready to exploit the advantages of being at the fringe of a centralised empire. The Baltics became the home of the Soviet avant-garde, with productions of Beckett and Ionesco, and in Tallinn in 1969 the daring publication of Russian writer Mikhail Bulgakov's satirical masterpiece *The Master and Margherita*. An uncensored edition of George Orwell's *Nineteen Eighty-Four* appeared in the mid-1980s. The thaw also produced notable opera singers and ballet dancers, including Mikhail Baryshnikov, from Rīga, and anti-Establishment poetry. Musicians managed to experiment with atonality and minimalism. The coincidence of modern ideas with folksong was cleverly exploited, as in the haunting compositions of Estonia's Veljo Tormis and the ritualistic rhythms of Lithuania's Bronius Kutavičius. The late Soviet period brought

Alfrēds Kalniņš statue, Rīga.

more abstractionism into painting, from Jonas Svazas and Dalia Kosciunaite in Lithuania to Latvia's Maija Tabaka and Ado Lill and Raul Meel in Estonia.

CONTEMPORARY MUSIC

Estonian music is flourishing at home and abroad. Best known is contemporary composer Arvo Pärt, exiled in the Soviet years but now back living in Tallinn. His minimalist, sacred works includes the widely acclaimed *Tabula Rasa*, written for the great Latvian violinist Gidon Kremer. Other Estonians with a reputation beyond their borders are the former rock musician-turned-avant-garde composer Erki Sven Tüür and a stream of world-class conductors, among them

> "When the musicians saw the score of Tabula Rasa, they cried out: 'Where's the music?' But then they went on to play it very well. It was beautiful. It was quiet and beautiful." Arvo Pärt

Neeme Järvi and his son, Paavo. The Latvian conductors Mariss Jansons and Andris Nelsons have made their names with, respectively, the Royal Concertgebouw Orchestra in Amsterdam

States, and contemporary dance now has a dedicated following in all three countries.

FILM AND VIDEO

Estonia has a particularly strong tradition in animated film, with directors such as Priit Pärn scooping prizes at international festivals. Other popular Estonian directors include Veiko Õunpuu, Jaak Kilmi and Toomas Hussar. Latvia's best-known film director is Laila Pakalniņa, whose work has been screened at Venice and Cannes. Latvia is also renowned for documen-

From the 2007 Latvian film, Defenders Of Riga.

and the City of Birmingham Orchestra. Lithuanian modernist Osvaldas Balakauskas also enjoys world renown, having earned the title of "Lithuanian Messiaen."

PERFORMING ARTS

Lithuanian theatre, currently favouring radical takes on the classics, has generated several world-class producers, among them Jonas Vaitkus, Juozas Nekročius and Oskaras Korčunovas. Lithuanian dramatist Marius Ivaskevicius and Estonia's Andrus Kivirähk both delight in poking fun at national identity, while Adolfs Žapiro and Pēteris Petersons are two very active, cosmopolitan figures in Latvian theatre. The National Opera in Rīga is the most dynamic in the Baltic

taries, a form championed by award-winning directors Ivars Seleckis and Herz Frank. Lithuania's best-known film director is Sarunas Bartas, whose philosophical and minimalist films have won international acclaim. The widely popular action comedy Redirected, which was written and directed by Lithuanian Emilis Vėlyvis, was a hit in 2014, screened in the UK and at many international film festivals. Bigger-budget historical films about the post-1917 fight for independence, the collapse of the first republics and post-war resistance are popular in all three nations.

Vilnius is home to the excellent Contemporary Art Centre, which has a reputation for being one of the most dynamic and innovative of its kind in the Nordic area, hosting the Baltic Triennial in 2009, when Vilnius was the European Capital of Culture.

In all three countries, video art has taken over from painting. Estonia's Raoul Kurvitz and Jaan Toomik and Lithuania's Deimantas Narkevičius have all contributed to the Venice Biennale. In Lithuania there has been particular focus on social issues and questions of female identity, as in a video by Egle Rakauskaite, which investigates the experience of eastern Europeans working in the United States.

Filmmakers are making their mark, too, not least because the three countries provide exceptional backdrops. The unspoilt towns and countryside are ideal for period dramas. The Rīga Film Fund was established in 2010, and shortly afterwards shooting in the city began in a joint venture between Latvia's Film Angels Studio and Indian Bollywood filmmakers Illuminati Films.

MODERN LITERATURE

Popular present-day writers include Latvian poet and writer Imants Ziedonis and prose-writer Zigmunds Skujiņš. Writers who were censored and repressed during the Soviet era and who have since won wide acclaim include Latvian poet and writer Vizma Belševica, poet Knuts Skujenieks and Lithuania's Juozas Aputis. Traditionally dubbed "land of poetry", prose and innovative essay-writing is now flourishing in Lithuania. The novels of Lithuanians Vytautas Bubnys and Vytautas Martinkus, though very different, show the continuing attraction of folk themes. Members of the younger generation of writers include Renata Šerelytė, author of short stories, award-winning novels and poetry, as well as Kristina Sabaliauskaite, mostly known for her bestselling historical trilogy Silva Rerum. Critics in Latvia have spoken of the "rebirth of the short story", a form championed by writers Andra Neiburga, Jānis Ezeriņš and Nora Ikstena. Estonia's Jaan Kross and the poet Jaan Kaplinski have an international following and have both been nominated for the Nobel Prize for literature.

Moving on from explorations of the Soviet era, writers such as Estonia's Tõnu Õnnepalu's, whose Border State explores the experience of a young homosexual in Paris,

examine contemporary life and adopt more experimental styles thanks to exposure to Western trends. Another good example of this trend are Kristiina Ehin's poems from her book The Scent of Your Shadow, which make for a perfect introduction to the Estonian way of life. The controversial Kaur Kender, often compared to Irvine Welsh, is yet another contemporary Estonian writer worth reading. His bestseller Petty God brutally explores the vulnerabilities of the modern society. Similarly, Lithuania's Jurga Ivanauskaite has tackled

In the Contemporary Art Centre, Vilnius.

in ironic and provocative fashion contemporary issues such as consumerism, advertising and the dumbing down of culture, while also exploring Buddhism following travels in Tibet. A mystic tendency in Lithuanian literature contrasts with a strong, continuing cult of the grotesque, the absurd and magic realism in Estonia.

SPREADING THE WORD

Inevitably, Baltic literature suffers from a dearth of translation into foreign languages, although extracts are regularly published by the countries' literature centres and cultural institutes, which will happily inform the curious about the latest trends in the arts.

FOLKLORE

From traditional tales, strange musical instruments and midsummer festivals to national costumes and sacred trees, the Baltic countries are steeped in folklore.

Folklore is at the very heart of Baltic culture. Indeed, until the 19th century, folklore in effect *was* Baltic culture, because German and Polish rule from the Middle Ages onwards had meant that no real indigenous literary culture had been able to evolve. In the 19th and 20th centuries, the Baltic scholars and writers who developed the new Baltic cultural identity primarily used peasant folklore as their starting point.

Fortunately this folklore was of immense richness, especially in the field of music. Songs appear to have played an important part in the worship of the ancient Baltic gods, and ever since have been at the heart of the Balts' sense of themselves. Almost every village has its own choir, many of a professional standard. State and public occasions often begin with folk songs. As a Latvian *daina*, or folk song, has it:
I was born singing, I grew up singing,
I lived my life singing.
My soul went singing
Into the garden of God's sons.

THE SINGING REVOLUTION

A visit to a folk performance is recommended for any visitor. From the beginning, folklore and the Baltic national movements were entwined. The first Estonian and Latvian song festivals, in 1869 and 1873 respectively, were also political events, celebrating the end of serfdom and symbolising

Traditional Estonian costume.

the reawakening and unity of the new nations. The republics between 1920 and 1940 turned them into great symbolic events. Folklore festivals became key symbols of the national independence movements in a process which has been dubbed, especially in Estonia, the "Singing Revolution". It was at the Baltica Festival in 1987 that the old national flags of the former republics were publicly displayed together for the first time under Soviet rule and without those responsible being promptly arrested. The national song festivals are astonishing affairs, with the choirs numbered in thousands and the audiences in tens or even hundreds of thousands. Folklore was also the key to rediscovering, or reinventing, the beliefs and society of the

Has a people anything dearer than the speech of its fathers? In its speech lies its whole domain, its tradition, history, religion and basis of life, all its heart and soul. Johann Gottfried Herder

pagan Balts that existed before the Christian conquest. These seem to have been based on the idea that the world was itself created partly through song and story-telling:

Once upon a time, the Lord God walked through the world, telling stories and curses, asking riddles...

The 14th-century priest Peter of Duisburg wrote that the Balts of his time "worship all of creation... sun, moon, stars, thunder, birds, even four-legged creatures down to the toad. They have their sacred forests, fields and

magnificent collection of portrayals of the devil by Lithuanian folk artists. Unfortunately, this is also a museum of historical anti-Semitism, since most of the devils are meant to be Jewish.

By the 18th century, awareness of the old Baltic religions as such had disappeared or become completely mixed up with Christian beliefs. Thus the great pagan festival of Midsummer's Eve was renamed St John's Eve, but it has retained many of the old pagan legends and customs, especially those connected with fertility. One of these is that on that particular night and only then, a flowering

Estonia's Voru Festival.

waters, in which they do not dare to cut wood, or work, or fish."

SPIRITS OF THE FORESTS

Until the 18th century, Catholic priests in Lithuania were still cutting down sacred oaks in an effort to stop their worship, and until the 20th century some of the ancient spirits lived on in folk tales about forest spirits such as the leprechaun-like *kaukai*, the *aitvarai* (who can lead people to hidden treasure) and the *barzdukai*, a form of bearded gnome. The *kaukai* were originally neutral spirits who could be won over with gifts. Later, however, they came to be identified with the Christian devil. The Devil Museum in Kaunas, unique in the world, contains a

⊘ JOHANN GOTTFRIED HERDER

Johann Gottfried Herder (1744–1803) was born in the Prussian town of Mohrungen (Morąg), in the former Polish-Lithuanian Empire. He recognised that language played a key role in both a person's identity and thought. While working as a teacher in Rīga, he produced *Tract on the Origins of Language* (1772), and his appreciation of the folk songs he collected was based on a belief that they represented a purity of spirit in peoples before civilisation. However, he warned against blind nationalism: "National glory is a deceiving seducer. When it reaches a certain height, it clasps the head with an iron band."

fern appears, and if a boy and a girl find it together, it will fulfil their heart's desire. Of course, ferns don't flower, but the tradition is a good excuse for young couples to go off into the forest at night.

For many centuries, Christian priests and ministers did their best to stamp out much of Baltic folklore, because it embodies so much paganism. The earliest records of Latvian folk songs are provided in evidence for 17th-century witch-trials, and it has been suggested that the "witches" of this period were the linear descendants of the old pagan priests and sorcerers.

"GOD IS A LATVIAN"

In the 1920s and 30s, efforts were made by some people to resurrect the old pagan religions. In Latvia, this took the form of the Dievturība movement, which continues to this day. Because in the 1930s the movement was closely associated with Latvian fascism, it was savagely persecuted under Soviet rule. Its ideology today remains intensely nationalist. "We have always believed that Latvia should be only for the Latvians," one of its leaders has said. "God is a Latvian – or at least, our god is."

Its theology maintains the existence of a single godhead who takes different forms. This, however, is a modern construct derived from the real, but now almost forgotten, ancient pagan religion. The Dievturi number only a few hundred, but their past sufferings and the purity of their folk singing gives them a prestige.

A certain holistic, pagan-influenced mysticism, a willingness to see divinity in all the works of nature, has characterised all three cultures up to the present day. This is true both of those authors who hark back to the ancient traditions, and those, like the Estonian poet Jaan Kaplinski, who render them into wider, universal terms – in his case, neo-Buddhist.

The new attitude to folk traditions in Europe dates to the later 18th century and the rise of Romanticism. Baltic folklore played a part in this cultural shift, because a key figure in the movement was the German philosopher Johann Gottfried Herder, who was moved by Latvian folk songs and stories when he was a Protestant minister and teacher in Rīga in the 1760s (see box).

ORAL FOLKLORE AND FOLK ART

Herder's influence led to generations of research by Baltic German scholars and, in the mid-19th century, the work was taken over by the first generations of native Baltic intelligentsia. Their task was the recording of this oral history. In Latvia, this process is linked above all with the name of Krišjānis Barons, who assembled the *dainas*, or Latvian folk songs. The 217,996 items form one of the largest collections of oral folklore in the world. After 1918, the governments and universities also set out to collect folk art. The Estonian National Museum in Tartu houses hundreds of thousands of examples, giving clues to an ancient tradition: for example, beer mugs

Celebrating the Summer Solstice in Latvia.

were decorated with "male" symbols, such as suns and horses.

Lithuania has a particularly rich tradition of folk carving, which is illustrated by the intricate wooden crosses outside many villages. Covered with ancient symbols, they resemble pagan totem poles. The carved crosses on the famous Hill of Crosses at Šiauliai is an apotheosis of Catholic piety and of Lithuanian nationalism, but also of ancient pagan symbolism.

However, the task of recovering the meaning of such figures, and the ancient Baltic tradition in general, is an intensely difficult one, both because of the suppressive effect of Christianity, and the effects of modernisation, especially Soviet rule. One reason why many Estonians

The Thinker (Rūpintojelis), a mournful carved wooden figure often seen by the roadside in Lithuania, is presented as Christ, but is in fact much older than Christianity.

wish to recover the area of Petseri, captured by Estonia from Russia in 1920 and transferred back by Stalin in 1944, is that the small Setu minority who live there have preserved folk tra-

The Kreutzwald Monument, Tallinn.

ditions which have been lost in Estonia itself.

The first major guide to Estonian folk stories was *Old Estonian Fairy Tales*, published in 1866. It is still popular in Estonia, and is held to have contributed to the creation of an Estonian prose style that is independent of the German models it previously imitated.

In 1861, Kreutzwald published the "national epic" *Kalevipoeg* ("Son of Kalev"), a reworking in verse of stories about a giant hero; the work was intended to help build up a national spirit, and prove to a sceptical world that the Estonian folk tradition was capable of producing an epic – considered at that time to be the highest form of literature. As with the Finnish *Kalevala*, debate has raged over the merits of the work ever since.

INVENTED GODS

The *Kalevipoeg* is still taught in every Estonian school, but otherwise its influence has progressively diminished. This has been far less the case with the Latvian national epic, *Lāčplēsis* (*The Bear-Slayer*), by Andrējs Pumpurs, in which another mythical hero is made a leader of the medieval Latvian resistance against the German invaders. *Lāčplēsis* has since become the theme of a verse play by Jānis Rainis, a rock-opera and several other works. Under the first Latvian republic, the Order of Lāčplēsis was the highest state award. Kangars, the traitor in the epic, has become a generic name for traitors, while Laimdota, Lāčplēsis' beloved, has given her name to boutiques and hairdressers, and ships and yachts are named after Spīdola, the witch.

Pumpurs also gave the ancient Latvians a pantheon of pagan gods, like the classical Olympus – quite unhistorical, but another passport to European respectability in his time. The contemporary habit of giving children "traditional" pagan names, such as Laima or Vytautas (after the Lithuanian medieval Grand Duke), dates from this period.

Today, this rich folkloric tradition is threatened by modern mass culture and by a danger that the over-use of folklore on official occasions, in schools and so on, may drain it of the joyous spontaneity which kept Baltic folklore alive and part of the region's life. Folklore traditions have therefore become diluted, but this is the price that has to be paid for joining the global capitalist community.

⊘ PAGAN GODS

Modern-day scholars have used surviving folk tales to try to establish the nature of the ancient gods and their worship. They have identified: **Dievs**, the principal deity; **Perkūnas** or **Pērkons**, god of thunder, akin to the Slavic Perun and the Scandinavian Thor; **Saule**, goddess of the sun; **Laima**, goddess of luck (good and bad, because Laima, like some Indian goddesses, also brings the plague); **Māra**, goddess of birth and death; **Usins**, the celestial charioteer, keeper of light; **Martins**, keeper of horses; **Janis**, who is responsible for the fertility of fields; and **Ausra**, goddess of the dawn.

THE SINGING TREE

A number of different instruments bring a distinctive sound to these lands of music and song; some have to be made with special rituals

Most traditional musical instruments are common throughout the Baltics and Eastern Europe: the goat-horn, whistle, flute, reed, violin, squeeze-box and zither. Other instruments belong to particular regions: the bagpipe in Estonia and Latvia's Protestant area, the hammer dulcimer in Lithuania and Latvia's Catholic part, and the hiukannel or bowed harp in the Estonian islands. But one instrument unique to the Baltic lands is a kind of board zither with between 5 and 12 iron or natural-fibre strings. Its history can be traced with some certainty back at least 3,000 years, and its Baltic names have supposedly originated from the proto-Baltic word kantlés, meaning "the singing tree": kantele in the Finnish language, kannel in Estonian, kåndla in Livonian, kokles in Latvian and kankles in Lithuanian.

This is a deified instrument and, according to folk beliefs, the tree for its wood must be cut when someone has died but isn't yet buried. In a fairy tale, a youth helps an old man who turns out to be God and rewards the good-hearted lad with this particular instrument.

The Apollonic, heavenly aura and the fine, deeply touching tone quality have made kokles a symbol of national music for Estonians, Latvians and Lithuanians. Unfortunately, the playing of the original instrument has almost died out. At the beginning of the 20th century, kokles developed into a zither of 25 to 33 strings, like a harp. "Modernisation" during the Soviet time resulted in a soprano, alto, tenor and bass kokles family. Compositions of questionable musical quality were played and presented as the national music.

MUSIC FESTIVALS

A folklore revival in the 1970s and 80s restored an interest in traditional instruments. Many of them, such as the bagpipe, jew's-harp, whistle, flute, reed, horn, clappers and rattles, are made by enthusiasts and played informally. It is now hard to imagine a celebration of calendar customs, folk-dance parties or folklore festivals without them.

The most important festivals are the summer and winter solstice celebrations, and there are large gatherings at such festivals as the Baltica, which involves all three Baltic republics. More local but no less exciting are Skamba (skamba kankliai in Lithuania) and the children's and young people's folklore festival, Pulkā eimu (pulkā teku in Latvia).

SONORIC MEDITATION

In Lithuania visitors should try to listen to sutartines, which is endless sonoric meditation, both vocal and

The Latvian national musical instrument, the kokle.

instrumental. The instrumental version of sutartines is played on kanklės, pan-pipes, trumpets or horns.

Primitive musical instruments are usually made by the players themselves. The more sophisticated ones such as the kokles, bagpipes, flutes, violins, accordions and zithers are made by a few skilled masters. These are not easy to obtain, though they can be found at fairs and folk-crafts festivals where there is also a good variety of bird-, devil- and animal-shaped clay whistles. The most popular instruments are the accordion and guitar, played at family celebrations and informal parties.

Catholic and Lutheran churches mostly have organs with distinctive characteristics. Rīga Dom's organ is recognised worldwide, while those in rural areas can have their own unique charm.

📷 SAUNAS AND SPAS

If you are ever invited to a sauna, don't pass up this very Baltic experience, and if you are not invited, you should seek one out...

Saunas have always been a way of life in the Baltic countries, and today they are undergoing a revival. Every farmstead once had one, usually by a river or pond for filling the pail for the fire and to cool off afterwards. Bathhouse walls were always made from logs, but the roof was often made from clay or earth with grass growing on top of it. There were two rooms, a dressing room at the front and a bathing room containing the oven and wooden benches.

The sauna was central to life: the goddess of fertility was thought to reside here, babies were born here and women would spend the eve of their wedding here. It was a spiritual as well as a healthy place: the word gars in Latvian means both spirit and the steam of a bathhouse.

Novices are advised to start off gradually, steaming for about 7–10 minutes, then cooling off and repeating the exercise three to five times. Only then should they start switching – a light flailing by birch branches – which helps blood circulation, increases perspiration, opens pores to help the skin to breathe and cleans out toxins. It is an excellent remedy for muscular pains and a good way to help get rid of extra weight. Either do this switching yourself or ask a friend – it's best to lie on the bench while someone else switches your back, starting from your feet and moving towards your head. Twigs should be soaked in cold water for up to 15 minutes before being used.

Cooling off can be done by taking a shower, relaxing for five minutes in a separate room or swimming in a lake. In winter, the hardy roll in the snow. But do take it easy after coming out of a sauna, as you might feel a little giddy. Herbal teas or beer are generally a part of the cooling-off process.

Water ladelled from a bucket is thrown onto heated coals, bringing the room temperature to around 70°C (158°F).

Ideally, a sauna will be built by a lake, which provides water to create the steam and a bath to cool off in. Traditionally, it was a place of life and death, where pagan spirits dwelt.

Felt hats come in various shapes and sizes and are worn to insulate the head from the intensity of the heat, allowing a longer period of steaming.

Mud is believed to have rejuvenating properties

Spas

For two centuries water cures and mud treatments in the Baltic countries have been offered in traditional spas, based on the healing power of the sea, mud and mineral water. The first one was at Druskininkai, an inland spa of curative waters opened by King Stanislav Augustus in 1794. The seaside resorts such as Jūrmala in Latvia and Pärnu in Estonia, began in the 1820s, developing from the sanatoria built for veteran officers of the Napoleonic wars of 1812, and subsequently popularised by the Russian royal family. The tsars and Tchaikovsky stayed at Haapsalu, famous for its mud treatments – the wooden Kuursaal (Resort Hall) here is the original from 1825. These spas were of the traditional European variety, not the kind one associates with pampering and mystic stones, but based on scientific balneotherapy. Under the Soviets they became institutions where Politburo members and chosen factory workers would be rewarded with a week or two of rest and relaxation.

Today, these centres have burgeoned into large spa holiday complexes, offering excellent modern facilities, and the idea of the spa has spread to the major hotels throughout the three countries. Now you are just as likely to be offered a bath in chocolate rather than in extremely smelly mud.

here is no river or lake, jump into a cold tub. This one scenic forest views. Novices are advised to start ing a sauna gradually, steaming for around 7–10 nutes, then cooling off, repeating the exercise three to times.

oating sauna on a lake, Estonia.

Felt hats, oak twigs, ferns and herbs: saunas are found in forests as well as in many modern hotels.

A roe deer in the Lithuanian forest.

NATURE AND WILDLIFE

Though lacking in dramatic scenery, the region has some of the most unspoilt spaces in Europe, which are wonderful habitats for all manner of flora and fauna.

In common with their neighbours in Scandinavia, people in the Baltics have an especially close relationship with nature. Many have a summer house and get away to the countryside during the warm weather as often as they can. A surprisingly strong sense of rural tradition permeates almost every aspect of Baltic culture, from popular music and food to the very way people think. And where many Westerners tend to romanticise nature, people in the Baltics enjoy it in a refreshingly hands-on and non-sentimental way. The average Balt is at ease working in a state-of-the-art office in the city one day and chopping firewood out in the sticks the next.

The three countries share many natural attributes: forests with deer and boar, bogs and lakes fit for ducks, and coasts with pines and dunes that see clouds of migrating birds. These are damp lands of lichen and fungi, of mires and flower-filled meadows. But there are many distinctive characteristics, too.

Peacock butterflies are common in all three countries.

ESTONIA

Situated on what is called a "boreo-nemoral" zone, Estonia is a transitional area where the coniferous Euro-Siberian taiga opens into a European zone of deciduous forest. The least populated of the three countries, it provides a truly unspoilt natural habitat.

One-fifth is covered by peat bogs, mostly in the central and eastern areas, which in spring echo with the croak of toads and frogs, and because much of the country is unsuitable for agriculture it has been spared environmental abuse. Wild, wooded meadows, found in few other countries, are particularly rich in plant life, such as orchids, and there are some 4,000 kinds of fungi.

Estonia's national flower is the cornflower, and the national bird is the swallow.

EXTENSIVE FORESTS

Forests and woodlands cover almost half the country and nearly half the forested land belongs to the state, which is a profit-making concern that considerably facilitates conservation efforts. Timber companies operate all year round for maximum efficiency, and illegal logging has been a problem. In 2010, to raise state funds, some 20,000 hectares (50,000 acres) were put up for sale in small plots.

There are still vast areas of untouched forest, and primeval forests remain in Järvselja in Tartumaa County and Puruni in Ida Virumaa

County, which, together with the wetland, provides a haven to all sorts of indigenous wildlife. A good indicator of the state of Estonia's forest ecosystems is the number of forest-dwelling predators, such as bears, lynx and wolves, as well as beavers, elk and deer. There are estimated to be stable numbers of all these at present, with some several hundred lynx, together with around 200 wolves and more than 600 brown bears. Forests are also home to the flying squirrel, an animal seldom found elsewhere in Europe. Ten species of rare and protected birds include the golden eagle, white-tailed eagle, spotted eagle and eagle owl, as well as the rare black stork.

LONG COAST AND MANY ISLANDS

The country has a long and, in many areas, dramatically beautiful coastline that covers some 3,794km (2,357 miles), most of which belongs to the 1,000-plus islands. The coast differs from the rough granite seaboard of its northern neighbour, Finland, and the sandy beaches of Latvia to the south. It changes from limestone cliffs in the north to sandy beaches and shelving coastal meadows in the west. These coastal meadows used to be widespread but today only a few are grazed; the rest have become overgrown with juniper or reed, and conservation programmes are under way to restore them.

For most of the second half of the 20th century, much of it was a restricted zone. This helped to preserve it from extensive development. Today, grey seals frequent the undisturbed shores and roughly one-fifth of the estimated 7,500 Baltic grey seals tend to keep close to the Estonian coast. During mild and ice-free winters, many give birth to their pups on the small islets.

The country is also a stopover point for Arctic waterfowl migrating along the East Atlantic Flyway. According to some estimates, up to 50 million water and coastal birds use the abundant coastal wetlands. Many stop here to prepare for the long journey to their Russian Arctic breeding grounds. During the first two weeks of

White storks are considered harbingers of good fortune.

⊘ TOP 10 NATURE SIGHTS

Lahemaa National Park, Estonia. Set beside the north coast, Lahemaa is a great place to see Estonian nature in all its rugged beauty. www.keskkonnaamet.ee

Lake Peipsi, Estonia. The fifth-largest lake in Europe is by far the best for fishing. www.visitpeipsi.com

Matsalu National Park, Estonia. A birdwatchers' paradise with observation towers and hiking trails.

Saaremaa Island, Estonia. This natural gem abounds in unusual flora and fauna. www.saaremaa.ee

Gauja National Park, Latvia. Around the spectacular River Gauja there is some wonderful hiking and impressive caves linked to local folklore.

Ķemeri National Park, Latvia. Part forest, part swamp, containing medicinal waters. A birdwatchers' treat. www.daba.gov.lv

Kolka, Latvia. Unique for many reasons – sublime beaches, remarkable lighthouse, great birdlife. www.kolka.info

Aukštaitija National Park, Lithuania. Nature trails through the many lakes and unspoilt forest. www.anp.lt

The Curonian Spit, Lithuania. Carved out by the wind and Baltic Sea, this is a natural miracle of pine forest and dune. www.nerija.lt

Žuvintas Biosphere Reserve, Lithuania. A boggy area rich in wildlife, it is known as the "kingdom of birds". www.zuvintas.lt

May, every small inlet teems with coots, grebes, ducks, geese and swans.

The biggest coastal wetland is Matsalu, a large bay surrounded by various coastal habitats, which has been turned into a national park (http://loodusegakoos.ee). During the spring migration, more than 2 million waterfowl pass through Matsalu, primarily long-tailed and other Arctic diving ducks.

The islands, which make up nearly 10 percent of the country's total territory, really set the country apart from its otherwise similar southern neighbours. The largest of these are Saaremaa and Hiiumaa, both of which are becomingly increasingly popular tourist destinations because of their raw beauty and unchanged way of life. There are hundreds of species of moss, and recently scientists were overjoyed to discover completely new species on Hiiumaa. But many of the islands are all but inaccessible in winter when, around January, the surrounding sea freezes over for about three months.

NATIONAL PARKS

There are five national parks in Estonia, as well as many nature reserves. Two of the most spectacular are Karula and Lahemaa National Parks. Karula National Park, near Valka in the south of Estonia, was established in 1993 to protect a unique landscape and its rich natural ecosystem. More than 70 percent of the territory is covered by forest, which varies from dry sandy pine forests to waterlogged swamp forests. This, along with many small lakes and streams, creates an ideal habitat for wildlife, including wolves, elk, otters, beavers, golden eagles and black storks.

Lahemaa is the oldest national park in Estonia and is the best developed for tourism, with a visitors' centre, well-marked trails and paths and

With a total area of around 500 sq km, the Matsalu National Park is an area of open floodplains, coastal pastures and wooded meadows as well as one of the most important autumn stopping grounds for the migrating birds in Europe – some 275 species can be seen in the park.

In one wooded meadow in Vahenurme in Pärnumaa County, Estonia, there are 74 different species of flora per square metre.

guided tours. The park has glimmering cliffs, broadleaf primeval forests, stone fields with giant boulders, small coastal lakes and bogs, as well as charming coastal villages, farms and old German manor estates with immaculately landscaped parks.

Wild boar.

Lakes produce whitefish, notably Lake Peipsi, and Võrtsjärv is famous for pike-perch and eel which are prized for the table.

LATVIA

Latvians' love of nature is particularly striking for its, well… naturalness. And it's apparent in everything from the way many people routinely adorn their homes with fresh flowers, to the fact that many Latvian surnames are derived from the names of various trees, flowers, animals and birds. It is mainly a low-lying plain, which is generally fertile, with lakes towards the east. More than 8 percent of the country is protected by law in four state reserves, three national parks and other protected areas.

Latvia's national flower is the oxe-eye daisy, and its national bird is the pied wagtail.

THE COAST

Latvia has an especially beautiful coastline, which stretches for some 494km (307 miles) along the Baltic Sea. Locals certainly make good use of the abundance of white sandy beaches during the summer, but you can always find a secluded stretch of beach for yourself if you're prepared to drive that little bit further on from popular tourist spots such as Jūrmala, Saulkrasti and Liepāja. In

Latvia is one of the few places in the entire Baltic Sea region where natural salmon spawning still occurs.

region, where many of these are found, is known as the "Land of the Blue Lakes". Nearly all inland waters ideally suited for swimming and fishing are pollution-free.

There are still a few beds of river pearl, a freshwater mussel requiring a pristine environ-

There are estimated to be around 400 lynx in the forests of Latvia.

the last century the resort of Jūrmala, which is just 20km (13 miles) away from Rīga, was considered one of the most prestigious summer spots in the entire USSR.

As in Estonia, the strict coastal restrictions during Soviet times helped preserve much of the natural beauty of the coastline, and there are still countless picturesque fishing villages strewn right the way along the shores where locals sell smoked fish and other seafood on rickety stalls by the roadside.

RIVERS AND LAKES

Latvia has more than 12,000 rivers, which together stretch for 38,000km (23,610 miles), as well as more than 2,000 lakes. The Latgale

ment to produce its pearls, which were once collected for royalty. Much of the river water, however, originates beyond Latvia's borders, over which they have no control, and occasionally industrial pollutants get into the larger rivers. Although some rivers have had their courses straightened, most large and medium-sized rivers retain their natural contours.

Many lakes provide feeding and breeding grounds for numerous bird species. Some of the most ecologically valuable of these are the shallow coastal lagoons along the Baltic coast. Places such as Lakes Pape, Liepājas, Engure, Babītes and Kaniera were cut off from the sea long ago and are now fresh water. Rare species of birds, such as the bearded tit, common and little bittern, corncrake, hen harrier, and little and spotted crake nest in Lake Pape and its surroundings. The lake and the nearby Nida marsh are important stopovers for bean and white-fronted goose and curlews during migration.

FORESTS AND MARSHLAND

Forests cover some 45 percent of Latvia's territory – compared, for example, with 8 percent in Britain. Most are mixed coniferous and broadleaf, with mainly pine, spruce, birch, aspen and black alder, though oak and lasts from late June until late September, the latter also being the time for gathering mushrooms, a favourite pastime – the Latvian word *sēņot* means "to go mushroom-picking". The most popular mushrooms are the edible boletus (very tasty with sour cream), orange cap boletus, chanterelles and rusulla. Best of all, the vast majority of forests, with a wealth of berries, mushrooms and hazelnuts, are free for everyone to enjoy.

Indigenous Latvian wildlife is similar to that of its Baltic neighbours. Some 4,000 Eurasian

Konik Polski wild horses in Pape Nature Reserve, Latvia.

lime trees are especially important in Latvian life. About a quarter of Latvia's forests feature extensive areas of wetland, habitats that have been mostly destroyed in other European countries. These so-called "swamp" forests cover large areas of low-lying ground that are permanently or seasonally flooded. Many rare plant and animal species belong here. Home to more than 1,000 pairs of black storks (about 10 percent of the world's population), 500 pairs of the lesser spotted eagle, woodpeckers and many other species, these forests are a dream for birdwatchers.

The forests also have a rich supply of berries – wild strawberries, blueberries, raspberries and loganberries. The berry-picking season otters live in the rivers. There are an estimated 200–400 wolves at large, as well as 400 lynxes. Beavers, which were hunted to extinction by the end of the 19th century, were successfully reintroduced into the country in the 20th century and now number an estimated 50,000–80,000.

Marshland makes up almost 5 percent of the country, most of which is unspoilt habitat. There are more than 20 protected plant species within this territory, and at least 15 species of bird that nest here, including the crane, golden plover, black grouse, whimbrel, merlin and peregrine. Marshes are also popular with berry-pickers for the cranberries, cloudberries, cowberries and bilberries that grow here.

NATIONAL PARKS

Nearly 7 percent of Latvia is protected by law. There are four nature reserves, four national parks and 240 protected areas – nature parks, protected landscape areas, restricted areas and biosphere reserves.

Teiči State Reserve (see page 256) is the largest protected marsh in the Baltic and a sight well worth seeing. A raised bog covers most of the territory, but there are also 19 lakes, hollows, mineral-soil islands, fens, swamps and natural meadows. It also has

LITHUANIA

Like its Baltic neighbours, Lithuania is predominantly flat. Its highest point is at Aukštójo kalnas, which stands an underwhelming 294 metres (964ft) above sea level. It lies on the western fringe of the East European Plain that stretches across Belarus and part of Russia. Much of the country is agricultural land, producing corn and root crops, while cattle include the indigenous Light Grey Lithuanian breed, found in the south and west of the country. As the country encompasses both coniferous and broadleaf

A honey buzzard with chick in nest.

the largest concentration of pre-migratory cranes in Latvia. An ancient Russian village of Russian Old Believers (people who adhere to the Russian Orthodox Church as well as old pagan beliefs) still exists on one of the marsh islands. The marsh can only be entered in the company of a guide.

Gauja National Park (see page 251) is one of the most spectacular places in Latvia and is named after Latvia's longest river. For 90km (56 miles) the Gauja flows through a breathtaking valley that is the heart of the park. Nowhere else in Latvia are there so many steep banks, ravines, streams, sandstone and dolomite cliffs, and caves. Sigulda makes a good starting point.

⊘ ENVIRONMENTAL CONCERNS

There have been a number of threats to the purity of the Baltic States' environment, starting with the Soviet withdrawal, during which aircraft fuel and oil from marine terminals were dumped. Power plants running off oil shale in Narva give Estonia unusually high sulphur dioxide emissions, and air pollution occurs around chemical and cement industries. There is also natural erosion of arable land by wind and water. Some 70 percent of Lithuania's wetlands have been lost through land drainage for agriculture, and mineral fertilisers washed from fields into the water is a big problem.

forests, it has a mixture of habitats sustaining a rich variety of wildlife.

Rue is Lithuania's national flower and the white stork is the national bird.

FORESTS

Once entirely covered with thick forests and bogs, about a third of Lithuania is still under tree cover. Most of the forest is coniferous, but in the central and southern parts of the country, small areas of Central European deciduous forests have survived.

The forests and wetlands are home to elk, wolves, lynxes and beavers, and the edible dormouse. The rare mountain hare can be found in marshy bog lands. Birds of prey include the white-tailed eagle, osprey, honey buzzard and lesser-spotted eagle. In 1969 a breeding centre was set up for the European bison, once common to the region, in Pasiliai Forest in the Panevėžys district. Their numbers, then diminishing, have all but disappeared.

BY THE WATER

Lithuania's glacial history can be seen in the country's abundance of rivers, lakes and wetlands. Up to 22,000 streams and rivers, including the 937km (582-mile) Nemunas, transform the landscape into a liquid latticework, and about 3,000 lakes cover some 1.5 percent of the country. Many of these are ideal for swimming. It's still possible to find your "own" lake, where few others go, even in the height of summer.

There are some 60 different kinds of freshwater fish, including native perch, tench and sea trout, as well as introduced species such as sturgeon. Lake Žuvintas in the south is an important breeding ground and migration resting ground for many kinds of water birds. It is also one of the few breeding grounds for endangered species such as the aquatic warbler and ferruginous duck.

Although Lithuania is the largest of the Baltic States, it has the shortest coastline at just 99km (62 miles). Most of it is taken up by the Curonian Spit, a thin stretch of sand composed mostly of dunes and pine forests that separates the Curonian Lagoon from the Baltic Sea. This precious natural habitat has a number or rare and protected plants, as well as a distinctive insect life, including a rich diversity

of butterflies, such as the Camberwell Beauty. There are also sea eagles here, and the largest colony of stalks in the country. Lithuania also boasts Europe's largest population of white storks: 13,000 pairs. Long-nosed seals are sometimes seen on the shore.

NATIONAL PARKS

There are five national parks and 30 regional parks, covering around 12 percent of the country. Aukštaitija National Park was the first one, designated in 1974, and covering an area of

As elsewhere in Europe, foxes have become common in suburban areas.

40,570 hectares (100,250 acres) around Ignalina, Utena and Švenčionys. The park is especially picturesque and perfectly encapsulates the lush, primeval beauty of Lithuanian nature.

The majestic Trakai National Park (www.seniejitrakai.lt), which lies 25km (16 miles) from Vilnius, was designated in 1992 and embraces the historic city of Trakai, together with the forests, lakes and villages in its vicinity.

Between all the various national parks and nature reserves, the sizeable protected natural habitat of Lithuania supports a huge variety of wildlife, including elk, deer, wolves, foxes and wild boar. Bird species include ospreys, white-tailed eagles and white storks.

OUTDOOR ACTIVITIES

From river rafting to sky-diving, snowboarding to Zorbing, the long coast, sleepy rivers and lush national parks are ideal places to get active and have some recreational fun.

Rural tourism and outdoor recreation are increasingly important in the Baltic economy. Estonia, Latvia and Lithuania continue to come up with good reasons for tourists to trek beyond the capital cities for some outdoor fun. The countries' nearly untouched ecosystem is scattered with small tourism enterprises, offering activities from hot-air ballooning to river rafting and horse riding on wild mares.

Regardless of the sport, and dramatic high ground notwithstanding, the countryside has sufficiently diverse beauty to create a playground for the outdoor enthusiast – and none are more enthusiastic than the Baltic peoples themselves.

GAUJA NATIONAL PARK

The national parks in all three countries are well equipped for outdoor activities, with hiking trails and tended waterways. Latvia's major playground, Gauja National Park, centred on the towns of Sigulda and Cēsis, is a particular magnet for outdoor adventurers. Like every state park in the Baltics, it is carved with hiking trails, observation points and camping sites, as well as historic landscapes that include castle ruins and archaeological excavation areas.

The River Gauja cuts through the park's ancient valley of sandstone and dolomite cliffs. There is water rafting, trail bungee-jumping, and a cable car for an overview of the scenery. Lacking dramatic white-water river rafting on the slow-moving Gauja is by no means dangerous, and offers an ideal way to enjoy the park's natural splendours with the family. Tourists can rent rafts that accommodate around 10 people with an accompanying guide, as well as private canoes and boats. The Gauja is riddled with small whirlpools, which swimmers

Cyclists on wooden hiking trail in Lahemaa National Park.

are cautioned about, and any skilled canoeist can work his or her way to a thrilling amount of speed on the 90km (55-mile) stretch of river.

Avid spelunkers will be able to find the largest cave in the Baltic States – Gūtmanis' Cave – in the centre of Gauja National Park. The cave's natural sand catacombs wind 18.8 metres (62ft) deep, 12 metres (40ft) wide and 10 metres (33ft) high.

Sigulda's most prized recreational feature is the professional 1,420-metre (4,660ft) long bobsleigh track (www.bobtrase.lv). Open year-round, it allows visitors to live out their dream of participating in one of the Winter Olympics' most popular sports. In professional bobsleigh and luge training and competitions, athletes reach speeds of up to 125kph (78mph). Amateurs, however, will fly through the concrete track at a much safer speed of 80kph (50mph) under the guidance of professionals. The tourist bobsleigh, called Vučko, is open from noon to 5pm every weekend between October and mid-March, and there is also a summer bobsleigh from May to September.

Lithuania is famous for its adventure and climbing parks, with the largest one in Druskininkai (http://unoparks.lt) offering trails for beginners as well as seasoned climbers (children and adults). A giant 21-metre (69ft) swing and an extreme

WATER SPORTS

During the summer months, the coast provides activities and relaxation in a variety of ways. Sailing between the mainland and Estonia's remarkable 1,520 islands is perhaps the most elegant way to enjoy the stunning coast. Visitors can splurge on a yacht trip to the island of Kihnu or spend a more casual day in the Bay of Pärnu watching the Baltic sunset over the boats. Or they might take a fishing trip. There is no shortage of sailing trips along the country's 3,794km (2,357-mile) shoreline.

Kayaking in Sigulda, Latvia.

55kmh (34mph) flight over the Nemunas River are definitely not for the faint-hearted. Fans of more laid-back outdoor activities will be delighted to find the beautiful area surrounding the historic resort and spa criss-crossed with cycling routes while families with children may spent the entire day at the amazing Aqua Park (http://akvapark.lt), which boasts six outdoor and indoor pools (including the sea-wave pool), 9-metre (29.5ft) palm trees, cascades and whirlpools, as well as 22 saunas and bathhouses. A 221 metre (725ft) -long slide adds a bit of a thrill to this tropical paradise. Even skiers will be able to practice their favourite sport in the middle of summer at the local Snow Arena (www.snowarena.lt) featuring indoor as well as outdoor skiing tracks.

Sea excursions are so popular, however, that booking should be made at least a few weeks in advance.

Yacht charters for both bareboat and skippered vessels are available at the main marinas, in Tallinn, Jūrmala and Klaipėda, but boating has not yet reached its full potential.

For those who prefer boating activities of a more sporty nature, speedboat, jet-ski and wake-board rentals are offered at most of the seaside resorts. Windsurfing, kitesurfing and kiteboarding (with its main hotspot at Svencele), are also popular coastal activities, and the relatively safe shallow waters are a good place to learn. Water temperatures seldom rise above 17°C (63°F) in summer. Diving centres in Tallinn,

Kipsala island on the River Daugava in Rīga, and from a base in Lithuania's Kaunas offer certified courses with trained professionals as well as open-water dives. There is diving in some lakes, too, but the best place for diving is off the coast, where one can explore the Baltic Sea's deep underwater secrets, including wreck sites. The wrecks in the Baltic are of special interest, but you need a guide, as there are unexploded World War II mines and munitions here. Countless rivers and lakes abundant in wildlife provide the perfect scenery for the kayaking and rafting

Hot-air balloons in Vilnius

trips which are highly popular here, particularly in Lithuania and Latvia.

EXTREME AND AIRBORNE SPORTS

Traditional daredevil activities include the annual ice-horse race on Lake Sartai, Lithuania. Kiiking, invented by Estonian Ado Kosk, in which participants are strapped to rigid poles and swing through 360 degrees, is also popular. In Rīga, you can imagine you are on the moon when you go catapult jumping.

Another staple is Zorbing, dry and wet. In Dry Zorbing the participant is strapped inside the ball and then tumbles around, hurtling down hills at speeds of up to 56kph (35mph). In Wet Zorbing the ball has some water in it, and the

participant slides about as the ball rolls around, much as in a water slide.

There is no better way to take in the patchwork countryside than from above. There are pleasure flights in Rīga, and the Kaunas Acrobatic Flying Club (www.aerokaunas.lt) offers delta-plane flights and paragliding for recreational enjoyment. Professional lessons are provided for beginners, though flights depend on weather conditions.

Skydiving has also, as it were, taken off. Founded in 1992 at Pociunai Airfield, the Kaunas Skydiving Club (www.skydive.lt) is the oldest parachute club in Lithuania and one of the most popular in the Baltics. The club is open every weekend from March to October and organises more than 5,000 jumps a year. Although the majority of skydivers are familiar to the sport, the club's professional staff offer training for beginners, who can choose a static-line or tandem jump. Skydiving is on offer in Rīga and Tallinn, too. Those who want to experience a freefall without having to jump out of the plane should head for Aerodium (www.aerodium.lv) situated less than 50km (31 miles) from Rīga, just before Sigulda. It is Eastern Europe's first vertical wind tunnel and was originally used for training military parachutists and astronauts, but is now a major tourist attraction. The flight simulator allows you to do acrobatic manoeuvres in the air and feel as free as a bird. A short flying lesson and essential equipment are provided.

Hot-air ballooning is a less intimidating way to enjoy the landscape from the air. A tradition that goes back for years, all three countries have

⊘ SOMETHING FOR THE BOYS

Fuelled by stag-party thrill-seekers and urged on by corporate team-builders, there are numerous activities for competitive (usually males), including the chance to pull the trigger of a Luger pistol or the infamous AK-47. You can paintball in a former Soviet base in Tallinn or join a military day and be "attacked" by the KGB. In Rīga, attractions include an F1 speed simulator, bobsleigh, go-karting, mud buggy races and hovercrafting, while 4x4 Extreme Action Days have competitors roaring through forest and swamp. You can go on quad safaris, enjoy aerobatics, karting, Zorbing, catapulting and just about anything else that will get the blood racing.

air-balloon festivals that bring a rainbow of floating ornaments to the skies each summer. The rides are an ideal way to enjoy a scenic evening of relaxation, with baskets comfortably carrying up to three people. For a cityscape ballooning trip visit Eurocentras in Vilnius. For a taste of rustic scenery, Nemunaitis village in the Alytus district of Lithuania is the best place to call.

HORSE RIDING

For centuries, horse riding has been the most traditional and best-enjoyed outdoor activity. Even today, Balts treasure this age-old way of getting around that carries a trail of culture and folklore behind it. The flatlands make hacking easy and, whether it's bareback riding along the coastal dunes of Latvia or keeping to the tame wooded paths of Estonia, riding is one of the most romantic ways to enjoy the outdoors. There are numerous stables and riding clubs throughout all three countries that offer lessons for every level, and many agriturismo farms have their own horses.

WINTER SPORTS

The polar freeze that strikes northeastern Europe from mid-November, lasting until late March, has earned quite a name for Baltic winters. Yet the long snowy days serve as the perfect excuse to head to the country for some winter sports and hot mulled wine. Temperatures in all three Baltic states sink to between 0 and –15°C (32 and 5°F) during the winter. With a generous snowfall, these temperatures create ideal skiing conditions.

There are no Alpine peaks – the highest it gets in the Baltics is 318-metre (1,044ft) Suur Munamägi (Big Egg Hill) in Estonia. Yet that same country's "winter capital", Otepää, has ski jumps and holds the World Cup Cross-Country Skiing Championship each January.

Winter sports such as skiing, snowboarding, hockey, ski-mobiling – even ice fishing – manage to keep Baltic inhabitants entertained all season long.

GOLF

Golf is a 21st-century arrival in the Baltic States. The rural landscapes, with an abundance of water hazards, woodland and wild areas, offer fine opportunities for inventive courses. Clubs tend to open from April to October. In Estonia Valgaranna (White Beach) Golf in Pärnu and the Niitväja Tallinn Golf Club are both 18 holes. Other courses near Tallinn include Estonian Golf and Country Club (EGCC) and Golf X Rae. The first course to open in Latvia was Ozo, just north of Rīga, in 2002. It

Snow-boarding in Otepää, Estonia's "winter capital".

has 16 ponds and 50 sand bunkers, and you will need to produce a handicap certificate. To the south of the city is Saliena Golf, with an 18-hole championship Club Course and a 9-hole Garden Course.

Lithuania's European Centre GC, opened in 2007, is an 18-hole championship-standard course, next to lake Girja, 20 minutes' drive from Vilnius. The 18-hole Capitals Golf Club between Vilnius and Kaunas, opened the same year, is also well located, in a rural setting with lakes and woodland. Another excellent golf site near Vilnius is the V Golf Club, offering an 18-hole modern course which blends the best features of Scottish Links and American design elements.

A classic Baltic lunch spread.

FOOD

Baltic food is fresh and wholesome, relying on the natural flavours of fish from its waterways, meat and dairy produce from its farms, a colourful array of fruit and vegetables from its gardens and juicy berries from the forests.

Baltic cooking today is basically pretty straightforward country fare. The plain, wholesome, unspicy dishes characteristic of all three countries – although especially Latvia and Estonia – demand little artistry, but nevertheless can be very good.

The best place to see what's in the Baltic larder is in Rīga, where, if your schedule allows, you should take an hour or two to peruse the Zeppelin hangars that house the city's massive – and extremely crowded – market. Scores of indoor stalls tout fresh and fermented dairy products: vast slabs of soft white cheese, harder yellow cheese, bottles of sour cream, yoghurt and cultivated sour milk. In another hall, high-quality fresh pork gleams pink, and many varieties of sausage and ham wait to be sampled. Smoked fish sells at one end of the market, while fresh fruit is on offer at the other.

Honey features regularly in local cuisine.

SUMMER HARVEST

In summer, baskets are piled high with early apples and pears – small irregular specimens that are not subject to the trading controls that are all too familiar in Western Europe; glass tumblers spill over with red and black berries and tiny yellow mirabelle plums. Look out for the different varieties of nuts, the dried fruit, the umbrils of caraway seed drying on the branch, huge bunches of fresh, strong, flat-leaf parsley, pots of honey, barrels of sauerkraut lined up for tasting and trays of fresh, home-made black, brown and white bread. These staple foods, which are brought in by private sellers from the nearby countryside, are the raw materials of traditional Baltic cooking.

These ingredients are usually served at the table with very little seasoning. In the vegetable hall you may smell dill and garlic – but for flavour Latvia mostly relies on fermented milk, smoked fish and cheese, and bacon, with a sprinkling here and there of caraway seed, rather than strong herbs and spices. Onions are considered too strong to feature heavily. Lithuanian cooking, partly influenced by the Orient, is the most pungent of the three.

This hint of oriental spice in Lithuanian cooking is a result of the country's complicated political past. From the 15th century exiled Crimean Tatars and refugees from the Golden Horde flocked to this powerful state to coexist with Russians, Belarusians and Poles under the leadership of the Polish/Lithuanian noble class. The results today are a half-forgotten legacy of exoticism and luxury, recipes which dare to include black pepper and nutmeg and marjoram. Spices were imported from the East; marjoram was probably brought into the country from Italy, via Catholic Poland.

With independence came a rediscovery of the richness of Estonian, Latvian and Lithuanian traditional country-style cooking. In each of the three capitals, countless traditional restaurants have opened, typically offering heavy butter-doused Lithuanian *cepelinai* and

Pickled herring and local mushrooms in Lithuania.

other local dishes. However, the best local cooking can usually still be sampled in private homes.

BREAD BASKETS

Excellent natural resources, quality farming and careful husbandry contribute to the goodness of Baltic food. The lush land provides rich harvests of grains and berries, dark forests provide the ideal environment for mushroom growth, fish populate the rivers, lakes and sea, and pig and dairy farming are important industries.

Rye bread, which has a strong rich taste, is enhanced by molasses, made from nativegrowing sugar beet, and caraway seed. This bread keeps well and is an ideal

accompaniment to the local beer, cheeses and pungent cured meat and fish. One type of pale rye loaf, which has a smooth, shiny, tan-coloured crust, is known as Rīga bread and is best eaten when it is fresh and sweet. (Most bakers hang a two-pronged testing fork beside their self-service shelves.)

Other Baltic speciality breads include the plain dark rye variety that is often served in hotels and which should not be judged by the dryness and sourness it exudes when left indefinitely exposed to the air. (Don't let this put you off.) Among the white breads are the robust and versatile French *baton*, not at all like its Gallic counterpart, and the creamy-coloured sourdough loaves that are usually home-made and well worth seeking out for their extraordinary muscular texture.

More than one Western traveller has made a meal out of bread alone, to the consternation of the locals, who cry: "But where's the sausage to go with it, or the butter?" (In the Baltics they love their meats and fats.)

PORRIDGE AND POTATOES

Although porridge used to be a staple food in these parts, porridges made from cooked grain are now rarely seen on menus except on special occasions. The ancient Latvian version, called *putra*, is made of barley (or a mix of barley and potato) and typically served with a ladle of bacon fat, some smoked meat or fish, or perhaps also with milk products, as a main course. In Estonia mixed-grain porridges are sometimes served with milk. There is also a breakfast speciality that is akin to Scottish porridge: *kama*, made of ground toasted grains and raw oats, is mixed with yoghurt or milk and eaten with salt or honey. *Kama* is good for upset stomachs. There is another dish that is similar to porridge, which is made of mushy peas and then eaten with bacon fat.

The Baltic Germans introduced the potato to the Baltics at the start of the 18th century, and the whole region fell for its charms, especially the Lithuanians. Today they eat boiled potatoes with everything from yoghurt to bacon fat, and, like the Poles and the Jews, they are fans of grated potato pancakes. The same grated potato is used to make a variety of filled rissoles, such as *cepelinai*, meaning that this potassium-rich foodstuff plays a part in most daily diets. Yeast-leavened wheat dough – the foodstuff from which genuine pizza bases are made – is another staple carbohydrate here. On street corners in Tallinn you can buy slightly sweet white dough made from this yeast-leavened wheat, which tastes deliciously fresh.

In Latvia the array of savoury baking is highly enviable. Special treats include cheese- and meat-filled yeast-dough buns

If a Lithuanian were asked to name his or her favourite dish, it would probably be something prepared with potato, particularly latkes, known in Lithuania as bulviniai blynai.

Although fat features so prominently in the Baltic diet, it is interesting to note that traditional food here is rarely fried. Vegetables and carbohydrates are typically boiled first and

Grūdenis is a thick country stew from Latvia that uses a pig's head.

and yeast-dough horns stuffed to the brim with minced bacon. If pizza makes you think of pasta, look no further than Lithuania, where cooking is strongly influenced by the Russian and Polish fondness for Slavic *koldūnai* – another Baltic treat.

FAT FEASTS

One of the hallmarks of Baltic food is the non-prevalence of protein. Meat and fish, at least in Latvia and Estonia, are eaten in very small quantities, almost as a dressing or garnish to the bread, pasta or porridge rather than the focus of a meal. Rich, fatty foods, rather than lean meats, tend to prove most popular at special feasts.

are then covered later with fat – whether it's in the form of bacon, cheese or, quite simply, with butter.

Pork is without doubt the most commonly eaten meat, though quality beef is also available, as well as game, including duck and sometimes hare. (The term pork covers salt pork, sausage and the black pudding – blood sausage – that Estonians eat every year on Christmas Day.)

In the 15th century Lithuania was highly renowned for its smoked wild boar. Domestic pig farming was later introduced by the Germans with exceptional results. This pork production industry was so successful that smoked lean pork from the Baltics, all pink, wrinkled, juicy and tender, is believed to have been the stuff of many a privileged Communist Party banquet. Smoked lean pork is certainly more inviting than the wedges of salted pork fat, the dietary mainstay of the labouring male peasant in the 1900s, which are still classed as a delicacy.

On commercial menus you will come across hot, fresh meat dishes more familiar to the visitor than anything mentioned so far. In many restaurants, meat cutlets, fried escalopes, meatballs and boiled and fried sausages are more often than not prepared by foreign chefs.

Strawberries, just one of many forest fruits.

FISH DISHES

If you like fish, you'll find there is much in the way of local delicacies to tempt you here. Local fish preparations, such as smoked saltwater salmon, pickled herring, smoked sprats and smoked eel, rank among the best fish dishes in the world. If you travel around the fishing villages, you will have the chance of sampling locally smoked fish, while around the inland lake districts you are likely to encounter freshwater fish dishes, notably those using trout, pike and pike-perch.

In Latvia and Lithuania fish is often cooked in bacon fat – a rare case of frying. Russian caviar, once the pride of every restaurant menu, is becoming increasingly difficult to find and is now

> *In Tallinn, look out for bars and restaurants that have won Silver Spoon Awards from the Gastronomy Society of Estonia. These are given annually in 10 different categories.*

very expensive. More affordable are the Estonian fresh fish soups, which are made with vegetables and thickened with flour and milk.

COLD DISHES

Until early in the 20th century two-thirds of traditional Baltic dishes were those for its cold table. This is something that seems to come especially into its own at breakfast, when a mix of cheese and meat, as well as vegetables and cream, is served. At other times of the day, the cold table is often supplemented with soup.

Salads are an important part of the cold table. They are usually accompanied by dressings and eaten with bread. One of the culinary highlights of a visit can be a bowl of tomatoes and cucumbers picked straight from a country garden, tossed with fresh dill and parsley and sour cream.

Sometimes strips of meat or cheese are used in the same way as raw vegetables to make composite salads for the cold table, but often these are covered in bottled flavourings. Unfortunately, they represent only a poor attempt at a quick urban cuisine adapted from the country.

SOUPS

Although there are old recipes in Lithuania for varieties of beetroot soup along the lines of the Russian/Ukrainian/Polish beetroot-based borscht, and for mushroom soup, this liquid dish is most typically found on the menus of cheaper eateries. Lithuanian beetroot soup has a sweet-and-sour base and is flavoured with sorrel, a rich source of iron and vitamin C.

Estonian food is generally fairly mild, and its soups are no exception. A classic Estonian soup contains milk, dried peas and buckwheat grains, and the majority of varieties of this are made with milk and vegetables, or with yoghurt and dill cucumber.

Under German influence, Latvia and Estonia used to make a sweet bread soup out of leftover fruit. Since the bread was probably sour and black the soup was closely related to the sour-sweet *ķīselis* made with summer berries. Beer soups belong to this curious category.

GARDEN PRODUCE

The country garden is something that is celebrated in all three states, and it cannot be stressed highly enough how vital a part it plays in Baltic culture. One of the most charming and notable poems in Lithuanian literature

Another crop that is increasing in importance in Latvia and Lithuania is sea buckthorn, which produces a juice full of minerals.

CAKES

At the opposite end of the spectrum from the healthy ideal of the country garden is the Baltic sweet trolley. Nowadays, cakes are generally more popular than desserts in the Baltics, and there are some excellent specialist chocolate shops. In Lithuania, look out for treecakes and honey cakes. Treecakes are made by adding

Cold borscht, a summer dish.

– one that is frequently, and many believe quite rightly, compared to Virgil's *Eclogues* – is called *The Seasons*, written by an 18th-century clergyman, Kristijonas Donelaitis. In the kitchen garden, which became popular in Donelaitis' time, the sweetest tomatoes, ridge cucumbers, courgettes, beets, kohlrabi, potatoes, swede and turnips grow in profusion alongside peas and cabbages and rhubarb. Somewhere near the vegetable garden you will also find apple trees and plum trees and, in an ideal world, a beehive. A guest might enjoy an inspiring summer tea made from baked sour windfall apples sweetened with clear plum jam and macaroons. Nothing is wasted.

⊘ BERRIES FROM THE FORESTS

Blueberries, bilberries, cloudberries, cranberries, lingonberries, raspberries, strawberries, whortleberries... there is a wonderful kaleidoscope of berries found in the Baltic forests and bogs. You can come across these in roadside stalls, as well as in restaurants and on the dining table. Try corn pancakes with berries and yoghurt for breakfast, or as pies and tarts or flavoured ice creams. There are juices and country fruit wines, and gins flavoured with berries – including juniper berries, which are often used in cooking. Anyone with a garden will grow berries and currants along with their flowers.

dough in layers to a rotating wooden pole in front of a hot fire. The result is a cake with many age lines and fungi-like appendages clinging to its outer "bark", where dollops of egg and lemon dough have been added. Despite its peculiar appearance, it is quite delicious.

In cafés, where many varieties of shortbreads, shortcrust and flaky pastries, and eclairs are sold, you can't help noticing that Latvians and Estonians have a penchant for eating large amounts of sweet whipped cream with their cakes. Chocolate cafés are the in-thing in Rīga.

Gira, a Lithuanian non-alcoholic brew made from dark rye.

DRINKS AND PICNICS

Coffee is one dietary feature that distinguishes Russia from the Baltics: coffee is far more prevalent here. Both tea and coffee are served without milk. Mineral water is normally good-quality (note that although tap water in Rīga is safe to drink it may sometimes come with an unpleasant smell).

If you are in the mood for something stronger, you'll find that the majority of bars and cafés serve beer on tap rather than in bottles. The main breweries (Kalnapilis and Utenos in Lithuania, Aldaris in Latvia and Saku and A. Le Cocq in Estonia) all have their loyal following. The local brews are available

> *Founded in 1870, Rīga's major chocolate manufacturer, Laima, makers of chocolate boxes, candies and biscuits, offers tours of its factory. See www.laima.lv*

on tap in most restaurants. The popular craze in Vilnius is for live beers from the nation's microbreweries.

Herbal eau-de-vie, Rīga Black Balsam (a dark brew, which tastes like a mixture of treacle and Campari), sweet Lithuanian liqueurs, locally produced Russian vodka and sparkling wines complete the standard alcoholic line-up. You may also find expensive wines from France and less costly but decent vintages from Georgia, Hungary and Romania.

Traditional food is considered by many Balts as something they make at home, but wouldn't necessarily look for when they go out, hence its scarcity in restaurants. The best local food is therefore enjoyed in private homes or as a picnic, composed of some of the delicacies offered at a typical Baltic cold table – excellent fresh vegetables, cold meats and tasty, albeit mild cheeses. Although the fare served in long-established hotels may seem rather heavy and fatty to the diet-conscious, health-obsessed Westerner, it can work wonders for an empty stomach. More imaginative chefs are beginning to look at how to use traditional ingredients in new ways.

⊘ SPECIAL OCCASIONS

Christmas Day is celebrated with pork dishes in Estonia, goose in Protestant Latvia, and fish and mushrooms in Catholic Lithuania. During midsummer, dairy products come into their own. A special dense yellow country cheese, smoked and flavoured with caraway seeds, is traditionally produced for midsummer (Jāņi, or St John's Day) in Latvia; a similar, spicier cheese is eaten in Lithuania, where *kugelis*, the national potato dish is in every home. You can sample both varieties of cheeses in Rīga's Central Market, and you should keep an eye out for local cheeses while travelling round the country.

Honeycomb and home-made cheese.

Watery landscape at Aukštaitija, Lithuania.

Figures outside the National Drama Theatre, Vilnius.

Autumn colours in Pärnu, Estonia.

Estonia, Latvia and Lithuania

INTRODUCTION

The principal sites in this detailed guide to Estonia, Latvia and Lithuania are clearly cross-referenced by number or letter to the maps.

Kõpu lighthouse, Hiiumaa island, Estonia.

Added together, the countries of Estonia, Latvia and Lithuania, each covering about the same area, are a little larger than England and Wales, or the size of Washington State. They sit side by side on the eastern edge of the Baltic Sea between Poland and the Gulf of Finland. Tallinn, the northernmost capital, is on roughly the same latitude as Scotland's Orkney Islands and southern Alaska. Vilnius, capital of Lithuania in the south, shares an approximate latitude with Newcastle and Newfoundland. This means that summer days lengthen into white nights and winter days are grey and short.

Although they have linguistic, cultural and historical differences, the three countries share a similar landscape. The overwhelming image is one of quiet roads and flatlands, rising in low, rolling hills towards the east, of myriad small rivers and lakes and of forests of the tallest pines. Scattered throughout are ancient hill forts and occasional boulders, "presents from Scandinavia" left by retreating glaciers. Like some of the oldest trees, these have frequently been bestowed with magical properties.

Midsummer Festival, Latvia.

The landscape is essentially rural, with vast tracts of arable and pasture lands, bogs and forests. Some of the remaining neoclassical manors, built by the occupying Russians, Scandinavians, Germans and Poles, have been converted into restaurants, hotels or cultural centres. In the cities, it is the legacy of these conquerors and their religions that prevail, in particular the Hansa merchants who for centuries monopolised trade. Urban development in Soviet times left the capitals' Old Towns largely untouched and now, spruced up and inviting, each is a Unesco World Heritage Site.

The Baltic Sea's "Amber Coast" is a wonder of endless white pristine beaches backed by dunes and pine forests. Its spas and safe swimming beaches have made its resorts popular for millions.

Travelling by public transport is not difficult, and a visit to one country can easily include a day or two in part of another.

Orjaku jetty, Hiuumaa island.

ESTONIA

The smallest of the three countries has a fairytale capital, hundreds of lakes and islands, ruined castles, restored manors and relaxed coastal spa resorts.

St Olav's church, Tallinn.

The northernmost of the Baltic States is Eesti Vabariik, the Republic of Estonia. It is also the smallest, least densely populated of the three countries. On the south side of the Gulf of Finland, its capital, Tallinn, is 85km (53 miles) from Helsinki and about 130km (80 miles) from St Petersburg. Finns have long taken advantage of Estonia's proximity and relative cheapness, making the ferry crossing in droves. Other European visitors have joined their ranks, particularly cruise-ship passengers and weekenders from the UK.

It is easy to see the attraction: Tallinn has the prettiest Old Town in the Baltics, a medieval enclave set on a hillock above its port. Within the fairytale walls and towers and beneath the Gothic spires are winding cobbled lanes leading to the old square. Beside this ensemble, a rapidly developing commercial district has redrawn the city's skyline and given locals more places to spend their new-found wealth.

Estonia has a second city in Tartu in the south, a distinguished university town that brims with student life. The historic, west-coast towns of Pärnu and Haapsalu are popular health resorts, and maintain a pace of life that's decidedly more relaxed than in the capital. A very different scene can be found in the industrial northeast of the country, particularly in the city of Narva, which has a high ethnic Russian population and is struggling to find its place in the new European Union economy. Much of the Russian border is taken up by Lake Peipsi, the fourth-largest lake in Europe, where a settlement of Old Believers flourishes.

A female elk in the birch woods of central Estonia.

Beyond the urban areas, nearly 40 percent of the country is forested with pine, spruce and junipers, and inhabited by elk, brown bears and beavers. The land is mostly flat and unpopulated, dotted with around 1,500 lakes. The largest islands are Hiiumaa and Saaremaa, rural backwaters where the earliest stone churches in the Baltics can be found.

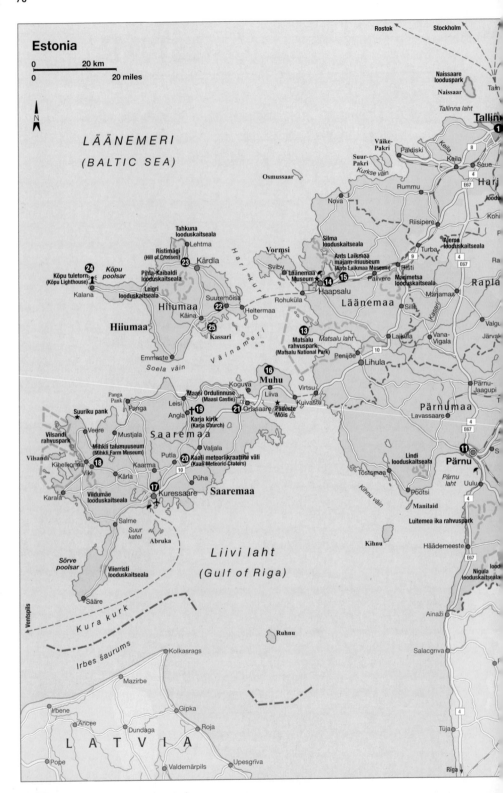

Estonia

0   20 km
0   20 miles

N

Rostok   Stockholm

Naissaare
loodusspark
Naissaar   Taln

Tallinna laht
Tallin

LÄÄNEMERI

(BALTIC SEA)

Väike-
Pakri   Paldiski   Keila   8

Suur-
Pakri
Kurkse väin   Keila   Saue   4

Osmussaar   Hari

Rummu   E67

Nova   loodu

Riisipere   Kohi

Silma   Alema
looduskaitseala   looduskaitseala
Turba   4

Tahkuna
looduskaitseala
Lehtma   Vormsi   E67   Ra

Ristimägi   Ants Laikmaa   Risti
(Hill of Crosses)   majam-muuseum
Köpu   Kärdla   (Ants Laikmaa Museum)
poolsar   Sviby   Rapla
Köpu tuletorn   Pihla-Kaibaldi   Läänemaa   Palivere   Marimetsa
(Köpu Lighthouse)   looduskaitseala   Museum   looduskaitseala

Leigri   Haapsalu
Kalana   looduskaitseala   Rohuküla   Läänemaa   Märjamaa
Hiiumaa   Suuremõisa   Silla
Heltermaa   Valgu
Hiiumaa   Käina   Järval
Kassari   Matsalu laht   Laikula   Vana-
Vigala

Emmaste   Matsalu
rahvuspark   Penijõe   10
Soela väin   (Matsalu National Park)   Lihula

Koguva   Muhu
Panga   Maasi Ordulinnuse   Liiva   Virtsu   Pärnu-
Pank   (Maasi Castle)   Jaagupi
Suuriku pank   Panga   Leisi   Kuivastu   Pärnumaa
Angla   Orissaare   Padeste
Vilsandi   Veere   Mustjala   Saaremaa   Mõis   Lavassaare
rahvuspark   Karja kirik   E67
Mihkli talumuuseum   (Karja Church)
Vilsandi   (Mihkli Farm Museum)   Valjala   11
Kihelkonna   Putla   Kaali meteoriikraatrite väli   Lindi   Pärnu
Viki   Kärla   Kaarma   (Kaali Meteoric Craters)   looduskaitseala
10   Tõstmaa   Pärnu
Karala   Viidumäe   Püha   laht   Uulu
looduskaitseala   Kuressaare   Saaremaa   Pootsi   4

Salme   Manilaid
Suur
katel   Abruka   Luitemea ika rahvuspark
Sõrve
poolsar   Kihnu   Häädemeeste
Viierristi   Liivi laht   E67
looduskaitseala
(Gulf of Riga)   Nigula   lood
looduskaitseala
Sääre

Ainaži
Kura kurk

Irbes šaurums   Ruhnu   Salacgriva

Kolkasrags

Mazirbe

Irbene   Gipka

Ancee   Roja   Tūja
Dundaga
LATVIA   4
Pope   Upesgriva
Valdemärpils   Riga

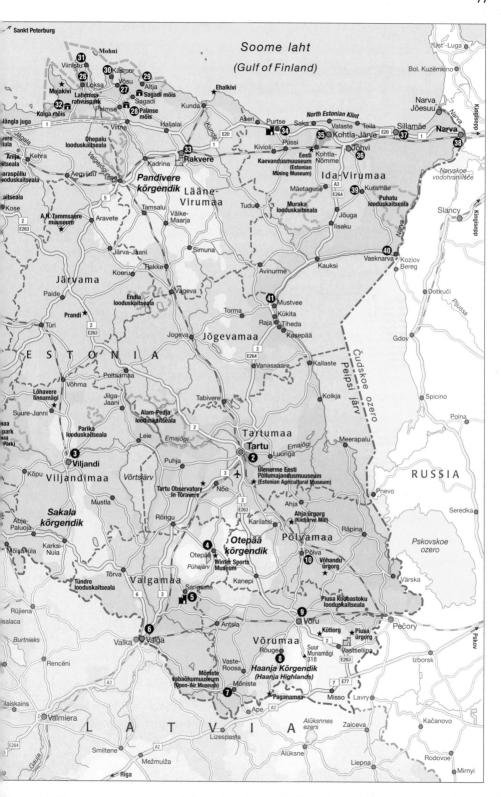

THE MAKING OF ESTONIA

Estonians' origins were "not of Europe", according to an early traveller. Nobody could have such a thought today of this courageous member of the European Union.

In the days when visitors to Estonia often arrived by sea, the first glimpse of Tallinn, the capital, made a lasting impression. Its ancient ruins and quaint houses with steeply peaked roofs, more Mediterranean than Baltic, captivated many visitors. In summer, it might have been the south of France, with early 19th-century Russians making an annual summer pilgrimage from St Petersburg. "I have seen delicate creatures," wrote an English visitor in 1841, "who at first were lifted from the carriage to the bathing-house, restored day by day, and in a fortnight's time bathing with a zest that seemed to renew all their energies."

In the evenings, "a band of military music plays, and restaurants offer ices, chocolate, etc., and you parade about and your friends join you, and you sit down and the gnats sting you; and if you don't like this, you may adjourn to the *salle de danse* close by, where the limbs so late floating listlessly on the waves now twirl round in the hurrying waltz."

Estonia had been a Russian province since 1721, and while the lot of the Estonian peasant had been pathetic for many years (and most ethnic Estonians were peasants), tsarist rule became increasingly repressive. By the late 19th century there were no more foreign tourists, Russians excepted, and as far as most foreigners were concerned, Estonia ceased to exist.

> In 1988 nearly a quarter of the population of Estonia gathered in Tallinn in a mass singing demonstration against the USSR, which became known as the "Singing Revolution".

At the peasant market in early 20th-century Pernau.

A CURIOUS RACE

A declaration of Estonian independence after World War I caught the world by surprise. Russia, torn apart by revolution, was unable to do much to counter the move. Authors of travel guides rushed in to appraise the reincarnated nation. "The broad visage of the Estonian," wrote one, as if reporting on a newly arrived specimen at a zoo, "has slanting eyes, low forehead, high cheekbones and projecting lower jaw." His conclusion was that Estonian origins were "not of Europe". Estonian independence lasted only until World War II. It then disappeared under the even heavier hand of Communist Russia and was presumed lost for all time. Rather suddenly in 1988, extraordinary reports were received in the West of a "Singing Revolution". Tens of thousands apparently spent that summer giving throaty voice to all the old Estonian songs and defiantly waving the long-hidden national flag. Within two years, although not without moments of nail-biting uncertainty, Estonia was independent again.

For all the ravages of a Soviet economic policy that had aimed at turning Estonia into an annexe of heavy industry, much of the character that delighted visitors of 150

A member of the Livonian Brothers of the Sword.

years ago had survived. Russians were still visiting the country in droves, but for the "Old European" atmosphere and the food rather than the beaches and swimming, which were prime casualties of environmental vandalism.

As for the newly independent Estonians, they had borne the burden of the previous half-century with fortitude. The "non-European" physical features of the ethnic Estonians are a reflection of Finno-Ugric ancestry. Because of the similarities between the Estonian and Finnish languages, Estonians had been able to follow Finnish television during the Soviet era. Its terms of reference did not flatter the Soviet system.

MIXED NATIONALITIES

Estonia's frontiers have been chopped and changed over the centuries. Their present configuration makes Estonia a country of some 44,000 sq km (17,000 sq miles), small enough to be covered by a day's driving in any direction, with a population of slightly more than 1.3 million, of whom about 69 percent are ethnic Estonians. The remaining 31 percent are predominantly Russians, most of whose families were sent in to man the industries that represented Estonia's role in the Soviet economic scheme. A few people living in the eastern part of the country are the descendants of 17th-century Old Believers, a sect that fled from Russia to escape, among other things, the tax that Peter the Great imposed on the beards they wore.

An additional group are the diluted remnants of Estonia's most influential settlers, the Germans. The latter came in two guises: the first were 13th-century Teutonic Knights who arrived ostensibly as bearers of Christianity but also as migrants with an urgent need to find somewhere to live, having recently fallen on hard times in the Holy Land; these people were followed by German craftsmen and merchants who formed the burgher class that ultimately monopolised the towns and cities. To an unusual degree, Estonians have taken a back seat while others have written their history. These 13th-century Germans were not the first to arrive, and many others followed after them.

⊘ RISE AND FALL OF THE MANOR

The most striking echoes of Estonia's feudal past can be found in the grand manor houses that dot the countryside. Some estates date back to the 13th century, when newly arrived Germanic lords staked out their holdings with wooden structures or fortified strongholds. In the 18th century, the manor house saw its heyday as families with the means built palatial Baroque and neoclassical complexes. Regular rows of chestnut or birch trees flank rural roads, indicating the approach to old manors. Many of them survived the Soviet era and have been spectacularly restored. See page 200.

HARDY BEGINNINGS

The future Finns and Estonians were among the first tribes to drift across Europe from Asia. Leaving the lower slopes of the Urals, they followed the river courses, subsisting mainly on fish, and clothing themselves in animal skins. They had already reached the Baltic coast when mentioned by Tacitus in the 1st century AD. "Strangely beast-like and squalidly poor, neither arms nor homes have they. Their food is herbs, their clothing skin, their bed the earth. They

the Danes were in danger of being routed. They were rescued, so the story goes, by a red banner with a white cross floating down from heaven – the image that was to inspire the future Danish flag. Their spirits up, they took possession of Tallinn.

Some years earlier, in 1200, around 500 heavily armed German knights had landed further south in the Gulf of Rīga with a commission to spread the word of God. They did so more efficiently than the Danes, who were themselves recent converts.

The Inner Fort of Tallinn, formerly known as Revel.

trust wholly to their arrows, which, for want of iron, are pointed with bone . . . Heedless of men, heedless of gods, they have attained that hardest of results, the not needing so much as a wish."

There seems to have been some pushing and shoving among new arrivals on the Baltic shores, especially when large numbers of Slavs turned up, but eventually the future Finns, Estonians, Latvians and Lithuanians took up positions in more or less the same pattern that persists today.

The first conquerors were the Danes under Valdemar II, who arrived with what should have been an invincible armada of 1,000 ships. The Estonians resisted the invasion so fiercely that

THE RULE OF THE KNIGHTS

In the end, the Danes asked the Teutonic Knights to lend a hand against the Estonian pagans. The knights tackled the task with customary efficiency and declared, in 1227, that, finally, the job had been accomplished. The knights transformed an economy, which had previously rested on primitive agriculture and products of the forest, into one of the best centres of farming and commerce of the Middle Ages. They constructed castles and founded towns everywhere, filling them with craftsmen and merchants recruited from Germany. Their social system was simple: Germans occupied the positions of noble, burgher and merchant; the Estonians were serfs.

This system survived political and religious change for seven centuries. In the year 1347, the Danish monarchy was desperate for cash. Tallinn, or Reval as it came to be known, was sold off to the efficient and prosperous knights. A large part of the commercial success of Reval and Narva, Estonia's two ports, was due to a virtual monopoly on trade to and from Russia. When Ivan III seized Narva and made it a Russian port it so alarmed the Baltic Germans that they sought the protection of Sweden. Under Gustavus Adolphus, Sweden was energetically

Sweden. A Russian force 35,000 strong made for Narva, held by a much smaller Swedish garrison in the castle. Charles, who was not yet 20, hurried to its aid. He arrived with 8,000 men and, in the middle of a snow storm, plunged straight into battle. The Russians were cut to pieces, losing every piece of artillery Peter possessed. Charles' advisers urged him to press on to Moscow, but the young leader had other ideas. "There is no glory in winning victories over the Muscovites," he said breezily, "they can be beaten at any time."

Reval [Tallinn], South Entrance to the Gulf of Finland, 1856.

bent on expanding its Baltic holdings, but there was no desire to tamper unnecessarily with a German infrastructure that worked so profitably. Later Swedish kings, particularly Charles XI, did interfere by taking over German-owned estates and either giving them to Swedes or, increasingly, keeping them for themselves. The dispossessed and disgruntled, who had previously turned to Sweden for protection against Russia, decided they now needed protection from Sweden. With perfect impartiality, they turned to Russia. Peter the Great readily agreed to help.

THE BATTLE FOR NARVA

The outcome was the titanic struggle between Peter and the equally legendary Charles XII of

⊘ THE ESTONIAN PEASANT

Early travellers were from the upper crust, and could not be expected to have much empathy with the working man. Lady Eastlake reported of the Estonian peasant, "Beyond his strict adherence to his church, we can find but little interesting in his character; excepting perhaps that of a servile obedience or cunning evasion... Provided he can have a pipe in his mouth, and lie sleeping at the bottom of his cart, while his patient wife drives the willing little rough horse... Offer him wages for his labour, and he will tell you, with the dullest bumpkin look, that if he works more he must eat more."

While Charles went off in pursuit of other enemies, Peter laid the foundations of Petersburg and planned a second attack on Narva. He entrusted the command to a Scot named Ogilvie, who not only succeeded in overwhelming the garrison but decided, apparently independently, to take no prisoners, military or civilian. A terrible massacre was finally stopped by the arrival of Peter the Great in the country. He is said to have ended the proceedings by cutting down some of the crazed attackers with his own sword. Moreover, he said, there was a perfectly good use for able-bodied Swedish prisoners: the conditions at the Petersburg building site were so bad that the workforce was dropping like flies.

ERA OF RUSSIAN DOMINATION

With Narva under his belt, Peter turned to Reval and its Swedish garrison. The defenders put up a great fight but ultimately they succumbed to thirst and an outbreak of plague. The Great Northern War between Peter and Charles was far from over, however, and in the course of fighting that swept across Europe the Baltic States were utterly devastated, the horror compounded by plague. With the Peace of Nystad in 1721, Sweden finally ceded its Baltic possessions, and Estonia, for one, prepared for its first taste of Russian rule.

Like the Swedes, Peter was not inclined to upset the way the German hierarchy ran Estonia, and the Estonians continued, according to one commentator, "to live and die like beasts, happy if they could subsist on dusky bread and water".

Nothing much had changed by the middle of the 19th century. The English writer Lady Elizabeth Eastlake, who moved in privileged circles during her stay, kept her eyes open and provides a wonderful insight into conditions. The ruling Tsar Nicholas I was so paranoid about revolutionaries – the insurrections of 1848 were just around the corner – that police surveillance everywhere was oppressive. If nothing else, though, it kept crime figures low. Over a whole year, Lady Eastlake reported, there had been only 87 misdemeanours among Reval's 300,000 population, "and five of these consist merely in travelling without a passport".

Most illuminating of all, perhaps, are Lady Eastlake's observations about the cloud that hung over young men in the form of military service in the Russian Army. The conscripts were chosen by ballot, No. 1 being the unlucky number. "From the moment that the peasant of the Baltic provinces draws the fatal lot No. 1, he knows that he is a Russian, and, worse than that, a Russian soldier, and not only himself, but every son from that hour born to him; for, like the executioner's office in Germany, a soldier's life is hereditary. . . If wars and climate and sick-

Estonian farming in the 1910s.

ness and hardship spare him, he returns after four-and-twenty years of service – his language scarce remembered, his religion changed, and with not a rouble in his pocket – to seek his daily bread by his own exertions for the remainder of his life."

IMPOSSIBLE CHOICES

The last years of the 19th century saw the emergence of the Young Estonians, a sign of awakening nationalism. The social order as they saw it was still dominated by the German hierarchy, but being anti-German did not make them pro-Russian. They were simply against the status quo, and for people in that mood Marxism was a very reasonable answer. The savage oppression of the St Petersburg uprising in 1905 destroyed any sympathy for the tsar. For most Estonians, World War I presented an impossible choice between Germany and Russia when, in truth, they would rather have been fighting against both. Nevertheless, tens of thousands found themselves in tsarist uniform, their plea to form their own units under their own officers falling on deaf ears.

The Russian Revolution in 1917 simplified the choice, the more so when it was announced that

Our Man in Tallinn: in its original outline, English novelist Graham Greene's famous work of spy fiction, Our Man in Havana, was to have been set in Tallinn in 1938.

with all the savagery associated with such a terrible event.

The tide eventually turned, although not without considerable clandestine help given

Signing the non-aggression pact with Estonia and Latvia at the Foreign Office in the Wilhelmstrasse in Berlin on 7 June 1939.

an Estonian national army was to be formed. About 170,000 volunteers immediately joined up, while many Estonians preferred to join the supposedly internationalist ranks of the Bolsheviks. From their various places of exile, members of a provisional Estonian government sent up a cry for independence.

Numerous fierce battles were fought over Tallinn between local Bolsheviks, who were backed by Red Guards, and the nationalist irregulars, who included schoolboys and the Tallinn fire brigade. The tide at first went in favour of the Bolsheviks and by the end of 1918 they held Narva and Tartu, and Russian comrades had advanced to within 32km (20 miles) of Tallinn. The struggle amounted to civil war, and this was fought

to the nationalists by the British Navy that involved using captured Russian destroyers and a series of raids by torpedo boats that penetrated the naval defences with which Peter the Great had ringed the Russian Baltic ports. The final battle was at Narva, and resulted in the nationalist coalition driving some 18,000 Bolsheviks across the Russian border. One year later, with the Bolsheviks still engaged in heavy fighting elsewhere, Russia renounced sovereignty over Estonia "voluntarily and for ever".

Communists were not inclined to accept the new government. There was an attempted putsch in 1924, which resulted in street fighting in Tallinn. Numerous other disturbances were countered by increasingly authoritarian measures. In the end these amounted to dictatorship and the sad conclusion that the country was not quite ripe for parliamentary democracy.

FARMS FOR ALL

Prior to the war, more than half of Estonia had belonged to 200 German-Balt families. An Agrarian Reform Law passed after independence took over all baronial and feudal estates, together with those belonging to the Church and the former Russian Crown lands. The land was redistributed and 30,000 new farms created. The lot of the previously hapless peasant was further improved by the establishment of the right to engage in trade.

Estonia was still struggling to find its feet when any gains were put in jeopardy by the secret protocol of the 1939 Nazi–Soviet Pact. Stalin and Hitler agreed that the Soviet Union would annex Estonia, Finland and Latvia, and Germany could claim Lithuania, although this was later amended to give Lithuania to Russia as well. A blatantly rigged election set the stage for an outright annexation on 6 August 1940, and almost immediately 60,000 Estonians went missing. They had been forcibly conscripted into the Soviet Army, deported to labour camps or executed.

The collapse of the Nazi–Soviet Pact naturally changed everything. German forces invaded in July 1941, meeting determined resistance in Estonia, where large numbers of Soviet troops were cut off. Estonia had only about 1,000 Jewish families, nothing like the numbers of Latvia and Lithuania, but even so 90 percent of these were murdered as Germany set about incorporating the country in the Third Reich.

By the end of the war some 70,000 Estonians had fled to the West. The population had dropped from more than 1 million pre-war to no more than 850,000. The educated classes did not wait to find out what would happen when the German forces in Tallinn surrendered to the Red Army on 22 September 1944.

RUSSIAN INVASION

Tens of thousands of those who did not flee were consigned to Soviet labour camps. The vacuum was filled by the arrival of comparable numbers of Russians with the dual purpose of manning

heavy industry and completing the Russification programme begun by the tsars. There was little Estonians could do except to turn their television aerials towards Finland to see how their Finno-Ugric cousins were getting along. At home, Soviet policies continued unabated, so that during the 1980s the proportion of Russians and other Soviet implants living in the country rose to 40 percent. With the whole of the country's industry under Moscow's remote control, no thought was given to the ecological impact of belching industrial works.

Soviet tanks thwart a German invasion of Estonia, from La Domenica del Corriere, *August 1941.*

With their stars firmly hitched to Moscow's wagon, Estonia's loyal Communist Party members were totally opposed to any sign of a nationalist revival in Estonia. The long-term implications of *Glasnost* and *Perestroika* were, however, not lost on them, and they took no comfort at all from the 2,000 demonstrators who summoned up enough nerve to mourn the anniversary of the Nazi–Soviet Pact in Tallinn's Hirvepark in August 1987. In this respect, the party hardliners and the large Russian minority were as one.

While members of the Estonian Heritage Society went about discreetly restoring national monuments, the radical-chic banner of environmental concern brought the independence movement to life. The first scent of this potential awakening came with the cancellation of plans for increased open-pit phosphorus mining in the northeast of the country. This was followed by demands for economic self-management and then, most extraordinarily, came the "Singing Revolution" (see page 59).

The extent to which the Estonian establishment fell into line with the new mood was revealed when the Estonian Supreme Soviet defied the USSR Supreme Soviet by endorsing

Communist Party HQ during a cultural festival, Tallinn

the legitimacy of a declaration of sovereignty. In the end it took a military coup attempt in Moscow to push the independence movement to its final conclusion. On 20 August 1991, with Gorbachev under house arrest and Russian tank units rolling into Tallinn, Estonia formally declared its independence. There were tense moments as the world waited to see whether there would be a repetition of the events in Czechoslovakia in 1968. In the event, the dissolution of the Soviet Union happened so rapidly that Estonia moved gratefully to the sidelines.

THE BALTIC TIGER AWAKES

Their long-awaited dream of regaining independence now realised, Estonians were faced with the daunting realities of post-Soviet existence: decaying factories, triple-digit inflation and a colossal environmental clean-up bill.

It was the swift and daring economic reforms carried out during these crucial days that laid the foundation for the country's "Baltic Tiger" economic growth in the mid-1990s. Aid and advice poured in from Western governments, while so-called "foreign Estonians" – those whose families had fled the 1944 invasion and settled abroad – flocked in from Sweden, North America and Australia, bringing their expertise and investment dollars. Most notably, in June 1992, the Bank of Estonia ignored IMF warnings and launched the Eesti kroon. It became the first stable currency of the former USSR, thanks in a large part to the country's pre-World War II gold supply, which, as fortune would have it, was still kept by the Bank of England and the US Federal Reserve.

Fuelling the cautious optimism of these heady and hectic times was the prospect of ridding the Estonian territory once and for all of its many remaining Russian military forces, a job that was finally accomplished on 31 August 1994. The joy of bidding farewell to Russia's troops was dampened three weeks later by the *Estonia* ferry disaster, which claimed 852 lives and left a lasting scar on the psyche of the young nation.

Along with fast-paced economic development, and the inevitable parliamentary scandals and corruption charges that came with it, the remainder of the decade was a time of reconnection with the West. On the international political level, an unpredictable and outspoken president, Lennart Meri, who served as head of state from 1992 to 2000, supplied world leaders with enough wry commentary on East–West relations to ensure that Estonia was never far from the minds of the major power players.

It was towards the end of the decade that the "little nation that could" hit the first serious pothole on its road to recovery. An economic slowdown in 1998, brought on by a monetary crisis in Russia, proved to any remaining doubters that, although Estonia could still fulfil its age-old role as a trade link between Russia and Europe, it was far wiser to keep its gaze firmly fixed westwards. It came as no surprise then when, in the September 2003 referendum, 67 percent

> *Finnish transmission of TV programmes from the West had a profound effect on Estonians, with Peyton Place a favourite programme of former president Lennart.*

of Estonians voted to join the European Union. Indeed, when the nation subsequently joined the EU – and NATO – the following year, many saw it as the final step in restoring Estonia's proper place in the family of Western European nations.

TRUE EUROPEANS

Membership of the EU turned out to be a mixed blessing for the small nation. As much-needed investment and development funds poured in, talent poured out, with many young, skilled professionals moving abroad in search of better opportunities. Their absence, though, did nothing to slow the breakneck pace of development that their country was experiencing. Driven mainly by a construction and real-estate boom, the economy rocketed to levels that even the most hopeful 1990s-era reformers would never have imagined. City skylines became obscured by builders' cranes, streets were suddenly awash with luxury cars, chic cafés opened and closed according to popular whims, and foreign tourists began visiting in droves.

The party was brought to a screeching halt by the worldwide economic crisis in 2008. Barring Latvia, no nation in Europe was harder hit by the downturn. The fragility of the nation's new-found wealth, much of which had been fuelled by cheap loans, became all too clear. Double-digit GDP growth turned into double-digit decline while inflation soared to 20 percent. Even the nation's famed IT sector, which had been making waves with innovations like Skype, couldn't keep the country from slipping into recession.

Some respite was provided by a reserve fund that a frugal government had put away during the fat years, but the first glimmer of recovery came after Estonia, once again defying Western advisers, refused to devalue its currency. Instead it tightened its belt enough to join the Eurozone. On 1 January 2011, the nation said goodbye to its beloved kroon, which had become a symbol of its post-independence success. Estonians

traded it in for a currency which they hope will bring them even deeper into the European fold and banish any notion, among investors at least, that they are "not of Europe".

From this point, Estonia quickly sprang back to its feet with the GDP growth reaching 2.1 percent and unemployment falling to slightly over 7 percent in 2014. The e-government programme became a widely praised model solution; Estonia is probably the only country in the world where 83 percent of the households have internet capabilities, while citizens may choose

Anti-Soviet demonstration, November 1988.

from around 4,000 online services provided by the government. In 2015 an e-residence aimed at stimulating foreign investment and facilitating business activity was added.

However, economic and technological achievements have been overshadowed in recent years by a growing tension in relations with Russia following its annexation of Crimea and intervention in Eastern Ukraine. In 2015, all three Baltic states asked NATO to deploy the alliance's permanent contingent on their soil while Estonia conducted its biggest military exercises ever. In 2017, NATO troops were finally deployed in Estonia, Latvia and Lithuania, under the Enhanced Forward Presence strategic objective.

📷 FESTIVALS

Festivals are a way of life, whether music, song, folk or religious. But some are more recent dates on the calendar, such as Tallinn's Rat Race and Kuldīga's midsummer naked run.

Music has long played an important part in the Baltic countries, and it was certainly crucial in the "Singing Revolution" that divorced the Baltic States from Moscow. In addition to the giant song festivals that occur every four or five years, music festivals dot the calendar. Jazz, classical and sacred music events ensure all tastes are catered for, and visitors should seek out performances in some of the many well-preserved buildings around the countries. There are large traditional folk gatherings at Võru in Estonia and at the Makslas Festival in Cēsis in Latvia. In summer, the coast sees big beach parties at Pärnu, Estonia, and in Liepāja, Latvia, where the Summer Sound Festival attracts bands from around Europe.

Festivals are not just to hear music. The June Rat Race in Tallinn, for instance, sees office workers in business suits and skirts run round the Old Town with computer keyboards and mobile phones, and the trotter horse race on a frozen Sartai Lake in February is a big equestrian get-together in Sartaii, Lithuania. On the coast, there are sea festivals in Salacgrīva and other Latvian villages, and around half a million people visit the Sea Festival in Klaipėda, Lithuania, in July, which is famous for its crafts stalls, music and boating events.

Catholic Lithuania can claim the most important religious festivals, including Užgavėnis (Mardi Gras), when an effigy of winter is burnt, winter and spring join in battle, and people in Vilnius dress as witches and ghouls to see winter driven out.

Pilgrimages take place in the Catholic south of Latvia at Aglona, and at the Madonna of the Gates of Dawn in Vilnius, Lithuania.

At an Estonian festival dancers show off well-stitched hems, finely embroidered skirts, sumptuous socks and elegant shoes.

Folk dancing in Lithuania's open-air museum at Rumšiškė. The three countries' outdoor museums are custodians of traditional ways of life and hold regular events.

Singing around the bonfire for Jani celebrations.

Midsummer

Midsummer's Eve, 23–24 June, is a magical time in the Baltic countries. Bonfires, lit by a person with any of the variants of the given name John, burn brightly and are leapt over for luck, On Estonia's islands old boats may be sacrificed in the flames. In Lithuania wheels are raised on poles at the centre of the bonfires. There are songs, dancing and games, and plenty to eat and drink, especially beer, as people head for the country in search of their pagan roots. Historically, midsummer marked the break between the sowing and harvesting seasons. Oak and flower wreaths are worn, young women bathe their faces in the morning dew, blossoms are set adrift on lakes and rivers, and couples go in search of glow worms and the elusive fern flower, which blossoms only on Midsummer's Eve – the fact that it does not exist allows couples to linger longer in the woods. In Estonia, Jaanipäev is so light that, with night banished, the two lovers Hämarik (dusk) and Koit (dawn) finally meet for a brief kiss. In Kuldīga, Latvia, a more recent tradition is the naked run over the Venta River bridge at 3am by a few score stalwarts wearing no more that oak wreaths.

There is a public holiday in all three countries on 24 June, and in 2010 the Estonian government added 23 June as national holiday, to commemorate the day that German troops were driven from Estonian soil in 1919.

ssed choirs are a feature of the Baltic countries. Here
usands of Latvians have come together to sing a
dful of the country's 1.2 million folk songs.

asker at Užgavėnės, the carnival, celebrations in
uania, where Morė, a huge effigy of winter, is paraded
ough the streets and burnt, while Lašininis, a fat figure
inter, is driven out by Kanapinis, who represents spring.

Marching drummers at the Sea Festival in Klaipėda, Lithuania's biggest event, with craft stalls, music and marine activity, including the international Baltic Sail rally.

View of St Nicholas Church and Alexander Nevsky Cathedral.

TALLINN

Estonia's fairytale port city has an enchanting, historic Old Town with a cosmopolitan outlook and a village feel. Tradition goes hand-in-hand with vibrant galleries and bars.

Estonia's capital is an exceptionally harmonious mix of the old and the new. Its historic Old Town, a Unesco World Heritage Site, far from being a medieval museum piece abounds in wireless internet zones and enjoys a cutting-edge club scene, while in the "new" downtown area, ancient wooden churches vie for space with gleaming glass high-rises. Its population is four times that of its next largest rival, Tartu, and though it has a cosmopolitan atmosphere, with only 450,000 inhabitants and a small city centre, **Tallinn** often feels more like a village.

Stretched along the rim of Tallinn Bay, just across the Gulf of Finland from Helsinki and midway between St Petersburg and Stockholm, the city holds a blessed maritime position that has made it a little bit too interesting over the centuries to other nations. Danes, German knights, Swedes and Russians have each held sway. The resulting layers of cross-cultural history have given the city its unique flavour.

Neighbourhood by neighbourhood, the surroundings change dramatically. Leave the Germanic, gabled houses of the Old Town in one direction and you find yourself among swanky 1930s offices. Chose another road and you'll see narrow, leafy streets that have changed little since they were home to factory workers in the late 19th century.

Strolling along Vana turg.

A couple of tram stops along and you're met with the sort of Baroque grandeur that would fit into any Tolstoy novel. Skirting this mosaic are districts of bland, Soviet-era housing.

In other outlying areas, such as Pirita, one can escape both the city's complicated history and its urban bustle and simply enjoy beaches and forests.

THE OLD TOWN

The first place to visit is the **Old Town** (Vanalinn), perched on a low hill by the shore. Set apart from the rest of the

⊙ Main attractions

Town Hall Square
Alexander Nevsky
  Cathedral
Toompea Castle
Bastion Tunnels
Kadriorg Park and Palace
Kumu Art Museum
St. Bridget's Convent ruins
Seaplane Harbour
  Maritime Museum

Maps on pages
98, 116

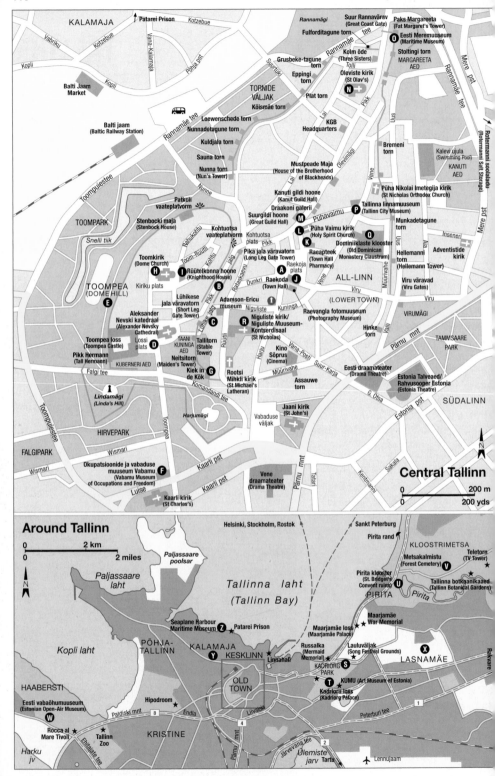

Central Tallinn

KALAMAJA

Patarei Prison
Kotzebue
Kotzebue
Vabriku
Vana-Kalamaja
Kopli
Kopli
Põhja pst

Balti Jaam
Market

Balti jaam
(Baltic Railway Station)

Toompuiestee

TOOMPARK

Snelli tiik

Patkuli
vaateplatvorm

Stenbocki maja
(Stenbock House)

Kohtuotsa
vaateplatvorm

TOOMPEA
(DOME HILL)

Toomkirik
(Dome Church) **H**

Kiriku plats

Ruütelkonna hoone
(Knighthood House) **I**

B

Lühikese
jala väravatorn
(Short Leg
Gate Tower) **C**

Aleksander
Nevski katedraal
(Alexander Nevsky
Cathedral) **D**

Toompea loss
(Toompea Castle)

Pikk Hermann
(Tall Hermann)

Falgi tee

KUBERNERI AED

TAANI
KUNINGA
AED

Tallitorn
(Stable
Tower)

Neitsitorn
(Maiden's Tower)

Kiek in
de Kök **G**

Rootsi
Mihkli kirik
(St. Michael's
Latheran)

Komandandi tee

Lindamägi
(Linda's Hill)

HIRVEPARK

FALGIPARK

Wismari

Wismari

Okupatsioonide ja vabaduse
muuseum Vabamu
(Vabamu Museum
of Occupations and Freedom) **F**

Luise

Kaarli pst

Kaarli kirik
(St Charles's)

Kaarli pst

Pärnu mnt

Harjumägi

Vabaduse
väljak

Jaani kirik
(St John's)

Vene
draamateater
(Drama Theatre)

Rannamägi
Rannamäe tee

TORNIDE
VÄLJAK

Suurtüki

Grusbeke-tagune
torn

Eppingi
torn

Plat torn

Pikk

Köismäe torn

Loewenschede torn

Nunnadetagune torn

Kuldjala torn

Sauna torn

Nunna torn
(Nun's Tower)

Nunne

Toom-Rüütli

Toom-Kohtu

Rahukohtu

Kohtu

Pühavaimu

Mustpeade Maja
(House of the Brotherhood
of Blackheads)

Kanuti gildi hoone
(Kanut Guild Hall)

Draakoni galerii

Suurgildi hoone
(Great Guild Hall) **M**

Pikk jala väravatorn
(Long Leg Gate Tower) **A**

Raekoja
plats

Raekoda
(Town Hall) **J**

Dunkri

Ratas kaevu

Rataskaevu

Niguliste

Adamson-Ericu
museum

Niguliste kirik/
Niguliste Muuseum-
Kontsertdisaal
(St Nicholas) **R**

Rüütli

Harju

Lossi
plats

Vana-Posti

Müürivahe

Kino
Sõprus
(Cinema)

Assauwe
torn

Kuninga

Kuninga

Suur-Karja

G. Otsa

Eesti draamateater
(Drama Theatre)

Suur Rannavärav
(Great Coast Gate)

Fulforditagune torn

Kolm õde
(Three Sisters)

Tolli

Oleviste kirik
(St Olav's) **N**

Paks Margareeta
(Fat Margaret's Tower) **O**

Eesti Meremuuseum
(Maritime Museum)

Stoltingi torn

MARGAREETA
AED

Rannamäe tee

Mere pst

Rotermanni soolaladu
(Rotermanni Salt Storage)

Olevimägi

KGB
Headquarters

Lai

Lai

Vene

Vene

Bremeni
torn

Kalevi ujula
(Swimming Pool)

KANUTI
AED

Inseneri

Ala

Uus

Uus

Püha Nikolai Imetegija kirik
(St Nicholas Orthodox Church) **P**

Tallinna linnamuuseum
(Tallinn City Museum)

Munkadetagune
torn

Püha Vaimu kirik
(Holy Spirit Church) **L**

K

Raeapteek
(Town Hall
Pharmacy)

Dominiiklaste klooster
(Old Dominican
Monastery Claustrum) **Q**

Hellemanni
torn
(Hellemann Tower)

Adventistide
kirik

ALL-LINN
(LOWER TOWN)

Viru

Viru väravad
(Viru Gates)

Raevangla fotomuuseum
(Photography Museum)

Hinke
torn

VIRUMÄGI

Pärnu mnt

Vaili

TAMMSAARE
PARK

Estonia Talveaed/
Rahvusooper Estonia
(Estonia Theatre)

Estonia pst

SÜDALINN

Estonia pst

Sakala

Kentmanni

Tatari

0 _____ 200 m
0 _____ 200 yds

N

Around Tallinn

0 _____ 2 km
0 _____ 2 miles

N

Helsinki, Stockholm, Rostok

Sankt Peterburg

Pirita rand

KLOOSTRIMETSA

Teletorn
(TV Tower) **V**

Metsakalmistu
(Forest Cemetery)

Pirita klooster
(St. Bridget's
Convent ruins) **U**

Tallinna botaanikaaed
(Tallinn Botanical Gardens)

PIRITA

Pirita

Paljassaare
poolsar

Paljassaare
laht

Tallinna laht
(Tallinn Bay)

Seaplane Harbour
Maritime Museum **Z**

Patarei Prison

PÕHJA-
TALLINN

Kopli laht

HAABERSTI

Eesti vabaõhumuuseum
(Estonian Open-Air Museum) **W**

Rocca al
Mare Tivoli

Tallinn
Zoo

Harku
jv

Hipodroom

Paldiski mnt

Ehitajate tee

KRISTINE

KALAMAJA

KESKLINN

Linnahall

OLD
TOWN

Russalka
(Mermaid
Memorial) **Y**

KADRIORG
PARK

Maarjamäe loss
(Maarjamäe Palace)

Maarjamäe
War Memorial

Lauluväljak
(Song Festival Grounds)

LASNAMÄE **X**

KUMU (Art Museum of Estonia) **T**

Kadrioru loss
(Kadriorg Palace) **S**

Endla

Liivalaia

Pärnu mnt

Järvevana tee

Ülemiste
jarv

Lennujaam

Tartu

Rakvere

Peterburi tee

city by old fortification walls, this is one of the purest medieval old towns in all northern Europe. Upper Town (Toompea), site of the original Estonian fortification, crowns the hill at 48 metres (157ft) above sea level. **Lower Town** (All-linn) spills out over an inclined horseshoe below. As they developed, each acquired distinct personalities: the ecclesiastical and feudal powers lived above, the merchants and guild members below.

The only practicable way to explore the winding, rough cobbled streets is by foot, so strap on robust walking shoes and head for the spires of the medieval district. There are several ways to arrive at the Old Town. Passing through the picturesque, 16th-century **Viru Gates** (Viru väravad) in the east and heading up the highly commercial Viru Street is the most travelled path into the Old Town. It is well worth taking a short detour to the narrow Müürivahe street (near Viru Gates) to climb the 14th-century Hellemann Tower (www.hellemann.ee; daily 10am–6pm) and walk a 200-metre (656ft) section of the original medieval wall. The three-storey tower – which used to be a prison and arsenal – now houses an art gallery and offers splendid views over the old fortifications. Return to Viru which quickly leads to **Town Hall Square** Ⓐ (Raekoja plats).

UPPER TOWN

One of Estonia's most famous legends holds that Toompea hill in the Upper Town is the burial mound of Kalev, the giant who founded Tallinn. When Kalev died, his widow Linda, in her immense grief, carried stone after stone to cover his grave until this massive hill was formed. It's no surprise that this spot is associated with the origin of the town – it was here during pre-Christian times that the first permanent settlement in Tallinn was built. The foreign empires that ruled the northern Estonian lands all used Toompea as their power base, stationing their respective political

representatives in Toompea Castle, now home to the nation's government.

Passage to Toompea from the Lower Town is provided by two scenic streets: **Pikk jalg** Ⓑ (Long leg) and **Lühike jalg** Ⓒ (Short leg), whose curious names have given rise to a tired joke, perpetuated by generations of tour guides, that Tallinn "walks with a limp". The long, sloping Pikk jalg is thought to be the oldest street in Tallinn, dating back to Viking times. It begins under the archway of the four-sided **Long Leg Gate Tower** (Pika jala väravatorn), built in 1380, and continues a straight, steady climb upward to Castle Square Ⓓ (**Lossi plats**). The extravagant mansions high up along the cliff to the right are a good indication of the wealth and power of Toompea's gentry, while the fortified defensive wall to the left is a testament to the political tensions and ill-will between the residents of Toompea and the Hanseatic Lower Town.

Lühike jalg, a narrow, winding lane with a staircase, was historically the main pedestrian passage into Toompea. Today it's flanked on both sides by

Ⓞ Tip

Though local women have become used to it, walking on Tallinn's cobblestoned streets in high heels is a recipe for disaster. Wear sturdy shoes when exploring the Old Town.

Alexander Nevsky Cathedral.

⊙ Where

The former industrial district of Rotterman's Quarter, located on the outskirts of the Old Town, has reinvented itself as chic neighbourhood with sleek modern buildings, trendy restaurants, cafés and shops. It is an excellent place for lunch or just a leisurely mid-day stroll.

Toompea Castle.

some of Tallinn's more intriguing art shops. At its top stands the **Short Leg Gate Tower** (Lühikese jala väravatorn), built in 1456. The sturdy wooden door you pass here is original and dates from the 17th century.

AROUND CASTLE SQUARE

Reaching Lossi plats at the top of these streets yields the dramatic sight of the grand, onion-domed **Alexander Nevsky Cathedral** (Aleksander Nevski katedraal; www.nevsky.orthodox.ee; Sun–Fri 8am–7pm, Sat until 8pm; free). Built from 1894 to 1900, the impressive structure now serves as the most important place of worship for Tallinn's Russian Orthodox faithful, and its interior has been beautifully restored with a massive iconostasis and several icons.

Originally, however, the church had a sinister political function. In the late 19th century, imperial Russia was carrying out an intense campaign of Russification in its outer provinces. As part of its drive to assert cultural dominance over the mainly Lutheran Germans and Estonians, the tsarist

government built this towering Orthodox cathedral directly in front of the castle, in the heart of what had been one of the city's best-loved squares. The name of the church is itself very telling – Prince Alexander Nevsky was the Russian military leader whose forces famously defeated the Baltic-based German crusaders in the "Battle on Ice" on Lake Peipsi in 1242, the climax of Sergei Eisenstein's classic 1938 film *Alexander Nevsky*.

During the construction of the cathedral, a rumour circulated that builders working on the foundation had stumbled upon an iron door bearing the inscription, "Cursed be anyone who dares disturb my peace." The story, with its obvious political undertones, was taken by superstitious locals to be a sign that old Kalev's grave had been discovered, and that he was not at all pleased with the building project. The notion soon gained further support when cracks began to appear around the building's base.

The cathedral somehow managed to escape Kalev's wrath and, more

miraculously, even survived the changing political winds of the early 20th century: after Estonia became independent in 1918, there was talk of removing the offensive structure. Reflecting popular sentiment, the writer Tuglas Friedeberg declared, "It looks like a samovar and should be blown up." Plans were put on hold because the new state lacked the necessary funds for demolition.

TOOMPEA CASTLE

Next to the cathedral stands **Toompea Castle** (Toompea loss), historic seat of power in Estonia and home to the *Riigikogu*, Estonia's parliament which can be visited (for details go to www.riigikogu.ee). As a permanent structure, the castle dates from 1229 when the Knights of the Sword built a square fortress surrounded by a circular, stone wall. In the 14th century this was rebuilt into a convent-style fortress with an inner courtyard, 20-metre (65ft) high walls, and four corner towers, three of which are still standing. The Baroque palace in front of you was built from 1767–73 on the order of Russian Empress Catherine the Great, and served as the administration building for the Russian provincial government in Estonia in tsarist times. The three-storey **Parliament Building** in the courtyard was built in 1922 on the foundations of the convent.

Around the castle's south side is the peaceful **Governor's Garden** (Kuberneri aed). This is the best place to view another Tallinn landmark, the 45.6-metre (150ft) **Tall Hermann** (Pikk Hermann) tower dating from 1371. Tradition dictates that whichever nation flies its flag on Tall Hermann rules Estonia.

To see the castle's most medieval-looking side, you can take a quick detour down Falgi Street, which passes south of Pikk Hermann. Only when you reach the bottom of the hill and look back do you begin to understand just how daunting Toompea's defences were. On the way down, paths on the left lead to the small Lindamägi (Linda's Hill), topped by a small statue of the mythical Linda, grieving widow of Kalev. Tallinn residents adopted

> **⊙ Tip**
>
> The city's discount card, the Tallinn Card (www.visittallinn.ee), gives free entrance to nearly all museums, free use of public transport and free tours as well as self-guided audio tour of the Old Town. It is available from the Tourist Information Centre, Kullassepa 4, and at many hotels.

Inside the Bastion Tunnels.

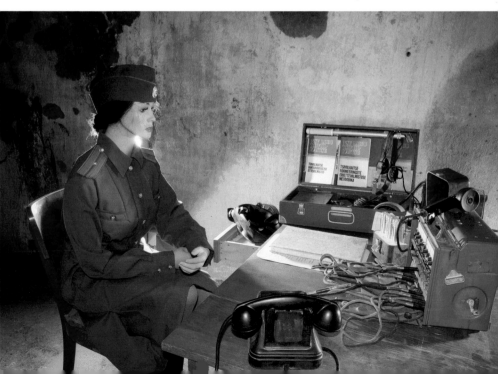

◎ Tip

Street finder: *tänav* means street, *väljak/plats* is square, *puiestee* is avenue, *mantee (mnt)* is road.

it during Soviet times as a kind of unsanctioned memorial to the thousands of loved ones who were deported to Siberia and never returned. Since there would be no gravesite for these victims, relatives would lay flowers here, at considerable risk to themselves if they were caught.

PEACEFUL TOOMPARK

The beautiful **Toompark** starts just to the north of this spot, and circles around the entire northwest side of **Toompea ❸**. With its forested pathways and moat, this is one of the town's most relaxing places for a summertime stroll, and yields unforgettable views of the town's medieval walls and towers.

INVADERS AND FORTIFICATIONS

Heading straight back up Falgi Street gives the opportunity for a different kind of detour. A right turn on Toompea Street leads to the awkwardly named **Vabamu Museum of Occupations and Freedom ❻** (Okupatsioonide ja vabaduse muuseum Vabamu; Toompea

Patkuli viewing platform.

8; www.okupatsioon.ee; May–Sept daily 10am–6pm, Oct–Apr Tue–Sun 11am–6pm), a high-tech and dramatic introduction to the 1940–91 period, when Estonia was occupied first by the Soviet Union, then briefly by Nazi Germany, then for another 45 years by the Soviets.

A return to the hill by the same route brings you firmly back into the medieval era. The sturdy-looking round tower on your right is **Kiek in de Kök ❻** (1475–6). Its name, which in Low German literally means "peek into the kitchen", refers to the tower's 36-metre (118ft) height. Soldiers stationed here joked that they could see right down the chimneys and into the kitchens of the houses below. During the Livonian Wars (1558–83), Ivan the Terrible's forces blew a massive hole in its top floor. As a memorial to the battle, six stone cannon balls were set into the tower's outer wall and are still visible today. Now the tower operates as a museum (www.linnamuuseum.ee/kok; Tue–Sun 10am–5.30pm) displaying the development of the town and its defences. The top floor café offers unrivalled views over the Old Town.

The tower also serves as the entrance to one of the city's most popular attractions, the **Bastion Tunnels** (Bastionide Käigud; book ahead, enquire at Kiek in de Kök museum or tel: 6446 686). When the Swedes were fortifying this side of Toompea with earthworks and high walls in the late 1600s, they included a string of hidden tunnels in order to move men and ammunition where they were needed. The tunnels never saw use in the 17th century, but found new life as World War II bomb shelters, and then as Soviet bunkers. Now refurbished, they are open to the public. Though adults may find the train to "future Tallinn" silly, the exhibits here provide a good historical overview of the city and the tunnels.

DANISH KING'S GARDEN

Another historic battleground is just steps away, along the wall that leads back towards Lossi plats. Crossing through a rectangular passage in the wall brings you to the **Danish King's Garden** (Taani kuninga aed), where, according to legend, King Waldemar II camped when his forces were first trying to conquer Toompea in 1219. It was here that a red flag with a white cross, which became the Danes' national symbol, supposedly floated downward from the heavens, spurring them on to victory. In reality, the battle was decided by a group of Slavic mercenaries who began attacking the Estonians from the opposite slope.

The two towers here, the small, round **Stable Tower** (Tallitorn) and the larger, square **Maiden's Tower** (Neitsitorn), both date from the 14th century. The name "Maiden's Tower" is ironic – the tower was a prison for prostitutes. For years it operated as a café, and employees claimed to have heard ghostly noises. After World War II the tower was a home

of Estonia's well-known architect Karl Burman.

DOME CHURCH

Both Toom-Kooli Street and Piiskopi Street lead from Lossi plats to Kiriku plats (Church Square) and the majestic Cathedral of Saint Mary the Virgin popularly known as **Dome Church**  (Toomkirik; http://toomkirik.ee; June–Aug daily 9.30am–5.30pm, Nov–Mar Tue–Sun 10.30am–3.30pm, Apr and Oct Tue–Sun 9.30am–4.30pm, May and Sept daily 9.30am–4.30pm), the prime Lutheran church of Estonia, established just after the Danes arrived in Toompea in 1219. When you step into the church, you will probably find yourself standing on the burial slab of Otto Johann Thuve, also known as "Tallinn's Don Juan". The hopeless playboy asked to be buried in this spot so that people entering the church would step on him, and by doing so wash away his sins. The church's Baroque interior is dominated by a huge collection of coats of arms. These traditionally accompanied the casket during funeral processions,

Cathedral of St Mary the Virgin, located in Tallinn, is Estonia's oldest church.

ⓘ Tip

Tucked behind the Town Hall is a museum of photography (a branch of the Tallinn City Museum), housed in the 15th-century Town Hall Prison (Raevangla fotomuuseum; www. linnamuuseum.ee/ fotomuuseum; Wed–Mon 10.30am–6pm), chronicling 150 years of Tallinn's photographic pursuits and displaying many antique cameras.

and were later kept in the church as a memorial. Along the northern wall, opposite the entrance, are the lavish tombs of some eminent historic personages, including Pontus de la Gardie, French-born head of Swedish forces during the Livonian Wars; A.J. von Krusenstern, a Baltic German explorer who in 1886 became the first mariner to circumnavigate the globe under the Russian flag; and Admiral Sir Samuel Greig of Fife, Scotland (1735–88), commander of Russia's Baltic Fleet and reputed lover of Catherine the Great. For amazing views of the city, climb the 69 metre Baroque church bell-tower.

Just outside the church is the green, two-storeyed, neo-Renaissance **Knighthood House ❶** (Rüütelkonna hoone), a grand structure with a distinguished history. Built in the late 1840s, it originally served as a meeting hall for the Knighthood, a guild-like organisation that united Toompea's noble families. It now hosts cultural events.

Kohtu Street to the right of Knighthood House leads down past some impressive houses once owned by Toompea's noble elite. The street soon ends at the **Kohtu Street viewing platform** (Kohtuotsa vaateplatvorm), from where there is a spectacular view of the red-tiled roofs of the medieval Lower Town, as well as the modern city and port beyond the town walls. The nearby **Patkuli viewing platform** (Patkuli vaateplatvorm) can be reached by turning right on Toom-Rüütli, then left at the end of that street onto a nearly hidden passage. This platform looks over the northern section of the Lower Town and gives an excellent view of St Olav's Church, the town wall and several of its towers. From the Patkuli viewing platform you can head straight down Rahukohtu Street to continue touring Toompea, or make your way down the Patkuli Steps and into the Lower Town.

THE LOWER TOWN

In medieval times, the area now called the Lower Town (All-linn) was the Hanseatic city of Tallinn (or Reval, as it was then known), a busy trading city of international stature. In 1248 it was

Medieval costumes at the Old Town Days festival.

granted autonomous status and from then on had its own government, local laws, social institutions and defence forces. More importantly, it was the domain of merchants and artisans, labourers and servants, all of whom would have contributed to the general bustle of commerce as they went about their daily routines.

For at least seven centuries, the social and cultural heart of Tallinn has been **Town Hall Square** (Raekoja plats), the attractive open area at the centre of the Old Town. Even now the square acts as the chief gathering place for the city's residents. In spring and summer it's invariably covered in café tables, and in winter there is a Christmas Market.

Presiding over the square is the **Town Hall** ❶ (Raekoda; http://raekoda.tallinn.ee; mid-June–Aug Mon–Sat 10am–4pm, Sept–mid-June by appointment). Historic records indicate that another town hall occupied this spot as early as 1322, but the present late-Gothic structure was completed in 1404. **Old Thomas** (Vana Toomas), the soldier-shaped weather vane on the spire, has been watching over the city since 1530 and has become a symbol of the town. The Baroque spire and the fanciful, dragon-shaped drainpipes are from 1627. Visitors in July and August should not pass up an opportunity to see the interior, with its vaulted ceilings and wood-carved benches. Summer visitors can also climb the 64-metre (210ft) Town Hall Tower (Raekoja torn; mid-May–mid-Sept daily 11am–6pm) for spectacular views of the Old Town.

Across the square from the Town Hall stands the **Town Hall Pharmacy** ❶ (Raeapteek; www.raeapteek.ee), one of the oldest continuously running pharmacies in Europe. Records first mention it in 1422, but it may have been established decades earlier. From 1580 to 1911 it was managed by 10 generations of the same family. Legend has it that marzipan was first made here. Some of the useful preparations sold here in centuries past included minced bat, burnt bees, snakeskin and powdered unicorn horn. These days the remedies sold are the same as in any modern pharmacy,

Inside the Town Hall.

⊙ CREEPY TALES

The tradition of sharing ghost stories in Tallinn goes back centuries and, if local legends are to be believed, just about every building in the Old Town has a resident spook. Even former prime minister Mart Laar can sometimes be seen giving VIP visitors ghost tours of this part of the city.

Of all the city's legends, the best known is that of "The Devil's Wedding" that supposedly took place at Rataskaevu 16. In the tale, a landlord, in desperate need of cash, unwittingly takes up the Devil's offer to rent out a room for his wedding party.

Later, stories arose about mysterious party noises from the flat. Adding to the intrigue today is a false window at the top of the house, which is in fact painted on the facade.

but there is a small exhibition room (Mon–Sat 10am–6pm; free) displaying archaic equipment and medicines.

HOLY SPIRIT CHURCH

Just a few paces from the square through the Saiakang (white bread) passage stands the **Holy Spirit Church** ⓛ (Püha Vaimu kirik; May–Sept Mon–Sat 9am–6pm, Mon–Sat rest of the year but hours vary greatly). In the 13th century it operated an Almshouse tending to the city's sick, elderly and poor. Unlike other churches, the Holy Spirit Church's congregation was made up of Tallinn's lower class and included ethnic Estonians. It was here that the first sermons in the Estonian language were given after the Reformation, and in 1535 the church's pastor, Johann Koell, translated and published what's thought to be the first book in Estonian. The building was completed in the 1360s, but its spire has been replaced numerous times following devastating fires, the last one in 2002.

The most eye-catching addition to the church is the large blue-and-gold clock near the main doorway. Created by well-known Tallinn woodcarver Christian Ackermann in the late 17th century, it is Tallinn's oldest – and by far most captivating – public timepiece. The church's interior is every bit as awe-inspiring, particularly the altar commissioned from renowned Lübeck sculptor and painter Bernt Notke in 1483. Figures of the Virgin Mary with Child, Apostles and saints, all painted in bright, clear blue, red and gold stand at the centre of the cupboard-type altarpiece. The pulpit dating back to 1597 is one of the oldest in Estonia.

PIKK STREET CURIOSITIES

Holy Spirit Church is on the corner of Pikk (Long) Street, which leads to the northern edge of the Old Town. This once-busy artery connected the port to the town's marketplace. The grand-looking building at Pikk 17, opposite the Holy Spirit Church, is the **Great Guild Hall** ⓜ (Suurgildi hoone), which served as a meeting place for Tallinn's Great Guild, a wealthy association of merchants that wielded considerable influence over town affairs. The hall is now used by a branch of the **Estonian History Museum** (Eesti Ajaloomuuseum; www.ajaloomuuseum.ee; May–Sept daily 10am–6pm, Oct–Apr Tue–Sun 10am–6pm), which chronicles the nation's developments up to the 18th century.

Architectural oddities along Pikk Street include the eccentric, Art Nouveau facade of the **Dragon Gallery** (Draakoni galerii; www.eaa.ee/draakon) at No. 18, with seahorse-tailed serpents and Egyptian slaves. Next to it is the Tudor-style **Kanut Guild Hall** (Kanut gildi hoone), with statues representing St Canute (Canute IV of Denmark, martyred in 1086) and the founder of Protestantism, Martin Luther. High up across the street from the Kanut Guild Hall, a man wearing a monocle gazes down. Popular legend says that a jealous wife installed it to break her husband's habit of spying on young women

Detail from the House of the Brotherhood of Blackheads.

s they practised ballet in the upper oors of the Guild Hall.

At Pikk 26 is the eye-catching **House f the Brotherhood of Blackheads** Mustpeade maja; www.filharmoonia.ee/ n/mustpeademaja; book at least 30 days a advance at the website). The exquisite enaissance facade is from 1597, and s beautiful carved wooden door, one of he most recognised architectural ele- nents in Tallinn, was installed in 1640.

A careful observer will notice some- hing eerie about the building at Pikk 9. Its cellar windows are completely ricked over – this was the **KGB Head- quarters** during the Soviet period. The lacard on the front of the building eads: "This building housed the head- quarters of the organ of repression of he Soviet occupational power. Here egan the road to suffering for thou- ands of Estonians."

T OLAV'S CHURCH

ust a few paces further along is Tal- nn's largest medieval structure, the normous **St Olav's Church N** (Oleviste irik; www.oleviste.ee; free). The church was first mentioned in historic records in 1267, and originally served a Scandi- navian merchants' camp that occupied this end of Pikk Street. An absurdly tall, 159-metre (522ft) Gothic-style pavilion steeple was built on the top of the tower in 1500, making St Olav's the tallest building in the world at the time. Numerous bolts of lightning hit the steeple through the centuries, and twice, once in 1625 and again in 1820, the church was burnt to the ground.

The steeple you now see was installed after the first fire, and is 124 metres (407ft) tall, 25 metres (82ft) shorter than the original. In spring and summer, able-bodied visitors can make the rigorous climb to the top of the tower (daily Apr–June and Sept– Oct 10am–6pm, July–Aug until 8pm) for spectacular views.

Humbler in size than the church but just as awe-inspiring are **The Three Sisters** (Kolm õde) at Pikk 71. This magnificently restored ensemble of three brightly painted 15th-century ter- race houses are a favourite for photog- raphers and now serve as the premises

The Three Sisters.

for a luxury hotel. Their less spectacular counterparts, **The Three Brothers**, are around the corner on Lai Street.

MUSEUM IN THE TOWER

Pikk Street ends at the **Great Coast Gate** (Suur Rannavärav) and its famous 16th-century **Fat Margaret's Tower** (Paks Margareeta). With a diameter of 25 metres (82ft) and walls up to 5 metres (17ft) thick, the cannon tower was a formidable part of the town's defences. It's now occupied by the **Estonian Maritime Museum** (Eesti meremuuseum; http://meremuuseum.ee; closed for renovation until autumn 2019). Four floors present an extensive look at the nation's seafaring history from Neolithic times to the present. Heading back to the square via nearby Vene Street brings you past a well-restored medieval house at No. 17, which contains the **Tallinn City Museum** (Tallinna linnamuuseum; http://linnamuuseum.ee/linnamuuseum; Tue–Sun Mar–Oct 10.30am–6pm, Nov–Feb 10am–5.30pm). This is one of the city's most modern and engaging history museums, chronicling Tallinn's

St Catherine's Passage.

development from its founding until today.

LATIN QUARTER

Further up Vene Street is the area that came to be called the "Latin Quarter". In medieval times it was the domain of the powerful **Dominican Monastery** (Dominiiklaste klooster; http://www.kloostri.ee; mid-May–mid-Sept daily 10am–6pm, mid-Sept–mid-May by appointment). Known as **St Catherine's Monastery**, it was founded here in 1246 by the Dominican Order, and played a key role in the town's religious affairs. The Reformation movement in 1525 closed it down, and in 1531 the abandoned complex was ravaged by fire. Though not all of the building remains, the monastery's beautiful courtyard and ancient corridors still give an impression of monastic life in medieval times. The corridors display a collection of medieval stonemasonry salvaged from elsewhere in the Old Town.

A separate museum known as Old Dominican Monastery Claustrum (Müürivahe 33; www.claustrum

u; mid-May–Sept daily 11am–5pm), ound the corner, gives access to the monastery's inner chambers, which xhibit additional stone carvings, as vell as archaeological finds from the monastery grounds.

Just south of the monastery, the arrow **St Catherine's Passage** (Katariina käik) that connects Vene and Müürivahe streets is absolutely not to e missed. One side of the picturesque assage displays some intriguing – if omewhat eerie – stone burial slabs hat were removed from the former t Catherine's Church, directly behind hem, during renovation. The lane eads to Tallinn's famous **Knit Market**, a section of the town wall where lderly ladies sell traditional woollen reations. From here, the **Viru Gates** re just a few steps away.

EEDLE-EYE GATE MEMORIAL

 walk down Harju Street, a few metres rom Town Hall Square, reveals a very ifferent aspect of the city's history: he devastation of World War II. About alfway down the street a terraced

park sits in a strangely empty block. This is where several buildings, including a hotel and a cinema, once stood. On 9 March 1944, with Nazi Germany still occupying Estonia, the Soviet Air Force bombed Tallinn, destroying entire neighbourhoods and leaving 20,000 homeless.

In 2008, when the block was being landscaped, planners restored one of the narrow lanes that ran between the houses on the west side of Harju. **Needle-Eye Gate**, as it was called, had remained buried since the war and now serves as a memorial. Glass panels allow visitors to peer into the cellars adjacent to the street, while a video display shows documentary footage of the area's history.

The **Church of St Nicholas** Ⓡ (Niguliste kirik) that lords over Harju Street was also destroyed in the 1944 raid, but it was reconstructed from 1956 to 1984. Dedicated to the patron saint of merchants and artisans, it was founded by a group of German settlers who had set up a trading yard here in the early 13th century. This was the only church

Tallinn harbour.

◎ Shop

St Catherine's Passage (Katariina käik), a narrow lane lined with craft studios, is worth a visit for shoppers and browsers. Enter through the archway just past Vene 12.

in the Lower Town that wasn't ransacked during the Reformation fervour of 1524, thanks to its head of congregation who kept the mobs out by pouring molten lead into the door locks.

The church now serves a purely secular function, operating as the **Niguliste Museum and Concert Hall** (http://nigulistemuuseum.ekm.ee; May–Sept Tue–Sun 10am–5pm, Oct–Apr Wed–Sun 10am–5pm), which showcases religious art from Estonia and abroad. It has the distinction of housing Estonia's most famous work of art, 15th-century artist Bernt Notke's mural *Dance of Death* (see page 46), a macabre masterpiece depicting people from various walks of life dancing with skeletons. Other treasures in the museum include awe-inspiring altars from the 16th and 17th centuries, a collection of Renaissance and Baroque chandeliers, and several curious 14th- to 17th-century tombstones.

Harju Street ends at **Freedom Square (Vabaduse väljak)**. After serving for decades as a car park (much to the dismay of patriotic Estonians), the square was refurbished in 2009 and now serves as a prime public space. At its head stands the Freedom Monument, which commemorates Estonia's 1918–20 War of Independence and continues to raise controversy due to its high cost and construction flaws.

AROUND TALLINN BAY

The Old Town is the tourists' favourite part of Tallinn, but at weekends the locals wander in the parks on the east side of Tallinn Bay. The best-loved of these is **Kadriorg ⑤**, a name synonymous with affluence, nature and, most of all, tranquillity. Nevertheless, music lovers appreciate numerous concerts traditionally held in in the park every summer. Kadriorg Park was laid out between 1718 and 1725 by the Italian architect Niccolò Michetti under the orders of Peter the Great, who named it in honour of his wife, Catherine. Most of it remains a wooded, informal park, planted with lime, oak, ash, birch and chestnut trees and punctuated by open fields. Among the more developed exceptions are the larg

Kadriorg Palace and Art Museum.

rectangular Swan Pond with fountains and a beautiful white gazebo, which provide a fittingly romantic introduction to the park. In the northeast corner of the park, a wonderful Japanese garden designed by internationally well-known landscape architect, Masao Sone, boasts the largest rhododendron collection in the region. Other attractions include cherry trees, orrises and irises. The jewel in the Kadriorg's crown is without a doubt the lavish, Baroque **Kadriorg Palace** ❶ (Kadrioru loss) that Peter had built in 1718. The palace is a stunning monument to imperial extravagance. In particular, its two-storey main hall, decorated in rich stucco work and grandiose ceiling paintings, is considered one of the best examples of Baroque design in all of northern Europe. Equally impressive is the manicured, 18th-century-style flower garden, with erupting fountains.

As the building is itself a masterpiece, it's appropriate that it houses one of the nation's top art museums. The **Kadriorg Art Museum** (http://kadriorumuuseum.ekm.ee; May–Dec Tue and Thu–Sun 10am–6pm, Wed until 8pm; Jan–Apr Thu–Sun 10am–5pm, Wed until 8pm) is the main home for the Art Museum of Estonia's foreign collection. While here, those interested in art should also visit the **Mikkel Museum** (http://mikkelimuuseum.ekm.ee; May–Dec Tue and Thu–Sun 10am–6pm, Wed until 8pm; Jan–Apr Thu–Sun 10am–5pm, Wed until 8pm), just across the street in what used to be the palace's kitchen house. Exquisite works include Flemish and Dutch paintings, Italian engravings, Chinese porcelain and etchings by Rembrandt.

A quick walk up the hill from the museums will take you to the **Presidential Residence** (1938) with ceremonial guards, and then to a small cottage, now a museum, where Peter stayed during visits while the palace was under construction.

KUMU ART MUSEUM

The road ends at Estonia's largest and most complete art museum, the **Kumu** (https://kumu.ekm.ee; Tue–Wed and Fri–Sun 10am–6pm, Thu until

Chatting outside Kadriorg Palace.

8pm). Opened in 2006, this sprawling, modern complex serves as the main building of the Art Museum of Estonia and a centre for contemporary art. Works produced by the nation's artistic heroes of the 19th and 20th centuries make up the permanent collection, while temporary exhibitions focus primarily on contemporary art. The facility itself, designed by Finnish architect Pekka Vapaavuori, is a fascinating, multi-functional maze of copper, limestone and glass that certainly deserves exploration. In 2008 the Council of Europe awarded Kumu the title of European Museum of the Year.

ALONG THE COASTAL PATH

The path from Kadriorg Palace to the sea leads to the angel-like *Russalka memorial*, built to commemorate 177 men lost when the Russian warship *Russalka* (Mermaid) sank en route from Tallinn to Helsinki in 1893. The dramatic monument is now a popular spot for Russian wedding couples to honour the tradition of laying flowers.

Kumu, the Art Museum of Estonia.

The wreck, incidentally, was discovered by Estonian researchers in 2003.

Opposite the monument, slightly further along the coast is the entrance to the **Song Festival Grounds** (Lauluväljak), scene of Estonia's "Singing Revolution". The Song Festival Arena with a distinctive, curving roof, was built in 1960 and is Tallinn's largest outdoor stage. Every five years it hosts an unforgettable event – Estonian Song and Dance Celebration festival which draws 34,000 performers and around 200,000 spectators. A nearby 42 metre Sound Ground Lights Tower (advance booking essential) offers a short photo exposition on the history of Song Festivals and breath-taking views of the city as well as ships on the sea through binoculars mounted at the observation deck.

Further north along the coast is the recently renovated **Maarjamäe Palace** (Maarjamäe loss), a grand pseudo-Gothic manor built by Count Orlov-Davidov in 1874. First used as a summer home, the "palace" changed hands several times, serving as a Dutch consul's residence, a prestigious hotel, an aviation school and a Soviet army barracks. It now houses the branch of the **Estonian History Museum** (Eesti Ajaloomuuseum; www.ajaloomuuseum.ee; May–Sept daily 10am–6pm, Oct–Apr Tue–Sun 10am–6pm) that chronicles developments in the 19th and 20th centuries.

Just beyond is the site of the sprawling **Maarjamäe War Memorial**, an overbearing, cement-filled park that could have only been born of the Soviet 1960s and 70s.

PIRITA DISTRICT

Pirita Tee, a pleasant place to stroll beside the sea, leads on to the Pirita district, home to the city's most popular beach. It is also the site of the Olympic Yachting Centre, which was built for the sailing events of the 1980 Olympic Games in Moscow and is still

used by locals. **St. Bridget's Convent ruins ①** (Pirita klooster; daily Apr–Oct 10am–6pm, Nov–Mar noon–4pm) lie over the River Pirita and across the road. It was built in 1407–36 for the Swedish-based St Bridget's order of nuns and in its time was one of the two largest buildings in Tallinn (the Dominican Monastery was the other). The convent was destroyed in 1577 during the Livonian Wars but the 35-metre (115ft) high western facade with an arched portal of flagstones is still quite beautiful, and the shell of the rest of the main church is intact. Peasants continued to live on the site for a considerable time after its destruction, and their gravestones are visible in its front yard. In 2001 a modern, smaller convent was opened on the site. Part of it can be visited (May–Sept Mon–Tue and Thu–Sat 7.30–8.30am, Wed 4.30–6pm, Sun 9.30–noon) while the closed area is where the remaining eight nuns live.

The Balts are fond of their cemeteries, and some say that the **Forest Cemetery ②** (Metsakalmistu) at Kloostrimetsa, down the road from Pirita, is the most beautiful place in all of Tallinn. It looks almost like a national park, with graves running up and down small hills under a deep forest of fir trees. In 1933, the writer Eduard Vilde was the first to be buried here, and most of Estonia's stars have since followed suit, including the singer Georg Ots (1920–75), the poet Lydia Koidula (1843–86), Konstantin Päts, Estonia's first president (1874–1956), and Lennart Meri, president of Estonia from 1992 to 2001.

Just to the east the space-age **Teletorn** (TV Tower; daily 10am–6pm) dominates the skyline; 314 metres (1,030ft) in height, it offers unforgettable views of the city and surrounding ports from its observation deck and café at the 170-metre (558ft) level. A few metres from the tower's base is the **Tallinn Botanical Garden** (Tallinna botaanikaaed; www.botaanikaaed.ee; daily May–Sept 10am–8pm, Oct–Apr 11am–5pm), covering 123 hectares (304 acres) of the Pirita Valley with its beautiful gardens and nature trails.

☉ Kids

Check out events at the Estonian Open-Air Museum, such as egg-painting at Easter, spring farm days in May, bonfires, swing songs and dancing on St John's Eve in June, an autumn fair in September and old-time festivities in the Christmas Village in mid-December.

An aerial view of Tallinn Botanical Garden.

On the western side of Tallinn and within easy reach of the city is the **Estonian Open-Air Museum** (Eesti Vabaõhumuuseum; http://evm.ee; daily late Apr–late Sept 10am–8pm, late Sept–late Apr 10am–5pm). Situated at Rocca al Mare on the Kakumäe Peninsula, overlooking the sea near some of the most exclusive property in town, the museum contains more than 72 buildings, brought here from all over the country, showing how life has typically been lived in rural Estonia. It hosts various events including dance, song, folklore and culinary festivals throughout the year.

SUBURBAN REALITY

To understand Tallinn fully, you must venture off into one of the residential neighbourhoods. Not far from the Forest Cemetery is **Lasnamäe** , an enormous concrete sea of nearly identical buildings with virtually no landscaping, which was the source of great controversy during the Soviet years. Begun in the late 1970s, it was nicknamed the "suburb

of Leningrad" because the housing authorities repeatedly installed new immigrants from Russia, no matter how long locals had been on the waiting list. It is now more than 70 percent Russian.

ARTISTIC KALAMAJA

A very different sort of residential area lies just beyond the walls of the Old Town, in the direction of the railway station. This is the **Kalamaja** district, a neighbourhood that has only recently become appreciated for its architectural value and bohemian charm.

Developed in the late 19th and early 20th centuries when a new rail connection from St Petersburg sparked an industrial boom, Kalamaja became the home of thousands of newly arrived factory workers from the countryside. A hotchpotch of wooden apartment houses sprouted up along the streets. Fire and rot meant that many of these homes didn't survive the Soviet era or turbulent 1990s, but the better houses were bought up and refurbished.

Tradition survives in Vabaõhumuuseum, the open-air museum.

Now Kalamaja has become the address of choice for artists and other young professionals, while edgy galleries are increasingly moving in. The attraction is easy to see: the stylish, colourfully painted houses lend the area a rustic charm that's impossible to find in most other areas of the city.

MARKET AND MUSEUM SHIPS

There are other draws for visitors as well, starting with the busy **Balti Jaam Market** (Mon–Sat 9am–7pm, Sun 9am–5pm) at the back of the railway station. Selling everything from apples to tombstones, it provides a glimpse of Estonian reality that's absent from most tourist brochures. A Kalaturg, or fish market, operates every Saturday (10am–4pm) at the Kalaranna square, selling various types of fish caught in local waters.

A long stroll down Vana-Kalamaja will bring you past the area's picturesque streets to the gates of **Patarei Prison** (http://patarei.org). Originally a fortress built in 1840, it was used to house inmates throughout the Soviet period. All access to Patarei was suspended in 2016; at the time of publication, in 2019, several possibilities for its future development and use were being discussed.

Just along the coast from here is Tallinn's Lennusadam housing **Seaplane Harbour Maritime Museum** ❷ (www.lennusadam.eu; May–Sept daily 10am–7pm, Oct–Apr Tue–Sun 10am–6pm). In addition to a minesweeper and a patrol boat, the collection includes Europe's largest steam-powered ice-breaker, dating from 1914, and the *Lembit* submarine, built in Britain in 1938. From its decks you can peer across at the Old Town's skyline and imagine what a tempting prize Tallinn would have been to any seafaring invaders. The seaplane harbour was built 100 years ago on orders from the Russian emperor Nicholas II to become part of Peter the Great's naval force. It was used for housing seaplanes until World War II. The Seaplane Harbour received numerous awards including the title of Estonia's Most Tourist-Friendly Museum.

Patarei Prison.

TARTU AND THE SOUTH

The brains of the country are nurtured in Tartu, the university town in the "real" Estonia of the south, where there are lakes, historic sights and the country's "winter capital", Otepää.

People often call southern Estonia the "real" Estonia. This is where ties to the land go back countless generations, the dialect is deep Finno-Ugric, and the locals have kept up a tradition of hospitality and generosity. The region is split roughly between the undulating Sakala, Otepää and Haanja highlands. Each has its own "metropolitan" focus – Viljandi, Otepää and Võru – but these cities have a rural feel. For the most part, industrial activity is secondary or subordinate to agriculture.

TARTU, CITY OF LEARNING

The largest city in the southern half of Estonia, with almost 98,000 residents, is **Tartu ②**, 187km (116 miles) south-east of Tallinn. Just as many say the south is the real Estonia, many call Tartu its real capital. At the very least, Tartu is the intellectual capital. Roughly a quarter of its population is made up of students, attending one of the city's 16 institutions of higher learning.

Chief among these is Tartu University, founded in 1632, which was a powerhouse for Estonian (as well as Latvian) intellectuals during their National Awakening. It has endured as the main seat of higher education in the humanities and currently has around 20,000 students.

Tartu was first recorded in 1030 as a stronghold built by Grand Duke

Yaroslav of Kiev. The city has been razed on several occasions since – by Estonians in 1061, Germans in 1224, the Great Northern War in 1708 and by fire in 1775 – and most buildings in the Old Town date from the 18th century.

The city has developed in a north–south fashion along the River Ema-jõgi, with most of the main university buildings sprinkled on the northern end where the Old Town lies. This district is immediately distinguishable by the wide, cobbled Raekoja plats (Town Hall Square), anchored by a pinkish

Main attractions

Tartu
Viljandi
Otepää Highlands
Pühajärv Oak
Mõniste Open-Air Museum
Haanja Highlands
Võru

Maps on pages 98, 136

Statue of the kissing students.

○ Tip

Tartu is especially proud of its nostalgic Toy Museum (www.mm.ee; Wed–Sun 11am–6pm) and the Science Centre AHHAA (www.ahhaa.ee; Mon–Thu and Sun 10am–7pm, Fri and Sat until 8pm) showing that the science can be really fun.

neoclassical **Town Hall** Ⓐ (Raekoda) at its head, from 1798. The grey clock tower rising from the middle of its roof was added in the 19th century to help the students be on time for classes.

In front of the Town Hall stands a fountain with a kissing couple under an umbrella. The statue, a symbol of Tartu's student population, was designed by the Estonian artist Mati Karmin in 1999 and quickly became a meeting point.

Along the northern side of the square is an unbroken row of pastel-coloured buildings greatly responsible for Tartu's reputation as the neoclassical prima donna of Estonia. The most noticeable is the "**Leaning House**" (1793) at No. 18. Erected on the old city wall and partly on marshland that later dried up, it leans markedly to the left. Inside is the branch of **Tartu Museum of Art** (Tartu Kunstimuuseum; www.tartmus.ee; Wed, Fri–Sun 11am–6pm, Thu until 9pm), with a collection that centres on the Pallas Higher Art School that ran in Tartu from 1919 to 1940.

At the foot of the square is the **Arched Bridge** (Kaarsild), which replaced the 18th-century Stone Bridge destroyed in 1944. Taking a daring walk over the bridge's top rail has become a time-honoured student tradition.

Tartu Ülikooli peahoone, the university's main building, lies just a couple of blocks north from the Town Hall, at 18 Ulikooli Street, a stately oasis in the cramped and crumbling side streets of the Old Town. Pale yellow with six white columns, the University Building is the most impressive neoclassical structure in Estonia. Completed in 1809, it was designed by the architect Johann Krause. Visiting its **Art Museum** (Kunstimuuseum; www.kunstimuuseum.ut.ee; Mon–Sat 10am–6pm) will allow you to take a peek at its impressive concert hall, classical statuary replicas, and a lock-up, where students were incarcerated for such infractions of conduct as duelling or insulting cloakroom attendants.

Further north on Jaani Street is the 14th-century brick Gothic **St John's Church** (Jaani kirik, www.jaanikirik.ee; Tue–Sat 10am–6pm). The renovation of the interior, which lasted for decades,

The Leaning House.

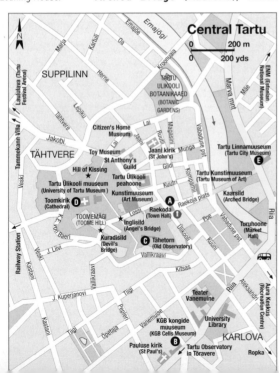

Central Tartu

Pallas

was completed in 2005. On the exterior you can admire hundreds of tiny terracotta sculptures. The 15 faces above its pointed portal represent the Last Judgement. On the same street is the 19th-century **Citizen's Home Museum** (http://linnamuuseum.tartu.ee; Apr–Sept Wed–Sat 11am–5pm, Sun 11am–3pm, Oct–Mar Wed–Sun 10am–3pm); in one of the oldest wooden houses of Tartu, it is an example of a middle-class citizen's home from the first half of the 19th century. **St Anthony's Guild**, on Lutsu 3 near St John's Church, is a collection of craft studios where visitors can watch artists at work. Concerts are held in its courtyard in summertime.

SOUTH OF TOWN HALL SQUARE

The neoclassical rule is further broken on the south side of Town Hall Square. First along Vabaduse Street is the grim, brown **Market Hall** (www.tarturg.ee; Mon–Fri 8am–6pm, Sat–Sun 9am–3pm). The bus station stands on the next block, and then the **Outdoor Market**, which is devoted half to foodstuffs and half to dry goods. The riverbank is dominated by modern glass high-rises. A short walk down the road is the **Aura Keskus** (www.aurakeskus.ee), a recreation centre with indoor swimming pools and water slides. Across the road on Riia Street is another set of modern buildings, comprising the Tartu Department Store and the Hansakeskus (Hansa Centre) with the Pallas Hotel (http://pallas.tartuhotels.ee) on its fourth floor.

A short walk uphill from here, at Riia 15b, brings you to the **KGB Cells Museum** B (KGB kongide muuseum; http://linnamuuseum.tartu.ee; Tue–Sat 11am–5pm). Built into what was the local NKVD/KGB in the 1940s and 50s, the museum covers themes of repression and the Estonian resistance movement.

The **Vanemuine Theatre** (1977; www.vanemuine.ee), at Vanemuise 6, and adjacent **University Library** (1980;

https://utlib.ut.ee), at W. Struve Street 1, are later touches. Both are white and functional, but the library is distinguished by the students perpetually gathered on its wide fountain-clad plaza for a quick smoke.

TOOME HILL AND PARK

It is a short, pleasant walk from here to **Toome Hill** (Toomemägi), the hilly park that dominates the Old Town. In the southern side of the park stands the early 19th-century **Old Observatory** C (Tähetorn; www.tahetorn.ut.ee; Tue–Sun 10am–6pm), which once had the world's largest refracting telescope. The historical telescopes are used for public observation at night (twice a month, Sept–May; free). The planetarium offers interesting shows (also in English) about the stars and their presence in folk culture, film and literature, as well as an array of hands-on exhibitions. Science buffs can also visit the **Tartu Observatory** (http://kylastuskeskus.to.ee) **in Tõravere**. From the west entrance on Vällikraavi Street, turn up under the grey Kuradisild

Statuary in Tartu's Art Museum.

⊘ Eat

Built into the side of Toome Hill, on the southeast edge of the park, the cavernous 18th-century Gunpowder Cellar, or Pussirohukelder, is now a popular beer restaurant serving local dishes (Lossi 28; tel: 7303 555; http://pyss.ee).

Street bookstall.

(1913) or **Devil's Bridge**. This is named after a Professor Manteuffel from Germany who, in the late 19th century, introduced Estonia to the use of rubber gloves in surgical operations, but whose name resembles the German "man-devil". You will find yourself between the University Internal Hospital (1808) and the University Maternity Hospital (1838). Straight ahead is the ochre **Angel's Bridge** (Inglisild), also named as a result of a linguistic confusion: **Toomemägi Park** was laid out in English style and the locals confused the words "English" and "angel".

Toomemägi is strewn with statues of people connected with Tartu University. In spring biology students traditionally wash the pensive head of Karl Ernst von Baer – a professor linked to Darwin – with champagne. The monument to the writer Kristjan Jaak Peterson – the first Estonian national to enter the university – is shown erect with a stick in his hand because he is said to have walked the 250 km (155 miles) from Rīga to Tartu. The "Romantic Corner" of the park lies to the left of the statue of Baer. It consists of a stone mound called the Hill of Kissing, to the top of which bridegrooms must carry their new wives, a low Bridge of Sighing with a well-worn cement bench, and a Sacrificial Stone where the lovelorn can leave a prayer to the ancient gods.

Sacred stones are found all over Estonia; people used to gather round them on a Thursday full moon, and leave (non-bloody) sacrifices. Tartu students have continued this ritual by burning their notebooks here at midnight on the Thursday before their exams.

TOOM CATHEDRAL

The monumental ruins of the **Toom Cathedral** ⓓ (Toomkirik; www.muuseum.ut.ee; May–Sept Tue–Sun 10am–6pm, Oct–Apr Wed–Sun 11am–5pm), which gives the hill its name, loom above this part of the park. Begun in the 13th century, this was once the largest brick Gothic church in the Baltic countries, but the majority of it was destroyed in the Livonian Wars (1558–83). The broken wings of 10 flying buttresses give an idea of its former grandeur. While

⊘ THE NAME GAME

Tartu residents possess a wry sense of wit that comes out in their penchant for nicknaming local buildings, particularly the newer, somewhat incongruous structures that have cropped up here since 2000.

The modern, glass Emajõgi Business Centre that stands adjacent to the market is locally known as "the flask" for its flat shape, and for similar reasons, the spiralling construction behind it is referred to as "the snail". The small ensemble of bank branches on the corner of Ülikooli and Vallikraavi has been sarcastically dubbed "Wall Street", while the oversized, cubical Kaubamaja department store nearby is jokingly called "Tallinn University" by students taking a jab at what they see as the ridiculous materialism of the capital.

the project to shore up the ruins continues, summer visitors can pay to climb its two renovated towers.

The huge choir on the church's eastern end was completely restored in the early 1800s under the direction of Krause. For a time it served as the university library, but it now contains the **University of Tartu Museum** (Tartu Ülikooli muuseum; www.muuseum. ut.ee; May–Sept Tue–Sun 10am–6pm, Oct–Apr Wed–Sun 11am–5pm; guided tours in several languages available, including outside opening hours). On each floor are exhibitions of the history of the university, from its opening in 1632 in honour of the Swedish King Gustavus Adolphus to the present day. A lovely white Baroque hall on the second floor is a public concert room with walls lined by cases of antique biological specimens. The most rare items are shown and carefully explained in the Treasury. Within the university are also the **University of Tartu Natural History Museum**, the **Botanical Gardens** and The Old Anatomical Theatre.

A trip across the Arched Bridge leads to **Tartu City Museum** ❺ (Tartu linnamuuseum; Narva Road 23; http://linnamuuseum.tartu.ee; Wed–Sun 11am–pm). Housed in a late 18th-century mansion, this museum covers the entire history of the town.

ESTONIAN NATIONAL MUSEUM

North-east of Tartu City Museum, at Muuseumi tee 2, is the **Estonian National Museum** (ENM; www.erm.ee; Tue and Thu–Sun 10am–6pm, Wed until 8pm) with the country's most important permanent folklore collection. The new museum building was inaugurated in 2016 on the grounds of the **Raadi Manor**, formerly home to the Baltic German von Liphard family. The building is ultra-modern and huge, complete with a cinema, library, restaurant and cafe. The manor park is open to the public (Narva maantee 177; daily 7am–10pm).

TARTU'S DISTRICTS

Lai Street separates the Old Town from **Suppilinn**, or Soup Town, so called because its streets are named after soup ingredients such as Bean and Potato. The industrial area south of the Old Town is the **Ropka district**, and the attractive **Karlova district** has cut-corner wooden houses built during the Estonian Republic as boarding houses. The area of stately homes behind Toomemägi Park – and very popular with university professors – is the **Tähtvere district**, where some of the architecture was inspired by the Bauhaus movement. Just beyond here are the Tartu Festival Arena (Laululava; http://arena.ee) where the first Baltic gathering was held in 1869. Today the stadium, with a canopy built in 1994, can hold 10,000 singers.

ARCHITECTURAL SIGHTS

Some of the most curious buildings in Tartu are ordinary houses. The weathered house at 65 Marta Street, beside the wooded park in which the beautifully restored **Karlova Manor** (private,

Tartu's part-ruined cathedral.

guided tours available only by request, tel: 569 72 225) stands, for example, is a marvel of wood and stone edging work.

At Riia 27, **St Paul's Church** (Pauluse kirik, 1919) was designed by the Finnish architect Eliel Saarinen. Created in red brick with a square tower, it looks a bit like a fire station. Another architectural curiosity is the constructivist **Tammekann Villa** (tours only by request; tel: 5537 102; http://granokeskus.utu.fi/enkehikko.html), built by Finnish architect Alvar Aalto in 1932 on Kreutzwaldi 6.

WEST OF TARTU

The small city of **Viljandi** ❸, 77km (48 miles) west on main road 92, clings to the slopes of a primeval valley plumbed by Lake Viljandi. Now the capital of the Sakala upland, with about 17,500 inhabitants, the site has been settled since AD 1000, but the Old Town is tiny; one small grid between Tallinna and Tartu streets and the **Castle Park** (Lossipark). Its appeal is its lakeland setting and the ruined castle perched on a series of hills above the water,

The start of the Tartu cross-country ski marathon.

but it is perhaps better known among Estonians for the Viljandi Folk Music Festival, held each summer.

A good place to start a tour of the town is the **Museum of Viljandi** (Viljandi muuseum; Kindral Laidoner Square 10; www.muuseum.viljandimaa.ee May–Aug daily 11am–6pm, Sept–Apr Tue–Sat 10am–5pm; guided tours in English), in the Old Town. This square used to be the marketplace, and its central fountain covers the town well. The museum is downstairs in Viljandi's third-oldest building, originally a pharmacist's shop (1779–80), and contains a model of the former castle. It also houses many painstakingly decorated old objects of daily use, such as tankards and horse yokes, as well as exhibitions covering Viljandi county's late 19th-century history and the period of Estonia's first independence (1918–40).

The 18th-century **Town Hall** (Raekoda) stands on nearby Linnu Street. The neighbouring **Old Water Tower** (Vana veetorn; May–Aug daily 11am–6pm, Sept Tue–Sat 10am–5pm, rest of

he year by appointment), dates from 911 and has been refurbished.

The entrance to Castle Park is just own Lossi Street, over a long wooden ootbridge. Begun in 1223, the **Order 'ortress of Viljandi** (Viljandi ordu-'nnus) is presumed to have been he largest fortress in the Baltics, 'esigned to stretch over three adja-ent hills, with its only entrance on he first hill, occupied by servants. The econd fold, once split between serv-ints and horses, is now a field edged vith bits of old wall. If you climb (care-ully) up on the stone by the edge, you vill get a great view over a long and narrow lake. The third hill supported he castle, the church and the prison. 'his final section has more ruins than he other two, and they stand out tarkly against the sky.

A bright red-and-white suspension oridge (Rippsild) leads from this end of the castle grounds into the rest of he park. Built in 1879, the 50-metre 164ft) bridge was brought to the town rom Rīga in 1931 by a German count vhose favourite daughter, the story joes, had persisted in racing her horse cross it.

The 15th-century church of the for-ner Franciscan monastery, **St John's Church** (Jaani kirik), has its own vooden footbridge, at the head of Cas-le Park just off Pikk Street. It is used also for concerts. The town's main _utheran church, **St Paul's** (Pauluse kirik, 1863–6), lies outside the park across Vaksali Road. Red brick with stone inlay, it has an industrial-age Gothic veneer.

By the lake's shore Viljandi has a dif-erent feel – it is considerably sportier, happier and younger. At one end are ennis courts and a town stadium, and here is also an athletes' hotel. Boats and pedalos can be rented from the pier beside the restaurant. It is advis-able to row out to the centre if you want to jump in because the bottom of the ake is so muddy.

OTEPÄÄ, THE WINTER CAPITAL

Estonia's entire southern region is dot-ted with pretty lakes, many of which are swimmable (though it is always best to check with a local). The largest, at 270 sq km (105 sq miles), is **Võrtsjärv**. It is, however, only 6 metres (20ft) at its deep-est. The lakes of **Otepää** in the **Otepää Highlands** help make this cosy town not just one of Estonia's most popular win-ter resorts but also a gracious rest spot during the summer months.

Otepää ④ is a short drive south-west from Tartu, but in its tranquillity it could be a million miles away from the city. Its population of around 2,000 easily doubles in winter. Tourism has become a mainstay of the economy in Estonia's "winter capital", and resort facilities include a ski jump, cross-country ski paths, three downhill ski-ing centres, a beach and hotels. The town's biggest events are the World Cup Cross-Country Skiing Champi-onship, which attracts around 10,000 participants each January, the Tartu Marathon involving 2,000–3,000 skiers in February, and an ice-fishing contest.

Orienteering at Otepää.

⊙ Tip

Otepää's two gentle downhill ski slopes lie south of the town, at Väike Munamägi (www.munakas.ee) and Kuutsemäe (www.kuutsemae.ee), where equipment can be hired.

The town and its surroundings have been designated a "protected area". Building above three storeys is forbidden, salt cannot be used against ice on the roads, and motorboating on Otepää's lakes and hunting and camping in its woods are restricted, though "bloodless" hunting – with a camera – is always allowed.

The town clusters up against these woods, and the centre has a pleasantly closed-in feeling, accentuated by a narrow triangular central park. The Tourist Information Centre is based nearby, at the bus station at 1 Tartu Street. The oldest building in town is **Otepää church**. Opened in 1608, it was built by Estonian peasants so they wouldn't have to attend the church of the German population. The folklorist Jakob Hurt was its first Estonian pastor (1872–80). The current steeple was added in 1860 and is 52 metres (168ft) high.

When the Estonian Students Co-operative was forbidden from consecrating its flag in Tartu in 1884, they defiantly brought it to the Otepää church. Their trek is honoured in the tiny **Estonian Flag Museum** (Eesti lipu muuseum; open by request; free) in the nearby rectory. Stone reliefs on the church's front doors that depicted this momentous nationalistic event were destroyed by the Soviets, but the locals replaced them with bronze casts in 1990. The "Monument to the 54" in front of the church, dedicated to the soldiers from Otepää who died in the War of Independence, was also blown up by the Soviets – once in the 1950s, and again in the 1980s – but each time it was replaced by the local people. There is also the **Winter Sports Museum** (www.spordimuuseum.ee; Mon–Fri 11am–5pm, Sat–Sun 11am–4pm) with a large collection of photos, medals and other items.

Linnamägi, former site of a 10- to 11th-century wooden stronghold and a bishop's 13th-century stone castle, is a small tree-covered hill a short walk south from the church past a municipal garden. The first level of the hill is marked with a large stone monument dated 1116, the year when Otepää first appears in the records. Locals use this spot for their midsummer celebrations. The excavated ruins of the castle stand on the shelf above. The expansive vista from here makes it easy to imagine why ancient warriors fought for the site.

PÜHAJÄRV OAK

In ancient times Estonians gathered under oaks whenever they had to make important decisions. One of the most famous oaks is a couple of kilometres outside the centre of Otepää. Standing wide and noble between a cow pasture vegetable patch and Pühajärv lake, the **Pühajärv Oak** is 22 metres (72ft) tall. Five people linking arms can reach around it. Its popular name is the War Tree (Sõjatamm), because of its part in independence history. In 1841, a local German landlord tried to force the Estonian peasants on his land to use heavier equipment than they felt their horses could draw. They refused, which resulted in a battle beneath the oak. The peasant

The magic Pühajärv Oak.

lost, but their act became a legend of Estonian solidarity. Incidentally, the biggest and oldest tree in the country, the Tamme-Lauri Oak, is located in Urvaste about 15km (10 miles) south of the town. It dates from 1326, and has a circumference of 8.25 metres (27ft).

Neitsijärv, or Virgin's Lake, which you pass on the way from the town to the War Tree, derives its name from the Middle Ages when the *droit de seigneur* meant that brides had to spend their first married night in the bed of the Pühajärv landlord. One young girl left her wedding for the manor and never appeared. In the morning, they found her bridal dress beside this lake, where she had drowned herself.

Pühajärv, the largest of the lakes in the area, literally means "Holy Lake". The public beach here is a well-maintained "blue flag"quality beach, and boats can be rented out. Soviet dissidents Andrei Sakarov and Alexander Solzhenitsyn both used to spend quiet weeks by Lake Püha and, if you ask, locals will show you where the prime minister of Estonia during the Soviet era kept his holiday home. He alone was allowed to use a motorboat here. His home is now a guesthouse owned by Tartu University.

THE SOUTHERN BORDER

About 20km (13 miles) south from here is **Sangaste loss ❺** (Sangaste Castle; www.sangasteloss.com; daily 10am–6pm), built in 1874–81 for Count Friedrich Georg Magnus von Berg as a small-scale copy of Windsor Castle in England. It is a particularly incongruous looking orange-brick mansion set back amid acres of agricultural plains. The manor was seized in the 1930s and most of the family fled to Finland. Sangaste has passed through many hands since, even housing hay and a tractor in its octagonal, multi-vaulted ballroom after World War II. In the 1970s, it was used as a Young Pioneers' Camp. Today it is a hotel and a conference centre.

Wide pastureland separates Sangaste from **Valga ❻**, the southernmost city in Estonia, whose main claim to fame is that it straddles the border with Latvia where it becomes Valka. When

> **⏱ Fact**
>
> Along Mäe tänav, on the edge of Otepää, stands a thick, wooden post decorated with metal bears. It marks the spot which, in 1992, local psychics determined was the best place to take advantage of the positive energy fields crisscrossing the area.

Growing flowers in a disused boat at Puhajarv Lake.

both countries became independent in 1918, the new border divided streets and in some cases, even houses. After a brief respite during Soviet times, border posts went up again in the early 1990s, and down again in 2007 when both countries adopted the Schengen accords. Many non-Estonians live here, and unlike other southern towns it is industrially developed.

If you edge southeast along the border for about 45km (30 miles), you will reach one of Estonia's largest forests. The **Mõniste Open-Air Museum** ⑦ (Mõniste vabaõhumuuseum; www.monistemuuseum.ee; May–Sept daily 10am–5pm, Oct–Apr Mon–Fri 10am–2pm) here contains a reconstruction of a 19th-century southern Estonian farmhouse. Between Mõniste and Võru is the peaceful hamlet of **Rõuge** ⑧. A picture of southern harmony, Rõuge curls in around seven clear lakes. One, called Rõuge Suurjärv, or Rõuge's Big Lake, is the deepest in Estonia (38 metres/125ft). The Rõuge church (1730), with a white exterior and red-roofed bell-tower, is delightful. Behind

the church lies the Valley of Nightingales, which attracts hundreds of these birds in spring.

HANNJA HIGHLANDS

To the east lie the **Haanja Highlands** Haanja is slightly higher than the Otepää and Sakala uplands and its forests are deeper, but it has also been widely tamed by potato fields and pastureland. Its summit is **Suur Munamägi**, or Big Egg Hill, due east of Rõuge. The highest peak in Estonia, reaching 318 metres (1,044ft) above sea level, it has a 35-metre (115ft) observation tower (www.suurmunamagi.ee; Apr–Aug daily 10am–8pm; Sept–Oct daily 10am–5pm, Nov–Mar Sat–Sun noon–3pm) on its summit, and the result is a view that is truly heavenly. On the clearest days, you can see all the way to Russia and Latvia.

It may also be possible to glimpse the ruins of **Vastseliina Castle**. To reach it, head east towards the "new" Vastseliina village, whose cultural centre is in an 18th-century manor house. The "old" village, called

Suur Munamägi is the highest point in the Baltic States.

Vana-Vestseliina, was built in the 14th century around the castle, but not much is left of either. The red-and-beige brick castle has been reduced to two towers and one section of wall, lost in an overgrown section of field. Sometimes there are night concerts in the castle. The 19th-century Vana-Vastseliina coach stop, where a tsar once stayed, has been turned into a restaurant and the former smithy is now a craft and coffee shop.

The folds of Haanja were created during the Ice Age, and the landscape is smooth and unending. Gentle pastures are edged by lone farmhouses and tiny lakes that appear then fade. The most popular place for fishing is **Verijärv**, or Blood Lake, a bit closer to Voru and filled with perch and pike. Large and picturesque, at the base of another steep, forested valley, it got its name because a servant supposedly once drove a cruel lord of the manor into its waters.

Võru ❾, the urban centre for the Haanja Highlands, sprawls around the biggest lake in the town, Tamula järv. Along with agriculture, Võru depends on forestry, furniture-making and dairy production. The population is about 12,300 and the local dialect, Võru-Seto, which is spoken by the southern Estonians from Võrumaa and Setuma, is considered as a separate language.

The town was officially established in 1784, and both the small yellow Orthodox church and St Catherine's Church (Katariina kirik) were built soon after. The most famous 18th-century structure in Võru is the **Friedrich Reinhold Kreutzwald Memorial Museum** (F.R. Kreutzwaldi memoriaalmuuseum; www.lauluisa.ee; Wed–Sun Apr–Sept 10am–6pm, Oct–Mar 10am–5pm) on Kreutzwald Street 31. This is where the Estonian writer and doctor lived for most of his life. Kreutzwald was born in the Rakvere region in 1803 and studied in Tartu from 1826 to 1833. However, he spent the next 44 years practising medicine in Võru where he compiled *Kalevipoeg*, the Estonian national epic.

The museum is divided between three houses. The first is where the small home of Kreutzwald's Estonian mother stood; she could not bear to

◉ Tip

Rôuge makes a good base for exploring southern Estonia. Ask at the local tourist office in Võru (tel: 782 18 81) for farm and rural accommodation.

House in the old town of Võru.

live in the same house as Kreutzwald's wife, Maria, who was from a wealthy German family in Tartu. This house has an exhibition of his life and many publications. His own home has been kept as it was when he lived there and it includes portraits of the family, who, ironically, spoke only German at home. On the walls of the low building at the back of the yard are interpretations of *Kalevipoeg* from a panorama of artists, including some of Estonia's best known, such as Erik Haamer, Juri Arrak and Kristjan Raud.

Kreutzwald Park runs towards the lake and a statue of Kreutzwald. The **Võru County Museum** (Võrumaa muuseum; www.vorumuuseum.ee; Wed–Sun June–Aug 11am–7pm, Sept–May 10am–6pm) stands at the start of the park. Exhibits range from the area's 5,000-year-old settlement to life in the 20th century. Art and handicraft displays change every month.

RETURN ROUTE TO TARTU

The drive from Võru back up to Tartu gradually becomes less hilly, but the

forests remain. Main road 2 is the most direct route, but the 64, an older road, is a more leisurely option. Just beyond **Põlva** ⑩ on the right is the impressive **Kiidjärve Mill**. Constructed in 1914 and trimmed with orange brick, it is the largest functioning watermill in Europe. The **Põlva Peasant Culture Museum** (Põlva Talurahvamuuseum; www.polvatalurahvamuuseum.ee; daily May–Sept 9am–6pm, Oct–Apr until 4pm) lies on the other side of the Tartu road, in the village of Karilatsi just beyond **Kiidjärve**. It has an old schoolhouse that is still set for lessons, a windmill and a garden designed to be a map of the region.

Outside Tartu, 7km (5 miles) from the city centre on the Võru road, is the well-presented **Estonian Agricultural Museum** (Eesti Põllumajandusmuuseum; www.epm.ee; Tue–Sun 10am–6pm; tourist information and café daily 9am–6pm). Fittingly, the surrounding landscape is anchored by far-flung farms, many of which have been renovated. It is a sign that the south is ploughing on, refusing to be shaken by the north's vagaries.

Midwinter at the Estonian Agriculture Museum.

E-STONIA

From inventing Skype to becoming a world leader in e-government, Estonia has firmly embraced the information age.

One of the first things visitors notice on arrival in Estonia is the overwhelming presence of all things high-tech. Everyone, from small children to senior citizens, appears to be linked, as if umbilically, to a mobile phone. And in Wi-fi-enabled cafés and bars, locals are busy tapping on their phones and tablets, or scrutinising their laptops.

These outward signs are just the tip of a technological iceberg. Over the past few years, Estonia has become enamoured – some would say obsessed – with the idea of remodelling itself into an information society. The result is that new technologies, particularly those involving internet and mobile phones, have worked their way into every aspect of life, from farming to dating to buying drinks at vending machines. Locals take these innovations in their stride, pointing out that this is, after all, the country that invented Skype.

INTERNET A UNIVERSAL RIGHT

Estonia has a high-tech history. In Soviet times this was where advanced software programming was developed, for espionage and space programmes, and Tallinn was a major centre for developing artificial intelligence. After independence, a "Tiger Leap" programme was introduced, to push the nation ahead by using computer technology in every field, and connecting every school to the internet. In February 2000, Estonia declared internet access a "constitutional right", and six months later, the government became the first in the world to convert cabinet meetings to paperless sessions, saving £200,000 a year in photocopying costs. A more recent programme has trained more than 100,000 adults, mostly retired people and blue-collar workers, in how to use the internet.

The mobile phone is almost universal here, and is used for far more than just talking. Nearly all customers paying for parking in central Tallinn do so by SMS text message, and other text-message systems are widely used for everything from buying bus tickets to checking bank balances to paying taxes and even voting. Most Estonians are regular internet users, and nearly all connections are broadband. There are over 1,360 Wi-fi "hot-spots" around the country, allowing laptop users high-speed net access in cafés, pubs, hotels, city squares, beaches, trains and inter-city buses.

Wireless connections are spreading broadband into rural areas where ADSL and cable connections don't reach. Farmers have been using the internet to track cow herds, and if rural dwellers don't have computers, they can look for official blue signs with the "@" symbol pointing to a place to log on.

ONE CARD DOES ALL

A smart ID card, which can serve as a passport within the EU, is doing away with both money and paperwork. It can be used on public transport and for filing taxes. Estonia is continually innovating, and a responsive public means that the country is often used by foreign companies as a test market for new technologies.

Linnar Viik, the Tallinn-born guru behind Tiger Leap, once told *Forbes* magazine: "People like to say, don't touch things that work. But Estonians like to look behind the thing and wonder whether there's anything we can change about it. In Estonia you might say, if it works, you can break it."

Estonia is a highly switched-on society.

Kite-flying on the beach at Pärnu.

THE WEST COAST

Estonia's west coast is famous for its spa resorts of Pärnu and Haapsalu, its ghostly castles, and the abundant flowers and birdlife in the Sooma and Matsalu National Parks.

The spas of Estonia's western shore used to be favoured by Russian tsars, and even under Soviet rule Russians flocked here for their summer holidays. Today they attract Western – and in particular Finnish – visitors.

Estonia's prime spa resort, **Pärnu** ⓫, is one of the few places outside Tallinn where people traditionally know how to deal with a tourist. Known as Estonia's "Summer Capital", the town of almost 40,000 inhabitants is 130km (80 miles) due south of Tallinn on the E67.

PÄRNU "OLD" AND "NEW"

The city's revival began in the 1990s when the majestic Rannahotell (1937; http://rannahotell.ee) overlooking the beach was refurbished, and the Art Nouveau gem, the Ammende Villa (http://ammende.ee), reopened, both buildings restoring touches of pre-war elegance to the beach area. More recently, the Hotell St Peterburg (www.stpeterburg.ee) has added some 18th-century class to the mix, and the modern Tervise Paradiis health resort (www.terviseparadiis.ee) has made a loud splash with its gigantic, indoor water park.

The long beachfront and numerous parks are restorative places to stroll, and the Old Town is ripe with structural curiosities. Younger Estonians particularly like Pärnu; throughout the summer the bars and cafés are hopping,

and the cultural calendar is packed with concerts and festivals.

The city proper, first noted in 1251, is divided by the River Pärnu. Rather confusingly, the Old Town lies on the south bank within what the locals refer to as the "new" city. The "old" city, north of the river, is where the majority of newer buildings are located. The reason for this is linked to Pärnu's complex history. During the 14th century, the area where the Old Town stands was occupied by a castle and fortification. But when the Swedes took power in 1617, they began

Map on page 98

Main attractions
Pärnu
Kihnu island
Soomaa National Park
Matsalu National Park
Haapsalu
Ants Laikmaa Museum

Pärnu's Tallinn Gate.

◉ Tip

The David Oistrakh Festival (www.oistfest.ee) is a highlight of the summer season in Pärnu. It takes place in the town's five-storey concert hall every July. Masterclasses by Estonian conductor Neeme Järvi are part of the festival.

to build across the river instead. The castle fell into decay and was finally destroyed during the Great Northern War (1700–21). This made the section on the north bank the oldest part of the city when, in subsequent centuries, development began to spill back over to the former castle area. This "old city" was, however, flattened during World War II, putting the area with the oldest buildings, or the "old town", back on the south side of the river.

PÄRNU'S OLD TOWN

Touring Pärnu's Old Town is far less complicated. For one thing, it isn't very large. Visiting would take only a couple of hours, if so many of the most eye-catching buildings didn't also contain enticing bars and cafés. Its main street, the pedestrianised Rüütli Street, runs nearly the entire length of the Old Town, and is by far the city's most active. Smaller cross-streets, however, provide some of the town's more interesting architectural finds.

Pühavaimu Street, running through the Old Town's centre, is one example.

Pärnu Town Hall and, in the distance, the spires of St Catherine's Church.

First on the block is a delicate yellow building (1670), fronted by an imposing balcony that bears four small lions' heads. Squeezed in next to it is an odd red- and mustard-coloured house (1877) that mixes everything from Corinthian columns to a flowery grey trim. It in turn merges into a green Baroque structure (1674) trimmed with courtly white and crowned with an old street lamp. The nearby **Almshouse** (Seegimaja), at Hospidali 1, dates from the 1600s. The grand, peaked edifice was built in 1658, and now operates as a restaurant.

Generally, the Old Town isn't so old; most buildings date from the 19th century. But it does have two intact 18th-century churches, which are perhaps most remarkable for their physical proximity but absolute disparity. **St Catherine's Church** (Ekateriina kirik, 1765–68) is a weird Orthodox conglomeration of knobs and ledges, with green roofing and unevenly soaring spires. The interior is almost lunatic in its iconography; silver shield-like icons crowd the white walls. Meanwhile, the

red-and-white Lutheran church, **St Elisabeth's Church** (Eliisabeti kirik, 1747) at Nikolai 22 a few blocks away, is austere by comparison, but nonetheless impressive. Its charming interior and acoustics have made it a much-used venue for classical music performances.

MEDIEVAL WALLS

There are two remnants of the original 14th-century fortifications. One is the **Red Tower** (Punane Torn), saved during the Swedish era to house prisoners. Tucked down a small alley off Hommiku Street, it is easy to miss, particularly since, contrary to its name, it is coloured a gleaming white. The other piece of the ancient walls is the **Tallinn Gate** (Tallinna Väravad). Grey and white with tall green doors, it sometimes doubles as a pub in summer.

Passing through the gate, you find yourself on a lovely, long, tree-lined walk beside a finger of the River Pärnu curled inwards to create a duck-filled pond. This is the beginning of the lush parks that surround the sanatoria in a rather awesome silence.

MUD TREATMENT

The sanatoria offer a wide variety of treatments, from aromatic massages to the more traditional mud baths for muscle and joint aches. Though no longer considered a cure-all, mud has been a mainstay of Pärnu's resort industry since the 19th century. The most striking symbol of this activity is the **Pärnu Mud Baths** (Pärnu Mudaravila), housed in a neoclassical building (1926) at the end of Supeluse Street. It has been the site of a boutique spa (www.hedonspa.com) since 2014.

The elaborate, mint-coloured **Beach Salon** (Pärnu Kuursaal; http://parnukuursaal.ee), next door at Mere Avenue 22, functions as a gigantic tavern, as well as a cultural centre with a bandstand behind it. Its front pavilion, facing the beach, has a picturesque fountain and a row of ornamental wicker arches, festooned with vines each summer.

These two buildings stand by the northwest edge of **Pärnu Beach**, beginning with the **Women's Beach**, where only women and small children are allowed so that they can sunbathe nude

⊙ Fact

The elegant Rannahotell in Pärnu was designed by the Estonian Functionalist architects Olev Siinmaa and Anton Soans. Pause over a drink on its front terrace and check out its style.

Pärnu Mud Baths.

in peace. You can walk for miles from here along the tree-lined promenade that parallels the beach; continuing north brings you through a collection of modern sculptures and finally fields of dank, waving reed, while a turn south leads to the more crowded sections of waterfront, ad hoc cafés, the Functionalist-style **Beach House** (Rannahoone) and a mini-golf course.

The Old Town has its own walks, the most famous of which is the triangular **Lydia Koidula Park**. The poet Koidula (1843–86) was born in a village outside Pärnu. She lived in the city from the age of seven until, at 20, she moved with her family to Tartu. Many consider Koidula's collection of verse, *The Nightingale of Emajõgi*, to be the foremost work of Estonia's period of National Awakening, and the pen-name Koidula, given to her by a fellow artist, means literally "singer of the dawn". Her real maiden name was Jannsen, and the modest wooden schoolhouse where her family lived is on Jannseni 37. The house itself is now the **Lydia Koidula Memorial Museum** (www.parnumuuseum.

ee/koidula-museum; Tue–Sat June–Aug 10am–6pm, Sept–May 10am–5pm), perfectly embodies the spirit of her times. Her father, J.V. Jannsen, also played an important part in raising Estonian national awareness and the development of Estonian journalism.

The **Pärnu Museum** (www.parnumuuseum.ee; Tue–Sun 10am–6pm; guided tours), on the other hand, is surprisingly rewarding. Located in a restored 19th-century townhouse, its outward appearance is somewhat dreary, but the artefacts within are worth a look. Archaeological finds date from as early as 8,000 BC. A 13th-century woman's costume, a 16th-century Gothic chalice and embossed-leather Bible, and 19th-century furniture are also on display. Culinary tours at the museum offer the possibility of tasting food served during different periods in the resort; these must be booked in advance.

PÄRNU'S ISLETS

A far more vivid glimpse of Estonia's past can be found on **Kihnu** and **Manilaid**, two small islands off Pärnu's

Floating sauna at Karuskose, Soomaa National Park.

coast. In summer, both can be reached by ferry (www.veeteed.com) from Munalaid harbour at the northwestern tip of Pärnu Bay.

Kihnu, the larger of the two, is unique in Estonia as its isolation has preserved a way of life that has long since vanished on the mainland. For centuries, while the men were away at sea, the women were tasked with running the island's day-to-day affairs. Nowadays, among Kihnu's 600 residents, it is they who carefully guard the islanders' cultural heritage, still wearing the same style of vivid woollen skirts as their grandmothers and great-grandmothers, and ensuring that traditional handicrafts, dances, games and music remain an integral part of everyday life. It is telling that the Kihnu wedding has been proclaimed a Unesco Masterpiece of the Oral and Intangible Heritage of Humanity.

At just 16.4 sq km (6.3 sq miles), Kihnu is small enough to navigate by bicycle – these can be rented at the harbour on arrival. There are four villages: Lemsi, Linaküla, Rootsiküla and Sääre. A 19th-century schoolhouse in Linaküla houses the **Kihnu Museum** (May–Aug daily 10am–5pm, Sept Tue–Sat 10am–2pm, Oct–Apr Tue–Fri 10am–2pm), which hosts exhibits on the island's history. Evidence suggests that seal hunters set foot on Kihnu around 3,000 years ago, while records of permanent habitation first appeared in the early 16th century. Opposite the museum stands a church where the island's legendary 19th-century sea captain, Kihnu Jõnn, immortalised in film and theatre, is buried.

The scenic coastline is dotted with giant boulders and fronted by islets, which are important bird habitats. A lighthouse, dating to 1864, stands at the island's southern tip.

Kihnu's little sister, **Manilaid**, known as Manija by the locals, is a far quieter affair. Its area is a mere 1.9 sq km (0.7 sq miles) and its population is just 31. The island remained uninhabited until 1933, when families from the then overcrowded Kihnu settled here. Manilaid's one tourist farm (www.manilaid.ee) attracts birdwatchers and visitors seeking a true sense of isolation.

NATIONAL PARKS

From Pärnu, a side-trip north to the **Soomaa National Park** ⓬ (Soomaa rahvuspark) provides a look at a landscape that's little seen elsewhere in Europe. At the end of route 59 through **Tori** and **Jõesuu**, signs direct drivers into the heart of the 371 sq km (143 sq mile) nature reserve. Soomaa literally means "land of bogs", and while the area is known for its floodplains and wildlife, its unique feature is its mysterious and often misty bogs – clear areas with peaty land, low trees and small ponds – a scene that doesn't look like it belongs on our planet. They can only be reached by carefully walking over specially built plank pathways. Soomaa's **Visitors' Centre** in Tõramaa (www.soomaa.com; May–Sept daily

Market on Kihnu.

10am–6pm, Oct–Apr Tue–Sat 10am–4pm) provides trail maps. Early June, when flowers are in bloom, is the best time to visit. In late June–August, mosquito repellent is a must.

Route 60 northwest from Pärnu leads to the small town of **Lihula**, which has a huge, Soviet-built cultural centre, a plaster-and-stone Orthodox church and a point-spired Lutheran church. Just 3km (2 miles) north from Lihula, the village of **Penijõe** is the gateway to the **Matsalu National Park ⑬** (Matsalu rahvuspark). Matsalu Bay has a range of habitats including reed beds, water meadows, hay meadows and coastal pastures. It was already noted for its birdlife back in 1870. Among the species found here today are avocet, sandwich tern, mute swan, greylag goose and bittern. There are also some white-tailed eagles. The reserve was formed from 39,700 hectares (98,000 acres) of the bay area in 1957. It can be visited by car or, since water covers some 26,300 hectares (65,000 acres) of this same area, by boat. Boat excursions of the rivers

Medieval Days festival in Haapsalu.

and the bay can be arranged though the **Matsalu Nature Centre** in Penijõe (mid-Apr–Sept Mon–Fri 9am–5pm, Sat–Sun 10am–6pm, Oct–mid-Apr Mon–Fri only; free), in a restored 17th-century manor house.

HAAPSALU AND MATSALU BAY

Matsalu Bay (Matsula laht) lies in the southern part of the coastal district of Läänemaa. One of the flattest sections of the already rather flat Estonia, it is also low in arable land, but the overall impression is certainly pastoral. The main town is **Haapsalu ⑭**, which has close to 10,000 inhabitants. A large military base and fishery were established here under the Soviets, and although the entire district has been under either Russian or Soviet control since 1710 (except for the 20 years of the republic), many locals identify with the Swedes, who ruled over them from 1581 to 1710. It was under the Russians, however, that Haapsalu became a spa of great repute and that many of its fanciest buildings were constructed.

The town originally centred around the **Haapsalu Episcopal Castle** (Haapsalu piiskopilinnus), which dates from 1279. The castle is partially ruined, but its courtyard has become a favourite spot for picnics and concerts, and technological additions mean that visitors hear sound effects emanating from various corners. The castle houses a museum (www.salm.ee; May–Aug daily 10am–6pm, Sept–Apr Wed–Sun 11am–4pm, courtyard open daily 7am–midnight; guided tours) chronicling the town's history, and its watchtower is open to the public.

The best-preserved part of the castle is the Romano-Gothic cathedral, one of only three functioning cathedrals in Estonia. Single-naved and towerless, it was built to double-up as a fortress, and its immense facade looks stubbornly impenetrable. Inside, the tall white walls and high-vaulted ceiling are almost bare. In a side chapel

s a baptismal font from 1634, with Adam, Eve and the serpent etched into its bowl – a vivid reminder of original sin to be washed away. Against its wall leans a sad wooden sculpture of a woman holding a child; a memorial to the people from Läänemaa deported to Siberia. The box beneath it, marked "1949–1989", contains Siberian soil. Directly above it is the window of the White Lady, focus of a Haapsalu legend (see box).

In front of the castle entrance is the large square that used to house the town market, and to the west is the space that served as the Swedish Market (Roosti turu). It now encloses a pleasant café, open in summer. On the square's east side is the **Lääne-maa Museum** (www.salm.ee; June–Aug daily 10am–6pm, Sept–May Wed–Sun 11am–5pm), within what used to be the Town Hall. Many of the artefacts come from the castle, and there are exhibitions about Haapsalu's days as a summer resort.

Across the street from the Lääne-naa Museum, **Ilon's Wonderland** (www.salm.ee; June–Aug daily 10am–6pm, Sept–May Wed–Sun 11am–5pm) shows off the works of one of Haapsalu's most famous residents, Ilon Wikland, illustrator of Astrid Lindgren's *Pippi Longstocking* books. Ilon was born in Haapsalu and, although she fled with her family to Sweden at the age of 14, she has depicted the town and the small house on Rüütli Street beside the Adventist church where her father was minister in many drawings.

The town has also been rich in handicraft artists, and the "Haapsalu Shawl", created of such fine wool that it can be drawn through a ring, is known throughout Estonia. A couple of shops specialise in local crafts, and one particular shop/museum near the Swedish Market allows visitors to try their own hand at craftmaking.

AFRICA BEACH

Just a couple of streets to the north is the seaside **Promenade** (Promenaadi). Here you can see the ghosts of Haapsalu's spa days by walking down to the "Africa Beach", so called because

Haapsalu Castle.

⊘ THE WHITE LADY

The "White Lady" is Haapsalu's favourite local legend. As the story goes, a monk from the cloister of the castle fell in love with a village girl and brought her into the castle disguised as a boy. When she began to sing in the choir, their treachery was discovered. As punishment, she was built into the walls and he was thrown into the cellar.

Every August, at full moon, the girl is said to return, and there are few villagers who do not claim to have seen her white reflection in the window of the cathedral. During this time, Haapsalu holds a "White Lady Festival" (www.valgedaam.ee), that climaxes with the audience walking to the southwest side of the cathedral where this window stands, with someone enacting the white lady's role.

Tip

Haapsalu's best beach is Paralepa, 1km (0.6 mile) west of the railway station.

locals sunning themselves here, covered with the town's famous curative mud, were said to resemble people from Africa. Additionally, in the early 20th century there used to be, along with little bathing houses, statues of wild animals set in the water. Although the water isn't safe for swimming any more, locals are still fond of strolling the path alongside it.

TCHAIKOVSKY BENCH

The restored **Resort Hall** (Haapsalu kuursaal), built in the 1900s, is an historic delight with green-painted timber, lacy cut-out porticoes and surrounding rose garden. For generations, concerts have been held in the bandstand beside it. Of interest here are a sundial and steps by the artist R. Haavamägi, who was born in Haapsalu, and the Tchaikovsky Bench. The Russian composer used to favour Haapsalu for his holidays and even used a motif from a traditional Estonian song in his 6th Symphony. The bench is decorated with the composer's likeness and, at the press of a button, it plays some notes

from the 6th. This is the spot where came every evening to watch the s set. The Tchaikovsky Festival is one a number of music festivals held he during the summer.

Continuing further down Sadam Road from this point will bring you the **Estonian-Swedish Museum** (Ra narootsi muuseum; www.aiboland.e May Tue–Sat 10am–6pm, June–A Tue–Sat 10am–6pm, Sun–Mon 10am 4pm, Sept–Apr Tue–Sat 10am–4pm where the history of the local seafa ing Swedish community comes to ligh Swedes settled along Estonia's coas and islands as early as Viking time and maintained a culture separat from the Estonians. Nearby, the Haa salu Yacht Club continues to thrive, b has been upstaged by a **Grand Hol Marina** (www.grandholmmarina.ee), whic has been built to cater for the summe Baltic yacht crowd, a few metres awa

Town activity has moved awa from the castle and beach down th lengthy Posti Street. However, if y wander the quaint backstreets the curious and creepy overgrow

Saxby lighthouse, Estonia.

d Town Graveyard – which lies on
osti Street – you find it easy to
nderstand the appeal that Haapsalu
as held for artists.

From Posti Street, Jaama Street
ads off to the right. At its end is the
lendid railway station, built in 1905 to
ceive Tsar Nicholas II on his summer
oliday. After years of neglect, it was
uced up for the town's 725th anni-
rsary celebrations in 2004. A number
antique locomotives are on display
the tracks, and the station's Emper-
's Salon houses a small branch of
e **Estonian Railway Museum** (Eesti
udteemuuseum; www.salm.ee; June-
ug daily 10am–6pm, Sept–May Fri-
n 11am–5pm). Further on, paths
ad through a park, ending at the
edy, calm Paralepa Beach.

AINTER'S HOME

eading out of town back towards
llinn will take you past the home
Ants Laikmaa, an influential early
th-century Estonian painter. Laik-
aa was an eccentric, and the home
e designed for himself, which has
been turned into the **Ants Laikmaa
Museum ⓯** (www.salm.ee; June–Aug
daily 10am–6pm, Sept–May Wed–
Sun 11am–4pm) is a peculiar blend
of red-and-white piping with a steep
moss-covered roof that has to be
seen to be believed. A small sign
points towards a bumpy road leading through the woods. The house at
its end, in a large yard, was begun in
1923 and was changed in design so
many times that it was never finished
during Laikmaa's lifetime. Laikmaa
was immensely popular in Haapsalu. He was known for known for his
handsome moustaches, for using carriages long after the advent of the car,
and for appearing in costume when
the mood struck him. He was also the
host of many unusual house parties.

From here Tallinn is about an hour's
drive northeast. If you feel that you
have not yet truly experienced the
sea, head west. At **Rohuküla**, 8km (5
miles) away, you can catch a ferry to
the islands of **Vormsi** or **Hiiumaa** (see
page 166), where the water is clean
and tourists are few and far between.

*The kuursaal in
Haapsalu.*

Kuressaare Castle on Saaremaa Island.

THE ISLANDS

Saaremaa and Hiiumaa, the two largest islands off Estonia's west coast, are idyllic rural retreats of windmills, fishing boats and farmhouse bed-and-breakfasts.

Most of the 1,500 or so islands off the coast of Estonia are mere hiccups, but two are so sizeable that island acreage ultimately accounts for some 10 percent of Estonia's total land territory. These larger islands, Saaremaa and Hiiumaa, are perhaps the most unspoilt and attractive corners of the country. Their pristine condition is due partly to the Soviet occupation. Clustered off the western shore, these islands were, rightly, considered likely points of escape to the West and were therefore kept for the most part incommunicado from the rest of the Soviet Union. At the same time, since they were clearly impractical for any industrial projects, they were spared the scars of heavy development. As a result, both islands are now prime destinations for Estonians in search of a bucolic, summer getaway, as well as for Finns, many of whom come to take advantage of Saaremaa's golf courses and luxury spas, or own summer houses on the islands.

DISTINCT WAY OF LIFE

Finnish pensioners were by no means the first of Estonia's neighbours to have territorial designs on Saaremaa and Hiiumaa. In the 13th century the islands were divided between the Oesel-Wiek (Saare-Lääne) bishopric and the Livonian Order. Three centuries later,

Saaremaa (Oesel) reverted to Denmark while Sweden took Hiiumaa. In 1645, Saaremaa was also assigned to the Swedes, and from then on they were destined to share Estonia's fate. Somehow, the islanders stubbornly retained a distinct way of life. They also began to stockpile impressive monuments left behind by the parade of conquering egos. The 13th-century churches and 18th-century manor houses that decorate their shores have now been mostly repaired, and have become mainstays of the islands' tourism industry. There

⊙ Main attractions
Muhu
Kuressaare Episcopal Castle
Angla Windmills
Hill of Crosses
Kõpu Lighthouse
Kassari island

Map on page 98

Angla Windmill at Saaremaa.

are some delightful farm bed-and-breakfasts from which to choose, too.

MUHU ISLAND

To reach Saaremaa, the largest of all the Estonian islands, it is necessary first to cross **Muhu** , where the ferry from **Virtsu** on the mainland docks. Estonia's third-largest island, Muhu is only 201 sq km (78 sq miles) and, along with about 500 smaller islands, belongs to the greater Saaremaa County. Muhu does not hold nearly as many attractions as its larger neighbour, but it does have sights worth stopping to see.

The most commercial of these is unquestionably **Pädaste mõis** (Pädaste Manor; www.padaste.ee). The estate, which dates from the 16th century, was once the home of the Baltic-German Buxhoveden family. Its Tudor-style main building (1875) is now being restored, and the beautifully decorated outbuildings have been turned into a luxury guesthouse and exclusive gourmet restaurant – reputed to be one of the best in the Baltics.

St Michael's church, on Saaremaa Island.

More down-to-earth sightseeing can be found in the village of **Koguva**, where the outdoor **Muhu Museum** (www.muhumuuseum.ee; mid-May–mid-Sept daily 9am–6pm, mid-Sept–mid-May Tue–Sat 10am–5pm) is located. The area nearby is thought to have been settled in the late Iron Age, but this still-inhabited fishing village was first documented in 1532. Of the 105 buildings that remain, parts of three date from the early and mid-18th century, making it the oldest preserved conglomerate of peasant architecture on the islands. A stroll through the village, with its thatched roofs, moss-covered rock walls and windmill, evokes images of a much quieter age.

Koguva is not far from the causeway that leads to Saaremaa. It is a beautiful road, and terribly romantic. The water on either side is filled by a beckoning green carpet of swaying reeds. In spring, it changes to white as thousands of swans come here to mate.

SAAREMAA ISLAND

Saaremaa is, at some 2,668 sq km (1,030 sq miles), a spacious, quiet and unassuming place. Much of its land has been cultivated, and the simple island roads are laced with field after field of livestock and wheat, interrupted only by patches of thick forest. Industry is at a minimum and, with the exception of those involved in tourism, those inhabitants who aren't at work on the land tend to be connected to the sea.

KURESSAARE'S GEMS

There is only one town of real consequence, **Kuressaare** , on the south side of the island, where some 13,000 of Saaremaa County's 33,000 inhabitants live. Kuressaare is said to have been particularly popular with party officials during the Soviet regime, and it certainly is extremely handsome.

Most of the buildings in the centre are gems of late 18th- and early

19th-century Neoclassicism, with pretty wooden houses and gardens mixed in beside them. Side streets reveal an ancient hand-pump for water or a freshly painted home with a paint-can tied proudly to its wooden gate. On Kaevu Street, an old windmill has been transformed into the unabashedly touristy Veski bar and restaurant (http://saare maaveski.ee).

Activity focuses around the triangular plaza where Tallinna Street turns into Lossi Street. At this junction are the market, the administrative halls and, after 9pm, the main spot for local youths to see and be seen. The yellow Town Hall (Raekoja, 1654–70) lies along the hypotenuse of this triangle, its entrance protected by stone lions. A peek inside is a good idea, as the building houses art exhibitions as well as the town's Tourist Information Centre.

To the left of the Town Hall stands an 18th-century fire station of burnt-brown wood. Opposite it is the Weigh House (Vaekoda), with a stepped gable.

Dating from 1663, the Weigh House is now a popular café and pub (www.vae-koda.ee), and encloses one side of the tiny Market Square. Here, in addition to jars of gooseberries in season you will find a range of distinctively patterned, hand-made woollen sweaters and mittens for sale, and items carved from the island's fragrant juniper wood. Sometimes there will also be a table or two piled high with slippery black mounds of the expensive Saaremaa speciality, eel.

A second, smaller square sits a few steps down Lossi Street. This has the County Seat and a monument for the fallen in the War of Liberation. It is actually the third such monument erected here; twice the Soviets tore it down only for the locals to reconstruct it.

Continuing down Lossi will take you past the **Apostolic Orthodox St Nicholas Church** (Nikolai kirik, 1790). Its fancy front gate tied with large silver-painted bows is unmistakable, and its white exterior is topped with rounded green spires. The interior echoes this

Monument at Kuressaare relating to the local legend of the giants Piret and Suur-Toll (Toell the Great).

Tip

The Vilsandi National Park Visitors' Centre (http://rmk.ee) is in Loona Manor (Loona Mõis; www.loonamanor.ee), 3km (2 miles) south of Kihelkonna. It has rooms to rent, tel: 454 6510.

colour scheme, and treads between neoclassical and Byzantine styles.

EPISCOPAL CASTLE

Kuressaare's main tourist attraction and its *raison d'être* is at the end of the street. The **Kuressaare Episcopal Castle** (Kuressaare piiskopilinnus) was built as the Bishop of Oesel-Wiek's foothold on Saaremaa, and first recorded in 1384. It is the only entirely preserved medieval stone castle in all of the Baltic nations. Ringed by a large and beautiful public park, a moat and imposing bastions erected during the mid-17th century, the castle is in the unyielding, geometric, late-Gothic style, made of white-grey dolomite quarried in Saaremaa. Each corner is crowned by a tower with an orange turret, and at the heart of the castle is a tiny, symmetrical courtyard. From the courtyard, stone steps lead down to basement rooms and up to a narrow, vaulted cloister. The former refectory lies on the west, and to the north are the austere former living quarters of the bishop.

Ten elaborate wooden epitaphs from the 17th century represent coats of arms of noblemen in Saaremaa and their individual occupations. One has oars, another tools, a third stags and arrows. Climbing the towers is worthwhile but requires fortitude; the watchtower in the southeast corner of the convent building is connected by a drawbridge suspended 9 metres (30ft) above the ground, and the defence tower is honeycombed with stone stairways. Some of the castle's upper rooms house the Saaremaa Museum (www.saaremaamuuseum.ee; May–Aug daily 10am–7pm, Sept–Apr Wed–Sun 11am–6pm; guided tours). This rich collection traces the inhabitants of Saaremaa from the 4th millennium BC and has a number of fascinating woodcarvings, including its pride and joy, the late 16th-century *Coronation of St Mary* attributed to Lübeck artist Henning van der Heide, and the oldest preserved wooden sculpture in Estonia: *Seated Madonna with the Infant* (1280–90). Other sections of the museum encompass the late-Tsaris

A Kaali meteor crater.

and pre-World War II period, as well as the island's natural history.

DOWN TO THE BEACH

From the castle, it is a pleasant walk down to the small, newly built yacht harbour. Nearby is Kuressaare's popular public beach. More secluded bathing can be found just a few minutes south of the town at the Mandjala-Järve beach.

Other spots to visit in Kuressaare include the restored Kuursaal (Resort Club), a grand, ornate, wooden recreation hall built for tourists in 1861. It stands not far from the castle. At Vallimaa 7 is the Aaviks' Memorial Museum (Aavikute majamuuseum; www.saaremaamuuseum.ee; Wed–Sun 11am–5pm), a tiny, old-fashioned house that was once home to a renowned linguist, Johannes Aavik (1880–1973), and his cousin Joosep Aavik (1899–1989), a musician and composer.

SAAREMAA ISLAND ROAD TRIP

Travelling to **Kihelkonna** in the west, and following the coast up to Leisi in the north, then back south to Kuressaare will take you into **Vilsandi National Park** (Vilsandi rahvuspark; www.keskkonnaamet.ee), which encompasses Vilsandi and 150 other offshore islets. Many of Saaremaa's interesting sites will be passed on the way. First stop is the **Mihkli Farm Museum** ⑱ (Mihkli talumuuseum; www.saaremaamuuseum.ee; mid-May–Aug daily 10am–6pm, Sept–mid-Oct and mid-Apr–mid-May Wed–Sun 10am–6pm) near the town of Viki. Although small, this open-air museum shows exactly what a typical farm in western Saaremaa is like. The main dwelling house (1834) stands with the other buildings in a circle enclosing a yard and a little flower garden. Most of the roofs are covered with reed, and the walls are of dolomite or wood. Original objects from the farmstead include household equipment with the Mihkli family emblem.

Turning at Kihelkonna north towards **Mustjala**, you will first catch a glimpse of the pointed red bell-tower of the

Vilsandi Lighthouse.

☉ Tip

With enough time and energy it's possible to cycle around Saaremaa, which has a poor transport system but some delightful rural bed-and-breakfasts. The most practical way to explore the island is by car.

medieval Kihelkonna church and then the ancient, weathered-grey Pidula watermill. From here it is a short drive to the **Panga Scarp** (Panga pank). This steep limestone outcrop is one of the highest points on the island and one of the loveliest. The water below is almost olive green, but so clear you can easily make out the thousands of pebbles that line the seabed. In the distance, the horizon stretches blue and endlessly, except for the tiny shadow of Hiiumaa island. In summer the sound of crickets fills the air.

Unsurprisingly, this very magical place has played a central role in island superstitions. In pre-Christian times, locals would throw one baby boy, born the winter before, off the cliff into the water every spring; this was an offering to the sea god with the prayer that he send back a lot of fish. In later times, they threw a ram instead, and even up to the 1930s, there are records of barrels of the island's famous beer being poured over the cliff's edge to ensure a good catch. Island brides have continued the tradition of "scarp pitching" to this day: on the eve of their wedding they often write their maiden name on a piece of paper, put it into a bottle and throw it off the cliff.

Turning east takes you to **Leisi**, an attractive rural town, from where the road heads south and in a few miles reaches the **Angla Windmills** (Angla tuulikud; www.anglatuulik.eu; daily May–Aug 9am–8pm, Sept 9am–6pm, Oct–Apr 9am–5pm). In the mid-19th century, there were about 800 windmills on Saaremaa, and the windmill has become the most recognised symbol of the island. Only a small proportion of the original windmills have survived, but at Angla five remain, rising into view suddenly on a slight swell amid windswept wheat fields. One of them was reopened as a working windmill after reconstruction in 2009. The small hermitage centre presents traditional crafts.

MEDIEVAL CHURCHES

Nestled behind a moss-covered stone wall on a sloping lawn across from fields of cattle 2km (1.25 miles) from here is one of Saaremaa's greatest treasures: the 14th-century **Karja church** ⑲ (mid-May–mid-Sept Mon–Sat 10am–5.30pm, Sun noon–6pm). Saaremaa is packed with some of the earliest churches in the Baltics, but no other has such marvellous stone sculptures still intact. These sculptures tell a thousand tales (see box).

If you head south again, turning right at the Liiva-Putla fork, you will reach the hamlet of **Kaarma**, site of another medieval church (May–Aug Wed–Sun 9am–5pm; free). Work began on Kaarma church in the latter half of the 13th century, but it was rearranged over subsequent centuries and is strikingly large. Its artefacts are more varied than those of Karja. The christening stone, for example, dates from the 13th century

☉ STORIES ON THE CHURCH WALLS

A relief on the first left buttress upon entering Karja church (Karja kirik) depicts village life. A woman listens to another with a pig on her back, symbolising gossip, while the man beside her has a rose behind his ear, representing silence. This is on the northern and thus colder side of the church, the side where the women sat because they were considered to be stronger.

St Catherine of Alexandria, to whom the church is dedicated, is carved into the northern arch before the altar. This 14th-century beauty, the legend goes, was wooed by King Maxentius of Egypt who was already married. She refused him and, enraged, he had her arrested and torn to pieces. The sculpture shows her with Maxentius' wife on her left, clinging to her skirt, St Peter on her right and the evil king crushed beneath her feet. Directly opposite is St Nicholas, the protector of seamen, and on his left are three village girls who were too poor to marry until he became their benefactor.

Painted on the ceiling above the altar is a table of Christian and pagan marks: the Star of Bethlehem and the symbol of Unity, both drawn with endless lines; the three-legged symbol of the sun; the "leg" devil; and two pentagons, symbols of gloom, which locals point out were also symbols of the Soviet Union.

the wooden "Joseph" supporting the pulpit is from around 1450, and the elaborate Renaissance pulpit was finished in 1645. Restoration work has exposed fragments of early mural painting. Other 13th- and 14th-century churches in the area worth visiting include Valjala church (June–Aug Tue–Sun 9.30am–6pm; free) and Püha church (Mon–Fri 8am–5pm, Sun 2–5pm; free) situated east of Kuressaare. The latter most clearly shows how these churches were built not just to be religious centres but also to serve as defensive strongholds.

If you turn left at the Liiva-Putla fork, you reach a much older landmark, the **Kaali meteoric craters** ⓴ (Kaali meteoriidikraatrite väli; http://kaali.kylastuskeskus.ee). These are not particularly beautiful – the largest one is referred to as Lake Kaali and looks like a big opaque green puddle – but it is remarkable to think that the bowl surrounding it was carved out by part of a 1,000-ton meteor that hit the earth here nearly 3,000 years ago. Eight smaller craters, made from other chips of the meteor, dot the woods surrounding it. There is a guesthouse and the Kaali Crater Museum of Meteoritics and Limestone.

MAASI FORTRESS

Finally, before leaving Saaremaa, a stop at the **Maasi Order castle ruins** ㉑ (Maasi ordulinnuse varemed), 4km (2.5 miles) north of **Orissaare** on the Orissaare–Leisi road, rounds out the story of the island's medieval struggles. The Maasi fortress was in many senses Kuressaare Castle's less fortunate sister. Established by the Livonian Order in the 14th century, it was meant to defend the island's eastern side. Denmark took possession when it purchased this part of Saaremaa in the 1560s, but more than once the fortress was taken over by attacking Swedes and used against the Danes. To prevent a repeat of this tactic, King Frederik of Denmark ordered it destroyed in 1576. Today, some exterior walls are still visible, and the newly excavated vaults have been restored to make it possible for visitors to enter.

Inside the Maasi Order castle ruins.

☉ Fact

In winter, when the sea is frozen, a 25km (15-mile) ice road links Hiiumaa to the mainland, though ferries continue to operate in the path they have kept clear.

HIIUMAA ISLAND

For natural beauty, **Hiiumaa Island** is perhaps more rewarding than Saaremaa. At 989 sq km (382 sq miles), it is Estonia's second-largest island, but has only slightly over 9,000 inhabitants, some 3,000 of them in the capital of Kärdla on the north coast. There is virtually no settlement in its heart, where there is a peat moor and swamp, and almost all agriculture focuses on the southern and western edge. Some yet to be cultivated areas in the south contain another natural oddity, "wooded meadows", and the rest of the island is overwhelmed by pines and junipers. A road rings the island, conveniently passing its most interesting sights, but there are so few cars on it that inhabitants typically drive on either the left or right according to whim.

Fishing is the most important industry, although the coast is notoriously treacherous to approach because of the shallow waters of endless shoals and rocks. This means that you have to walk out quite a way over pebbles simply to get your stomach wet, but don't let this deter you from taking a swim in the clean, peaceful waters.

HISTORIC SUUREMÕISA

The eastern harbour of **Heltermaa** has been slightly dug out, and it is here that the ferry arrives from the mainland, from **Rohuküla** by Haapsalu. Just inland is the historical hamlet of **Suuremõisa** ㉒. Hiiumaa once had around 25 stately manor houses, but most have either been destroyed or have irreparably deteriorated. The **Suuremõisa manor** is one exception. Built by a Swedish family called Stenbock in 1772, then bought by O.R.L. von Ungern-Sternberg – for decades Hiiumaa's richest and most powerful landowner – this manor still has its main building, stable-master's home and stables, outbuildings and cellars, and expansive front and back lawns. Under the trees there are gravestones for the family's much-feared guard dogs. Inside the main building are 64 rooms, some with original painted ceilings and ceramic fireplaces. A primary school and an agricultural school are

A Hiiumaa guesthouse owner shows off his smoked fish.

oused here, but in summer the building is open to tourists free of charge.

Just down the road is the attractive
ühalepa Church. Built of timber in the
mid-13th century, then replaced with
tone in 1770, its tall white bell-tower,
opped by a hexagonal brown roof, has
een extended three times since then.
urned into a cellar by the Soviets, the
hurch resumed services on Christmas
ve 1990.

On its south side stands a rather
quat white chapel containing the tomb
f Ebba Margarethe Gräfin Stenbock,
uuremõisa manor's first owner. On
s north side, strewn amid alders, are
tumble of other old graves. Around
e northeast corner is a log set in the
hurch wall; this is the spot through
hich the priest used to hand out
read to the poor and needy. A few feet
own the gravel road to the north, away
om the main road, brings you to the
ontract Stones, otherwise known as
Hiiumaa's Stonehenge". The origin
f this large pile of boulders, which
ere evidently brought here by hand,
unclear. One popular theory is that

before going out to sea local sailors
would bring a heavy stone to this spot,
and by doing so make an agreement
with God to ensure a good voyage and
a safe return.

Back up the coast in the main town
of **Kärdla** is the Rannapaargu Café
(www.rannapaargu.ee). To reach it, you
must walk down Lubjaahju Street past
yet another Hiiumaa peculiarity, the
giant swing. Found in villages all over
the island, the swings are particularly
busy on Midsummer's Eve. A new holiday centre is another place for summer activity in Kärdla, offering horse
riding, and a spot where visitors can
catch trout and have them prepared
on the spot. The **Hiiumaa Museum**
(http://muuseum.hiiumaa.ee; May–Aug
daily 10am–5.30pm, Sept daily 10am–
5pm, Oct–Apr Mon–Sat 10am–5pm) is
housed in Kärdla's 19th-century Pikk
Maja (Long House).

HILL OF CROSSES

Outside town, 5 km (3 miles) west on
the road to the **Kõpu Peninsula**, is a
more sombre attraction, the **Hill of**

⊘ Fact

At the end of the
Saaretirp headland
nothing remains but a
needle point and a large
heap of stones: if you find
a pebble with a hole in it,
make a wish and place it
on the pile, and your wish
may come true.

The Angla Windmills.

Crosses ㉓ (Ristimägi). Like many Estonian coastal areas, Hiiumaa was populated for centuries by a large group of Swedes, who, by a time-honoured arrangement with the Swedish Crown, were given a special status as freemen. In 1781 Stenbock, with the help of Russian Empress Catherine the Great, arranged for 1,000 of Hiiumaa's Swedes from the village of Reigi to be stripped of their land and rights, and forcibly resettled in Ukraine. Their last church service was held on this hill. According to legend, a local farmer marked the spot with a small, wooden cross. Later, a tradition was established that each new visitor would add his own cross, made from sticks found on the ground. The site is now eerily covered with thousands of crosses.

Some of Hiiumaa's most interesting structures are the lighthouses that twinkle along the shore. The most remarkable is the **Kõpu Lighthouse** ㉔ (Kõpu tuletorn; May–mid-Sept daily 10am–8pm), halfway out along the thickly forested Kõpu Peninsula, on the windswept western wing of the island. This soaring four-cornered and red-crested white lighthouse looks like a cross between a space rocket and a pyramid. First lit in 1531, it is considered to be the oldest continuously operating lighthouse in the world.

KASSARI ISLAND

Understandably, many of Estonia's best-known artists and writers keep summer retreats on Hiiumaa; conductor Eri Klas, for example, has his on Kõpu. But the most popular spot for summer cottages is **Kassari** ㉕, just southwest of Heltermaa. Kassari is one of between 200 and 400 islands (depending on the water level) that cling to the coast of Hiiumaa. It curves in so close to the shore by the town of Käina that it has been incorporated into the larger island with two short bridges. The bay between them, Käinu Bay, is rich in sea mud that attracts birds, including golden eagles and other rare species. You may even see an eagle or two flying over the road. These birds, in turn – along with the island breezes and the sea – are

Kassari chapel.

responsible for the richness of flora all over Hiiumaa.

In fact, the island has about 975 different species of plants, some of them, such as the orchids, also quite rare. Kassari, however, is richest in junipers, whose berries and bark might be called the island staple. Its uses include the wood for butter knives that keep butter from turning rancid; the branches for sauna switches to perk up the kidneys; the berries for a vodka spice, a source of vitamin C; and for medicinal purposes. This scraggy dark bush has even been fashioned into furniture.

Junipers crowd the pebbly projection of Saaretirp with special determination. This mile-long promontory is a favourite place to picnic or ponder. The island's sheltered position makes the water warm, and beside it the apples crop early. The last owner of the former Kassari manor house, Baron Edvard Stackelberg, had an especially large orchard, though neither it nor his home still remains. But the small servants' house directly opposite where it

stood is in good shape and houses a branch of the Hiiumaa Museum (opening hours as above). The exhibition contains a huge light reflector from the 19th-century Tahkuna lighthouse, maps of island history and traditional fishing tools.

ANCIENT CHAPELS

Down one more pebble-laden lane is the **Kassari chapel** (mid-June–Aug Fri–Sat 11am–4pm, open upon request only rest of the year, tel: 566 064 05; free), the only stone chapel surviving in Estonia with a roof of thatched reed. Carefully restored in 1990, it is illuminated by a simple central candelabra and candles on each blue-coloured pew.

One final church to note back on Hiiumaa island, just inland from Kassari, is the **Käina church** (Käina kirik), built between 1492 and 1515. Although it was heavily bombed during World War II, it is still a very moving spot. The wind rushes through the limestone shell and over the old tombs that are set directly into its floor.

Yacht by the frozen harbor at Orjaku, Kassari.

The ballroom at Palmse Manor.

EAST OF TALLINN

Two of Estonia's important wildlife regions lie to the east of the capital: Lahemaa National Park and Lake Peipsi, the fifth-largest lake in Europe. Beyond them rises industrial Narva.

East from Tallinn on the E20, the Narva Highway, the capital's industrial sprawl gives way to a scene more typical of the country – vast, flat stretches of road flanked on both sides by forests and ponds. About an hour's drive from the capital, this road becomes the southern border of **Lahemaa National Park** (Lahemaa rahvuspark; www.keskkonnaamet.ee), a truly peaceful and intriguing area of the country close enough to Tallinn to make it a practical day trip. More than 75 percent of the 72,500-hectare (180,000-acre) park is woodland, and the population is fewer than 20 per square kilometre. There are remains of ancient settlements, freshwater lakes, wetlands, a few farms, fishing villages and four manor houses. Sheltered bays dip between craggy promontories that jut into the Gulf of Finland. It is an important wildlife area with deer, elk and bear, and during the migration season, for special species such as the black stork. Plant life abounds, and among the 850 documented varieties is the rare arctic bramble.

Loksa 26 and **Võsu** 27 are the park's two main towns. They are the best stopping points for food shops and cash machines, though neither are of intrinsic interest. Loksa is much the larger, with a cargo port, and a mainly Russian population. It is easy to make trips around the park from either town,

but one can just as easily use the E20 itself as a starting point.

PALMSE MANOR

The turn-off at **Viitna** leads north, to Lahemaa's most famous landmark, the striking **Palmse Manor** 28 (Palmse mõis; www.palmse.ee; daily 10am–6pm). The beautiful house and grounds are a testament of 18th-century aristocracy, but this land's history goes back much further. In 1286, a group of nuns from the Cistercian Order of St Michael in Tallinn were given the land by the King

Main attractions
Lahemaa National Park
Palmse Manor
Viinistu
Jõhvi
Sillamäe
Narva
Pühtitsa Convent
Lake Peipsi

Map on page 98

The Manor dates from the 18th century.

Tip

The 16th-century Vihula Manor, 5km (3 miles) from both Altja and Sagadi Manor, has been beautifully restored and is now among the most picturesque destinations in Lahemaa. La Boheme Restaurant makes an elegant lunch or dinner stop (tel: 326 4100; www. vihulamanor.com).

of Denmark. The pond they built here for their fish farm is still in use. In 1673, the Von der Pahlen family, Baltic-German nobles, bought the estate, and in 1730 built the manor house. It was rebuilt in 1782, and was their home until Estonia's first independence in 1918, when the property was nationalised.

After World War II, the manor served as a Soviet Pioneer camp and fell into disrepair. Renovation lasted between 1972 and 1985, and today the estate is a perfect period piece, filled with Empire furniture. Visitors are welcome to stroll the grounds, where they'll find a peaceful swan pond, landscaped gardens, a smart restaurant, a tavern serving Estonian dishes and a café.

The estate also boasts a nice orangery with over 130 species of exotic plants, an exhibition devoted to the production of spirits in Estonia and an exhibition of a 19th-century ironwork, which visitors are encouraged to try and work themselves. There also a lot of activities for adults and children. Across the courtyard is the **Lahemaa Visitor Centre** (daily 9am–5pm,

mid-Sept–mid-May Mon–Fri only Here you'll find information in Englis on the park's sights and nature walk and more importantly, detailed maps a necessity in this area of small, con fusingly marked roads.

A turn from Palmse to the northwe leads to another impressive Germa estate, **Sagadi Manor** (www.sagadi.e daily May–Sept 10am–6pm, Oct–Ap 10am–4pm). It was built in 1749 an renovated at the end of that century a classical style. Like Palmse Mano it has been decorated to reflect 18th century elegance. One of the renovate outbuildings is a hotel and restauran another is a museum of forestry. stroll behind the house leads to a pon and swathes of lawn where interest ing and often bizarre modern woode sculptures are on display.

SEASIDE ALTJA

Most of Lahemaa's other attraction can be found to the north, in the forr of several tiny seaside hamlets that do the area's four rocky peninsulas. On of these gems is **Altja** ㉙, a wonderfu

Restored wooden buildings, Altja.

:ample of a timeless Estonian fish-
g village. The old, thatched-roofed
ooden buildings were restored in
e 1970s, and the village has since
ecome a popular local tourist spot.
u'll find a 19th-century inn, a tradi-
onal village swing and several paths
ong the coast. The headland is dotted
ith attractive sheds for storing fish-
g gear.

Another coastal village, **Käsmu** ㉚,
much less typical. This is called
:aptains' village" because of the lav-
h houses that sea captains built here,
ving it a decidedly affluent look. A
rive through the village reveals some
' the most unusual and beautiful
:sidential property in Estonia. There
a slightly dark side to all this beauty,
owever. The village's original eco-
omic prosperity is linked to its resi-
ents' salt-smuggling activities in the
9th century. In the 1920s, when Fin-
nd imposed the prohibition of alco-
ol, the economic focus here shifted
alcohol-smuggling. Käsmu is now
so known for its **Maritime Museum**,
oused in what was a school of

navigation in the late 19th and early 20th
centuries. The musty and somewhat
jumbled museum displays a collection
of sailing artefacts, as well as works by
local artists and a few Saku beer bottles from a century ago. It offers also a
trip in a Viking boat.

VIINISTU ART MUSEUM

Like Käsmu, the tiny village of
Viinistu ㉛, north of Loksa, also made
a good share of money from smuggling
alcohol, but what puts it on the map
nowadays is something else entirely
– art. This village of just 150 is home
to the **Viinistu Art Museum** (Viinistu
kunstimuuseum; www.viinistu.ee; summer daily 11am–6pm, winter Wed–Sun
11am–6pm), which has the largest private art collection in the country, with
between 200 and 300 19th- and 20th-
century Estonian paintings on display,
easily rivalling the state-owned museums in Tallinn.

The reason the collection is here
is that former resident Jaan Manitski
fled as a child with his family to Sweden during World War II. After making

*"Old Jüri" boulder,
Käsmu.*

his fortune as financial adviser to the famous pop group ABBA, he returned to Viinistu, eventually converting the town's Soviet-era fish collective into this art and cultural centre. The village has a modern guesthouse and restaurant, as well as a respectable, old-fashioned tavern. The road that leads through the village ends in a small trail that follows its rocky coastline. Offshore, **Mohni island**, an uninhabited nature reserve, is visible.

On the western side of the park another manor, **Kolga mõis** ㉜, remains unrestored due to a lack of funds. The graceful 18th-century building is a cliché of a crumbling pile, with falling plaster, peeling wallpaper and a cracked exterior. Rejoining the E20, one can either head back west to the modernity of Tallinn, or turn east, towards the Russian border and what was Estonia's heavy industrial zone during Soviet times.

INDUSTRIAL ESTONIA

If Estonia were a jigsaw puzzle, the northeast corner would be the one piece that didn't fit. Ida-Viru County, which straddles the main transport routes leading to Narva at the Russian border, is the heavily industrialised region of Estonia. It is rich in energy-producing oil shale and supplies more than 90 percent of the nation's electricity. During the Soviet period, thousands of ethnic Russians were settled in the region to work its plants and mines, and small villages suddenly became factory towns filled with rows and rows of apartment blocks. When Soviet industry collapsed, this area was hardest hit. Most jobs here disappeared, leaving decaying buildings, environmental hazards and a population of mainly ethnic Russians whose role in the newly independent Estonia was far from clear.

So many years later, the situation has been slow to improve. The area's economy still lags far behind that of the rest of the nation, and the eyesores of the last century – dilapidated buildings and enormous hills of mining waste – line the roads. For this reason Estonians from other areas have written off the northeast as not worth visiting. But it is for this same reason that many foreigners find it fascinating. It offers the chance to see a side of Estonia ignored by most guidebooks, and to glimpse the Soviet past without a Russian visa. It also has its own medieval castles, natural beauty and some sights that aren't found anywhere else in Estonia.

CASTLES OF THE NORTH

The E20 leads into the area from the direction of Tallinn. Before reaching the heart of Ida-Viru County, it passes some points worth mentioning. One of these is **Rakvere** ㉝, the country's seventh-largest city, located at the mid-point between Tallinn and Narva. For Estonians, the name Rakvere is always associated with the town's meat-processing plant, but its main attraction for tourists is **Rakvere Castle** (Rakvere

This statue, built to mark Rakvere's 700th anniversary, recalls the fact that the town was once known as Tarvaspää – literally "Bull's Head".

nnus; www.rakverelinnus.ee; May–
ug daily 10am–6pm, Sept Wed–Sun
0am–6pm, Mar–Apr and Oct Wed–
un 10am–4pm).

The castle was built in 1253 on
he site of a wooden one that was
estroyed during the Livonian Wars.
or better or worse, it is the most
ommercially developed of Estonia's
astles. It not only has the obligatory
istorical displays in its interior, but
lso features such crowd-pleasing
menities as a tavern, wine cellar and
medieval torture and horror cham-
er. In summer, its front courtyard has
number of smithies, a petting zoo,
rchery range and other activities.
ther sights in Rakvere include the
uins of a Franciscan monastery dat-
ng from 1515 and several charming
treets of late 19th-century buildings.

The much smaller castle at
urtse ③ (www.purtsekindlus.ee; Sat
oon–9pm, Sun noon–6pm, other
ays on request) is another medieval
ight worth seeing. It is easily missed,
s it stands several hundred metres
way from the highway in the midst of

several other buildings. The red-roofed
edifice dates from 1533, the Swedish period, when Purtse was a free
port. Although the castle was partially
destroyed during the Great Northern War (1700–21), it was inhabited
until 1938, and fell into disrepair. Now
restored, it serves as a café, concert
hall and exhibition centre.

HANDS-ON AT KOHTLA MINE

Kohtla-Järve ③, the heart of Estonia's
mining region, is further east. Though
by population it is Estonia's fourth-
largest city, it has a decidedly sleepy,
residential feel, and other than a large
monument to miners, it has virtually no
points of interest.

The area's real gem, by far one of
Estonia's most fascinating museums,
lies instead 10km (6 miles) south of
here in the village of **Kohtla-Nõmme**.
The short drive past forlorn, abandoned houses and emaciated cock-
erels leads to the **Estonian Mining
Museum** (Eesti Kaevandusmuuseum;
http://kaevandusmuuseum.ee; tel: 3324
017; June–Aug daily 11am–6pm,

Rakvere Castle.

Sept–May Wed–Sat 11am–5pm; guided tours; pre-booking by phone is required, last entry two hours before closing time). Opened in 1937, the Kohtla mine was one of a dozen shale mines that operated in Ida-Viru County during Soviet times, and grew to encompass around 60km (37 miles) of tunnels. After it closed in 2001, about 1.5km (1 mile) of it was turned into this hands-on "under-ground museum". Visitors are given hard hats, electric lamps and over-alls before descending into the tun-nels. The tour guides, all former mine workers, demonstrate the gigantic digging and clearing machines, give children rides on the tiny train that once carried miners to their stations, and let guests put a few holes in the rock with a large mining drill.

COMMERCIAL JÕHVI

The road reconnects with the E20 at **Jõhvi ㊱**, the administrative centre of Ida-Viru County. Many Estonians wryly refer to this town of almost 11,000 as "the real border of Estonia", since it is the last where the majority ar Estonian-speakers, and all towns t the east of it have a decidedly mor Russian feel. Apart from Narva, Jõh certainly has more commercial activit than anywhere else in the county, bu it also has its historic sites, such a the charming green-topped **Orthodo Church of the Epiphany** (Issanda Ris timise kirik). It was built in 1895, an Alexy II, Patriarch of Moscow and all o Russia from 1990 to 2008, was the rec tor here in the 1950s.

Jõhvi's more impressive churcl however, is St Michael's (Mihkli kiril in the centre of town. Built in 1364, served as a church and fortress unt it was destroyed in the Livonian War in the 16th century. Its present forr comes from a 1728–32 reconstruc tion. Inside is the **Jõhvi Fortifie Church Museum** (Jõhvi kindluskirik muuseum; Tue–Fri 11am–4pm, May Oct also Sat 11am–3pm), which out lines the church's history and display archaeological finds from the loca tion. The 30-minute CD tour is avai able in English.

Narva Castle.

More than anything, Jõhvi is a regional hub. From here, roads lead in several directions and into very different types of territory. To the north lies some truly spectacular scenery. The coastline from **Toila** to **Ontika** and **Saka** is made up of dramatic high cliffs, rising up to 56 metres (184ft) out of the sea. This natural monument is a symbol of Estonia, and is referred to as the **North Estonian Klint**. It is the edge of the vast limestone plateau on which this region sits. The waterfall in **Valaste** is Estonia's highest at 26 metres (85ft), but is somewhat artificial in that it was created by diverted water.

Toila is home to the picturesque **Oru Park**. The large regional park contains more than 200 different plants, as well as nature walks and a pebble beach. The land is on the former property of a German baron who had a manor house built here in 1899. Estonia's first president used the house as a holiday retreat, but it was destroyed in 1943. The park remains, and many of the paths pass through manicured gardens and statuary.

STALINIST SILLAMÄE

East from Jõhvi is **Sillamäe** ③, an intriguing, Soviet-era relic that should not be passed up. The entire town is a perfect museum piece of Stalinist-style architecture. Though there was a village here as far back as 1502, Sillamäe really came into being during the Soviet period, when it was a centre for mining and processing uranium. The town, which retains its look of a grandiose, planned city from the early 1950s, was a secret military area, populated exclusively by Russians and not marked on local maps.

Its main street, Kesk, cuts through the small town centre, where nicely trimmed gardens, a town hall and a community centre are accented with an unmistakably Socialist-Realist statue of a bare-chested man holding an atom aloft. A grand formation of steps leads to the park-like Mere Avenue, and then towards the seaside promenades. A block west, at Majakovski 18a, is the **Sillamäe Museum** (www.sillamae-muuseum.ee; Tue–Fri 10am–6pm, Sat 10am–4pm) where, among the various

Valaste waterfall.

minerals and Soviet banners on display, is a recreated apartment from the 1950s. The constantly changing museum offers temporary exhibition and a lot of activities.

ON THE BORDER

The E20 reaches the Russian border at **Narva** . With just 56,000 inhabitants, it is Estonia's third-largest city, and its least Estonian. Nearly 96 percent of its inhabitants are Russian-speakers. Here more than anywhere in Estonia, questions of citizenship and of the role of minorities in the Estonian republic become acute. Many residents feel that they are neither part of Estonia nor Russia, living in a kind of no-man's land.

Indeed, the border itself is the city's most striking feature. **Ivangorod Castle** and **Narva Castle** stand facing one another across the River Narva like sentries guarding their respective lands. The **"Friendship Bridge"** stretches across the river between them, with EU flags on one side and Russian flags on the other. Ignoring geopolitical concerns, locals casually

Puhtica orthodox monastery in Kuremäe.

stroll across to the Russian side for cheaper grocery shopping. Western visitors wishing to follow them will need a Russian visa, something that takes several days and considerable expense to procure.

The city was first mentioned in 124 when it was listed in census record compiled by the Danes, who built For Narva. They sold the castle, along with the rest of northern Estonia, to the Teutonic Order in 1346. In 1492, the year the Russians finally repelled the Mongols, Tsar Ivan III built a fort a Ivangorod on "his" side of the river.

Narva flourished in the Swedish period, taking over Tallinn's position a the primary trading port between Russia and the rest of Europe. It continue to flourish under tsarist rule as well By the late 19th century Narva was a industrial giant and a major seaport Its largest company, Kreenholm Texti Manufacturing, employed more than 10,000 people in its factories: Estonia first strike was organised here in 187.

During the first republic Narva remained part of Estonia. The ci was affected by economic depression during the 1920s and 1930s, and suffered terribly during World War II. O 17 August 1941 the Germans entere Narva and when, in July 1944, they were finally driven out, 98 percent the city had been destroyed. After th war, the Russians set about rebuildin the town. Two electric plants that wer subsequently constructed now produc most of Estonia's energy.

NARVA'S BASTION

Almost nothing remains of Narva's Ol Town, which is filled with block apart ments. The **Town Hall**, built by the Swedes, was one of the few building that survived the war, but is now in serious state of neglect. Narva Castl to the right of the bridge, is the city only real tourist attraction. Narva statue of Lenin stands in the ground of the castle; it is hidden on th

eft-hand side of the compound, symbolically facing east across the river owards Russia. The walls around the ort are walkable, and photographers should note that in the late afternoon he southwest corner bastion offers superb views of both forts. Inside its multi-storey tower, the **Narva Museum** (daily 10am–6pm) displays artefacts rom the town's history, as well as exhibitions on Estonian history and modern art. Of particular interest are he photos of Narva's Old Town taken before the war.

The 15km (9-mile) drive north along the river leads to **Narva-Jõesuu**, a popular beach resort town in the 19th century. It is trying, with very limited success, to recapture some of its past glory, despite intrusive factory smokestacks and other post-Soviet debris. The town is still filled with early 20th-century gingerbread houses, and one of the most colourful is just off Ranna Street. The Orthodox Church, created from rough-hewn logs, is a gem. Two spa resorts operate here in summer.

SOUTH TO TARTU

Backtracking to Jõhvi, the final spoke of the Ida-Viru County hub leads south, through an area where nature and spirituality replace the noise of human development. Highway 3 provides the quickest access to Tartu 132km (82 miles) away, but a small detour on Highway 33 leads to **Kuremäe** ㊴, home of the striking Orthodox **Convent of Pühtitsa** (Kuremäe jumalaema uinumise nunnaklooster; guided tours on request), the only Eastern Orthodox nunnery in the Baltic States.

Approaching Kuremäe, the green domes of the Pühtitsa Cathedral beckon through a forest of oak and pine. Pühtitsa is Estonian for "holy place", and indeed the convent is built on a site that has been sacred since the 16th century, when a peasant saw a vision of the Virgin Mary on the top of a hill. An icon was found beneath an ancient oak tree near the same spot, and the icon of the Assumption of the Mother of God is still the convent's most prized possession, surrounded by precious gems and

Swedish Town Hall, Narva.

○ Eat

Look out for *sudak* (pike-perch) on the menu in local restaurants – it is one of the main catches of Lake Peipsi.

mounted on a pillar to the right of the cathedral altar.

The first nun was sent to Pühtitsa in 1888 to establish the convent, and the complex of buildings, circled by a high granite wall, was designed by Mikail Preobrazhensky, a professor at the St Petersburg Academy of Arts. The five-domed, three-aisle Cathedral of the Assumption, which can accommodate up to 1,200 worshippers, was finished in 1910. There are five other churches in the complex, including a small one just outside the main walls, which is used for funeral services. Today there are more than 100 nuns in residence. Some 24 hectares (60 acres) of the 75-hectare (187-acre) property are farmed. Cash is raised from the sale of icons and other religious items made by the nuns. From Kuremäe either take a road that links up with Highway 3 at **Jõuga** to continue south, or extend the detour to historic **Vasknarva** ㊵, at the Russian border. The town was founded in the 12th century as a waystation on the trade route linking the principalities of Novorod

Lake Peipsi.

and Pskov with Tartu and Tallinn. All that remains of its Livonian fort are two broken walls.

LAKE PEIPSI

Either route leads to the shore of **Lake Peipsi** (Peipsi järv), where there are forests of tall conifers and white beaches of bleached oyster shells. There are occasional fishing villages strung along the water's edge, their attractive clapboard houses painted a variety of colours, each fronted by banks of vibrant flowers and backed by greenhouses which are used to extend the short growing season.

Mustvee ㊶, 65km (40 miles) north of Tartu, is Lake Peipsi's largest town, and the centre of Estonia's community of Old Believers. These are Russians who fled to Estonia in the 17th century to avoid religious persecution, and they have since developed their own distinct culture and traditions. There are approximately 15,000 Old Believers by birth in Estonia today and about 2605 according to the census from 2011, most of them living here along the shore of lake.

The town itself has two churches and several incongruous modern apartment blocks. Just south of Mustvee, the 7km (4-mile) village street that connects **Kükita**, **Raja**, **Tiheda** and **Kasepää** is perhaps more indicative of the Old Believer culture. It is lined with two-storey houses, most with small towers or balconies. Every one of these houses should traditionally have an icon inside and a spade in the yard. The Old Believers Museum (Kolkja Vanausuliste muuseum; https://vanau sulised.weebly.com; tel: 5662 980; May–Sept Wed–Sun 11am–6pm, Oct–Mar by appointment) in **Kolkja** will provide more insight into the history and practices of this group.

From Raja, the highway to Tartu leads away from the lake and the realm of Russian village life, and back into 21st-century Estonia.

Winter in Lahemaa National Park.

Afternoon light in Slītere
National Park.

Girls in traditional Latvian dress prepare for a cycle in the country.

Folk dancers in the Old Town of Rīga.

LATVIA

Sandwiched between the two other countries, Latvia has the largest capital city, superb Art Nouveau architecture and a great recreational national park.

A carved detail of a mythical Pan-like face.

The main highway of the Baltics is the 1,030km (640-mile) River Daugava, which starts in Russia and arrives, via Belarus, in the south of Latvia near Daugavpils. German crusaders arrived near the river's estuary at a place they called Rīga, and made it their base for the conquest of the Baltic peoples and the expansion of Hansa trade.

Today, Rīga is the most exciting city in the Baltics. It is rich with the architecture of the medieval merchants, who built and funded gabled homes and storehouses. In the expanded late 19th- and early 20th-century city there are exquisite Art Nouveau buildings, many designed by Mikhail Eisenstein, father of the filmmaker Sergei Eisenstein, who was born here. Slightly over 700,000 of the country's 1.95 million population live in Rīga, and there is no other city in the country approaching its size. It also has the best market in the Baltics and one of the most popular seaside resorts at nearby Jūrmala.

Strudels for sale.

Second to the Daugava is the River Gauja, which is the centre of a fine national park north of Rīga. To the east are the more remote blue lakelands of Latgale, a Catholic stronghold and place of pilgrimage where you can find excellent local pottery. To the west is Kurzeme, the former domain of the Duchy of Courland, where you can explore the well-preserved medieval towns of Liepāja and Ventspils on the Baltic coast and, inland, Kuldīga. To the south is Zemgale, home to the nation's most stunning Baroque treasure, the Rastrelli-designed palace at Rundāle.

The soul of Latvia and the Latvians is not in buildings but in the countryside among its magic oaks and ancient hill forts. People are happiest spending a weekend on the family farmstead tending vegetable gardens, singing songs and drinking beer by a bonfire or just relaxing in a steamy sauna. In a country with countless rivers and lakes and almost 500km (300 miles) of pristine beaches, it is not difficult to imagine why many Latvians prefer nature to urban living.

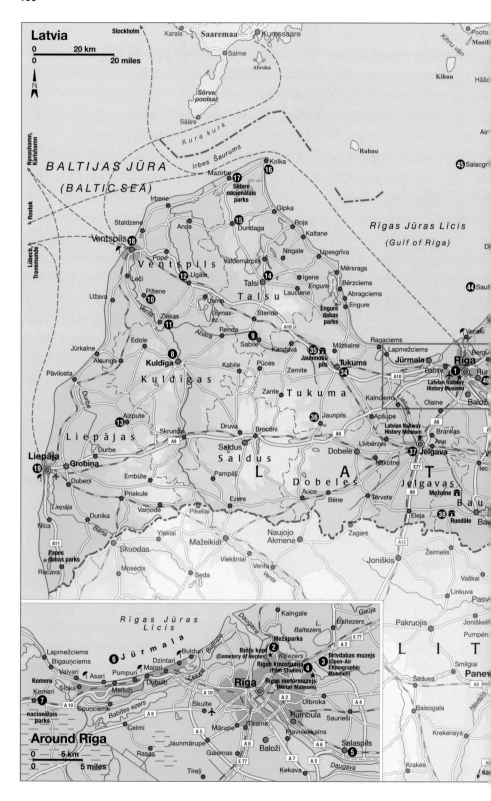

Latvia

0 — 20 km
0 — 20 miles

N

BALTIJAS JŪRA
(BALTIC SEA)

Stockholm

Karala   Saaremaa   Kuressaare

Salme

Abruka

Sõrve
poolsal

Sääre

Kura kurk

Irbes Šaurums

Mazirbe   17   16   Kolka

Slīteres
nacionālais
parks   15   Gipka

Irbene

Staldzene   Ande   Dundaga   Roja   Kaltene

Ventspils   18   Pope

Leči   Valdemārpils   Nogale   Upesgrīva

Piltene   12   Ugāle   Mērsrags

10   Talsi   14   Igene   Bērzciems

Užava   Usma   Laucene   Engure   Abragciems

Zlēkas   Usmas-   Stende   Engure   Engure

11   ez.   Engure
dabas
parks

Abava   Renda

Jūrkalne   Edole   Sabile   9   Kandava   Milzkalne   Ragaciems

Alsunga   Kabile   35   Jaunmoku   Lapmežciems

Pāvilosta   Kuldīga   8   Kabile   Pūces   Zemīte   pils   Tukums

Durbe   34

Kuldīgas   Zante   Tukuma   Kalnciems   Apšupe

Aizpute   13   Jaunpils   36

Liepājas   Skrunda   Druva   Broceni   Livbērzes   Brankas

Durbe   Aizpute   Saldus   Dobele   Nakotne   Āne   Jelgava   37

Liepāja   Grobiņa   Saldus   Jelgavas

19   Dubeņi   Pampāļi   L   A   T

Embūte   Auce   Bēne   Tērvete   Eleja   Mežotne

Priekule   Ezere   Rundāle   38

Liepāja   Vaiņode   Pikeliai   Naujojo   Žagarė   A12

Dunika   Ylakiai   Mažeikiai   Akmenė   Joniškis   Žeimelis

Papes   Skuodas   Viekšniai   Venta

dabas parks   Mosėdis   Seda   Venta

Rucava   Jonišķeli

Rīgas Jūras Līcis
(Gulf of Riga)

Poots   Manil

Kihnu vāin

Kihnu   Hāāc

Ruhnu   Air

45   Salacgri

44   Saul

Veči

Bergi

Jūrmala   Rīga   1   Rur

Babite   46

Latvian Railway   Baloži
History Museum

Olaine

A10

Latvian Railway
History Museum

A8   Iec

A9   Bau

E77   Jelgava   A8

Pakruojis   L   I   T

Smilgiai   PANE

Šeduva   A9

Baisogala

Krekenava

Krakės

Around Rīga

0 — 5 km
0 — 5 miles

Rīgas Jūras
Līcis

Lapmežciems   Jūrmala   Kalngale   L.   Baltezers   Gauja
Baltezers

Bigauņciems   6   Buldurī   Mežaparks   2   A E 77

Vaivari   Dzintari   Brāļu kapi   Ķīšezers   3   Brīvdabas muzejs
(Cemetery of Heroes)   (Open-Air

Kemeri   Asari   Pumpuri   Majori   Rīgas kinostudija   4   Ethnographic
(Film Studios)   Museum)

Slokas   Dubultī   Rīgas motormuzejs
(Motor Museum)

Kemeri   7   Melluži   Rīga   Ulbroka   A4

nacionālais
parks   Spunciems   Babītes ezers   A10   Skulte   A2   A4

Celmi   A9   Mārupe   Tīraine   Rumbula

Jaunmārupe   Pļavniekkalns   Saurieši

Rasas   A5   A8   Baloži   A6   Salaspils   5

Tīreļi   E77   Gaismas   A7   A5   Ķekava   Daugava

Kalngale

Rīga port in the second half of the 17th century.

THE MAKING OF LATVIA

The Baltic States' first woman president was elected in a country shaped by Hansa traders, Russian maritime ambition and warring neighbours.

When Latvian independence was self-proclaimed in 1918, the country had to be assembled like a jigsaw puzzle out of territory inhabited by Lettish-speakers. This amounted to the southern half of what had previously been Livonia together with Latgale and the Duchy of Courland.

To complicate matters, the city of Rīga, Latvia's capital, had hitherto been for all practical purposes an independent city-state with an overwhelmingly foreign population. It was a German city from the day the crusaders landed, and it had remained a predominantly German city of Hanse merchants through all the vagaries of Polish, Swedish and Russian rule. The Latvians managed to restore themselves to a majority between World Wars I and II, but independence was then snuffed out by Soviet annexation.

Against the backdrop of massive impending change in Eastern Europe and the Soviet Union, Latvians knew they were in a private race against time. It had been the Kremlin's intention all along to obliterate the 1918 frontiers so that Latvia, like Estonia and Lithuania, was in effect an unbroken extension of Russia itself. The struggle which ensued was a replay of events leading up to World War I, the reincarnation of the land of the Latvians.

Between the World Wars, Latvians comprised 75 percent of the population, but under Soviet annexation the combined effect of mass deportations and Russian immigration reduced the Latvian majority to 52 percent by 1989.

The banner of the first all-Latvian song festival, held in 1873.

CRUSADERS' ARRIVAL

Curious events had led to the arrival of the German crusaders in 1200. Almost 1,000 years after Christianity had been adopted as the official religion in Armenia and then Rome, it had still not reached the eastern shores of the Baltic, and there was rather a rush among the Pope and various Christian princes to make up for lost time. To this end, a number of missionary monks were dispatched. Meinhard of Bremen established a colony at Ikšķile, 25km (15 miles) upstream from present-day Rīga in 1180 and persuaded Latvians to be baptised in the river in such numbers that he was made a bishop. The test came when he informed his converts that the price of salvation was the payment of a tithe.

They not only abandoned the faith en masse but put the bishop in fear of his life. He implored Pope Clement III to send help, but died before any was forthcoming. His successor, Bishop Bertold, called for a holy crusade in the Baltics, but met his end on the tip of a pagan spear.

The Pope had other problems. The crusade in the Holy Land had gone disastrously wrong and large numbers of crusaders, expelled from their strongholds, were homeless. Led by Bishop Albert (Albrecht von Buxhoevden), they were dispatched to the Daugava where they went

A knight of the Livonian Order.

about their business with Teutonic efficiency. "All the places and roads were red with blood," wrote a chronicler of the Knights of the Sword.

THE HANSA CONNECTION

Rīga's wealth in the late Middle Ages was in part due to its joining, in 1282, the Hanseatic League, Europe's first free-trade organisation. The league was started by German merchants' societies (Hanse) to protect the herring trade in Lübeck and its vital salt suppliers in Hamburg. The alliance soon developed into a powerful one of more than 150 port-cities that came to control the shipping of fish, flax, fur, grain, honey and timber from Russia and the Baltics, and cloth and other goods manufactured by Flemish and English guilds.

Hansa cities had their own legal systems, armies and privileges. Rīga had exclusive rights to transport goods along the Daugava, and Livonia had its own Hanseatic diet or parliament.

Almost at once, Rīga had a defensive wall, a fortress and at least one church. By 1211, Bishop Albert was ready to start building a cathedral. Word was sent to the Pope that the Daugava mission had been accomplished and that a contingent of knights was being sent north – to Estonia – where the Danes were experiencing similar difficulties with truculent pagans.

The Knights of the Sword were in due course amalgamated with other orders; these came to be known collectively as the Teutonic Order. Having discharged their divine duties, they tackled the secular task of creating a city-state for themselves with immense zeal. They imported fellow Germans not merely to build the city and port but also to organise the region's agriculture. The Latvians were excluded from the process except as labourers.

LOOKING TO LITHUANIA

The military power of the Teutonic Order was eclipsed in the 15th century, but by then the German economic and landowning oligarchy was thoroughly entrenched in Latvia. It was safe as long as Russia was kept out of contention by the Mongol Empire. With the demise of the latter, however, an alarming threat materialised in the person of Ivan the Terrible. The only recourse was to seek the protection of Poland-Lithuania, and then there was a price to be paid. Lutheranism had made inroads in Latvia under the German influence and Poland was uncompromisingly Catholic. The Jesuits were to be given a licence to bring Latvians back into the fold.

The way the Jesuits went about their task revived memories of the Teutonic Order, and this was coupled with a rigid Polish feudal order that was harder on the peasants than anything previously experienced. The country was sharply divided on the desirability of Polish protection. Rīga profited enormously by being elevated to the role of Poland's principal port, so the merchants had no reason to complain.

The landed gentry and the peasants, however, were paying the price, and they became increasingly desperate for protection against the protectors. Protestant Sweden seemed the most likely

> *The Swedish–Polish War was followed by the bitter winter of 1601 in which 40,000 Latvian peasants died from cold and hunger.*

candidate. The resulting Swedish–Polish war saw the Swedes repulsed, but Latvia was left a wreck.

Gustavus Adolphus tried to topple the ruling order again 20 years later, and this time Poland, much weakened by events elsewhere, suc-

(James) had been named after his godfather, James I. He had been a great shipbuilder, and at Ventspils he built an impressive navy, turning out 24 men-of-war for France and 62 for Britain. With unbounded ambition he acquired territory for the duchy in the Gambia and Tobago.

The duchy brought a degree of stability to the south of the country. In the north there had been few tears when the Jesuits were sent packing by the Swedes. Historians consider this period of Scandinavian rule, which brought with it unprecedented construction of schools and hospitals, the

RIGA.

Copperplate engraving of Rīga, 1638.

cumbed. The Swedes rebuilt Rīga Castle, added barracks outside the Swedish Gate and built castles on the River Daugava. Poland remained in charge of Latgale in the east and, in the south and west, the Duchy of Courland.

In 1561 this small slice of Latvia had been awarded to Gotthard Kettler, the last Grand Master of the Teutonic Order, who, fearful of Russian incursions on his land in the north, had submitted to Poland, and had been granted a degree of independence. Its importance grew under Duke Jacob, who became a prince of the Holy Roman Empire.

A DUKE'S EMPIRE

Though Protestant, the Kettlers had been friends of the English Stuart kings and Jacob

implementation of a code of laws and the translation and publication of the Bible in Latvian, a golden age. The barons, however, were horrified when their estates were expropriated and given to the Swedish aristocracy. Hoping to be third time lucky, they looked again for a more sympathetic protector: their choice this time was Russia.

THE GREAT NORTHERN WAR

The Great Northern War of Sweden versus Russia, which began in 1699, was a titanic struggle that swept across the entire breadth of Europe. In and around Latvia, the Swedish Crown sought to finance the war by taking 80 percent of the estates, dispossessing both the Swedish barons, who had only just been given them, as well as the remaining Germans. These lands were squeezed for all they were worth and reached the point where they were providing the Swedish Crown with more revenue than all other sources put together.

Peter the Great's ally Augustus II, the odious Elector of Saxony, launched an invasion of Livonia in 1700 that got as far as Rīga before it was halted. Peter the Great was called on for help, but his forces were tied down at Narva in Estonia. In the event, the Russians were defeated at Narva and the victorious Charles turned his

Festivities on Midsummer's Eve, 1842.

attention to Augustus. The Elector of Saxony was in no position to resist, and he surrendered.

SERVANT GIRL BECOMES EMPRESS

Sweden was not destined to hold on to Latvia or its neighbours for much longer. Peter the Great's ultimate victory in his duel with Charles XII opened the way to realising his dream of Russian control of the eastern Baltic. By then he had another, purely personal, interest in the region. Some years earlier, he had been struck by a woman called Martha who had arrived at court on the arm of first one and then another of his ministers, the second being Prince Menshikov. She was a servant, the daughter of a Lithuanian peasant, who had been employed by a Protestant pastor

in Latvia before marrying a Swedish army officer. The marriage had failed and Martha was pursuing other interests among the Russian nobility.

Menshikov loyally relinquished the lovely Martha and she became Peter's mistress. On embracing the Orthodox faith, she changed her name to Catherine and after eight years of companionship he married her. Peter changed the law to allow him personally to crown her Empress in 1724. On Peter's death, Catherine was proclaimed empress in her own right. The accession to the Russian throne of a Latvian peasant was all the more extraordinary because there was practically no social or economic mobility in Latvia: ethnic Latvians weren't even allowed to own property in their own capital. Martha's change of name and religion is an indication of the way in which ambitious Latvians had to leave behind the indigenous culture in order to break out of a rigidly tiered system. The result was that the Latvian language and everything that went with it was pushed further and further into rural backwaters.

BALTS AT THE RUSSIAN COURT

Catherine I died after a reign of only two years, but the Latvian connection with the Russian Crown was renewed when Peter's niece Anna acceded to the throne. While Catherine was undoubtedly fast, Anna was considered downright debauched. More to the point, she was the dowager Duchess of Courland, and she brought German Balts from Jelgava, Rīga and elsewhere to the Russian court en masse. Jelgava, then called Mitau, was the capital of Courland. Anna's father-in-law was Duke Jacob's son, and he had introduced French opera and ballet into its social milieu. Anna granted the first Russian constitution in Jelgava in 1731, but it was her chamberlain and lover, Ernst Johann Biron, who has left the greatest mark. An opportunist and a scoundrel, he became the Duke of Courland after Anna's husband died and was a power behind the throne. He was responsible for sending some 20,000 to Siberia.

The German Balts in Russia's courts used their influence to restore the port of Rīga after the depredations of the Russo-Swedish Wars. This care did not extend to other parts of the country. It was said that, Rīga apart, Latvia was ruled by wolves for a century afterwards.

Neglect and ghastly conditions led, in 1802, to a peasant uprising led by "Poor Conrad" who, reflecting the revolutionary mood in France, was called "the Lettish Bonaparte". The revolt was put down ruthlessly and Poor Conrad died an excruciating death. There was a repetition in 1840, with the peasants directing their fury at the Lutheran Church.

Four centuries after the demise of the Teutonic Order, the Latvian establishment was still dominated by German aristocrats and burghers. The country had subsequently been ruled by Poland, Sweden and Russia, but the old German system had somehow endured despite efforts to dis-

Empress Anna's lover, the Duke of Courland, managed to find enough money to bring in Bartolomeo Rastrelli, the future architect of St Petersburg's Winter Palace, to construct the sumptuous palace at Rundāle.

economic sphere to counteract German influence. The Russian railways were extended to the Baltic coast, and Rīga handled a large share

Town Hall Square, Rīga, 1819.

lodge it. To rebellious 19th-century peasants, the Lutheran Church was a symbol of German domination. The Russian Orthodox Church hastened to exploit anti-Lutheran feelings. The Orthodox catechism was translated into Latvian and given away free in large numbers. German landowners retaliated by refusing to make any more land available for Orthodox churches. German–Russian rivalry took on a life of its own, and the role of the German Balts sparked a furious row between Tsar Alexander III and Bismarck. Lutheran pastors were locked up or sent to Siberia, and as many as 30,000 of their flock were formally advised that they were henceforth Orthodox.

The Latvian peasant derived some benefits as the region was drawn into the Russian

of Russia's trade. At the same time there was a remarkable sprouting of literary activity in Latvian. Rich Germans held on to their positions, but the lower rungs had to make room for Latvians. All of this increased Latvian political awareness, but satisfaction at overcoming the old German obstacles did not make organisations like the New Latvians pro-Russian. Political sympathies on the workshop floor in Rīga were more inclined towards Karl Marx.

THE BALTIC REVOLUTION

The Baltic Revolution of 1905, which coincided with the St Petersburg uprising, was aimed with equal venom at everything German and Russian. Order was restored in Rīga only by the intervention of the Imperial Guard. The tsar had no qualms about letting the outraged German barons take their revenge, and when they had done so he rewarded them with concessions, such as granting permission to reopen five German schools. One way or another, the German element clung on, and at the onset of World War I, the population of Rīga was still at least 50 percent Baltic-German.

The wounds of the rebellion had not yet healed when World War I broke out. The country was at first occupied by a defensive Russian

Latvian women in traditional costume, 1936.

Army. In 1915 the Latvians were permitted to raise a national army. When the Russians withdrew in confusion after the Bolshevik revolution, the Latvians put up a spirited defence of Rīga against the advancing Germans at the cost of some 32,000 casualties. When the Germans took Rīga, it was not the prize that they were hoping for. The port was inactive, the machinery having been shipped to Russia.

A secret national organisation bent on Latvian independence was formed within the first months of German occupation and was in contact with refugees in Russia and exiles who had fled after the 1905 rebellion. The Allied victory in November 1918 simplified matters. A state council simply proclaimed independence and offered citizenship to all residents apart from Bolsheviks and German Unionists. The fly in the ointment was that 45,000 German troops still occupied Rīga. When they withdrew, the Bolsheviks arrived and there was no organised force to stop them. They declared Latvia a Soviet republic. The situation was rescued by Estonia, which drove the Bolsheviks off its soil and then crossed the border to help the Latvians do likewise.

Independent Latvia was in a sorry state. The population was a third below pre-war levels, industrial output was virtually nil, and many children had never been to school. A land-reform programme expropriated the German baronial estates and redistributed them in parcels to Latvian peasants.

Agrarian reform was supplemented by a takeover of industry and commerce, or what was left of them. The Latvian was of course given official status, and there was a general revival of Latvian culture. Perhaps the most significant statistics were the changing population ratios. By 1939, Latvians enjoyed one of the highest standards of living in Europe and were once again in a commanding majority in the country, as high as 75 percent.

THE NAZI–SOVIET PACT

Progress came to a jarring halt in 1940. The Bolsheviks undertaking to respect the independence of the Baltic States "voluntarily and for ever" vanished with the Nazi–Soviet Pact of 1939. A Soviet invasion was followed by annexation. The Nazi–Soviet Pact was short-lived, and in June 1941 the German Army drove out the Soviet forces. Latvia, together with Estonia and Lithuania, was made part of Hitler's Ostland. The consequences for Latvia's 100,000 Jews were horrific: 90 percent were murdered in the Holocaust.

Rīga was reconquered by the Soviet Army on 8 August 1944, and with that the NKVD set about restoring order in its customary manner. An estimated 320,000 people out of a population of just 2 million were deported to the east; most never returned. Tens of thousands more fled westwards only to be forced to work in German factories under daily bombardment by the Allies. Active guerrilla resistance to the Soviet regime continued until as late as 1951, but little news of it leaked out to the West.

More executions and deportations followed in the purge of so-called bourgeois nationalists in 1949–53, and all the time Russians were surging in ostensibly to man the industrial machinery of the Five-Year Plans. Khrushchev purged 2,000 influential locals who raised their voices in protest, replacing them either with Russians or so-called *Latovichi*, Russians who purported to be Latvians on the strength of a few years' residence in the country. Notorious *Latovichi* such as Arvīds Pelše and Augusts Voss rigorously enforced Russification policies. Even folk singing was driven underground. Signs of a revival surfaced in the 1980s. It began with the unobtrusive restoration of derelict churches and the odd historical monument. Poets and folk groups also performed discreetly.

The principal catalyst that brought protest out into the open was the green movement. Environmental concern served as cover for the formation of nationalist pressure groups, and before very long the underground press was addressing such taboo subjects as the activities of the secret police and human-rights violations. The breakthrough occurred in 1986, when public protest managed to stop the construction of a hydroelectric scheme on the River Daugava.

With this victory in hand, and a softer line on public protest coming from Moscow, the resistance movement grew. The National Independence Movement of Latvia (NIML), founded in June 1988, maintained that the illegal annexation of 1940 invalidated the Soviet regime. A census taken in 1989 revealed that Latvians were on the brink of becoming a minority in their own country – they represented a mere 52 percent of the total population, around 30 percent in Rīga. The Russian minority rallied in opposition, forming an organisation known as Interfront.

RETURN OF THE REPUBLIC

The Soviet Union eventually collapsed so quickly and so passively that it is all too easy to forget how bravely Latvians demanded "total political and economic independence" and, specifically, a free market economy and a multi-party political system. Nor will Latvia forget the five killed by Soviets at the Ministry of the Interior in January 1991, nor the freezing cold nights on makeshift barricades against Soviet tanks in Old Rīga. Elections gave the nationalists a two-thirds

majority, and the country was renamed the "Republic of Latvia".

The regaining of independence in 1991 was the first step in a sequence of events that would reunite Latvia with the rest of Europe. In 1994 Latvians celebrated the final withdrawal of Russian troops with the demolition of a Cold War radar station in Skrunda. Cultural life returned to the sovereign nation, and a free market economy struggled with bank crises and privatisation scandals, often involving politicians and prominent members of society, but eventually experi-

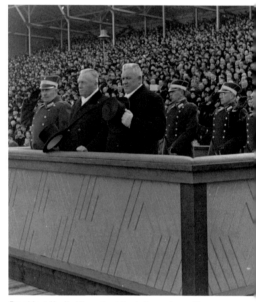

President Karlis Ulmanis at the Independence Day military parade in 1935.

enced unparalleled, and necessary growth. The question of citizenship for Russian residents has largely been resolved, but not without acrimony. Parliament also experienced growing pains, with the collapse of 11 governments in nearly as many years. But in June 1999, Vaira Vīke-Freiberga was elected president by the *saeima*,

Kārlis Ulmanis, President of Latvia in the 1930s, was arrested by the Soviets in 1940. He probably died in Turkmenistan, but his remains have not been found.

the first woman head of state in the post-Communist world. She was in place in time to steer the country through negotiations to join both NATO and the European Union in 2004.

After EU membership the economy soared, with annual GDP growth reaching 11 percent, and a property boom attracted unprecedented foreign investment to the country. But the populist government ignored the warnings of economists and did nothing to put out the fires of runaway inflation and an overheating economy. A real-estate bubble financed by the loose

Philippe Halsman was born in Rīga in 1906 and lived in the building on Kaļķu Street that now houses a T.G.I. Friday's restaurant. A friend of Einstein and Dalí, his photographs graced the magazine covers of Time and Life.

lending policies of both local and Scandinavian banks fuelled this impending disaster. The ripple effect of the Lehman Brothers collapse in 2008 became a tsunami in Latvia that left the nation's economy in ruins.

Unlike more prudent Estonia, Latvia spent its windfall tax revenues recklessly and put no money aside for a rainy day. It also decided to bail out the nation's largest privately owned bank, Parex Banka, with taxpayers' money, infuriating the local populace. The IMF and EU agreed to loan Latvia €7.5 billion. A peaceful anti-government demonstration on Cathedral Square in early 2009 ended in a riot by drunken hooligans. The coalition government collapsed and the opposition New Age Party took the reins, making tough decisions to save what was left of the economy. Government employee salaries were slashed by nearly half as unemployment soared to over 20 percent.

The drastic austerity measures paid off and the Latvian economy swiftly rebounded, mainly due to a strong export market. In 2012 Latvia saw 5.6 percent growth – the fastest in the entire EU. By 2014, the government had nearly completed the privatisation process, started accession negotiations with the OECD, raised minimum salaries and joined the euro zone. However, some problems remain, namely the high unemployment rate exceeding 10 percent and a demographic crisis which has reduced the country's population in recent years to 1.95 million – a loss of more than 600,000 citizens since 1989. Geopolitical tensions with Russia over the conflict in Ukraine pose yet another challenge to Latvians fearing that their hard-won independence may yet again be under threat. In 2015, Latvia, together with Lithuania and Estonia, asked for a permanent presence of NATO troops on its soil; in 2017 NATO troops were deployed in all three countries as part of the Enhanced Forward Presence strategic objective.

Former president Vīķe-Freiberga.

⊘ THE FIRST WOMAN PRESIDENT

Born in Rīga in 1937, Vaira Vīķe-Freiberga fled the country with her family ahead of the invading Soviet Army, arriving in Germany where she spent much of her childhood in a displaced-persons' camp. The family emigrated to Canada where she gained her bachelor's and master's degrees in psychology and a PhD in experimental psychology. In 1998, repatriated to Latvia, she became director of the Latvian Institute and a year later was elected Latvia's president. Since leaving office she has joined numerous international organisations and became the president of the World Leadership Alliance Club of Madrid, a non-profit organisation promoting worldwide democracy, in 2014.

In the Russian quarter of Rīga, 1991.

MANOR HOUSES AND CASTLES

There are hundreds of manor houses scattered throughout all three countries, but it is only recently that work has begun to restore them.

Architecturally, the manor houses of Estonia, Latvia and Lithuania come in a mix of styles, from Baroque to neoclassical, neo-Gothic to neo-Renaissance, reflecting the tastes of successive owners, foreign influences and passing whims. They are also reminders of feudal times under foreign occupation: these were the homes of the landowning Danish, Swedish and German aristocracy, of merchants, Russian counts and governors on whom much of the population, long enslaved, had to depend.

A number were destroyed in the first Russian revolution of 1905, a peasants' revolt against the landowners. After confiscation during the first independence, many houses were left without the resources to keep them standing. Little respect was given to their finery under the Soviets, who turned them into collective farms, schools and medical or social institutions, while in the 1990s the newly independent nations looked on them as vestiges of an occupation force. But within a dozen years, a realisation had begun to grow that some of these buildings played an inherent part in the nations' stories, and should be cared for and preserved.

In Estonia, 200 manor houses are now under state control, half of them in daily use; in Latvia they are increasingly being converted into country-house hotels, like Rumene Manor in Courland, which has been refurbished by the architect Zaiga Gaile, Latvia's former first lady. In Lithuania, where the Manor House Preservation Programme was introduced in 2003, a number are being transformed into museums which explain their history and purpose. In some cases attempts are being made to revive stables and farmwork and, should you imagine yourself living in splendour, you will find some manors are for sale.

Kukšu muiža in Latvia is a fine example of a restored manor house. Now a hotel, the riverside building has metre-thick cellar walls and dates from the 16th cent. It fell into disrepair under the Soviets when it was use a collective farm.

The interior of Kukšu muiža, whose restoration was helped by a list of furnishings compiled in 1855. Wallp was removed to reveal late 18th-century wall painting four of the rooms.

Vana-Vastseliina Castle in Estonia dates from the 14th century and, like many castles, it was destroyed in the Great Northern War.

Castles

Each Baltic capital rose around a medieval castle, which came with the crusading Orders and the proselytising Church, whose timber strongholds across the country were soon replaced by sturdier stone. The various power struggles that went on for centuries ensured that they remained fortified, though many today are no more than weed-covered ruins, while others have been incorporated into domestic estates. Notable is the stronghold of the Bishop of Saare-Lääne (Oesel-Wiek) at Haapsalu, in Estonia, which contains the Cathedral of St Nicholas, and his Episcopal Castle at Kuressaare on Saaremaa island, the only complete medieval fortress in the Baltics.

Cēsis, in Latvia, is the place to go to feel the crusading Livonian Brothers of the Sword, who built their headquarters here. Their castle looks romantic, despite damage during the Great Northern War.

Most distinctive are the red-brick Gothic castles. Without stone, they lack carvings, but there was no choice in areas with nothing to quarry and only bricks to bake. Adornments had to be made in the form of wooden balconies, jetties and balustrades. In this style are Turaida, built in 1214 under Archbishop Albert, the founder of Rīga, and, in Lithuania, Kaunas Castle and the magnificent island castle of Trakai, rebuilt from ruins during the 20th century.

Greatest of the northern European Gothic red-brick castles is Malbork (Marienburgas in Lithuanian), now in Poland, and headquarters of the Association of Castles and Museums Around the Baltic Sea.

…oclassical Veliuona Manor in the historic Lithuanian …n of the same name was designed by Mykolas Zaleckis … completed in 1820. It is one of the largest wooden …dings in the region and today it houses a local …eum of archaeology and ethnography.

…s castle, headquarters of the Livonian Brothers of the …rd, is one of Latvia's top sites.

Old Turaida castle in Sigulda, Latvia.

A birds'-eye view of the old town.

RĪGA

The largest of the three countries' cities is the most diverse. Set beside the wide River Daugava, Rīga has a Unesco-status Old Town with Art Nouveau buildings and a massive Central Market.

With a population of 704,000 **Rīga** ❶ is the largest and most cosmopolitan city in the Baltic States. It almost seems too big for the country it occupies: roughly a third of the nation lives in the Latvian capital. Spread either side of the River Daugava, the city lies some 8km (5 miles) from the great sagging dip of Rīga Bay, and for some 3,000 years these warm waters have provided both a gateway and an outlet for the continental heartlands. Like Tallinn in Estonia, its skyline is an impressive collection of towers and spires. Expertly manicured parks, a meandering canal that once served as a moat and tree-lined boulevards separate the Old Town from the sprawling "new" city. Rīga's status as a Unesco World Heritage Site is more than evident in its medieval churches, guild halls and winding cobblestoned streets, as well as in its ornately decorated Art Nouveau buildings, many of which have been lovingly restored to their original 19th- and early 20th-century grandeur.

A final blessing for Rīga's citizens and an ever-growing number of foreign visitors is Jūrmala, the lovely sandy beach just a half-hour's drive from the city centre (see page 223). This collection of seaside residential towns spread out over 20km (12 miles) has been favoured by generations of holidaymakers from its beginnings as a 19th-century spa to its heyday as

a fashionable haunt in the 1930s and later the premier destination for rest and relaxation in the Soviet Union.

THE OLD TOWN

Rīga is not a difficult town to get around, and nearly everything of merit can be reached on foot. The dead-straight Brīvības iela (Freedom Street), is the main artery of the city and leads directly to the **Freedom Monument** Ⓐ (Brīvības piemineklis, see page 215), the perfect place to begin a tour of Old Rīga – known locally as Vecrīga.

◉ Main attractions
Old Town
Occupation Museum
Church of St Peter
Mentzendorff House
Rīga Cathedral
Museum of the History of Rīga and Navigation
Rīga Art Nouveau Museum
Central Market
Pārdaugava and the National Library
Kipsala

◉ Maps on pages 188, 206

Strolling in the city.

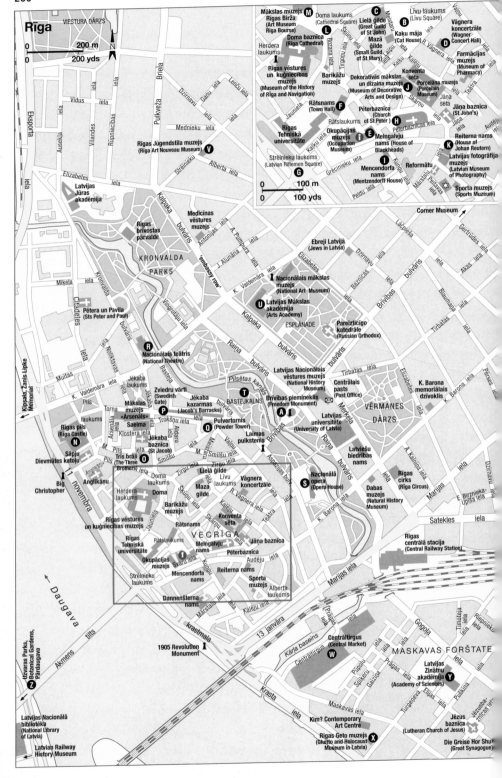

Walk down Kaļķu iela (Lime Street) to **Līvu Square** B (Līvu laukums), named after the now nearly extinct Finno-Ugric people who founded a fishing village here long before Germans or even Latvians arrived on the scene. Today the square is the city's liveliest, populated by buskers and souvenir touts and hundreds of locals and tourists taking advantage of the fantastic views provided from a large concentration of summer beer gardens.

On the opposite side of the square is the yellow **Cat House** (Kaķu māja), whose two felines perched on top of its towers caused quite a stir nearly 100 years ago. Local lore has it that the owner of the building was engaged in a dispute with the powerful Great Guild across the street. To show what he thought of them, he turned the cats around so that their backsides faced his foes. The dispute was later settled and the cats were returned to their original positions where they remain to this day.

THE GREAT AND SMALL GUILDS

The city's two guild halls are on the west side of the square. Traditionally only Germans were allowed to belong to the **Great Guild of St John** C (Lielā ģilde), a merchants' guild founded in 1384. The building was last redesigned in 1866 by the city architect J.D. Felsko and today is the home of the Latvian Symphony Orchestra (http://lnso.lv). The **Small Guild of St Mary** (Mazā ģilde; www.gilde.lv/maza) was for artisans and was started in the mid-14th century. Both functioned until the 1860s, but they were not finally dissolved until the 1930s.

To the left of the guild halls, on Richard Wagner Street is the **Wagner Concert Hall** D (Vāgnera koncertzāle), the concert hall named after the illustrious German composer, who conducted in the building for two years before he fled to avoid his creditors. The clandestine journey on the stormy, unforgiving Baltic Sea would inspire him to write the *Flying Dutchman*. Beyond the courtyard at No. 13 is the **Museum of Pharmacy** (Farmācijas muzejs; http://fm.mvm.lv; Tue–Sat 10am–5pm, Sun 10am–4pm) that displays old bottles, many of which still contain their original ingredients. Of equal significance is the building's Rococo doorway, one of the few examples of the style in Rīga.

TOWN HALL SQUARE

Continue walking up Kaļķu iela until you reach the next square. Rātslaukums encapsulates all of Latvia's history and in its centre stands the **House of Blackheads** E (Melngalvju nams; www.melngalvjunams.lv; closed to visitors). This historic gem was heavily damaged during World War II. The remains were destroyed by the Soviets after the war, but the Dutch Renaissance guild house was rebuilt with private donations and opened in time for the city's 800th anniversary in 2001. Founded in the 13th century, the brotherhood organised the city's social life and the house became a meeting place for bachelor merchants arriving

Tip

Rīga's Tourist Information Centre in the Town Hall Square is open daily 10am–6pm (May–Sept 9am–7pm). There are also information kiosks at the airport, main bus station and in Livu Square. See www.liveriga.com

Statue of Roland outside the House of Blackheads.

from abroad. One of the community's patron saints was St Mauritius, who was black and gave the brotherhood its name. Since 2012 it's been home to the chancellery of the President of Latvia. The next building houses a **Tourist Information Centre**. The historic **Town Hall** ⑤ (Rātsnams) opposite, also rebuilt, is the seat of local government. A third floor was added to the original architectural plan, as well as a modern wing behind the building.

OCCUPATION MUSEUM

Next to the Blackhead Brotherhood house is an ugly black building, the former Museum of the Latvian Red Riflemen, home to the excellent and chilling **Occupation Museum** (Okupācijas muzejs; http://okupacijasmuzejs.lv; daily 11am–6pm; free). The museum retraces Latvia's plight under the Nazi and Soviet occupations from 1940 to 1991, with explanations in English, German and Russian. The moving exhibit depicts the life of Latvians deported to Siberia and those who fought the Soviets in the forests.

The museum is important for anyone interested in recent Latvian history. Another branch of the museum is the chilling, former KGB building which now houses the **Corner Museum**. It presents the history of the Soviet security agency and is located at the corner of Brīvības and Stabu Streets.

In front of the Occupation Museum, facing Akmens Bridge is **Latvian Riflemen Square** ⑥ (Strēlnieku laukums) with a red granite Monument to the Latvian Riflemen in its centre. This controversial landmark was once dedicated to the riflemen who joined the Bolsheviks after the revolution. In a time of dramatically changing fortunes, the Latvian Riflemen split, some remaining true to the tsar, others joining the Latvian freedom fighters and still others swearing allegiance to the Reds. Some of the latter gained respect as the bodyguards of Lenin and infamy as the executioners of the Romanov family in 1918.

CHURCH WITH A VIEW

Facing the Blackheads' house is the elegant steeple of the **Church of**

St John's church in the old town.

Peter  (Pēterbaznīca; http://peter-baznica.riga.lv; Tue–Sat 10am–6pm, Sun noon–6pm, May–Aug until 7pm). A lift glides heavenwards to a viewing platform 72 metres (236ft) up in the 122-metre (380ft) steeple. The first church here, made of wood, was built by the city's craftsmen in 1209. Two centuries later it was rebuilt in stone. In 1709, 15 years after the steeple was completed, the city fell to the Russians and Peter the Great took a special delight in climbing to the top of the tower, then the tallest wooden structure in Europe. When it was struck by lightning in 1721, he personally helped to put out the fire.

MENTZENDORFF HOUSE

In the corner of the square, at Grēcinieku Street 18, is the half-timbered **Mentzendorff House**  (Mencendorfa nams; www.mencendorfanams.com; May–Sept daily 10am–5pm, Oct–Apr Wed–Sun 11am–5pm), which offers a good idea of what life was like in a prosperous German's home in the 17th–18th century, though the building itself dates back to the 16th century. Among its former

owners was Andreas Helm, head of the Small Guild, and Rheinhold Schlevgt, master of the Order of the Blackheads, who established a pharmacy on the premises. Its restored interior has *trompe l'œil* wall decoration and painted ceilings inspired by Jean-Antoine Watteau. The rooms have been furnished with period pieces from the Museum of the History of Rīga and Navigation.

ST GEORGE'S AND ST JOHN'S

Facing St Peter's on the north side are two other important churches. **St George's** now houses the **Museum of Decorative Arts and Design**  (Dekoratīvās mākslas un dizaina muzejs; www.lnmm.lv; Tue and Thu–Sun 11am–5pm, Wed until 7pm), and it should be visited if only to see the building's interior. This was the original church in the city, founded by the crusading Bishop Albert of Bremen in 1204 as a chapel for the Sword-Bearer's Order. It stood beside the castle complex which launched the first crusades against the Baltic people. Rebuilt after a rebellion in 1297, it was

⊙ **Tip**

Street finder: *iela* means street, *laukums* is square, *bulvāris/prospekts* is avenue, *ceļš* is road.

Church of St Peter.

the first stone building in the city and it remains one of the few examples of Romanesque. It has not been used as a church since the Reformation, when it was turned into a storehouse.

Next to St George's is **Jāṇa Sēta**, a small square abutting part of the old red-brick city wall, on the other side of which is the red-bricked **St John's** (Jāṇa baznīca; www.janabaznica.lv; Tue–Sat 10am–5pm, Sun 10am–noon; free), which is distinguished by a steeply stepped Gothic pediment. The church started life in 1234 as the chapel of a Dominican abbey. In 1330 it was enlarged and its buttresses became the dividing walls of the new side altars. It was taken from the Dominicans during the Reformation, and in 1582 a divine service in Latvian was held here for the first time. On the south wall, facing St Peter's, is a grille covering a cross-shaped window behind which two monks were cemented up during the building of the church, and for the rest of their short lives they were fed through the small gap.

Opposite the entrance to the courtyard is the **Statue of the Bremen Town**

Dome church with St Peter's.

Musicians from the Grimm's fairy tale. It was a gift from the city of Bremen, home of Bishop Albert, founder of Rīga. Sandwiched between the two churches is Ecke's Convent, which once belonged to the mayor of Rīga. In 1596, after allegations of embezzlement circulated around town, Ecke was forgiven after donating his lavish home to an Order of nuns that cared for widows who could no longer support themselves. It currently houses a teashop and small hotel (http://ecke. konvents.besthotelsriga.com). Behind the building is a further courtyard, **Konventa Sēta**, which is now home to an upmarket hotel, dozens of shops and cafés as well as the **Rīga Porcelain Museum** (Rīga porcelāna muzejs; http://porcelanamuzejs. riga.lv; Tue–Sun 11am–6pm, Wed until 7pm in summer). Its medieval architecture has been lovingly restored, making it difficult to imagine that this complex of houses once supported a convent that looked after the city's poor.

BAROQUE MANSIONS

Head southeast to the corner of Audēju iela (Weavers' Street) and Mārstaļu iela

⊙ THE BURNING OF RĪGA

For nearly 100 years before Peter I's arrival, the city had been under the control of the Swedes, who had rebuilt its castle, the flag-topped citadel to the north just by Vanšu Bridge. Rīga had been the largest city in their empire, bigger even than Stockholm.

After the Swedes had been driven out in a nine-month siege by Peter's Russian army, the city was in no great shape, and two-thirds of the population had died. Among them were many Latvians who were barred from living within the city walls. Since the arrival of the German crusaders and the construction of the city in stone, the Latvians had been relegated to the lands beyond the city walls, and to Pārdaugava on the river's far bank, where they lived in buildings that had to be built out of wood. Each time the city was threatened, as it had been by the Russians, they had to burn their property and accept the protection of the city walls.

The eighth and last time this happened was in 1812 when an eagle-eyed watchman on St Peter's belfry spotted a distant cloud of dust heralding the French invasion. Four churches, 705 houses, 35 public buildings and hundreds of acres of vegetable plots were torched before it became clear the dust was caused by a herd of cows. Napoleon crossed Latvia via a different route.

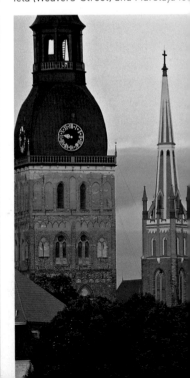

and look out for the **House of Johan Reutern**  (Reiterna nams) where exhibitions are often held. It was built by a rich German merchant in 1685, during the Swedish occupation, and beneath the roof is a frieze showing the Swedish lion devouring the Russian bear. At No. 21 is another Baroque mansion, which was built in 1696 for Reutern's son-in-law, a burgher named Dannenstern. Both have fine doorways by the local stonemason Hans Schmiesel, who was responsible for the handsome if rather out of place portal on St Peter's Church.

Nearby is the **Latvian Museum of Photography** (Latvijas fotogrāfijas muzejs; www.fotomuzejs.lv; Wed and Fri–Sun 11am–5pm, Thu noon–7pm), which has a collection of late 19th-century photographs of rural landscapes as well as some impressive pictures from World War I. A highlight of the museum is the Minox spy camera produced in Latvia just prior to the war and later manufactured by the famous German firm Leica.

Just past the museum on the left is Peitavas Street, where a **Jewish synagogue** (www.jews.lv; Mon–Fri 7.30am–4pm, Sun 8.30am–3pm) has been beautifully restored. The only Jewish place of worship in Rīga that survived the Nazi occupation of Latvia, it was spared for fear that a blaze might spread to other nearby buildings. It is open to visitors, and services are held here every Saturday.

CATHEDRAL AND SQUARE

All streets in the Old Town lead to **Cathedral Square**  (Doma laukums), the cobbled focal point of the Old City, where tourists pose for photos in front of the largest church in the Baltics and then spend far too much money for a drink at a beer garden with a view. **Rīga Cathedral** (Doma baznīca; www.doms.lv; May–Sept Mon–Tue and Sat 9am–6pm, Wed and Fri 9am–5pm, Thu 9am–5.30pm, Sun 2–5pm, Oct–Apr Mon–Sat 10am–5pm, Sun 2–5pm), or St Mary's, is a magnificent red-brick structure, with a gable like a Hanseatic merchant's house and a bulbous dome of northern Gothic solemnity. Steps lead down to the north door because the

A market in Cathedral Square.

⏲ Fact

The beautiful decorative arts in the Museum of the History of Rīga and Navigation give an insight into the rich and cultured life of merchants in the city.

Rīga Castle.

city's constant rebuilding has meant the ground level has actually risen over the years.

The cathedral was begun by Bishop Albert just after St George's, in 1211, and he is buried in the crypt. The plaques, tombs and headstones decorating the interior show just how German the city remained, no matter who owned it. Especially notable is the 6,768-pipe organ, which was, at the time of its completion in 1884, one of the world's largest. It was such a grand project that the tsar himself donated money to the cause and Franz Liszt composed music for its inauguration.

The cloister gardens are surrounded by a 118-metre (387ft) vaulted gallery (hours as for cathedral), one of the most outstanding examples of north European medieval construction work, which also houses hundreds of pieces of local history including tombstones, the original Dome cockerel and a huge stone head thought to be an ancient pagan idol.

Next door, with its entrance at Palasta Street 4, the **Museum of the History of Rīga and Navigation** (Rīgas vēstures un kuģniecības muzejs; www. rigamuz.lv; May–Sept daily 10am–5pm; Oct–Apr Wed–Sun 11am–5pm) is a eclectic collection of historical item and memorabilia, and does not hav too much to do with the sea. Its scop is very wide and it is one of the bes museums in the city, reflecting th wealth of its merchants. It was the firs public museum in the Baltics when opened in 1773 and it was based o the collection of Nicolaus von Himse a medical practitioner who had die nine years earlier at the age of 35.

RENAISSANCE STYLE

Pils iela (Castle Street) leads o Cathedral Square in front of an ele gant, 19th-century Venetian Renais sance building housing the **Ar Museum Rīga Bourse**  (Māksla muzejs Rīgas Birža; www.lnmm.lv; Tue Thu and Sat–Sun 10am–6pm, Fri unt 8pm), which opened in 2011. Opulent decorated interiors have been smart adapted to the needs of the Latvia foreign art collection. Highlights of th museum include 17th-century norther uropean paintings, western European orcelain from the 18th and 20th cenries (also from the Meissen Royal orcelain Factory) and an Oriental art ollection.

In the corner of Anglikāņu Street off astle Street is a smart brown Renaisnce-style building, which belongs to e **Danish Embassy**. It was built as the ritish Club for expatriates, merchants nd sundry travellers (Napoleon called ga "a suburb of London"), and every ick and detail of the Anglican church ehind it was brought from Britain, cluding a shipload of earth to provide e foundations. Women were allowed the club once a year.

ĪGA CASTLE

ls Street arrives at **Rīga Castle ** Rīgas pils), which the Swedes redegned in 1652. The first castle was uilt here in 1330 by the Livonian rder, who later decamped to Cēsis. 1481, in one of many internecine ars within the city, it was razed by e townspeople, but the Livonian rder returned to besiege the town

34 years later, eventually prevailing and forcing the locals to rebuild it. Today it is the official residence of the President of Latvia. In 2011, a fire destroyed some of the building, including the Red Hall. Fortunately, the museum art collections kept in the building weren't damaged.

THE THREE BROTHERS

Opposite the castle, Mazā Pils Street dives into the narrow lanes of the Old Town again. The most attractive group of buildings here are the three buildings known as **The Three Brothers ⊙** (Trīs brāļi). These are the oldest residences in the city, merchants' homes of almost doll's-house proportions dating from the 15th century. They have been colourfully restored, and they show how the families would live on the lower floors while leaving the upper areas for storage. One of them is home to the city's small **Museum of Architecture** (Arhitektūras muzejs; www.arch museum.lv; Mon 9am–6pm, Tue–Thu 9am–5pm, Fri 9am–4pm; free).

The Three Brothers.

Nearby is the red-brick **St Jacob's** (Jēkaba baznīca; daily 9am–7pm; free), the principal Catholic church. Its 73-metre (240ft) thin green spire, topped by a gold cockerel, is one of the three sky-pricking steeples that shape the city's skyline. In 1522 it became the first church in Latvia to hold a Lutheran service, but 60 years later, when the Polish King Stephen Bathory took the city for a brief spell, it was handed to the Catholics. In front of it is the peach-coloured residence of the archbishop, and on the north side is the parliament building on Jēkaba Street which was blockaded against Soviet attack in 1991. One of the original cement barricades erected to protect the building is displayed in front of the church.

SWEDISH GATE

Turn right along Trokšņu Street, leading directly to the charming **Swedish Gate** (Zviedru vārti). Built in 1698, this is the only gate left in the city walls, and through it the condemned were led to their fate. The executioner lived in the apartment next to the gate;

he would place a red rose on his window ledge on any morning he had to perform. The street on the far side of the gate is lined by the yellow **Jacob Barracks** (Jēkaba kazarmas), erected for the occupying Swedes. Turn right up Torņa Street past the old houses built against the red-brick city wall that has been partially restored. At the end of the street is Pulvertornis, the **Powder Tower**, the last of 18 city towers. Its round red-brick walls and concave conical roof, topping 26 metres (85ft), are reminiscent of Lübeck, queen of the Hansa cities. The **Latvian Museum of War** (Kara muzejs; www.karamuzejs.lv; daily 10am–5pm, Apr–Oct until 6pm; free) is housed inside.

AROUND THE PARKS

To say that the Old City is an island is rather fanciful, but it is entirely surrounded by water. The old moat that encircles it on the landward side is now a small canal running through a series of attractive parks from the ferry terminal in the north on the far side of the castle, to the railway station and

The Swedish Gate.

market in the south. To the north, on Kr Valdemāra Street, is the **National Theatre Ⓡ** (Nacionālais teātris). To the south, between Brīvības and Kr Barona Street, is the fine 19th-century **Opera House Ⓢ** (Nacionālā opera; www.opera.lv), formerly known as the German Theatre, which has been lovingly renovated with private donations. You can take guided tours, included "Richard Wagner, the legend of Rīga" dedicated to the places related to this famous composer.

In the park just to the north of Brīvības is **Bastejkalns Ⓣ**, the high spot of the city and not much more than a hiccup with little waterfalls and pleasant summer terraces by the canal. Five inscribed stones nearby commemorate the film cameramen and policemen killed here during the Soviet attack in January 1991. Cruise the canal on boats that depart from the quay at Bastejkalns, and enjoy the panorama of the old town (www.rigabycanal.lv).

The rallying point for the nation is the **Freedom Monument** (Brīvības piemineklis) on Brīvības, the elegant lady designed by K. Zāle in 1935. Locally known as Milda, she holds aloft three golden stars representing the three regions of Latvia: Kurzeme, Vidzeme and Latgale. An honour guard keeps watch over Milda while Latvians lay flowers at her feet, an act that once held the prospect of a one-way ticket to Siberia. Beyond the monument on the left is the **Russian Orthodox Church** (Pareizticīgo katedrāle), which was gutted by the Soviets for use as a planetarium. The restoration that began in the late 1990s is still ongoing. Also located on Brīvības 32 is the temporary site of the **National History Museum** (Latvijas Nacionālais vēstures muzejs; http://lnvm.lv; Tue–Sun 10am–pm, June–Aug Tue 11am–7pm), which was moved from Rīga castle after the fire there. On the other side of splendid Vērmanes Garden Park, between Elizabetes, Dzirnavu and Marijas street, is the elegant Bergs Bazaar (www.bergabazars.lv; built 1887–1900), full of shopping and dining options, and the Saturday Farmers Market.

The Esplanade park behind the Orthodox Church leads to the 19th-century **Arts Academy Ⓤ** (Latvijas Mākslas akadēmija; www.lma.lv) and the recently revamped **Latvian National Art Museum** (Latvijas nacionālais mākslas muzejs; www.lnmm.lv; Tue–Thu 10am–6pm, Fri 10am–8pm, Sat–Sun 10am–5pm). It has a permanent exhibition of paintings by 18th-century Baltic Germans and the Latvian masters Rozentāls, Annuss, Valters, Padegs and Liberts, and frescoes by the nation's most revered artist, Vilhelms Purvītis. There are also numerous 20th-century Latvian paintings on display. Outside is a statue of Janīs Rozentāls (see page 216).

Just off the park on Skolas is **Jews in Latvia** (Ebreji Latvijā; www.jewish-museum.lv; Sun–Thu 11am–5pm, May–Sept also Fri), a museum dedicated to the achievements and history of the Latvian Jewish community.

Freedom Monument.

ART NOUVEAU FACADES

Elizabetes iela at the top of the park should be followed for a while to appreciate its Art Nouveau and National Romanticism buildings. Nos 10a, 10b and 33 were designed by Mikhail Eisenstein, father of Rīga's most famous filmmaker, Sergei Eisenstein, director of the 1925 epic *Battleship Potemkin*. But most of his work can be seen in Alberta iela to the northwest (second right and first left after Kr Valdemāra), where he was responsible for nearly all the houses on the right side plus No. 13 opposite. After years of neglect during the Soviet era, many of the buildings have been renovated. At the end of the street is Strēlnieku iela, with another Eisenstein masterpiece at 4a, which has his typical bright blue touch.

MUSEUM OF ART NOUVEAU

On the corner of Alberta iela and Strēlnieku iela was the house that the Latvian architect Konstantīns Pēkšēns built for himself. **The Rīga Art Nouveau Museum ⓥ** (Rīgas Jūgendstila muzejs; www.jugendstils.riga.lv; Tue–Sun

An Art Nouveau facade featuring Pan, mythical birds, a lion and other motifs.

10am–6pm) is on the ground floor and is intended to look like the original apartment designed by Pēkšēns, who lived there. All seven rooms, including the bathroom and kitchen, contain Art Nouveau fixtures and furniture. Two other famous people lived here: the artist Janīs Rozentāls (1866–1916) and the writer Rūdolfs Blaumanis (1863–1908). The **Rozentāls and Blaumanis Museum** (Jaņa Rozentāla un Rūdolfa Blaumaņa muzejs; http://memorialiemuzeji.lv; Wed–Sun 11am–6pm, June–Aug Wed until 7pm) is on the top floor. The flat is filled with household effects and Rozentāls' paintings of early 20th-century Rīga, his family and friends and their holidays in Finland.

At the southwesterly end of Elizabetes on Merķeļa iela is the **Natural History Museum** (Dabas muzejs; www.dabasmuzejs.gov.lv; Wed–Fri 10am–5pm, Thu until 7pm, Sat–Sun 11am–5pm, free last half an hour and Thu 5–7pm) which displays all manner of objects from rare fossils to freaks of nature preserved in glass jars.

CENTRAL MARKET

Beyond the railway station are the five 20-metre (66ft) high Zeppelin hangars, built by the Germans in Vainode southwestern Latvia, in World War and brought here in the 1920s to house the **Central Market ⓦ** (Centrāltirgus; www.rct.lv; daily 7am–6pm) – one of the real wonders of Rīga.

The city's market had for three and a half centuries been sited beside the Daugava and even then it was one of the largest in the Baltic region. It must still be a contender for the title of Europe's largest market, with more than 3,000 vendors. It is built over a large underground storage system, and each hangar has its speciality: meat, dairy products, vegetables and seafood. Cream is sold in plastic bags, there are barrels of sauerkraut, fancy cakes, pickled garlic, dried herbs and mushrooms, smoked fish and whole stalls selling nothing but tins of sardines.

Beyond the pavilions, the old flea market spreads across acres of pavement. Open every day, it is at its busiest on Friday and Saturday.

MOSCOW DISTRICT
The market is at the edge of the **Moscow district** (Maskavas forštate), known locally as "Little Moscow", where for centuries, ethnic Russians have lived. Among the oldest of its communities are the Old Believers who settled here after fleeing from the late 17th-century religious persecution in Russia. The area was also a vibrant centre for Jewish life in Rīga, extinguished under the Nazis. Unlike the orderly German-influenced streets and manicured parks of the city centre, the Moscow district always had a wild streak and character of its own. The warehouse quarter known as Spīķeri, just beyond the Central Market on Maskavas iela, has become a trendy place full of cafés, bars, clubs and art galleries housed in renovated yellow-brick buildings, and is well worth a visit after a stroll through the market.

During the regeneration, which was completed in 2013, the Daugava's riverside was transformed into a broad promenade with wonderful views over the old town. It's worth visiting the three-storey contemporary art centre **Kim?** (www.kim.lv; Wed and Fri–Sun 2–6pm, Tue and Thu until 8pm; Tue free), at Maskavas 12/1, showing exhibitions by famous artists. At Maskavas 14a (entrance from Krasta iela) you will find the eye-opening **Ghetto and Holocaust in Latvia Museum** ❌ (Rīgas Geto muzejs; www.rgm.lv; Sun–Fri 10am–6pm), within the former ghetto limits and commemorating 70,000 Holocaust victims.

In the middle of the Moscow district is the squat, brown, Empire State replica belonging to the **Academy of Sciences** ❓ (Zinātņu akadēmija; observation deck Apr–Nov daily 9am–10pm), and just beyond, in Jēzusbaznīcas Street, is a fascinating octagonal wooden **Lutheran Church of Jesus** (Jēzus baznīca), built in 1822 from solid, wide boards. At the end of the street are the ruins of the **Great**

The Academy of Sciences building.

Synagogue (Die Greise Hor Shul), which was burnt to the ground on 4 July 1941 with dozens of Jews inside. Next to it is a **monument to Žanis Lipke,** who saved 50 Jews during the war (see page 218).

The Moscow district is typified by dilapidated 19th-century wooden buildings, Soviet concrete monstrosities and post-independence prosperity that has run amok in the form of shiny glass car dealerships and shopping malls. But some things never change, and among them is the only gold dome in the city peeking out from the skyline in a clump of lime trees. Named after its principal benefactor, the businessman Alexei Grebenschikov, **Grebenščikova baznīca** is the place of worship for the Old Believers. The church now has the largest parish of the faith in the world, with a congregation of approximately 25,000.

THE LEFT BANK

On the opposite bank, across Stone Bridge (Akmens tilts) from the Old Town, is the attractive suburb of **Pārdaugava**, which has many, recently renovated, wood-built houses. This is a lively and trendy place with a lot of cultural events on offer and a seasonal food and craft market held on Saturdays (for more information, see http://kalnciemaiela.lv). From here there is a good view of the Old City skyline. The modern, impressive building rising on the bank in the form of a glass hill is the **National Library of Latvia** (Latvijas Nacionālā bibliotēka; www.lnb.lv; guided tours on request: ekskursijas@lnb.lv), also known as the Castle of Light, designed by the famous Latvian architect Gunārs Birkerts and opened to the public in 2014. It was the main venue of Latvia's EU presidency in the first half of 2015.

Victory Park (**Uzvaras Parks**) has a Soviet victory monument and is popular with Russians. Near the park is a railway museum (www.railwaymuseum.lv), and about a mile from the bridge are the **Botanical Gardens ❷** (www.botanika.lu.lv; daily May–Aug 10am–9pm, Apr and Sep 10am–7pm, Oct–Mar 10am–4pm) with a palm house.

KIPSALA

Kipsala, an island on the left bank of the Daugava river, just 20 minutes walk from the old town and connected by the cable-stayed Vanšu Bridge, is a pleasant place for a stroll. The well preserved old wooden fisherman houses, some from 18th century, are the main attraction. The best known inhabitant of the island is Žanis Lipke, who saved over 50 Jews during World War II by hiding them in a bunker under his shed. The **Žanis Lipke Memorial** (www.lipke.lv; Tue–Wed and Fri–Sun noon–6pm, Thu until 8pm), a simple, dark wooded construction shaped like the river boat, next to the Lipke's house, makes you ponder on the suffering of people who hid for so long underground.

Central Market.

ART NOUVEAU

Rīga experienced great affluence as Art Nouveau became fashionable, and the city is littered with examples of this flamboyant style.

Art Nouveau, the architectural style that brings such an unexpectedly decadent air to Rīga's streets, celebrated the triumph of the bourgeoisie at the end of the 19th and beginning of the 20th century. In highly developed Rīga more than in any Russian city, the new urban middle classes found prosperity.

A new wave of architects jumped at the task of designing residential blocks, academies, schools, department stores, libraries, banks, restaurants and factories. The result is that nearly one in three buildings in Rīga – some 40 percent of the boulevard city that grew up in the 1900s – is in Art Nouveau or Jugendstil.

EISENSTEIN'S ORNAMENTATION

Rīga hosted a mixture of new, often decorative approaches to building. The residential houses in Alberta Street, built by civil engineer Mikhail Osipovich Eisenstein, father of the great Russian filmmaker, are saturated in finishing details. Inside the entrance to 2a Alberta Street the exterior decoration evolves into a turquoise hall of columns, embroidered with leaves and curves.

Eisenstein's "decoratively eclectic Art Nouveau", a staggering synthesis of rationality and ornament, is shared by other contemporary Rīga architects, including the Baltic Germans Friedrich Scheffel, Heinrich Scheel and Reinhold Schmaeling. All studied in St Petersburg, where Art Nouveau flourished. The entrance hall to Scheel and Sheffel's residential block with shops at 8 Smilšu Street shows a characteristic affinity with the Arts and Crafts movement. That thread takes the curious visitor back to one of Rīga's most important architects, the Baltic German Wilhelm Bockslaff. Bockslaff built the graceful Stock Exchange (1905), on Kalpaka Boulevard. Since 1919 the building has housed the Latvian Arts Academy. Its pastel-coloured ceiling, embroidered after the style of William Morris, is a treasury of stained glass, and the whole building is a fine monument to the eclecticism of Art Nouveau.

Houses, shops and banks on Brīvības Street and nearby Ģertrūdes and A. Čaka streets employ the perpendicular to express the solidity and the excitement of town life. Architects of this so-called "rational" Art Nouveau from the mid-1900s include Latvians Jānis Alksnis, Eižens Laube, Paul Mandelstamm and Konstantīns Pēkšēns.

LATVIA'S ROMANTIC STYLE

Laube, Mandelstamm, Pēkšēns and Aleksandrs Vanags all graduated from Rīga Polytechnical Institute, which encouraged them to develop a specific Latvian style. A general heaviness, in some cases as if the building had been poured out of a mould, in others as if it were a test-run for different building materials, including stucco, wood, stone, brick and plaster, characterises this National Romanticism. It incorporated stylised ethnographic ornaments, and the natural materials used in an urban setting, together with tapered window recesses and steep roofs, suggested a continued link with rural life.

The individual features of scores of these buildings, testaments to high-spirited urban living, make a walk around Rīga a joy. A visit to the Rīga Art Nouveau Museum on Alberta Street is an absolute must to see how furniture, flatware and even plumbing fixtures were embellished in this style. www.jugendstils.riga.lv

Dramatic figures on Elizabetes Street.

AROUND RĪGA

Just a short bus or train ride from the centre of Rīga are a number of places in which to have fun, from the Open-Air Ethnographic Museum to the city's seaside playground at Jūrmala.

⊙ Main attractions

Lake Ķīšezers
Rīga Zoo
Open-Air Ethnographic
  Museum
Salaspils Memorial Park
Jūrmala
Ķemeri National Park

Map on page 188

When high society in London and Berlin was only thinking about green spaces to live in, Rīga's wealthy elite were already designing **Mežaparks** ❷ (Forest Park), one of Europe's first garden cities. Tired of the overcrowding and squalor of the city proper, prosperous Germans created this place, known then as Kaiser Park, beside **Lake Ķīšezers** to the north, where only summer cottages and entertainment facilities were permitted. Neglected during the Soviet era, many of the impressive Art Nouveau properties have been renovated, and the park is once again inhabited by the cream of local society, its property commanding some of the highest prices in the country.

The park is also home to **Rīga Zoo** (Zooloģiskais dārzs; http://rigazoo.lv; daily 10am–5pm, Apr–Oct until 7pm; feeding shows June–Aug 11.30am–2.15pm), which has brown and polar bears and is well worth a visit. **Mežakakis Adventure Park** (www.kakiskalns.lv; May–Sept Mon–Fri 11am–8pm, Sat–Sun from 10am) with five rope courses, and the **Song Festival Stadium** (Lielā estrāde), which can accommodate 10,000 singers and 25,000 spectators. They gather every five years for a major festival as they have done since 1873. A small beach on the lake is a popular destination for swimmers and sunbathers.

Aktīvās Atpūtas Centrs (Pāvu iela; http://aac.lv) on Lake Ķīšezers is an activity centre where you can hire bicycles and roller blades, and go boating, jet-skiing, windsurfing, water-skiing and parasailing. "Ice boating" was first held on Lake Ķīšezers in 1926, and it was here that the Rīga Yacht Club devised the rules for the sport.

OPEN-AIR MUSEUM

Perhaps of greatest general appeal is the **Open-Air Ethnographic Museum** ❸ (Brīvdabas muzejs; www

Lake Ķīšezers.

brivdabasmuzejs.lv; museum daily 10am–5pm; grounds May–Sept until 8pm), 10km (6 miles) northeast along Brīvības Street. More than 100 buildings are set out in 100 hectares (250 acres) of woodland beside Lake Jugla. The idea for the museum arose in the wake of the desolation of the countryside after World War I, and work began on it in 1924.

The most impressive building is the 18th-century Lutheran church (Usmas baznīca) just to the left of the entrance. The whole building, including its figurative woodcarvings, was made with axes. There is a special, highly decorated seat beside the altar for the local German landlord, and the front pews were reserved for imported German workers. Attending church was obligatory for all workers at that time, and those caught skiving were put in the stocks or the pillory exhibited outside. Before the 19th-century organ was installed, the only music would have been an accompanying drum.

The museum display is divided into Latvia's ancient regions and it shows the contrasts between the rich Kurzeme farmers and those of poorer Latgale. Farmsteads were built for the family unit, which usually meant three generations. Costumed figures populate the village, and a blacksmith, potter and spoon-maker often perform. There are occasional folk gatherings here, and a major crafts fair is held on the first weekend in June – it's very entertaining and should not be missed.

FILM STUDIO AND MOTOR MUSEUM

In the same direction is the Motor Museum, about 5km (3 miles) from the centre of town along Brīvības iela. Šmerļa Street leads down to it from Brīvības, passing by the city's **Film Studios ❹** (Rīgas kinostudija; www. studio.lv), which operate an open-door policy. Since 1940 the studios have produced mainly documentary films, and its protégés included Juris Podnieks. His 1989 film about the Soviet Union, *Hello, Do You Hear Us?*, which won the Prix d'Italia, included extraordinary footage of the Chernobyl disaster. This

◉ Tip

For both the zoo and for Lake Ķīšezers, take tram No. 11 from Barona iela to the Mežaparks stop.

The Open-Air Ethnographic Museum.

is also a great place to rent costumes and film props.

Just beyond the film studios, the street forks right into Sergeja Eizenšteina Street, where the glistening facade of the recently restored **Motor Museum** (Rīgas motormuzejs; www.motormuzejs.lv; daily 10am–6pm) stands out like a brand new Rolls-Royce radiator grille. Rīga has been a key player in motor manufacturing in eastern Europe: its Russo-Balt factory, for example, presented Russia with its first car and tank.

A STROLL IN THE CEMETERIES

Just to the south are the great cemeteries of the city (take tram No.11 from Barona iela in the centre of Rīga), which are highly regarded by Latvians who use them almost like parks: the **Cemetery of Heroes** (Brāļu kapi) for the casualties of World War I and the War of Independence (1915–20); **Raiņa Cemetery** (Raiņa kapi) for the great and the good of Latvian literati; and the old **Forest Cemetery** (Meža kapi),

final resting place of heads of sta as well as common folk.

Although overgrown and neglecte the Russian **Pokrov Cemetery** (Po rova kapi) is also worth a look. Th epitaphs on its ageing headston chronicle the life of tsarist-e bureaucrats, while at the far en near Sencu iela, is the final res ing place of fallen Soviet soldier marked by an enormous gold-paint concrete statue of a marching Re Army infantryman holding aloft flag bearing the hammer and sick of the USSR. You can also take a lo at the Orthodox chapel in the midd of the grounds.

The **Great Cemetery** (Lielie kap is located nearby and includes th remains of large crypts of prom nent Rīga families dating back the late 18th century. The graves the revered Latvian folk-song colle tor Krišjānis Barons and the equal important educator and Nation Awakening icon Krišjānis Valdema can be found here.

The beach at Jūrmala.

ALASPILS

he A6 follows the right bank of the iver Daugava for 16km (10 miles) outheast to **Salaspils** ❺, where the ivonian Order built its first palace, in he 14th century, and in 1412 signed an mportant agreement with the Bishop f Rīga, establishing shared rule over he capital. On this site in 1605 the wedes suffered a crushing defeat by he Poles. But Salaspils is destined to o down in the history books primarily s the site of a nightmarish World War concentration camp.

A 40-hectare (100-acre) **memo-ial park** was opened in 1967, centred n a long, sloping concrete building iscribed: "The earth moans beyond this ate." On the far side are half a dozen nonumental statues and a lengthy, low lack box where wreaths are placed. emits a continuous and eerie ticking oise, supposed to represent a beating eart. The sites of the former barracks re marked, and an inscribed stone indi-ates the place of the gallows. Around ,000 people were murdered at the alaspils camp during the Holocaust.

JŪRMALA

The word *jūrmala* in Latvian simply means seaside, and this is the name given to the Baltics' most famous resort, extending west from **Lielupe**. **Jūrmala** ❻ has long been the play-ground of Rīga, from its 19th-century spa days to its heyday in the 1930s. Peggie Benton, an English diplomat's wife, was in Rīga at the outbreak of World War II, and like many people from the city rented a villa at Jūrmala for the summer. "The Latvians kept up the delightful Russian custom of bathing naked," she wrote in *Baltic Countdown*. "One soon learned not to worry and got used to strolling up to a policeman, tightly buttoned into his uniform, to ask how much longer until the red flag went up and we had to put our clothes on again."

During the Soviet era Jūrmala became *the* destination for holi-daymakers from across the USSR, and ugly concrete hotels began to overshadow the quaint European atmosphere which attracted so many people here.

Jūrmala villa.

Today, Jūrmala is still a favourite for Russian tourists, especially among the Russian elite and although many of the buildings have been restored or renovated, a slightly Soviet atmosphere, and mentality, remains.

Not actually a proper city, rather a collection of small seaside towns, Jūrmala stretches along a narrow strip of land, pressed against the beach by the River Lielupe, which follows the coast for about 8km (5 miles) before emptying itself into Rīga Bay just west of the mouth of the Daugava.

The main beaches at Majori and Dubulti have both been awarded Blue Flags guaranteeing water purity and a variety of services such as changing stations, toilets, fresh water for rinsing off and emergency medical support, not to mention seaside bars and cafés. On a typical summer day you can expect the beaches to be packed and to see football and volleyball games as well as the occasional woman in nothing more than a bikini and high heels using the beach as her personal catwalk. Topless sunbathing is fairly common, but nude beaches are rare. The spas around town are yet another reason to visit.

MAJORI AND DUBULTI

A casual stroll down the main pedestrian street of Jomas iela in **Majori** will afford every visitor with countless opportunities to eat, drink and shop 12 The cultural high point of Majori is **the Rainis and Aspazija Summer Cottage** (Raiņa un Aspazijas memoriālā vasarnīca; http://memorialiemuzeji.lv; Tue–Sat 10am–5pm), a recently restored attractive wooden house once lived in by the poet, playwright and journalist Jānis Rainis in a street called J. Pliekšāna iela, which was Rainis' real name. He lived here during his last three years, from 1926 to 1929, and a museum preserves his effects, which include more than 7,000 books in 11 languages. In fact, he usually rented out the large house to holidaymakers, opting to live and work in the smaller house next door where he used to complain about the noise from his tenants' gramophone. His wife, the

A variety of ships off Jūrmala.

et and writer Aspazija, is also com-
emorated at the house.

There is an abundance of seaside
ntertainment all along this coast, but
st strolling round brings rewarding
ghts such as the renovated Lutheran
hurch in **Dubulti** (Dubultu luterāņu
aznīca), whose towering steeple can
e seen from a great distance, and the
right-blue wooden Orthodox church
earby. Jūrmala is also home to doz-
ns of spa hotels that offer mud baths
nd other health treatments often used
y German and Finnish pensioners.
he urban centres provide top-notch
estaurants and nightlife as well as
xcellent examples of wooden Art Nou-
eau buildings. To the east, in Bulduri,
the **Līvu Water Park** (www.akvaparks.
— with dozens of water slides and
ools, both indoors and out — not to
ention a popular poolside bar, sau-
as and hot tubs.

ETTING TO JŪRMALA

nyone driving to Jūrmala, or even
rough it, needs to buy a permit for
e day from the roadside offices on its

outskirts. Most people take the trains,
which leave Rīga station roughly every
20 minutes, or the cheaper minibuses
that depart from the terminal across
the street from the train station.

There are a dozen train stops to
choose from between Lielupe and
Ķemeri ❼, a spa town set back from
the sea. In its heyday the grand Ķemeri
Hotel had a cosmopolitan air, hosting
international chess championships and
social events, and although it is scheduled to reopen in the near future its
renovation has been plagued by construction problems and legal battles.

Majori is the central stop, with cafés,
restaurants, souvenir shops and an
outdoor concert hall, all within easy
reach of the railway station.

VECAKI BEACH

Although not as popular with tourists
as Jūrmala, the beach at **Vecaki**, 20km
(12 miles) north of Rīga, is a Latvian
favourite with a few beachside bars and
beach volleyball courts as far as the
eye can see. Take a Carnikava-bound
train (40 minutes) from Central Station.

Fanciful wooden villa near Jūrmala beach.

⊘ HIKES IN ĶEMERI NATIONAL PARK

Without its grand 1930s Art Deco hotel to attract upmarket tourists,
gamblers and spa-goers, the old resort of Ķemeri, just west of Jūrmala,
has become something of a backwater. The town itself owes its existence to the park's sulphur springs and the curative properties of the
mud. These days Ķemeri attracts more nature-lovers than spa-goers,
as it is the perfect starting point for a hike through the Ķemeri National
Park (Ķemeru nacionālais parks; www.kemerunacionalaisparks.lv).

Founded in 1997, this 380 sq km (147 sq miles) park is only a short
distance from the sea. Made up of wetlands, swamps, raised bogs, forests
and lakes, it is the perfect breeding ground for rare and not so rare species of flora and fauna. More than 250 species of birds, including endangered black storks, sea eagles and white-backed woodpeckers, inhabit
the park, as well as mammals such as wolves, lynx, elk and deer. Of the
900 plant species, 86 are protected, including two types of wild orchids.

The park offers a variety of different nature trails with bird-watching
platforms and several kilometres of wooden boardwalks over the swampy
terrain. The park service provides an information centre at the Meža māja
(May and Sept Sat–Sun 11am–5pm, June–Aug Wed–Sun 11am–6pm) in
the centre of the town where you can ask about specific routes through
the park. Some boardwalks may be closed due to renovation.

Field of poppies and cornflowers,
Kurzeme Region, Courland.

KURZEME: THE WEST COAST

To the west of Jūrmala lies a rural area of "blue" cows and amber-washed beaches that was once owned by the powerful dukes of Courland.

Kurzeme is the westernmost region of Latvia, a healthy agricultural area half-surrounded by sea. It was once known as Courland (Kurland in German), named after the Kurši, the amber-rich seafaring people who dominated the coast before the arrival of the German crusaders. Not unlike their contemporaries, the Vikings, the Kurši often supplemented their incomes by sailing across the sea to Sweden, and even as far as Denmark, to wreak havoc on local populations, stealing everything that was worth taking. Several of their exploits are mentioned in Scandinavian sagas.

In 1561, after the break-up of Livonia, Courland came into its own. It became a duchy under the sovereignty of Poland, and included the region of Zemgale (formerly Semigallia) to the south of Rīga, plus a small corner of modern Lithuania.

POWERFUL DUKES

Courland's dukes enjoyed a degree of independence, building castles for themselves and Lutheran churches for the people. Many became rich and powerful, notably Jacob Kettler (1642–82), who went empire-building and collected a couple of outposts, one in the Gambia, West Africa, the other the Caribbean island of Tobago. Kettler amassed his fortune largely from the trees that grow exceptionally tall and

straight. The most impressive forests are in the Slītere National Park (Slīteres Nacionālais parks; see page 232) and along the sandy coastal region, which was once below the sea. Trees grow to around 35 metres (110ft), and some of them are up to 500 years old.

Kurzeme's thriving shipbuilding and trading activities were conducted at the two important ice-free ports of Ventspils and Liepāja, which have once again become major trading hubs, rivalling even Rīga. The coast around Kurzeme is a continuous white sandy

⊙ **Main attractions**
Kuldīga
Pedvāle Outdoor Art Museum
Ugāle church
Dundaga estate
Slītere National Park
Ventspils
Liepāja
Pape Nature Park

Map on page 188

In Kuldīga.

beach, from just north of the major Lithuanian resort of Palanga up to the Kolka Peninsula and down to the fishing village of Mērsrags and Lake Engure in the Bay of Rīga. Beyond this is Jūrmala, Latvia's riviera, and Zemgale.

For 45 years, until 1991, most of this coast was used by the military and was therefore inaccessible; today, even in the heat of summer, much of it remains completely deserted save the occasional kite-flyer or windsurfer. Between the coastal lowland in the west and Rīga Bay in the northeast, towns, villages, churches and estates are tucked in the valleys and wooded corners of a landscape that rolls between rivers and hills. Kuldīga and Talsi are the principal inland provincial towns.

KULDĪGA

The town of **Kuldīga**  is 160km (100 miles) west of Rīga, and is a good centre for exploring the region. A castle was first built here in 1242, and in 1561 the town, known then as Goldingen, was made the capital of Courland

Ventas waterfall, the most elongated in Europe.

by the first duke, Gotthard Kettler. The castle was built beside the River Venta, which was navigable all the way to Ventspils and the sea.

The city declined after the Great Northern War (1700–21) and the castle was reduced to little more than a ruin: only a park and an engraved stone marking its location remain. The churches are worth exploring: **St Anne's** (Sv Annas baznīca) has an impressive neo-Gothic spire, **St Catherine's Lutheran Church** (Sv Katrīnas luterāņu baznīca) has a fine wooden altar and pulpit from 1660, and there is a grand view over the town from the top of its 25-metre (85ft) tower. The **Holy Trinity Catholic Church** (Sv Trīsvienības katoļu baznīca) in Raiņa Street also has an impressive altar which was donated by Tsar Alexander I in 1820.

Part of the town's charm is derived from the Alekšupīte, a tributary to the River Venta, which runs by a mill and between wooden houses that date from the 17th century. Most of the old red-tile roofed buildings are centred around the square overlooked by the 19th-century town hall, but the main pedestrian street today is Liepājas which runs from Raiņa Street a few roads back. With a wooden building that looks as if it might be a Wild West saloon, this street leads to the main modern square, dominated by two Soviet-style buildings housing a hotel and supermarket – practically the only eyesores in an otherwise charming medieval town.

At the 19th-century brick bridge over the Venta you can see the Ventas rumba, Europe's widest waterfall, extending the 110-metre (360ft) width of the river. In the park overlooking the river is the **Kuldīga Museum** (Kuldīgas novada muzejs; www.kuldigasmuzejs. Tue noon–6pm, Wed–Sun 10am–6pm) its building more interesting than its exhibits. It served as part of the Russian pavilion at the 1900 World's Fair

Paris and was bought by a wealthy usinessman who had it shipped to uldīga as a gift to his fiancée.

OMA VILLAGES ND VINEYARDS

pleasant drive leads northeast of uldīga, to Sabile and Kandava, towards ukums. These villages are known r their Roma population. **Vīna kalns** Vine Hill), in **Sabile ❾**, features in ie *Guinness Book of Records* as the ost northerly place in Europe where nes are grown. The town has one of e region's few surviving synagogues, hich is now an arts centre. On the other de of the river is the **Pedvāle Outdoor rt Museum**, created in 1992 on a for-er baronial estate (Pedvāles brīvdabas ākslas muzejs; www.pedvale.lv; daily ay–late Oct 10am–6pm, late Oct–Apr)am–4pm). Visitors can explore 150 ectares (370 acres) of rolling hills cov-red in sculptures and modern art on a rand scale and can even book a room at ie museum's guesthouse.

Kandava has a pleasant Old Town, ut only a fortification wall and powder tower remain of its origi-nal castle. It does, however, have the oldest fieldstone bridge in Latvia. Due south of Kandava at **Zante** you'll find the **Kurzeme Fortress Museum** (Kurzemes cietokšņa muzejs; Wed–Sat 10am–5pm, Sun 10.45am–3pm), where you can explore restored trenches, bunkers and military machinery, including a Soviet tank and aeroplane, from the two World Wars.

Between Kuldīga and Ventspils is the small town of **Piltene ❿**, the seat of a bishopric that retained its independ-ence from 1234 to 1583. The remains of its castle of the Livonian Order lie behind the church, built in 1792.

Danish craftsmen were imported via Piltene, and art historians detect their hand on the robust folk carv-ings of the altars and pulpits of local churches. But the principal carvings at Piltene, which have not survived, were by the 18th-century master carvers from Ventspils, Nico-las Soeffren the Older and Younger, ship carvers who turned their skills to church work.

Small-town Kuldīga.

ZLĒKAS

Among other local churches with fine carving is **Zlēkas** , between Piltene and Kuldīga. This is the largest church in Courland and it has a fine black-and-gold Baroque pulpit and altar, which were carved by local craftsmen. Its confessional dating to the late 16th century is the oldest in Latvia. At **Ēdole**, on the opposite side of the main Ventspils road and about 20km (12 miles) northwest of Kuldīga, there is a church that dates from the 17th century. It also has a restored 13th-century castle converted into a hotel (Ēdoles pils; http://edolespils.lv).

UGĀLE CHURCH

One of the most interesting churches is at **Ugāle** , directly north of Kuldīga on the road between Tukums and Ventspils. Built in 1694, its organ was installed four years later, making it the oldest in the Baltic. Is has 28 stops, including the only surviving Baroque register. It was built by Cornelius Rhaneus from Kuldīga.

The beautiful, unpainted lime-wood carvings by Michael Markwart from

Sabile is home to vineyards.

Ventspils include stars that once revolved and angels' wings designed to flap. The neighbouring village of Usma is the origin of the 18th-century **Lutheran church** in Rīga's Open-Air Ethnographic Museum, and its location on the shore of Lake Usma makes it an excellent destination for water sports including fishing and sailing.

AIZPUTE

After Courland's incorporation into Russia in 1795, the small town of **Aizpute** , about 130km (80 miles) to the south, earned the nickname "Klein Danzig" because nearly two-thirds of the population were Jewish. The town makes a pleasant stop, and has a church dating back to 1254, castle ruins from the same period, a watermill complex, stone bridge, castle, manor house and the recently rebuilt Dom Tavern (16th century).

AROUND TALSI

The region northeast of Kuldīga is **Talsi** , centred on the market town of the same name. Like a painting on a chocolate box, it is a pretty, tranquil idyll tucked under hills beside a large pond. Not surprisingly, it has long been an artists' haunt. In its cobbled streets is a small local museum and a Lutheran church, whose pastor Karl Amenda was an accomplished musician and a friend of Beethoven.

North of Talsi is a series of former large country-house estates. The palace at **Nogale** (Nogales pils) is a particularly good example. It was built in 1880 for Baron von Firks as a summer residence and hunting lodge, and from 1920 to 1980 it was a school. It has now been restored and is once again privately owned. The two-storey neoclassical building overlooks a lake and 7 hectares (170 acres) of parkland.

The neighbouring village to the west is **Valdemārpils**, where the main estate is now a school. It takes its name from Krišjānis Valdemārs, one of the leading

lights of the National Awakening, who was born in nearby **Cīruļi** in 1825. He became enchanted by the sea near here at Roja and went on to found Latvia's first seamen's school at Ainaži, right up by the Estonian border.

Outside his country manor in Valdemārpils is one of the oldest lime trees in the country and the biggest in the Baltics, a huge and crippled beast that once served as a pagan holy site for worship and sacrifice (Elku liepa).

DUNDAGA ESTATE

The largest estate in the whole of the Baltics was **Dundaga** ⑮, the northernmost village of any size on this cape. In the 18th century the castle's lands stretched for 700 sq km (270 sq miles), and today is well preserved. The crozier and sword, symbols of the Church and the Sword Bearers, are inscribed on its entranceway, and the main door inside the courtyard is guarded by a statue of a bishop and a crusader. The estate belonged to the bishops of Courland, the last of whom was Herzog of Holstein, brother of Germany's Friedrich II.

Today the building houses two schools and a tourist information centre, and is used as a venue for local events and concerts and as a cheap accommodation.

The local church (Dundagas baznīca), which is dated 1766, has woodcarvings by Soeffren and an altar painting by Latvia's great 20th-century artist, Janis Rozentāls. Memorials to several members of the Osten-Sachens family are scattered in the church grounds, but the most notable memorial (Krokodils), located on the north side of Dundaga, is dedicated to local boy Arvīds Blūmentāls, who emigrated to Australia and, after hunting 10,000 crocodiles, served as the prototype for the character "Crocodile Dundee".

SECRET COAST OF THE LIVS

On the Rīga Bay side of the cape, the road from Jūrmala continues through pine trees of extraordinary stature, which have provided masts for many ships throughout the ages. Dozens of sleepy fishing villages, which were completely isolated during the Soviet

The distinctive memorial to Arvīds Blūmentāls, the original "Crocodile Dundee".

era, dot the coast. Even today, one has the feeling that not much has changed here save a rejuvenation of traditional summer sea festivals.

All around this peninsula, which encircles the carefully controlled **Slītere National Park** (Slīteres nacion-ālais parks), there is scarcely any sign of life. The reserve is an important wildlife area caring for a number of endangered plants, and supporting the busiest birdlife in the region; in April some 60,000 migrating birds congregate here. It also provides a habitat for swamp turtle and natterjack among other species. A Landscape Protection Zone has been organised to conserve the forest landscape and biological diversity along the sea coast, while allowing visitors to enjoy the area. **Kolka** ⑯ is the main centre for information about the park.

At the top of the peninsula, just beyond Kolka, is a point where the waters of Rīga Bay meet the Baltic Sea. The marked line where the seas meet runs out past the half-washed-away lighthouse to the horizon, and

Forest at Slītere National Park.

when the wind blows, the waters ar whipped up into a great crashing wall Kolka is also home to the **Liv Centre** which is part Liv history museum, par information centre (Kolkas līvu centrs Mon–Fri 9am–4pm; free), where yo can learn about the proud people tha once populated the coastline.

Continuing down the western, Balti side of the coast are a further series c former fishing communities. Typical i **Mazirbe** ⑰, where farmlands stretc back from the dunes of the bleache sand, which is strewn with smal cockle and mussel shells. If you'r lucky you might even find a chunk c amber. A white wooden hall built wit help from Estonia serves as a meetin place for the last of the Liv community

VENTSPILS

The heyday for **Ventspils** ⑱ was unde Duke Jacob, who launched his ship for the Caribbean and West Afric from here. But, after his death, Vent spils went into decline and followin the plague of 1710 was reduced to jus seven families. It enjoyed a cultura

⊘ HOTELS, POLITICS AND ROCK 'N' ROLL

For centuries Liepāja, or Libau as it was known, was dominated by Germans, Poles, Russians and, of course, Latvians, but today the biggest influence on the city appears to be Danish. In fact, one Danish rock musician in particular is leaving a lasting mark. Louis Fontaine, born Steen Lorenz, first visited the city in the 1990s as part of a European tour for his rock band and fell in love with the place. Eventually, he moved to the city, opening up Latvia's first boutique hotel, the Fontaine Hotel (www.fontaine.lv), as well as the Fontaine Palace, a 24-hour rock club.

As Fontaine's business interests grew, he came into contact with what he deemed corruption in local politics and became a vocal opponent of the city's mayor. He later ran for office on an anti-corruption platform, claiming that if he were elected there would be a "new sheriff in town". He even created a music video for his campaign in which he was dressed as a cowboy with a ten-gallon hat, a six-shooter in one hand and a bottle of Jim Beam bourbon in the other.

Fontaine was elected to the city council, but did not replace the incumbent mayor. Today he owns restaurants, clubs, bars, hotels, a spa and a travel agency in Liepāja. He also organises the annual Fontaine Festival on the Promenade in August, featuring acts from both home and abroad.

renaissance during the years of independence, and after World War II the Soviet Union built it up as an industrial centre. In the 1990s Russian petrodollars made the tiny town the wealthiest in Latvia, and its manicured parks, tidy streets and renovated buildings are a testament to this prosperity. The pipeline has dried up in the wake of worsening relations between the two countries, and the city now survives on revenues from oil tankers at its portside terminal.

Ventspils' charming historical centre is tiny and can easily be explored on foot. The town's most striking attraction is the restored **Livonian Order Castle** (Ventspils pils) dating back to 1290, which houses the **Ventspils Museum** (Ventspils muzejs; http://muzejs.ventspils.lv; Tue–Sun 10am–6pm) and a medieval restaurant. Behind the castle is the promenade on the bank of the River Venta where visitors can watch ships passing by or, in the summer, take a short cruise from the east end. The 18th-century Baroque **Town Hall** is also worth a visit, as well as **St Nicholas' Church**, built in 1835 on the opposite side of the square.

Sunbathers can take advantage of the city's Blue Flag beach, and a few hours can be whiled away at the **Seaside Outdoor Ethnographic Museum** (Piejūras brīvdabas muzejs; http://muzejs.ventspils.lv; May–Oct Tue–Sun 10am–6pm, Nov–Apr by appointment tel: 6362 4467), where the main attraction is a working narrow-gauge railway. Nineteenth-century houses and fishing boats hundreds of years old are also on display.

LIEPĀJA

The other significant port on this coast **Liepāja** ⑲, 130km (80 miles) south of Ventspils, with almost twice its population (70,000). Liepāja is a centre of metal-smelting and was a major Soviet military base with submarine pens. Known throughout the nation as

the city where the wind is born, Liepāja was Latvia's Gdansk, where the first organised grass-roots opposition to Soviet rule began in the 1980s.

The city is also a major cultural centre, claiming some of the nation's best musicians and artists as its own.

There's plenty to see and do in Liepāja. Start in the Old Town at the 18th-century **Trinity Lutheran Church** (Sv Trīsvienības luterāņu baznīca), built in 1758, with an unusual Baroque facade and elaborate Rococo interior. Its most impressive asset is its organ dating from the same period, which, until 1912, was one of the world's largest, with 7,000 pipes and 131 registers. Head down Lielā iela to Rožu laukums, the main square, designed in 1911 with more than 500 rose bushes, giving it its name. Walk down Zivju (Fish) Street for a look at 17th-century warehouses and wooden homes with red-tiled roofs. To the left, on the corner of Kungu and Bāriņu streets, is the old **House of Peter I**, Madame Hoyer's former hotel, where Peter the Great once slept. Ironically,

Wooden stocks at Ventspils Castle.

across the street is another historic home where the Russian tsar's adversary, Charles XII, King of Sweden, supposedly spent the night. At the end of Zivju Street is **St Anne's Lutheran Church** (Sv Annas luterāņu baznīca), Liepāja's oldest place of worship, dating to the early 16th century, with a beautiful altar carved by Nicolas Soeffren.

The **Liepāja Museum** (Liepājas muzejs; http://liepajasmuzejs.lv; daily 10am–6pm; free), housed in a fine 19th-century house on Kūrmājas prospekts, is also worth a visit. The street ends at the Blue Flag beach, ,where a monument to mariners lost at sea was erected in 1977. Just south of the bronze statue are the main beach, seaside park and concert hall.

A NIGHT IN THE CELLS

North of the canal separating the Old from the New City is the fascinating **Karosta** (http://karostascietums.lv; guided tours of the port and bicycle excursions) or military naval base built in 1893 by Tsar Alexander III. It was a city unto itself, with its own housing, schools and churches, but now is a collection of empty administrative and apartment buildings and military barracks. The only building that seems to have withstood the test of time is the colourful **St Nicholas' Orthodox Church** (Sv Nikolāja pareizticīgo katedrāle; daily 8am–5pm). The **Old Prison** (Karostas cietums, location as above; June–Aug daily 9am–7pm, May and Sept daily 10am–6pm, Oct–Apr Sat–Sun noon–4pm) is now a museum, and the years of suffering have supposedly left their mark on the building as it is purported to be haunted. Daring visitors and sceptics of the supernatural can participate in "Behind Bars", a theatrical performance where tourists are locked up in cells overnight. This can be arranged at the tourist information centre. Just north of the city, ruined fortifications slowly recede into the sea, creating an eerily beautiful landscape.

BREEDING GROUND

To the south of Liepāja, the immaculate beach continues its drift towards distant Lithuania, passing eroded sand banks and dunes on the coast before crossing the border and arriving at the large resort of Palanga.

Birdwatchers and nature-lovers who might have enjoyed the Slīter National Park should also stop at the **Pape Nature Park** (Papes dabas parks; www.pdf-pape.lv) at **Rucava**, the last town before the Lithuanian border. With money from the World Wildlife Fund, the pristine seaside breeding ground for birds and other animals has been preserved. Wild cattle and horses that have been reintroduced in this thriving ecosystem also inhabit Lake Pape and its surrounding swamps. A bird-watching tower has been erected and several miles of hiking trails have been created to make the park accessible. Accommodation can also be arranged at the Rucava tourist information centre.

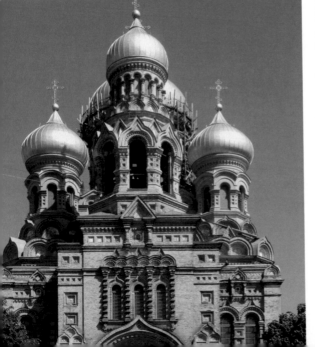

St Nicholas' Orthodox Church.

Storm clouds over the Baltic, Liepāja.

Village houses on Daugava River, Jekabpil.

LATGALE

Ceramics, glassware and local produce are the rewards for exploring this land of myriad lakes, gentle uplands, outposts of Old Believers and a deep Catholic faith.

atvia's easternmost region is "The and of the Blue Lakes". A mass of eciduous trees makes it not just uer, but greener, too. It is the poor- st and the most remote of the regions. s people, who speak a dialect some gard as a separate language, have rger families and are more gregari- us. They sometimes like to think of emselves as the Irish of Latvia. If ere is any festival or gathering here will be lively. Traditionally, the people Latgale had homesteads adjoining ach other, rather than isolated coun- y homes as in the rest of Latvia. They ontinue their established crafts, espe- ally ceramics, making big, chunky gs and candelabra which are thickly azed and seen everywhere.

Rubbing up against Russia, Belarus nd Lithuania, Latgale's geography has ven it a different history, too. While urzeme and Zemgale were being cruited to the Lutheran cause by the ukes of Courland, the Swedes in Rīga nd Vidzeme were banishing practis- g Catholics, and many of them came Latgale, where Catholic Poland eld sway. They left their mark in the aroque Jesuit style of their grand hurches: St Peter's in Daugavpils, t Ludwig in Krāslava, the Holy Cross Pasiene and the huge white coun- y church at Aglona, where Catholics om all over Europe gather in their

thousands on the Feast of the Assump- tion. Among these slightly distant lands is Daugavpils, Latvia's second- largest city, tucked in the far southeast 224km (140 miles) from Rīga, and the best part of a day's train ride away.

PĻAVIŅAS TO LĪVĀNI

The town of **Pļaviņas** is the last on the A6 from Rīga before Latgale. Here the River Daugava spreads out like a vast mirror in the summer, and in win- ter it is the place to see the collision of huge ice sheets. Just beyond Pļaviņas

Main attractions
Open-Air Ethnographic Museum, Jēkabpils
St Peter's Church, Daugavpils
Sts Boris and Gleb Church, Daugavpils
Daugavpils Mark Rothko Art Centre
Krāslava History and Art Museum
Ludza Castle ruins
Pasiene church

Map on page 188

A boy plays with his dog near Razna lake.

the road follows the Daugava upriver to **Jēkabpils** , named after the Courland duke. Beside the road on this north bank is **Krustpils Castle** (Krustpils pils), built in 1237. Once a fortress of the Livonian Order, it came into the possession of the Korf family in the 16th century and remained their property until it was seized by the Latvian government in 1921 as part of the land reforms and used as a military base. It is now home to the **Jēkabpils Museum** (Jēkabpils muzejs; http://jekabpilsmuzejs. lv; Mon–Fri 9am–5pm [May–Sept until 6pm], Sat–Sun 10am–4pm [May–Sept until 5pm]).

The town of Jēkabpils, marked by the dome of a **Russian Orthodox Church** (Sv Gara pareizticīgo baznīca) of 1887, lies on the far bank of the river. It was a main river staging post for logging and the fur trade and had a settlement of Old Believers. It is famous as the birthplace of Jānis Rainis (1865–1929), the most important literary figure of the National Awakening. His father was an estate overseer and he built Tadenava, the

house where Jānis was born. T[ ] building is now the **Rainis Museu[ ]** (Raiņa muzejs; http://memorialiemuzeji[ ] May–Oct Wed–Sun 10am–5pm), co[ ] taining the family's household item[ ] Of all local attractions, the **Open-A[ ] Ethnographic Museum** (Sēļu sēt[ ] Only May–Sept Mon–Fri 10am–6p[ ] Sat–Sun 10am–5pm, Oct Mon–F[ ] 9am–5pm, Sat–Sun 10am–4pm; http[ ] jekabpilsmuzejs.lv), displaying old far[ ] buildings and antiquated agricultur[ ] contraptions, is the most interesting

Līvāni , the next town upstrea[ ] is known for its excellent blown-gla[ ] art, some of which was used as dec[ ] ration in the Olympic village in Athen[ ] produced at the now defunct Līvān[ ] stiklu fabrika. Call ahead for a tour [ ] the **Glass Museum** (www.latgalesam[ ] nieki.lv; tel: 6538 1855).

DAUGAVPILS

Daugavpils , near the Lithuani[ ] and Belarus borders, is at a cros[ ] roads between the Baltic and Bla[ ] Sea routes, and the road and railw[ ] from Warsaw to Moscow. This form[ ] capital of the Duchy of Pārdaugav[ ] known as "Polish Livonia", has [ ] sprinkling of 18th- to 19th-centu[ ] mansions and the odd bright splas[ ] of Art Nouveau. The city has be[ ] attracting "foreigners" for many ce[ ] turies, from the Old Believers, th[ ] sect exiled from Moscow in the 18[ ] century, to others just coming to th[ ] relatively prosperous town to fi[ ] work. Many left, too, including Mark[ ] Rothkowitz, who went to the USA [ ] 1903 at the age of 10 and became th[ ] painter Mark Rothko (see page 23[ ] It is an industrial town, and Russi[ ] cation under the Soviets was intens[ ] Prior to World War II one-third of th[ ] 40,000 population was Russian or Po[ ] ish. Now there are 95,000 inhabitant[ ] only a small percentage of whom a[ ] Latvian. The industries that the So[ ] ets built up – textiles, bicycle man[ ] facture and locomotive repair she[ ]

Travelling the old way near Daugavpils.

have suffered economically, but its importance as a service and transportation hub has grown.

CHURCHES

The stunning white Catholic church of **Peter's** (Sv Pētera katoļu baznīca) is perhaps the most striking attraction in the centre, apart from a series of bars and cafés on the city's busy pedestrian street of restored 19th-century apartment blocks named after the Latvian capital. This mid-18th-century former monastery building is an example of a fortress church and its twin-towered facade is a mark of the Jesuit Baroque, which was brought in from Lithuania. It is a basilica with three naves, the middle one rising to an impressive tunnel vault. At the end of the street by the river is the **Daugavpils Museum** (Daugavpils novadpētniecības un mākslas muzejs; www.dnmm.lv; Tue–Sat 10am–6pm, Sun–Mon 10am–4pm), which is worth a quick stop.

The three most impressive structures in Daugavpils are located outside the centre. Follow the main street next to the river across the train tracks to see two beautiful churches: the 10 onion domes of the Orthodox **Sts Boris and Gleb Church** (Sv Borisa un Gļeba pareizticīgo katedrāle), built in 1904, are only outdone by the blue pastel colour of its facade, and the Catholic church (Dievmātes katoļu baznīca) across the street looks like a smaller copy of the basilica at Aglona (see page 240). Daugavpils' pride and joy is the huge red-brick **fortress** (Daugavpils cietoksnis), the only example of this type of architecture to have survived in the Baltics.

MARK ROTHKO ART CENTRE

In the arsenal building of the fortress is the **Daugavpils Mark Rothko Art Centre** ㉔ (Daugavpils Marka Rotko mākslas centrs; www.rothko center.com; Tue and Sun 11am–5pm, Wed–Sat 11am–7pm), which opened in 2011. The centre presents not only the life of the famous abstract expressionist but also contains some original paintings donated by his

Sts Boris and Gleb church, Daugavpils.

◎ Drink

The people of Latgale are famous for their hospitality, but this usually involves toasting with the region's home-made spirit, *kandža*, a potent grain alcohol that can leave you more than a little tipsy.

The ruined castle at Ludza.

family. In the growing museum collection there are works by other contemporary Latvian and international artists. On the bank of the Daugava River is a monument to the painter by Romualds Gibovskis.

Some 45km (30 miles) east of Daugavpils is the town of **Krāslava** ㉕, and in its centre is Krāslavas pilsmuiža (www.kraslavaspils.lv), one of the finest examples of an 18th-century Polish manor house. The beautifully restored complex consists of the manor house, an art and craft centre and the **Krāslava History and Art Museum** (May–Oct Wed–Fri 10am–5pm, Sat 10am–4pm, Sun 10am–2pm, Nov–Apr Tue–Fri 10am–5pm, Sat 10am–4pm). The surrounding park with grottos and a lake is also worth a visit. The distinguished local church, **St Ludwig's** (Sv Ludviķa baznīca), was completed in 1767 in Baroque style.

LAKELAND REGION

Rolling lands of rivers and lakes spread north from Krāslava, towards Rēzekne, Latgale's capital. Just

above Krāslava, lying next to t[...] Hill of the Sun, (Sauleskalns), **Drīdzis** ㉖, probably the most bea[...] tiful and certainly the deepest Latvia's lakes at 65 metres (213f[...] **Ežezers** ㉗ (hedgehog) lake, fu[...] of little islands, is to the northea[...] and nearby is Velnezers (the de[...] il's lake) whose crystal-clear blu[...] waters are so unusual that for ce[...] turies locals have claimed that it h[...] mysterious properties, thus ear[...] ing its dubious name. **Rāzna** ㉘ ju[...] south of Rēzekne, is the country[...] second-largest lake at 56 sq km ([...] sq miles), and there are plenty [...] local houses to rent as well as son[...] campsites. Northwest of Rēzekne [...] Latvia's largest lake, **Lubāns** ㉙ b[...] much of its 82 sq km (32 sq miles) [...] hardly more than marshland maki[...] Rāzna all the more impressive.

AGLONA PILGRIMS

Northeast of Daugavpils, down sto[...] tracks on the east side of the road [...] Rēzekne, is the village of **Aglona** [...] which is much too small for its gra[...] Baroque church (Aglonas bazilik[...] to which thousands of pilgrims ma[...] their way on the Feast of the Assum[...] tion (15 August) each year, on foot, [...] gypsy cart, car and charabanc.

The object of their veneration is [...] picture of the Virgin Mary, kept behi[...] the altar, which is said to have hea[...] ing powers. The picture is report[...] to have been presented by Manu[...] Palaeologus to Lithuania's Vytauta[...] who gained favour with the Byzanti[...] emperor when he brought Benedi[...] tine monks to the country. In 17[...] the picture was copied and either t[...] copy or the original, depending [...] which camp you follow, remained [...] Lithuania while the other came he[...] to Aglona the year that the chur[...] was founded. Money came fro[...] Ewa Justyna Szostowicka (Justī[...] Šostovicka), a local Polish aristocr[...] whose portrait hangs on the prese[...]

basilica's west wall. The church was built to accommodate Dominicans from Lithuania whom Szostowicka invited to teach, heal and convert.

This is the second church on the site. The first one, made of wood, burnt down in 1787 and a two-towered Italianate creation rose up around the original organ, which was saved. A monastery and cloister are attached to the church; Dominicans lived here for 150 years until the tsar forbade people from becoming involved in the church.

For a more secular sight, it's worth visiting the interactive and entertaining **Aglona Bread Museum** (Mon–Sat 9am–6pm) to learn more about the bread-making process and sample local produce, washed down with herbal teas, as well as the **World War II Exhibition**, which has a vast collection of weapons and other war memorabilia.

RĒZEKNE

Although modern and rather unprepossessing, **Rēzekne** 🟤, 60km (38 miles) north of Daugavpils, is a relaxed place and a good centre for exploration. Its population of 31,200 is about one-third that of Daugavpils, but Rēzekne is the capital of Latgale.

The **Regional Museum** (Latgales kultūrvēstures muzejs; June–Aug Wed–Sat 10am–6pm, Sun 11am–5pm, Sept–May Tue–Sat 10am–6pm) is just up from the trio of churches on the main street, and has a nostalgic look at the town as it used to be before it was largely destroyed in World War II. The statue in the middle of the road, *Latgales Māra*, which symbolises the liberation of Latgale from the Bolsheviks in 1920, was destroyed twice by the Soviets in 1940 and 1950, but was erected for the third time on this spot in 1992. Rēzekne is one of many ceramics centres in the region, and typical pottery makes an attractive souvenir

from shops and workshops in and around the town.

On a steep hill overlooking the city you'll find a lonely stone arch, practically all that remains of an ancient castle (Rēzeknes pilsdrupas).

Some 25km (15 miles) southeast of Rēzekne is **Ludza** 🟤, one of the most attractive towns in the country and home to one of the most picturesque **castle ruins** (Ludzas pilsdrupas). Perched upon a hill overlooking two lakes, a three-storey brick wall marks the place where the largest fortress in Latgale protected Teutonic crusaders since the 14th century. A museum has local ceramics and finds from the 10th century onwards.

From Ludza the road goes east to Russia at Zilupe. To the south is the fourth of Latgale's great Catholic churches, **Pasiene church** 🟤 (Pasienes katoļu baznīca). An echo of the church at Daugavpils, it's a twin-towered wedding cake built in 1761, 67 years after a Dominican mission was founded. From here there is a magnificent view across the plains of Russia.

A procession at Aglonas Basilica during the Feast of the Assumption.

ZEMGALE

Latvia's smallest region stretches from Rīga Bay south through fertile plains that have produced a number of glittering palaces, most notably Rastrelli's Rundāle.

The region of Zemgale was for a time linked with Courland, and from Lithuania in the south to Lake Engure, halfway along the west side of Rīga Bay, it borders the modern region of Kurzeme. Skirting Rīga, it then slips below the River Daugava and slides along the length of the Lithuanian border, tailing away to the far southeast. Apart from the northerly area around Tukums, most of Zemgale is characterised by a dead flat, fertile plain, part of the central lowlands that in places actually sink below sea level. This is the breadbasket of Latvia.

The main river is the Lielupe, which flows through the ancient towns of Bauska and Jelgava, Zemgale's capital, which the dukes of Courland and Semigallia made their home. There are a number of large 18th- and 19th-century estates in the region, but this was the frontline in World War I, and many were burnt by the retreating Russian Army. One exception is the palace at Rundāle, near Bauska, which has been magnificently restored and is now the finest in the Baltics. All of these places are within easy striking distance of Rīga.

WEST TO TUKUMS

The region of Tukums lies to the west of Rīga and Jūrmala, and is a stepping-stone into Kurzeme and the Baltic coast. Heading west from the capital,

the A10/E22 passes through scenes of World War I conflict, notably at Ložmetējkalns, site of the "Christmas battles", heroic attacks by the Latvian Riflemen on a strong German position in late 1916/early 1917.

Tukums ❸❹ is the first town of any size on this road. It has a castle mound and was originally a Liv settlement. It has a pleasant old centre, and a tradition of weaving, which is carried on in an artisan's workshop on Tidaholmas iela (www.tukumamuzejs.lv; Tue–Sat 10am–5pm; individual and group courses). In

> **Main attractions**
> Tukums
> Jaunmoku pils hunting lodge
> Engure Lake and Nature Reserve
> Jaunpils manorial castle
> Jelgava History and Art Museum
> Rundāle Palace
> Bauska Castle ruins

Map on page 188

Rundāle Palace's elaborate landscaping.

Harmonijas Street is the Tukums Art Museum (www.tukumamuzejs.lv; Tue–Fri 11am–5pm, Sat–Sun 11am–4pm) which has a collection of works by the most important 20th-century Latvian artists, including Rozentāls. The Lutheran church dates from 1670.

To the south of the town is the 17th-century **Durbe Castle** (Durbes pils; www.tukumamuzejs.lv; 20 Apr–20 Oct Tue–Sat 10am–5pm, Sun 11am–4pm, 21 Oct–19 Apr Tue–Fri 10am–5pm, Sat–Sun 11am–4pm), set in a park with a collection of textiles and agricultural implements. Another manor house, **Šlokenbeka Castle** (www.slokenbeka.lv), to the north of Tukums, is near **Milzkalne**, on the highest spot in the region with a view over Rīga Bay. It was built as an estate in the 15th century, and its buildings were erected in a square formation and surrounded by walls to serve as a fortress. It is the only example of this type of medieval architecture left in the Baltics. Now it's a hotel, there are guided tours, Degole cheese tasting and wine degustation on offer. An odd museum here is dedicated to

road-building in Latvia with exhibits of antique machinery (May–Oct Tue–Fri 9am–4pm, Sat–Sun 10am–5pm, Nov–Apr Mon–Fri 9am–4pm; free).

A few miles past Tukums on the Ventspils road is **Jaunmoku pils 35**, a renovated hunting lodge. It was built in 1901 by Wilhelm Bockslaff, who designed the Art Academy building in Rīga for George Armitstead, one-time mayor of the capital. Its most striking features are its ceramic stoves, built by the firm of Celms & Bēms, especially one imprinted with old postcards of Rīga from the city's 700th anniversary celebrations in 1901. On the first floor is the **Museum of Hunting and Forestry** (www.jaunmokupils.lv; daily 9am–5pm), which includes a collection of around 40 different animal horns from all over the world. The lodge, now a 3-star hotel, provides facilities for hunters' holidays in the area.

A short distance southwest is the town of Kukšu, with a prime example of a manor house: the **Kukšu Muiža**, now functioning as a hotel (www.kuksumuiza.lv) following a lengthy restoration.

Jaunmoku pils hunting lodge.

COASTAL COMMUNITIES

From **Lapmežciems** to **Bērzciems**, most of the communities on the coast have names ending with *-ciems*, meaning village. Their attractive farm buildings stand near the sea and lurk in the wood. The **Engure Lake and Nature Reserve** lies beyond the thatched church tower roof at the little port of Engure. This beautiful body of water stretches along the coastline separated from the sea only by a narrow strip of land. Some 50,000 birds visit this 18km (12-mile) -wide, shallow lake every year, and nearly 170 different species inhabit the reserve.

South of Tukums, on the road to Dobele, is **Jaunpils** ㊱, a village with a lakeside manorial castle (www.jaunpilspils.lv) and church dating back to the 16th century. This was the estate of one Baron Reke, whose coat of arms is hung over the church altar. Visitors can also spend the night at the castle and dine at the medieval tavern where all dishes are made in accordance with an 18th-century recipe book loosely translated as *How to Cook for Nobility*.

Dobele's chief claim to fame is a ruined castle of the Livonian Order.

JELGAVA, THE DUKES' TOWN

South of Rīga, the only town of any size is **Jelgava** ㊲. Though you would not know it to look at it, Jelgava is a historic town, formerly called Mitau, that once rivalled Rīga. The history of the town, and of the 11 dukes of Courland and Semigallia, who were friends of the Russian Romanovs and influential at court in St Petersburg, is laid out in the **History and Art Museum** (www.jvmm.lv; Tue–Sun May–Sept 11am–6pm, Oct–Apr 10am–5pm). This is housed in the Academia Petrina, built for Duke Peter von Biron in 1775 and once an important educational and scientific centre. Exhibits include gold and silver ducats minted here and a waxwork of Duke Jacob. The museum lies just behind the landmark tower of the ruined **Holy Trinity Church**. In recent years the tower, reconstructed with EU funds, has become a popular attraction with an exhibition hall and observation deck on the 9th floor, a restaurant on the 8th floor, ethnographic and

⊙ Tip

Accompanied by guides, ecotourists to Lake Engure can camp overnight, use the small boat marinas and ride on horseback through the reserve. Further information from the tourist information office in Tukums (www.visittukums.lv; tel: 6312 4451) or Talsi (www.talsitourism.lv; tel: 6322 4165).

Re-enacting the past at Jaunpils.

historical displays on the 5th, 4th and 3rd and a tourist information office on the 1st floor. Also in the old part of town is **St Ann's Church**, from 1619, which has an altar painting by Janis Rozentāls. On the same side of the river there is an interesting **Latvian Railway History Museum** (Latvijas Dzelzceļa Vēstures Muzejs; www.railwaymuseum.lv; Wed, Fri–Sat 10am–5pm, Thu 11am–7pm) housed in a former railwaymen's residential house. Besides exhibits of the personal belongings of former railway workers and other small objects they used in their job, the tour around the exhibition (approximately 40 minutes) also takes in a former depot and engines.

The wide, slow Lielupe, which slips north into Rīga Bay, has always carried river traffic. Past the bridge on the right is the Rastrelli-designed Jelgava Palace (May–Aug Mon–Fri 9am–5pm, Sat 9am–6pm, Sun 11am–4pm, Sept–Apr Mon–Fri 9am–5pm; palace currently undergoing renovations until 2020), a large and solid Italianate building on the site of the town's original castle (1265). Since 1957 this three-storey,

Interior decorations at Mezotne Palace.

brick-red and cream building set around a square has housed an agricultural college. It is an impersonal resting place for the dukes of Courland and Semigallia, but their tombs, restored in recent years, are worth a look.

Frederick-Wilhelm, the penultimate of the Kettler dynasty of dukes, altered the family's fortunes when he married Ivan V's daughter Anna Ivanova, in St Petersburg in 1710. The 17-year-old newlyweds had just started back to the young duke's palace in Jelgava when he became ill and died. Reluctantly, Anna was obliged to continue her life in Jelgava. Bored and confined in what to her must have seemed something of a backwater of wooden homes and flat farmlands, she began an affair with Ernst Johann Biron, an ambitious Courlander on the palace staff. In 1727 Anna became Empress Anna of Russia, peopling her court with German Balts and making Biron a count.

RUNDĀLE PALACE

Within nine years of Biron becoming a count, he was wealthy enough to employ Bartolomeo Rastrelli (1700–71), the architect who later built St Petersburg's Hermitage or Winter Palace, to design a manor for himself at Rundāle, to the south of Jelgava, which he at first called Ruhental, meaning Peaceful Valley in German.

Rundāle Palace ㊳ (http://rundale.net daily May–Oct 10am–6pm, Nov–Apr 10am–5pm; Garden May and Oct daily 10am–6pm, June–Sept daily 10am–7pm, June–Aug Fri–Sun until 9pm; guided tours available in English) is an imposing, well-restored palace of 13 rooms, approached through a grand drive flanked by twin semicircular stables. At the height of its construction between 1736 and 1768 it employed 1,500 labourers and artisans. Work on the building and grounds, some of which have still to be restored, was interrupted first in 1738, after Biron had achieved his ambition of becoming

uke of Courland and diverted Ras-
elli into turning Jelgava Castle into
elgava Palace. The second interrup-
on was more serious when, after
ecoming regent of Russia for a year
llowing the empress's death, Biron
as banished to Siberia for 23 years.

In the 19th century it was used by the
arist governors, and the new govern-
nent took it over in 1920, restoring its
ar damage. Its stairways, galleries,
ndings, rooms and halls are gracious
nd well decorated. The wall paintings
re by the Italians Francesco Martini
nd Carlo Zucchi and the exquisite
ecorative moulding is by Michael Graff
om Berlin. His oval Porcelain Study
particularly striking. On the ground
oor there is a collection of period fur-
iture and ornaments.

The finest rooms are upstairs, where
ome interesting Dutch, Flemish and
panish paintings from the 17th and
8th centuries are hung. The dukes'
hrone stood in the Gold Hall, which is
natched in magnificence by the White
lall or ballroom, where the intricate
tucco work includes a delicate heron's

nest on the ceiling. The gardens: Rose,
French and Dutch Bosquet, still under
reconstruction, are also impressive.

MEŽOTNE MANOR

Rundāle was the apogee of the fusion
of German and Russian society which
came together and flourished in the
region in the 18th and 19th centuries.
A number of important manors were
built in this accessible area. The one
at **Mežotne**, on the River Lielupe a
few kilometres northeast of Rundāle,
which was given by Tsar Paul I to his
children's governess, Charlotte von
Lieven, in 1797, has been restored and
is now an elegant hotel and conference centre (www.mezotnespils.lv). One
of the grandest houses otherwise was
at **Eleja**, due south of Jelgava on the
main road to Vilnius, but it is now just
a forlorn ruin; only a tea house and a
former cemetery has survived.

TĒRVETE WRITER'S MUSEUM

The flatlands of Zemgale were originally inhabited by the Semigallians,
who in the 13th century produced one

*Rundāle Palace and its
restored grand facade.*

of the greatest Latvian leaders, Viesturs. The centre of his domains was to the west of Rundāle in **Tērvete**, but the tribe was pushed south by the German crusaders who built a castle on the site of their stronghold, some of which still remains. Nearby is the **Meža Ainavu Park**, which has a museum called **Sprīdīši** (www.spridisi.lv; May–Oct Wed–Sun 10am–5pm), dedicated to one of Latvia's most respected writers, Anna Brigadere, who lived here from 1922 to 1933. Beside the museum is a guest house. Her most famous creation was Sprīdītis, an impish character who overcomes great obstacles to gain the heart of the woman he loves. The park has a vast selection of foreign and domestic trees, wooden sculptures of characters from many of Brigadere's literary works and castle ruins. A number of walking trails begin in the town.

BAUSKA

To the east of Rundāle is **Bauska**. On arrival there is a car park just beyond the bridge over the River Mūsa. The river shortly converges with the Mēmele, helping to form half a moa for the Livonian Order's castle(http: bauskaspils.lv; May–Sept daily 9am–7pm, Oct daily 9am–6pm, Nov–Ap Tue–Sun 11am–5pm; guided tours i English, including Dressing Cultur in the Duchy of Courland), which wa not rebuilt after its destruction in th Great Northern War. The huge rec brick ruins at the confluence of th two rivers are among Latvia's larç est and most picturesque. Climb th tower for a good view from the to (closed for renovation at the tim of writing) or explore the renovate duke's residence.

The castle hosts an array of musi and arts festivals, some with a med eval theme. There is a small museun in the castle, and another in the tow where there is also a synagogue. Bee aficionados can tour the local brewer Bauskas Alus (www.bauskasalus.lv).

From Bauska the road leads direct north back to Rīga, past **Iecava**, whic is best known for its large egg factor fine Lutheran church from 1641 an neighbouring cemetery.

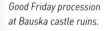

Good Friday procession at Bauska castle ruins.

A view of the countryside from Bauska Castle Ruins.

Turaida castle.

VIDZEME

The River Gauja runs through the rural heartlands of eastern Latvia to make Gauja National Park the country's great outdoor leisure area, centred on Sigulda and Cēsis, while quiet villages harbour the country's folkloric and literary heritage.

Lying to the east of Rīga, Vidzeme is the largest of the country's four regions. In the north it stretches from the Bay of Rīga all along the Estonian border, and in the south it lies beside the right bank of the Daugava from the capital to the eastern region of Latgale. Beside the river's banks, there are castles and remains of ancient settlements, pointers to a powerful past.

At the heart of the region is another river route which, though less exalted, is just as ancient and rather more beguiling. This is the River Gauja, which runs through a deep gorge at the centre of the **Gauja National Park** (Gaujas nacionālais parks; www.enter-gauja.com). It is Latvia's showcase rural attraction, rich in wildlife, full of prehistoric hill forts and containing one of the most important archaeological sites. They call it "Little Switzerland", and have installed a bobsleigh run, but "little" is the key word. The Baltics' second-highest point is in Vidzeme: it just 312 metres (1,025ft).

GAUJA NATIONAL PARK

Gauja National Park begins at **Sigulda** ③, 50km (30 miles) northeast of Rīga, and is an easy day trip from the capital by the A2 or by public transport. From Sigulda the park extends north through Cēsis to Valmiera. Sigulda and Cēsis are the main centres for

information about activities and excursions such as walking, biking and boating, particularly canoeing on the River Gauja, which is a popular way to appreciate the park.

The park covers around 900 sq km (350 sq miles) along more than 100km (60 miles) of river, and is divided into sections with varying degrees of access. All boating activity is popular on the river, and organised parties embark in inflatables for overnight camps, taking three days to travel from Valmiera to Sigulda. Logging on the

⊙ Main attractions
Gauja National Park
Sigulda
Ungurmuiža wall paintings
Cēsis
Āraiši archaeological site
Alūksne
Lake Alauksta

📍 Map on page 188

Cēsis.

river ended when the area was designated a national park in 1973.

There is something rather sedate about Sigulda. It is a pristine and airy little town which hides its affluent past beneath a film of cleanliness. It became popular during the National Awakening as a place where Latvians from Rīga could discover their rural roots. It has more recently become a winter sports centre, with a bobsleigh run and ski slopes on the far side of the railway crossing.

Sigulda Castle (Siguldas pilsdrupas) is through the town on the left. Deeply moated and once incorporating a convent, it was built by the Crusaders' Order of Sword Bearers, who came here as soon as they arrived in Latvia in 1207. They used large boulders and stuck them together with mortar mixed with eggs and honey. Today, it is a crumbled ruin with an open-air concert hall in its midst. Since 2012 it has been possible to ascend the North and Main Gate Towers (May–Sept daily 9am–8pm, Oct Mon–Fri 9am–5pm, Sat–Sun 9am–7pm, Nov–Apr daily 10am–5pm). The attractive

country house beside it is the mode "castle" (Siguldas pils), built in 1878. now houses the district council. Arti and writers of the Awakening used come for inspiration, and Rozentāls a other painters used to like hiking up Gleznotāju kalns, Painters' Hill, just the east, which has one of the best vie over the Gauja (walk from the car park the far side of the old castle). Kronval Atis (1837–75), a prominent Young La vian and teacher, is remembered by statue outside the new castle; some the stained glass produced during h lifetime is still in situ in what is now sanatorium. Located in a former brewe of Sigulda manor, there is a sand art ga lery by local Artist Elmārs Gaigalnieks

LĪGATNE NATURE TRAILS

One of the best places to see wildl and natural scenery, with possibiliti of sighting at least a deer, is just nor of Sigulda in **Līgatne**. There are al some rare plants here, such as Lady Slipper orchids, Linnaea borealis a woodland tulips, and in spring it is ca peted with lily-of-the-valley. Turn l

New Sigulda Castle.

Līgatne through **Augšlīgatne** on the gulda to Cēsis main road, turning left again just before the river, where there re two parking spots and day tickets the parks can be bought (www.enteruja.com; Mon–Fri 9am–6pm, Sat–Sun am–7pm). Nature trails are mapped ut, and a ferry takes cars over the ver. From Sigulda there are two ways cross the Gauja. The road goes over a ridge, and every 30 minutes a cable ar swings alongside it, 40 metres 35ft) above the river, taking 4 minutes cover the 1km (0.6-mile) distance. n the far side, the road falls away to e right to reach the side of the river, here day tickets to the park can be ought in the car park. At the Rehalitation Centre Ligatne and Skalupes, ere is a unique opportunity to see a ell-equipped, **Soviet underground uclear bunker** (www.bunkurs.lv; guided urs Sat and Sun at noon and 2pm), hich was kept secret until 2003.

ŪTMANIS' CAVE

ne banks of the Gauja are characterised by red sandstone cliffs and caves, the deepest of which is **Gūtmanis' Cave** ⓴ (Gūtmaņa ala; www.entergauja. com; visitors centre daily May–Sept 9am–7pm, Oct–Apr 9am–6pm), found opposite the car park. Scratched by graffiti more than 300 years old, the cave is 19 metres (62ft) deep and the fresh spring water that wore it away still bubbles into it, tasting strongly of iron. The cave is named after a healer called Gūtmanis who first used the water as a cure.

Some 10 minutes' walk further up the road is **Turaida Castle** (Turaidas pils; www.turaida-muzejs.lv; daily, May–Sept 9am–8pm, Oct 9am–7pm, Nov–Mar 10am–5pm, Apr 10am–7pm, open-air exhibitions, the Main Tower and tower-shaped South Block 9–10am and 6–7/8pm, general and themed guided tours in English available by prior request), a fort of red bricks and a single round tower, which breaks up through the forest heights. This is all that remained after lightning ignited the castle's gunpowder store in the 17th century.

In the language of the ancient Livs who first settled this valley, Turaida

A monument to Kaupo.

⊘ KAUPO AND THE CHRISTIANS

The church at Krimulda, a 20km (12-mile) drive north from Sigulda, was erected in 1205 and is the oldest working house of worship in Latvia. At the time, a Liv tribe ruled by a chieftain named Kaupo populated the area. Unlike many of his contemporaries, Kaupo decided to embrace the new Christian faith brought by the German crusaders and even travelled to Rome, where he met Pope Innocent III. The Pope recognised him as the Christian ruler of the Livs and sent him back to Turaida with 100 pieces of gold, with which he began construction of the church.

Although the Livs weren't happy with the new arrangement, Kaupo remained loyal to his new religion and the crusaders until his death in 1217 at the Battle of Viljandi in present-day Estonia. He is said to be buried either somewhere within the church or in a nearby wood where a memorial has now been erected in his honour.

It will never be known whether or not Kaupo was a true believer or just a shrewd ruler who wanted a strong ally against neighbouring Latvian and Estonian tribes. Today you can visit the beautiful little church any time of the day or night, explore nearby nature trails and caves, or take a look at the 18th-century wooden Minister's House on the opposite bank of the stream.

means "the Garden of the Gods". Inside the castle there is a gallery and a small museum charting its history. On the path to the castle are a wooden Lutheran church (1750), the oldest in Vidzeme, and a few yards away, beneath a large linden tree, a black marble slab marks the grave of Maija, the Turaida Rose (Turaidas Roze), a young woman murdered in 1620.

DETOUR TO BĪRIŅI

From Turaida the road continues to **Inciems**, where it meets up with the road to Valmiera. Time allowing, a pleasant detour on the P9 to **Bīriņi** is also recommended. The 19th-century neo-Gothic manor house at Bīriņi (Bīriņu pils; www.birinupils.lv), a hotel today, is surrounded by a beautiful park with a lake and a charming tavern – a perfect place for lunch.

Back on the A3, the next small town along this road is **Straupe**, where there is something familiar about the old castle (Lielstraupes pils), dating from 1263. The square tower, which rises in a dark dome and lantern, and the scrolled and

stepped gable of the building below are reminiscent of the cathedral Rīga. The castle is in a pleasant setting beside a large pond near the River Bra sla, and today it is used as a clinic fo rehabilitating substance abusers.

In the grounds are a bell-tower and Lutheran church that has some interes ing 17th-century painted panels. Tom stones and tablets mark the passing of generations of the von Rosen fami owners of the castle and fierce prote tors of the German Baltic way of life. Th present generation is scattered, thoug some have helped in its restoration. has an organ made in Rīga in 1856 by th firm of Martin, and the acoustics make a good recital venue.

Another German monument nearby at **Ungurmuiža** ⑪ (www.ung muiza.lv; Tue–Sat 10am–6pm, Su 10am–4pm, restaurant Tue–Su noon–10pm; guided tours), on th way to Cēsis. This belonged to the vc Campenhausens who had it built 1751, now it houses a hotel and a res taurant. It is the only existing woode Baroque building of this period left

Latvian girls in traditional dress in front of the castle at Cesis.

atvia, and although it has been pil-
ged many times over the years, its
ntastic 18th-century wall paintings on
e second floor have been restored to
eir former glory. A park surrounds
e building and many ancient trees
n be seen here.

ĒSIS

urrounded by nature trails, **Cēsis** ⓰
a major centre of leisure activities in
oth summer and winter. A pleasant,
ide-open town, it was a popular cul-
ral centre during both the National
wakening and first independence.
s attractive yellow-and-white, two-
nd three-storey buildings date back
everal centuries, and a Lutheran
urch, **St John's** (Sv Jāņa baznīca),
as started in 1281. There are several
otels and good places to eat, but don't
ave without tasting the local Cēsu
eer from northern Europe's oldest
rewery (Cēsu alus darītava), which
as been in operation since 1590. Once
roduced in the castle, brewing opera-
ons have moved a few streets away to
ldaru laukums or Beer Square.

Cēsis was a walled town and a mem-
er of the Hanseatic League, and its
story is well documented in the **Cēsis
useum of History and Art** (Cēsu
estures un mākslas muzejs; http://cesu
s.lv; May–Sept castle daily 10am–6pm,
useum Tue–Sun 10am–6pm, Oct–Apr
astle and museum Tue–Sat 10am–
om, Sun 10am–4pm), which occu-
es the Medieval Castle, Cēsis Manor,
e New Castle and Coach House. The
astle is a chalky-white fortified con-
ent that served as a power base for
e Livonian Order. In the castle you
an learn more about ancient Latvian
wellery at the smithy, enjoy a special
orkshop of experimental archaeol-
gy run by the Master of Applied Arts,
aumants Kalniņš, and visit a medieval
ctivity centre (Fri–Sun). The beauti-
l castle park is a favourite place for
stroll. Look out for a couple of black
vans who live at the pond.

Cēsis also has the distinction of
being the birthplace of the Latvian
flag. At the end of the 13th century, an
ancient chieftain was killed in battle
and was laid out on a white sheet. His
blood stained the sides, leaving a white
stripe in the middle.

ĀRAIŠI ARCHAEOLOGICAL FINDS

The locality was inhabited by Baltic
Finns until the Letgallians moved in
around the 6th century, and it has provided much archaeological information.
But the most impressive digs have been
in **Āraiši**, 7km (4 miles) to the south of
the city. It was here that the Letgallians
built a large lakeside fortress in the 9th
century, and its excavation has been one
of the most important finds of this kind
in northern Europe. Burial barrows have
been uncovered as well as graves, and
today you can visit the reconstructed
fortified town of tiny wooden buildings
on the lake (Āraišu ezerpils; http://amata.
lv/archeological-museum-park-araishi; Apr–
Oct daily 9am–7pm, Nov–Mar Thu–Sun
9am–4pm).

ⓞ Fact

Several cities in Vidzeme
were once part of the
prestigious Hanseatic
League, Europe's first
organised international
trade organisation,
including Cēsis, Koknese,
Limbaži, Sigulda,
Straupe, Valmiera and, of
course, Rīga.

*Strolling Cesis's
streets.*

○ Tip

Teiči Bog in the Teiči Nature Reserve, 25km (15 miles) north of Madona, is the largest moss bog in Latvia, with a range of wildlife from golden eagles to brown bears. To book a three-hour excursion (June–Oct), contact mobile: 371 291 39677; www.madona.lv.

Beyond Cēsis, reached by a popular cycle path, is **Valmiera** ⓯ which also has an ancient castle and church and was once a member of the Hanseatic League. An observation tower gives a good view of the valley. North of the town up towards **Strenči** is one of the most picturesque stretches of the River Gauja. To the northwest is **Mazsalaca**, an attractive, out-of-the-way town on the River Salaca.

COASTAL ROUTE

The Gauja was strategically important as the main route to Tallinn and St Petersburg. Today, the most pleasant way to drive to Tallinn is up the scenic coast, around the eastern edge of Rīga Bay, which allows views of the Baltic Sea through the pines. Unlike the rest of Latvia's coast, its sandy beaches are scattered with boulders and stones. From Rīga the A1/E67 goes past summer villas north to the resort town of **Saulkrasti** ⓮ or "sunny shores", beyond which lie small communities, such as Dunte where the infamous, tall tale-teller Baron von Münchhausen (1720–97) lived from

1743 to 1750. Although the roadsid tavern and museum where he onc drank burnt down, it was rebuilt (www minhauzens.lv; May–Oct Mon–Thu 10am 5pm, Fri–Sun 10am–6pm, Nov–Ap Wed–Sun 10am–5pm), and the charm ing **Liepupe Church** (Liepupes baznīca where he married is open to the publi

Salacgrīva ⓯ provides a conveni ent stopping point, and between her and Ainaži, the coast takes on a di ferent aspect as meadows push ou into the sea. Ainaži is right up by th border, and was put on the map as th port where Krišjānis Valdemārs chos to base Latvia's Maritime Academy i 1864. Ainaži flourished for a while a a port and shipbuilding centre, bu now it has returned to being a back water, with a small museum chartin its moment of seafaring glory (Ainaž jūrskolas muzejs; www.ainazumuzejs.l May–Sept Wed–Sun 10am–5pm, Oct Apr Tue–Sat 11am–5pm).

ALONG THE DAUGAVA

To the southeast of Rīga the A6/E2 follows the north bank of the Daugav

Gulbene rail station.

aving Rīga through the Moscow dis-
ict with its Old Believers and tradi-
onal Russian community. Just beyond
is **Rumbula** ㊻, where the big week-
nd market draws people from miles
ound; mostly a car mart, its reputa-
on is a touch below spotless and tour-
ts are not encouraged to browse.

The road continues towards the big
xtile town of Ogre, past **Ikšķile** ㊼,
hich in the Liv language was called
xküll. The first settlement is on an
land on the Daugava, accessible to
e passing traveller only by boat in
e summer and on foot in the winter
hen the river is frozen over. It bears
e remains of the oldest stone church
Latvia (Ikšķiles baznīcas drupas),
uilt in 1186.

At **Ķegums** ㊽ the country's first
ydroelectric scheme, built between
e World Wars, has pushed back the
ver's banks and created a long lake.
he change of landscape is a source of
egret to the historians and traditional-
ts who converge at its centre, around
ielvārde ㊾. Staburags, a natural
onder mentioned in the *Lāčplēsis* epic

and a source of national pride, is now
submerged in the River Daugava.

Lielvārde is the home of this Latvian
legend, recorded in a 19th-century epic
written by Andrējs Pumpurs (see page
62). Its protagonist and namesake,
Lāčplēsis, was brought up by a bear
until found by Lielvārdis, who adopted
the young boy. On one occasion he
saved his father from a rogue bear by
tearing it apart with his bare hands,
giving him the name "bear-slayer". He
was last seen in a fatal struggle with
the Black Knight, symbolic of the Teutonic crusaders, but he will return, it is
said, to throw the enemy into the sea
and make the land free again.

As you approach Lielvārde you'll
notice a reconstructed wooden fortress (Uldevena pils; Apr–Oct Thu–Sun
10am–6pm) on the right side of the
road. Inside you can see how ancient
Latvian tribes once lived, and it's also a
great place for a picnic by the river. Just
outside the city centre you can visit the
Andrējs Pumpurs Museum (Andrēja
Pumpura muzejs; Tue–Sat 10am–5pm,
Sun 10am–3pm), where the writer

Cottage for rent, Cēsis.

once lived. There is an old church and the ruins of a 13th-century castle in the same park overlooking the river.

Before the A6/E22 meanders into the Latgale region, it is worth noting the 13th-century crusader castle at **Koknese** ⑩, which was once perched high on a hill above the river, but is now at the water's edge. Following the river downstream past a white Lutheran church set on a wide sweep in the river, the road comes to the ruins of the two-storey castle (Kokneses pilsdrupas) where the Pērse meets the Daugava.

MADONA TO ALŪKSNE

Madona ⑪ to the north is the next town of any size, a quiet spot with a renovated inn from the 16th-century Swedish days. Just north of Madona is **Cesvaine** ⑫. Its impressive late 19th-century "castle" (Cesvaines pils), a mix of neo-Gothic with an Art Nouveau interior, was the hunting lodge of Baron Adolf von Wolf, who had no fewer than 99 estates in the Baltics. The castle was badly damaged in a fire in 2002 but has since been restored to its former glory

and now houses a museum (May–O daily 10am–6pm, winter until 4pm) a tourist information centre.

West of Madona is Gaiziņkaln the highest hill in Latvia, 312 metr (1,025ft). You can climb up to its sur mit for a 360-degree view of the lake pastureland and acres of deep gre forest, not to mention an ugly new pr vately owned recreation area.

North of Cesvaine is **Gulbene** ⑬ where a manor house with a fine po tico lies in ruins: bullet holes still pe per its facade. In 1944 the Germa blew up the church tower before the advancing Russians to deprive the of a viewing platform: it fell on the church, destroying the roof. Beside it the only statue of Martin Luther in the Baltics. In two buildings of the man there is a small museum.

From Gulbene a narrow-gau railway (www.banitis.lv) runs up to the attractive town of **Alūksne** ⑭, whi is centred on a ruined 14th-centu Livonian castle (Livonijas ordeņa pi on a lake. It sits on an island reach across a small wooden bridge and

Cesvaine Palace was built in 1896 for the German baron Emil von Wulf in the late Tudor Neo-Renaissance style.

devoted today to sports activities. A granite rotunda was built on top of the site of an ancient Letgallian fort on the southwestern shore of the lake by the Vietinghoff family to honour the dead of the Great Northern War.

One of the town's main claims to fame is that its pastor Ernst Glück adopted Martha Skavronska, the daughter of a Lithuanian grave-digger. She went on to marry Peter the Great and become Catherine I of Russia.

Glück also produced the first Latvian translation of the Bible, in 1689, and a copy of it, one of only a dozen left in the world, is kept along with many others in the **Bible Museum** (Ernsta Glika Bībeles muzejs; Pils 25a; http://visitaluksne.lv; Mon–Fri 9am–5pm, Sat 10am–5pm, Sun 10am–1pm). The earliest Latvian religious tract, God's Word, dates from 1654, and a copy is also in the museum. When Glück first arrived in Alūksne, he lived in the castle, but he later moved to a single-storey wooden manse behind the Lutheran church, and his plantation of oaks is still standing.

LITERARY TRAIL

Between these eastern towns and the Gauja National Park, a number of Latvian literary figures, who play such an important part in the country's nationhood, are remembered in a pastoral setting that can have changed little since they knew it more than 100 years ago. Beneath shady trees are several wooden barns, cottage gardens full of flowers and small platforms for the delivery vehicles to collect and return the milk churns.

Beside **Lake Alauksta** ⑤ is the **Skalbe Museum** (Kārļa Skalbes memoriālais muzejs "Saulrieti"; mid-May–mid-Oct Wed–Sun 10am–5pm), which contains local painted furniture. Kārlis Skalbe (1879–1945), a writer of fairy tales, died in Sweden where he had fled the Soviet invasion. His remains were returned in 1992 and

buried beneath a stone overlooking the lake.

The museum (Brāļu Kaudzīšu memoriālais muzejs "Kalna Kaibēni"; mid-May–mid-Oct Wed–Sun 10am–5pm) at the nearby village of **Vecpiebalga** ㊹ celebrates the Kaudzīte brothers, Reinis and Matīss, who jointly wrote Latvia's first major novel, *The Time of the Land Surveyors* (1879). Much of the house, Kalna Kaibēni, was designed by the brothers, and the lathe used by Rainis is one of the earliest surviving in the country. A granary and sauna are part of the well-preserved home. Not far away is a museum dedicated to the composer Emīls Dārziņš, with an exhibition of writers and composers who have emigrated (Emīla Dārziņa muzejs "Jāņaskola"; mid-May–mid-Oct Wed–Sun 10am–5pm).

At **Ērgļi** ㊲ there is a museum (Rūdolfa Blaumaņa memoriālais muzejs "Braki"; www.braki.lv; 10 May–Oct Tue–Sun 10am–5pm) where the playwright Rūdolfs Blaumanis was born. **Indrāni**, nearby, is the setting of one of his most famous plays.

Alūksne's castle ruin.

Farmer in rural Lithuania.

Trakai, the island castle
stronghold of the dukes of the
Grand Duchy.

A Lithuanian beekeeper.

LITHUANIA

The southernmost Baltic state, bordering Poland, Belarus and the Russian exclave of Kaliningrad, has a Baroque capital and a fabulous sandy coast.

he Lithuanian coast has o shortage of long sandy eaches.

The people of Lithuania are predominantly Catholic, a fact that's impossible to miss. Vilnius, the capital, owes its Baroque flavour to the Jesuits who built its university as well as its many splendid churches. Outside the capital, the astonishing Hill of Crosses, just north of Šiauliai, is the biggest testament to the country's faith.

These shrines are an extension of a pagan tradition of wood-carving, seen everywhere, from the Witches' Hill on the Curonian Spit to the monuments commemorating the victims of the crimes committed during the Soviet occupation. Sometimes the recent tragic past doesn't seem so far away. Some will always think of Vilnius as the Jerusalem of Lithuania, a once-vibrant Jewish community and centre of Yiddish publishing wiped out during the Holocaust.

In spite of their Catholicism, the ethnic Lithuanians were the last people in Europe to convert to Christianity. At the height of its history the Grand Duchy of Lithuania famously stretched from the Baltic to the Black Sea. Such grandeur can be glimpsed at the dukes' castle at Trakai.

Vilnius today is a lively capital with nightlife to rival many cities in the West. The country's second city, Kaunas, is where you'll find some of the best museums, including one devoted to Lithuania's towering artistic figure, Mikalojus Konstantinas Čiurlionis.

Colourful wooden houses.

The River Neris, which connects Vilnius with Kaunas, runs down to a lagoon where it is separated from the Baltic Sea by the Curonian Spit. This exceptional sandbar of small fishing villages stretches south into the old region of Königsberg, now the Russian exclave of Kaliningrad. Further north, Klaipėda, Lithuania's third city, is the centre of coastal activities and as different to its two bigger relations as can be.

Add to this a rural landscape that's barely changed in the last century and the result is one of the most endearing and mystifying countries in Europe.

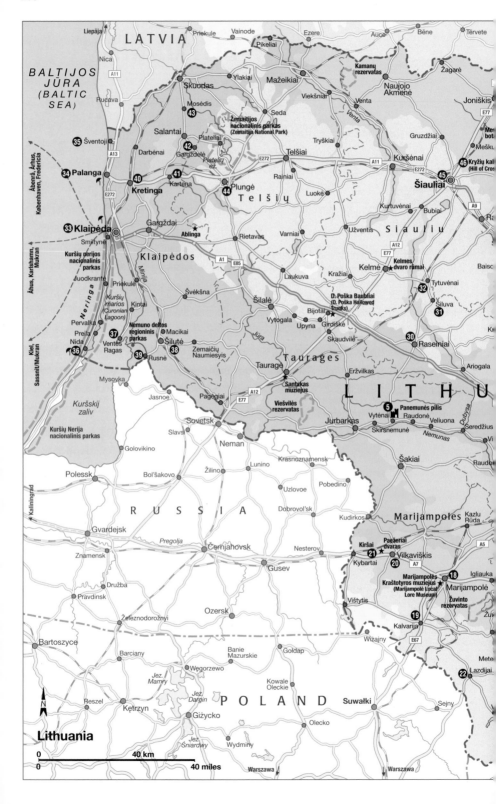

Lithuania

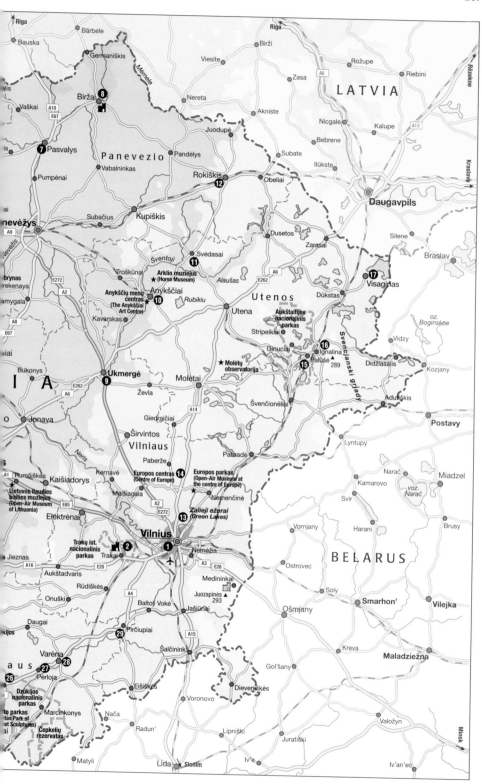

Logging on the River Nemunas
in the mid-20th century.

THE MAKING OF LITHUANIA

One of Europe's most devout Catholic countries, Lithuania did not at first take willingly to the baptismal font, nor to the succession of foreign powers that left their mark on this proud nation before it finally won independence.

The story of modern Lithuania could easily begin in 1385 with the unhappy tale of the 11-year-old Princess Jadwiga of Poland (c. 1373–99), who was due to marry young Wilhelm von Habsburg. The wedding was to take place in Kraków, then capital of Poland. The festivities were in full swing when, unexpectedly, a delegation of Lithuanian nobles arrived and went into urgent conference with their Polish counterparts. The outcome was that the archbishop headed for the castle with unsettling news for little Jadwiga. The wedding was called off and she was going to marry another man instead.

For the Polish nobility, if not for Jadwiga, the proposal just put forward by the Lithuanian delegation made more sense than her marrying a Habsburg. A conjugal union between Poland and Lithuania would create a force capable of seeing off the Teutonic Knights who were grabbing ever more of the Baltic lands. Jadwiga must have seen things differently; at least the Habsburgs were Christians. The Lithuanian Grand Prince she was now supposed to marry was a pagan. The Lithuanians had resisted every attempt to convert them to Christianity. Moreover, Prince Jogaila was three times her age and it was known that he had already murdered a number of close relatives. Jadwiga watched helplessly as the castellan of Kraków entered the castle, seized the downcast von Habsburg and banished him from the kingdom.

Mindaugas, King of Lithuania.

For his part, Jogaila had no more love for the Poles than he did for their religion. The Lithuanians were proud to be pagans. Jogaila had distinguished antecedents including Mindaugas, the first to unite the peoples of Lithuania in 1230. In 1251 Mindaugas was baptised into Christianity and on 6 July 1253 he was crowned King of Lithuania. Both Christianity and the idea of the king didn't really take; Mindaugas was the only crowned King of Lithuania and, though baptised, his adherence to Christianity was minimal at best. Most of the country remained pagan.

FOUNDER OF VILNIUS

The next strong leader to emerge was Gediminas (1316–41), the founder of the Gediminaičiai,

> *Eagle-eyed visitors to Lithuania will soon spot its rich ethnic history. Look around and you'll see bricks, drain covers and the like illustrated in a beguiling array of former rulers' languages.*

or as it was later called the Jogailaičiai (Jagiellonian) dynasty that ruled Lithuania and Poland for the next 250 years. He founded Vilnius, where he built his hilltop castle overlooking the Neris and Vilnel (or Vilnia) Rivers. Though he remained pagan he brought in Dominican and Franciscan teachers and he also encouraged the immigration of artists and craftsmen. By the time he died, Gediminas had so successfully fought against the Tatars of the east that the Lithuanian Empire reached down to the Black Sea. In the west, the coast around Klaipėda

> The Order of the Lithuanian Grand Duke Gediminas, reinstituted after independence, has been awarded to Olympic boss Antonio Samaranch, philanthropist George Soros and musician Mstislav Rostropovich.

called him Władysław Jagiełło), and three days later he married an unhappy Jadwiga. The following month they assumed the crowns of both Poland and Lithuania. The marriage, alas, did not have a fairy-tale ending. Jadwiga hated her husband from beginning to end and sought consolation in burying herself in good works for the poor. She died leaving her fortune to the educational establishment in Kraków, which later became the Jagiellonian University.

King Ladislaus II – Jogaila's full title – fulfilled one of his contractual obligations by going straight to Vilnius and smashing Perkūnas' statue. What followed was the usual fusion of old pagan beliefs and newfangled Christianity. Perkūnas' mother was transformed into the Lithuanian Madonna. A bishop was appointed, and mass baptisms were organised at which converts were presented with a white smock and given a Christian name.

LAST OF THE GREAT RULERS

The new king's previous position as Grand Prince of Lithuania per se was given to his cousin Vytautas (Witold, c.1350–1430), another grandson of Gediminas, who was the last of the great Lithuanian rulers. He built the impressive red-brick island castle at Trakai after the nearby castle of his father, Kęstutis, had been attacked once too often by the German crusaders. He drove back the Turks and mustered a bodyguard of Turkic Karaites whose descendants live by the castle today. In 1410 he and Jogaila decisively defeated the German crusaders at Grunwald/Tannenberg (Žalgiris), and under Vytautas' rule the Grand Duchy became one of the largest states in Europe, occupying Belarus and Ukraine. Even with shared privileges, the rivalry between the Polish and Lithuanian nobilities see-sawed for many years. The union was considerably strengthened by Jogaila's son Casimir (by a later wife), who held the position of both

Equestrian statue of the Grand Duke Gediminas, Vilnius.

(Memel in German) had been seized by knights of the Livonian Order in 1225. Before the orders merged, however, they also had to fight the Teutonic Knights of the southern lands that became Prussia, as well as Lithuania's dukes.

Poland was very much Rome's champion, and the marriage of Jadwiga and Jogaila was not agreed without conditions. First Jogaila would have to become a Christian. Second, he would have to convert his empire to Christianity. The terms of the marriage also required Lithuania to make some territorial concessions to Poland and release all Polish prisoners and slaves.

On 15 February 1386, Jogaila bowed his head for a splash of baptismal water, assumed the Christian name Ladislaus (the Poles afterwards

King of Poland and Grand Duke of Lithuania. The union was solidified by two sets of "Lithuanian Statutes" and finally written down in constitutional form agreed in 1569 at the Union of Lublin. The two countries were to share a king and a two-tiered government, but Lithuania kept a separate administration and its name.

Although Lithuania was territorially the larger of the two partners, Poland exerted the greater cultural influence. The Lithuanian nobility were Polonised and spoke Latin at court and Polish at other times. For the other social strata, the

were beaten for leaving the estate without permission, for brawls and misdemeanours, and for non-observance of religious practices. A dungeon, together with chains, shackles, stocks, hooks and instruments of torture, were part of the regular inventory."

SHARED HISTORY WITH POLAND

The history of Lithuania right up to the partition of the union by Prussia, Russia and Austria at the end of the 18th century is therefore tied to Poland's. Lithuania's separate identity had

Portrait of John II Casimir Vasa (1609-1672), King of Poland and Grand Duke of Lithuania.

effects of the union were more painfully felt. The Polish social order was rigorously imposed throughout the joint empire. Unlike the nobility, the Lithuanian bourgeoisie did not assume the status of their Polish counterparts. They were summarily demoted, disenfranchised and lost the right to own land.

The Lithuanian peasant had even more reason to rue the Polish takeover. "Common cruelty was an established feature of social life," argues the historian Norman Davies. "Faced with the congenital idleness, drunkenness and pilfering of the peasantry, the nobleman frequently replied with ferocious impositions and punishments. The lash and the knout were the accepted symbols of noble authority. The serfs

⊘ PAVLOVO RESPUBLIKA

A bizarre testament to the country's historical reputation as a land of tolerance, the Pavlovo Respublika was a fully independent "state" of several farmsteads, existing from 1769 until 1795. The brainchild of the Polish priest Paweł Brzostowski (1739–1827), the republic had its own president, printed its own money, had its own flag and was recognised by the last Polish-Lithuanian parliament before the country was absorbed into the Russian Empire. The ruins of the 18th-century building that served as the republic's headquarters can be visited by those with a taste for the quirky past. Find it on route 3937, 30km (19 miles) southeast of Vilnius.

grown progressively weaker, and the partitions made matters worse. Little Lithuania or Lithuania Minor, which included Königsberg (modern-day Kaliningrad) and the coast, was given to Prussia; Russia took the rest. Tsar Alexander I toyed with the idea of reconstituting the Grand Duchy – with himself as Grand Duke – but was prevented from pursuing his idea by Napoleon's invasion. Welcomed as a liberator, Bonaparte was given the keys of Vilnius on his march with his 500,000-strong Grande Armée towards his 1812 defeat in Moscow.

To begin with, it was the Lithuanian nobility and educated classes who fretted under the Russian yoke. They joined the Polish uprising of 1830–1, and paid dearly. Next time round, about 30 years later, it was a stirring among the peasants, which the Russian government quelled with reforms giving peasants the right to hold up to 50 hectares (120 acres) of land each. This satisfied some of them, but others were firmly under the thumb of the Roman Catholic clergy and could not accept with good grace anything on offer from Orthodox Russia. The Russian

Napoleon's Grande Armée crosses the Nemunas at Kaunas, 1815, at the start of his Russian campaign.

⦿ NAPOLEON'S GRAND FROZEN ARMY

The northern Žirmūnai suburb of Vilnius was the focal point of historical fanfare in early 2001 when workers from a building development stumbled on a mass grave. At first, the remains were thought to be victims of the Soviet regime. A second trench with nearly 20,000 skeletons was unearthed a few months later, revealing coins and army uniform fragments that made it clear these were soldiers from Napoleon's Grande Armée.

In June 1812 the soldiers had marched through Vilnius on their way to Moscow. Welcomed as liberators from the Russian occupation, they were embraced by the city's residents. However, on their defeated trail back to Paris from Moscow five months later, the

remaining half-starved and sickly soldiers arrived when the city's temperature was –30°C (–22°F). The army of nearly half a million – the largest ever raised in Europe – had been reduced to 40,000. That winter in the freezing city a further 30,000 died. As the corpses littered the streets, residents did not know how to dispose of them.

When Russian forces reoccupied the city, the corpses were placed in the thawed ground of trenches the French soldiers had dug on their advance to Moscow, hoping for the first major confrontation with the Russians. They had dug their own graves. The bones were placed in a mass grave in Antakalnis Cemetery, where they have been commemorated with a statue.

administration responded by decreeing that only Orthodox subjects were to be employed by the state, even in the most menial capacity.

RUSSIFICATION

From 1864 onwards, the tsars did their utmost to Russify their Lithuanian holdings, and it was the declared policy of Muraviev, the Russian governor, to eradicate the traces of ancient Lithuania once and for all. That generally took the form of imposing Russian Orthodoxy. Non-Orthodox nobles were not allowed to buy property. They were permitted to rent it, but only for 12 years. Peasants could not buy land without a "certificate of patriotism", for which one of the qualifications was that they were Orthodox. An otherwise qualified landowner could lose his privileges simply by taking a non-Orthodox wife. Land for Jews was out of the question.

The programme of Russification reached its extreme in education. The university was closed down and only Russians were admitted to schools above elementary level. The use of the Lithuanian language was banned for all official purposes, and the Latin alphabet, in which Lithuanian was written, was also prohibited. It became a punishable offence to have a prayer book that was written in Latin characters.

The Russian revolution of 1905 gave the Lithuanians a chance to reclaim some of their dignity, if not their independence. Resolutions were passed demanding the creation of an autonomous state with a *seimas*, or National Assembly, with Vilnius as the capital. Threatened with a campaign of passive resistance, concessions were made such as the reintroduction of the Lithuanian language in schools. National literature sprouted with amazing rapidity, but the great symbolic victory was that Vilnius, effectively part of Poland for five centuries, was restored as the Lithuanian capital. Just as it seemed that the country might be freed of its shackles, World War I broke out.

Driven out of East Prussia, the Russian Army rampaged through Lithuania, burning, plundering and taking away all Lithuanian men of military age. The German troops in pursuit were received almost as liberators, but it was quickly apparent that Germany also considered Lithuania a source of cheap labour. The various claims submitted to the conference by a Lithuanian

In 1948 future President Valdas Adamkus won two gold and two silver medals in the track and field events of the "Olympic Games of the Enslaved Nations".

delegation were made to look irrelevant as the Russian revolutionary war, not to mention the activities of a renegade German force under General Bermondt, overflowed into Lithuania. A

Count Muraviev, Russian Minister of Foreign Affairs.

combined force of Estonians, Poles and Lithuanians managed to repel a Bolshevik invasion, but while they were thus engaged the Polish Army marched into Vilnius and was able to hold the capital. This takeover was in direct violation of the 1920 Suwałki Treaty signed by both Polish and Lithuanian governments. Polish forces held on to it even as the Bolsheviks swept towards Warsaw. In the end they surrendered it to the Bolsheviks rather than to Lithuania, and Kaunas became the interim capital. It was a small compensation when Lithuania reclaimed Klaipėda (Memel) and the coast from Germany in 1923.

The possession of Vilnius (Wilno in Polish) bedevilled relations between Poland and Lithuania. The city was undoubtedly the ancient capital of the Lithuanian state, but over the course of 500 years it had become overwhelmingly Polish in every other respect. In 1910 a controversial Russian census broke down the population as 97,800 Poles, 75,500 Jews and only 2,200 Lithuanians. The argument centred on the issue of whether language determines nationality. After five centuries of Polonisation and Russification, the Lithuanian language tended to be spoken only in rural areas and among peasants. The national revival did not take off until the first quarter of the 20th century. The Red Army occupied Lithuania in 1940

thing left to working people in the towns and in the country has been unemployment, insecurity, hunger, indigence and national oppression." The majority of the Lithuanians steadfastly denounced the Soviet annexation as illegal.

The first Soviet deportations of Lithuanians began in June 1940. Soon after, Lithuania, together with Latvia and Estonia, was occupied by the Germans. The 150,000 or so Jews in Lithuania all but vanished in Hitler's grim Final Solution, as Germans and Lithuanians set about the systematic murder of the Lithuanian Jewish

The Jewish quarter of Vilnius before World War II.

under the terms of the secret Nazi–Soviet Pact. "Whether you agree or not is irrelevant," Molotov told the Lithuanian government, "because the Red Army is going in tomorrow anyway." The invading troops had an approved government trailing in their wake. The existing parties were dissolved, and those leaders who had not already fled were sent to Siberia.

The Soviet propaganda machine then went into action. The previous government, it said, was "indifferent to the real interests of the people, has led the country into an impasse in the fields of both domestic and foreign policy. The vital interests of the Lithuanian people have been sacrificed to the mercenary interests of a handful of exploiters and rich people. The only

population. Lithuania lost another 200,000 people to Stalin's deportation orders.

SOVIET TANKS ROLL IN

When the three Baltic States moved almost in unison out of Soviet control in the late 1980s the lead in Lithuania was taken by Sąjūdis, a breakaway movement sanctioned by the Kremlin. Its objective was full independence. There was no need to consult the Soviet Union, it said cheekily, because no one had ever recognised the 1940 annexation. This was too provocative even for the easygoing Soviet leader Mikhail Gorbachev and, on the day that the parliament voted for unilateral independence, Soviet tanks drew up outside. Despite the freezing temperatures, thousands found themselves on the streets. There were shootings at the Television Tower in Vilnius where 14 were killed and 700 injured.

In July 1991 seven border guards were killed in Medininkai, in the south of the country, by Soviet special forces. But on 21 August Soviet troops began to leave the country and the statue of Lenin in Lukiškiū Square was torn down. By September all three Baltic countries had been admitted into the UN. Kaunas-born Vytautas Landsbergis (b.1932), a doctor of music and author of a number of books on Lithuanian artists and musicians, served as de facto head of state until 1992, when elections for the presidency took place.

AN INDEPENDENT STATE

Through the hardship of the 1990s, self-esteem began to return, Pope John Paul II paid a visit almost as soon as he could, in September 1993, clearly delighted once more to be united with such a faithful congregation who were busily looking for funds to restore their churches. In Vilnius hard work was rewarded in the granting of Unesco World Heritage status to the Old Town.

The economy slowed at the end of the 1990s, following Russia's crisis, but recovered in the first decade of the 21st century. Lithuania's own crisis struck in 2003 when Rolandas Paksas, a populist president, was impeached for corruption involving the awarding of Lithuanian citizenship to a rich Russian financial backer and gaining him the distinction of being the first political leader in Europe to have been judicially removed from office.

A former president, Kaunas-born Valdas Adamkus, who had had a career with the Environmental Protection Agency in the US, was re-elected in time to preside over Lithuania's admission into the EU and NATO in 2004. Relations with its neighbours were beginning to normalise, too, with agreements reached with Moscow about Russian citizens travelling across the country to reach the Russian exclave of Kaliningrad.

The year 2009 was a milestone. Celebrating 1,000 years since the word Lithuania was first used in written texts, it was also one of the toughest after independence. Vilnius was awarded the title of European Capital of Culture just in time for the national airline to go bust and the global economy to nosedive, meaning the

city never received the visitors it badly needed. In July Dalia Grybauskaitė was elected the country's first female president, setting the tone on austerity measures to come by taking only half her salary. Following in the footsteps of its Baltic neighbours, Lithuania swiftly recovered from the brink of bankruptcy and by the end of 2011 was one of the fastest growing EU economies. Four years later it adopted the common European currency to become the 19th member of the eurozone. This success was overshadowed by the ongoing crisis in Eastern Ukraine and Moscow's

Former president Valdas Adamkus casts his vote after the scandal that ousted his predecessor in 2003.

support for Ukrainian separatists, which stirred echoes from the tragic past not only in Lithuania but elsewhere in the region. Amid these concerns, in 2014 Lithuanians elected the incumbent president Dalia Grybauskaitė – a staunch critic of the Russian president Vladimir Putin – to a second term in office, while the government decided to reintroduce compulsory military service, a practice that had been abolished in 2008. Lithuania, along with Poland, Latvia and Estonia, also asked for a permanent presence of NATO troops on its soil; in 2017, 1,000 NATO troops deployed in Lithuania and, in the same year, also in Latvia, Estonia and Poland, as part of NATO's Advanced Forward Presence strategic objective.

Vilnius's historical centre.

VILNIUS

A beautiful city, both ancient and modern, Lithuania's capital is renowned for its Baroque churches and an Old Town that is both a delight and an education to explore.

Lithuania's capital lies rather inconveniently in the far southeastern corner of the country only a couple of dozen kilometres from Belarus. **Vilnius** grew up on a hill beside the River Neris, near the point where it is met by the smaller River Vilnel. It was a stronghold against first the Teutonic Knights and then a Tatar invasion that never came.

The Neris flows westwards towards Kaunas, Lithuania's capital during the period in the 20th century when Vilnius and the surrounding area was annexed by Poland. For 17 years the two countries were not on speaking terms. Poland and Lithuania had been joined by marriage in 1386. In 1795 Vilnius was swallowed into the Russian Empire, and as Russification followed Polonisation many churches the Jesuits had built, evolving a local Baroque style, were given over to the Russian Orthodox belief.

HERITAGE SITE

In spite of many decades of neglect, Vilnius has one of the largest Old Towns in eastern Europe, bristling with the confident and robust Gothic, Baroque and Renaissance towers of churches that seem too large and too numerous for the 547,000 population. In 1994 the Old Town was designated a Unesco World Heritage Site, ensuring

Pedestrianised Pilies Street.

that the maintenance and upkeep of these churches, along with the streets, is considered an important aspect of the city's budget.

About half the population is Lithuanian, while smaller percentages of Poles (16.5 percent), Russians (12 percent), Belarusians (3.5 percent) along with others comprise the majority of the city's various ethnic groups.

Before World War II Vilnius was one of the great Jewish cities of Europe, and a centre of Yiddish publishing. New streets and buildings in its centre mark

Main attractions
Cathedral
Old Town
St Anne's Church
Užupis
Madonna of the Gates of Dawn
Holocaust Exhibition
National Art Gallery
Antakalnis Cemetery

Maps on pages 266, 280

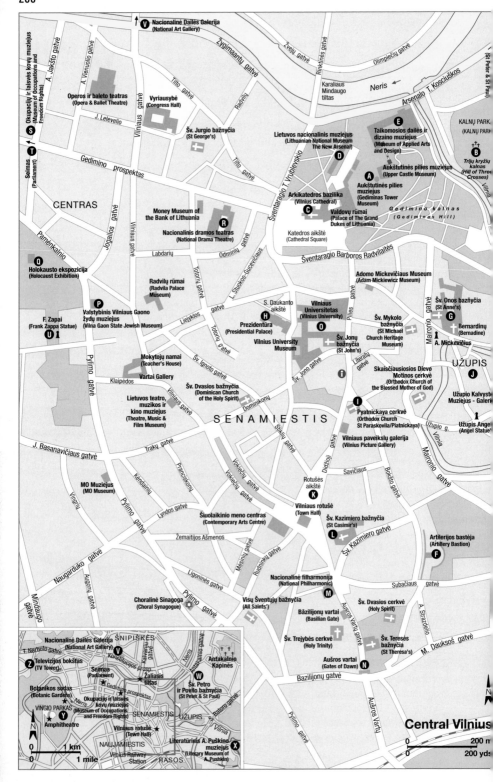

e site of their ghetto: some 150,000 its inhabitants were killed by the zis and their Lithuanian henchmen. Besides the variety of churches, the y's historical legacy can be viewed in very hands-on and real way by visits the 16th-century Gates of Dawn, with icon believed to work miracles, and the former KGB and Gestapo head-arters, which is now a museum. ost pleasure is to be had from specting the churches and simply lking the cobbled streets. These are ightened by antiques shops, restau-nts, bars and cafés. There are sev-al outstanding restaurants. The beer rs that in summer tend to bloom on e city's streets and the cavernous llars that become the city's pulse in lder months are also an important pect of Vilnius' charm.

ASTLE HILL STARTING POINT

e best place to start a tour of the ty is from the top of the **Gediminas wer Ⓐ** (Gedimino bokštas) on **Cas-e Hill** (Gedimino kalnas), overlook-g the red-tiled roofs and the church wers of the Old Town, the Cathedral, e administrative buildings along the ain avenue, Gedimino prospektas d the modern business and shopping ntres on the right bank of the Neris, retching to the Television Tower in e Karoliniškės district and beyond.

The castle on Castle Hill, the oldest ttlement of Vilnius, was built by Grand uke Gediminas (Giedymin, c.1275–41) at the confluence of the Neris and lnelė Rivers. It was to this spot that he vited merchants, artisans and friars om various Hanseatic towns. Accord-g to legend, Gediminas dreamed of a werful iron wolf howling from a hill at e mouth of the Vilnelė, a dream which gnified that at this spot a magnificent rt and a town would arise.

All that remains are the ruins of e southern part and the western efence tower, Gediminas Tower, which uses the **Gediminas Tower Museum**

(Aukštutinės pilies muziejus; www.lnm.lt; daily Apr–Sept 10am–9pm, Oct–Mar 10am–6pm). The restored 14th-century, three-storey octagonal brick tower houses a small exhibit of archaeologi-cal finds and the history of the castle, which is one of the symbols of Lithua-nia's independence. The independence movement scored its first victory when the old Lithuanian yellow, green and red tricolour was raised on the obser-vation platform on 7 October 1988.

On the nearby **Hill of Three Crosses Ⓑ** (Trijų kryžių kalnas) are the symbols of Lithuanian mourning and hope, which were rebuilt and unveiled on 14 June 1989. The first crosses were erected on the hill in the 17th century in memory of martyred Franciscan monks. During Stalin's time they were removed and buried. The crosses standing today are reproductions of the originals.

At the foot of Castle Hill lies the reconstructed **Palace of The Grand Dukes of Lithuania** (Valdovų rūmai; www.valdovurumai.lt; Sept–May Tue–Wed and Fri–Sat 10am–6pm, Thu 10am–8pm, Sun 10am–4pm, June–Aug

Ⓞ Tip

Available at Tourist Information Centres and on-line (www.vilnius-tourism.lt), the Vilnius City Card, comes in two basic versions: a 24 or 72-hour, costing €30/20 (with and without public transport) and €45/35 (with/without public transport) respectively. Discounts are available when cards are purchased at the Vilnius Tourist Information Office. The card entitles holders to free museum entries as well as discounts on restaurant meals, concert tickets and hotel bookings.

Gediminas Tower.

⊙ Tip

Visiting the top of Castle Hill is a must, although the walk can be tiring for many. A funicular-type vehicle operates, which you'll find in a hidden courtyard west of the Museum of Applied Arts and Design.

Mon–Wed and Sun 10am–6pm, Thu–Sat 10am–8pm), a replica of the original 15th-century building demolished by the Russians at the start of the 19th century. Currently it is a national museum, offering four different tours for visitors including the one presenting the history of the palace and sections of original walls and the one showing the ceremonial halls and their evolution in time. The highlight of this tour is the Treasury Hall. Interesting temporary exhibitions are also often held at the palace.

THE CATHEDRAL

The settlement's original church, which became the **Cathedral ⊙** (Arkikatedros bazilika; www.katedra.lt; daily 7am–7pm), was built in the 13th century by the order of King Mindaugas. After his death the church reverted to its original use as a pagan shrine until the structure was recommissioned in 1387 by Grand Duke Jogaila (Jagiełło). The structure then became a symbol of Lithuania's conversion to Catholicism. It occupied the northern part of the castle complex and it was rebuilt 11 times.

The present white neoclassical building by Laurynas Stuoka-Gucevičius (Wawrzyniec Gucewicz, 1753–98) dates from 1777–1801, when it was given a dominating portico of six Doric columns topped with the imposing renovated statues of Sts Helen, Stanislaus and Casimir, supposed symbols of Russia, Poland and Lithuania. The facade has large Baroque statues depicting Abraham, Moses and the four Evangelists. The interior has three naves of equal height divided by two rows of massive pillars. The main altar is classical, and there are several interesting chapels to the right, especially the Baroque chapel of St Casimir (1623–36), which now contains the mausoleum of Kings Alexander and Ladislaus IV. As the patron saint of Lithuania, Casimir is believed to have had miracle-working powers, hence the ex-votos, the silver body parts left by the faithful as a prayer for the release from some particular ailment.

Also of interest is the **Cathedral Crypt** (www.bpmuziejus.lt; Mon–Sun 10am–5pm; guided tours only), which serves as the final resting place for

The altar at St Casimir's Church.

many of the country's leaders, noblemen and archbishops. In 1985 a fresco was found along the crypt's wall. It is believed to have been painted at the end of the 14th century, making it the country's oldest painting.

In the Soviet era the Cathedral served as a picture gallery. As a symbol of national revival, it was the first church to be reconsecrated, on 5 February 1989. The 52-metre (170ft) **belfry** (Mon–Sat May–Sept 10am–7pm, Oct–Apr 10am–6pm) which stands to the front and to the right of the Cathedral, was originally part of the city's defence walls. It is a distinctive landmark and a good meeting point.

Walk away from the Cathedral towards the Neris to find the main building of the **Lithuanian National Museum, The New Arsenal D** (Lietuvos nacionalinis muziejus; www.lnm.lt; Tue–Sun 10am–6pm), the country's biggest museum. Founded in 1855, closed by the tsarist authorities and reopened in 1968, the exhibits therein illustrate the history of the people of Lithuania from the Stone Age to 1945.

There are costumes, farming and fishing equipment and recreated interiors of houses from different regions along with weapons and armour. In front of the museum sits a statue of King Mindaugas (Mendog, c.1200–63), unveiled on the 750th anniversary of his coronation on 6 July 2003. Further round the hill on the right at No. 3 Arsenalo is another branch of the National Museum, **The Old Arsenal** (details as above) with an exhibition on prehistoric Lithuania.

Next to it, at No. 3a, is the **Museum of Applied Arts and Design E** (Taikomosios dailės ir dizaino muziejus; Tue–Sat 11am–6pm, Sun 11am–4pm). The museum has a number of changing exhibitions as well as a permanent collection of paintings and folk pieces, for the most part focusing on wooden sculptures and other Christian art. The fashion design collection is also interesting.

THE OLD TOWN

Covering 269 hectares (665 acres), Vilnius **Old Town** (Senamiestis) is

Vilnius Cathedral's distinctive architecture.

Eat

Take a break from sightseeing at the lively Užupis Café (Užupio kavinė; daily 10am–11pm; www.uzupiokavine.lt), located among the sculptures dotted around the riverbank.

one of the largest in eastern Europe. The main artery running through the medieval city was Pilies gatvė (Castle Street, of just plain Pilies), which begins at the southeast corner of Katedros aikštė (Cathedral Square) and runs into Didžioji gatvž (Great Street), past Town Hall Squares and on into Aušros vartai (the Gates of Dawn), the only remaining gates of the town fortifications built against the Tatar invasions in the early 16th century. Only a few parts of the town wall remain in Bokšto, the street with the **Artillery Bastion** 🅕 (Artilerijos bastja; Bokšto 20; ww.lmn.lt; Tue–Sun 10am–6pm), which currently forms part of the National Museum. There is a beautiful view over the Old Town.

On cobblestoned Pilies lie numerous historical buildings, and from the balcony at No. 26, Lithuania's independence was declared in 1918. The building is now the **Signatories' House** (Signatarų namai; www.lnm.lt; Tue–Sat 10am–6pm), which houses a small museum dedicated to the events and to the history of the Lithuanian revival

Bernardine Monastery.

movement. It is well worth venturi into the side streets and courtyar for a glimpse of the 19th-century c There are a number of antiques sho cafés and cellar bars tucked aw down these quiet lanes.

ST ANNE'S CHURCH

Bernardinų, at the northern end Pilies, leads to **St Anne's Church** (Šv. Onos bažnyčia; Maironio 10; Ma Sept Tue–Sat 10.30am–6.30pm, S 8am–7pm, Oct–Apr Tue–Fri 4.3 6.30pm, Sat 10.30am–6.30pm, S 8am–5pm; donation), one of the be examples of Gothic architecture Lithuania. Its western facade is pa terned with 33 different varieties bricks, making it amazingly grace and harmonious. The chapel was bu in the 16th century during the rei of the Jagiellonian king Žygimant Augustas (Zygmunt August, 1520–7 The church has no foundations; rests on alder logs. The original in rior was destroyed by fires and is minor interest. Napoleon Bonaparte said to have been so enraptured by Anne's that he exclaimed his desire bring the church back to France in t palm of his hand and set it down ne to Notre-Dame.

PRESIDENTIAL PALACE

Napoleon stayed in Vilnius on the w to and from Moscow during his ill-fat campaign of 1812, at the Bishop's Pa ace in Daukantas aikštė, behind t university, which is now the **Preside tial Palace** 🅗 (tel: 370 706 64 073; ww lrp.lt; free guided tours in English, 4.15–5.30pm and Sun 9am–12.45p prior registration required). The Fren writer Stendhal was in charge of fo and provisions, and it was in Vilniu he said, that he learned to drink li a Russian. The euphoria that greet the Grande Armée's arrival evap rated on their retreat when the c was plundered by the starving troo In early 2001, workers from a housi

development in the north of the city stumbled on a mass grave of about 30,000 Napoleonic soldiers. Some of their bones now lie in a communal grave at Antakalnis Cemetery.

The palace was built for merchants in the 16th century and redesigned at the end of the 18th century by Laurynas Stuoka-Gucevičius, whose monument stands in front of the nearby 16th-century **Church of the Holy Cross** (Šv. Kryžiaus bažnyčia). In tsarist times it was the residence of the governor general, and under the Soviets it was the Palace of the Art Workers. Today it is the official **residence of the President of Lithuania**. Every day at 6pm there is a changing of the guard ceremony, while each Sunday at noon a Flag Replacement Ceremony is held, with soldiers dressed in modern uniforms and some clad in medieval armour.

Next to St Anne's is the **Bernardine Church and Monastery** (Bernardinų bažnyčia ir vienuolynas); the order came here from Poland in 1469. It has a Gothic roof and a Baroque belfry, and being built on the edge of the town it was fortified with gun ports. The nearby statue represents the Lithuania-born Polish writer Adomas Mickevičius (Adam Mickiewicz, 1798–1855), educated at Vilnius University, who wrote the epic *Pan Tadeusz* about the society of the Polish–Lithuanian Commonwealth.

Facing St Anne's is the former **St Michael's Church** (Šv. Mykolo bažnyčia), built between 1594 and 1625 in the style of the Lublin Renaissance as a family mausoleum for Leonas Sapiega, Chancellor of Lithuania. The building now houses the **Church Heritage Museum** (Bažnytinio paveldo muziejus; www.bpmuziejus. lt; Tue–Sat 11am–6pm, guided tours in English available), containing a wealth of exhibits charting the rise of the Catholic Church in the country. The highlights include the treasury of Vilnius Cathedral and Lithuanian goldsmith masterpieces.

The many churches in the Old Town are signs of Vilnius' geographical situation on the border of Catholicism and Orthodoxy. The **Orthodox Church**

Town Hall Square.

of **Paraskovila Piatnickaya**  (Pyatnickaya cerkvė) on Didžioji Street was constructed for the first wife of Grand Duke Algirdas in the 14th century, and Peter the Great reputedly baptised Alexander Pushkin's great-grandfather here. Further up the street, the **Orthodox Church of the Blessed Mother of God** belonged to Algirdas' second wife.

UŽUPIS

Opposite St Anne's on the far side of the small River Vilnelė lies **Užupis** , the first suburb outside the fortified city walls. This slightly scruffy but up-and-coming district, once dubbed the Montmartre of Vilnius because of its arty population, has designated itself as the independent Republic of Užupis (Užupio Respublika). On 1 April, the appropriate day of their declared independence, border patrols are set up and passports must be shown to their fake policemen. Their antics have been tolerated to such an extent that the Lithuanian Ministry of Foreign Affairs has opened up diplomatic relations with them. The area is as fun-loving

The Gates of Dawn.

as its residents. The tongue-in-chee Užupis Constitution can be seen i Paupio Street and is translated int English and several other languages.

Explore the main workshop and a gallery of the republic, the **Galera Ga lery** (UMI Galera; www.umi.lt; Užup 2; Mon–Fri 11am–5pm), which als houses a gift shop where unique Užup souvenirs can be bought. A bright painted crumbling ruin of a buildin the gallery is hard to miss. Outsi find sculptures on the riverbank ar in the river itself, while the intern. gallery space is given over to all mar ner of media, from children's finge painting to experimental photograph The **Angel statue** at the intersectio of Užupio and Malūnų is a symbol the republic. The area is known f its traditional arts, and several worl ing galleries of jewellery, cerami and other crafts can be found here. Užupio 26 there is a small, but interes ing **Museum and Gallery of Blacksmi Art** (Tue–Fri 10.30am–6.30pm, S 10.30am–4.30pm) showing an authe tic 19th-century blacksmith workshop

TOWN HALL SQUARE

Town Hall Square  (Rotušės aikšt was the political, cultural and ec nomic centre of Vilnius. The origin 15th-century **Town Hall** (Rotušė; ww vilniausrotuse.lt) didn't survive, ar the present one, which was designe by Laurynas Stuoka-Gucevičius, th architect of the city's Cathedral, w completed in 1799. In the 19th ce tury it was frequently used for cu tural events, and in 1845 it becam the first town theatre. Now it's rente out for public events and houses a art gallery.

Past the Town Hall Square Didžioji lies **St Casimir's Church** (Šv. Kazimiero bažnyčia), the olde Baroque church in Vilnius, built 1604–15 and named after the patro saint of Lithuania. The saint was th son of Casimir IV of Poland; the crov

on the church roof represents his royal connections. The church has long been an object of persecution. Under the tsars it was converted into the Orthodox Church of St Nicholas and the crown of St Casimir was replaced by an onion dome; during World War I the occupying Germans turned it into a Protestant church, and the Soviets subsequently made it the Museum of Atheism and History of Religion. St Casimir's reopened for public worship in 1989 and has been magnificently restored to its original splendour.

Didžioji Street leads into Aušros vartai. The **National Philharmonic** (Nacionalinė filharmonija; www.filhar monija.lt), built in 1902, is at No. 5. This is one of the city's main music venues, with both a concert hall and chamber music hall, where the national orchestra and choir regularly perform.

GATES OF DAWN

The street rises to the only remaining city gate, the **Gates of Dawn** (Aušros vartai; Ostra Brama in Polish, daily 6am–7pm). In 1671 Carmelite nuns from neighbouring St Theresa's built a chapel above the gates to house a holy image of the Virgin Mary, said to have miraculous powers. Its artist is unknown and it has been encased in gold and silver by local goldsmiths, leaving only the head and hands uncovered. The chapel's interior was refurbished in the neoclassical style in 1829, and from the street below pilgrims can be seen singing and praying in front of the Virgin. Thousands of votive offerings decorate the walls, and many pilgrims of both the Catholic and Orthodox faiths come to pray, queuing up on the stairs installed in the 18th century to connect the chapel to the adjacent **Church of St Theresa** (Šv. Teresės bažnyčia). Mass is held in Polish and Lithuanian.

On the way up to the Gates of Dawn, in the courtyard of the only Russian monastery to operate during the Soviet era, stands Vilnius' most important Orthodox church, the **Church of the Holy Spirit** (Stačiatikių Šv. Dvasios cerkvė; daily 10am–5pm). It was built in the 17th century to serve the Russian

Tip

Street finder: *gatvė* means street, *aikštė* is square, *prospektas* is avenue, *kelias* is road.

Looking out over the university.

Orthodox community, and it bears similarities to Catholic architecture. Before the altar stands a glass case containing the well-preserved bodies of Saints Anthony, Ivan and Eustachius, martyred in 1347 because of their faith, at the behest of Grand Duke Algirdas. The three saints are clothed in white during the Christmas period, black during Lent and red on all other occasions. However, on 26 June the bodies, believed to have healing powers, are left naked.

VILNIUS UNIVERSITY

A tour of the Old Town should include a visit to **Vilnius University** (Vilniaus Universitetas), founded in 1570 by the Jesuits and one of the most important centres of the Counter-Reformation. For almost 200 years the Jesuits' college was the source of enlightenment, science and culture. It was closed under the tsarist regime in the 19th century. Today, some 20,000 students study at its 12 faculties. The four-storey building with an observatory tower dates back to 1569 and its windows are Rococo. The library contains nearly 5 million volumes, making it the richest collection of Lithuanian books, as well as 180,000 manuscripts from the 13–16th century. Soon after it was founded, it became one of the best-known libraries in eastern Europe. There are 13 courtyards in the grounds. The first is named after the poet and humanist Motiejus Kazimieras Sarbievijus (Maciej Kazimierz Sarbiewski, 1595–1640). To better preserve the university heritage, the **Vilnius University Museum** (www.muiejus.vu.lt; Mar–Oct Mon–Sat 9am–6pm, Nov–Feb Mon–Sat 9.30am–5.30pm) was created in 2010. The entrance to the University Architectural Ensemble is at No. 3 Universiteto. The museum's collection consists of rare books and manuscripts, including the 14th-century *Psalterium Mariae* and documents bearing the signatures of Lithuania and Polish rulers, as well as numismatics, medals, instruments and objects from three Lithuanian Masonic Lodges. The telescopes from the university observatory and old terrestrial

Choral Synagogue is the last remaining place of Jewish worship in the city.

globes are on display in the White Hall of the library.

Adjacent to the university is **St John's Church** (Šv. Jonų bažnyčia), named after St John the Baptist and St John the Evangelist. It was built in 1427, but its present Baroque look is from restoration work from 1737. Its 68-metre (223ft) bell-tower is the tallest structure in the Old Town (www.muziejus.vu.lt; May–Sept 10am–7pm), it's worth climbing up the stairs for the view; there is also a lift. During the Soviet occupation the church was used as a Museum of Scientific Thought. Today the working parish church has kept some flavour of its former incarnation, as exhibits, including a 1613 map of the country along with some scientific books from the 14th century, can be found within its six chapels. The church also functions as a regular concert venue.

Opposite the church is a passageway leading to the Observatory Courtyard and the university's **Observatory**, founded in 1753, when it ranked third in importance in Europe after those at Greenwich, London, and the Sorbonne, Paris. The top of the facade is crowned with the signs of the zodiac. Further on, in Daukanto Courtyard, the offices of **the Yiddish Institute** are helpful to walk-in visitors who are investigating their Jewish past in Lithuania or surrounding countries.

THE "JERUSALEM OF LITHUANIA"

An essential part of pre-war Vilnius was its massive Jewish population, which made up nearly half of the city. Today little remains of the Jerusalem of Lithuania, as Vilnius was once called. The Great Synagogue and the Schulhoyf, the traditional centre of Jewish culture around today's Vokiečių, Žydų and Antokolskio streets, suffered heavy damage during the Holocaust. The ruins of the synagogue, which dated back to 1661, remained for some years before the Soviet authorities decided to

blow up what was left to make way for a kindergarten and a basketball court, and despite the small present-day congregation, there continue to be proposals to see it rebuilt. The only remaining synagogue for the small surviving Jewish community is the **Choral Synagogue** (Choralinė Sinagoga; Mon–Fri 10am–2pm) at Pylimo 39.

THE HOLOCAUST EXHIBITION

The **Vilna Gaon Jewish State Museum of Lithuania** Ⓟ (Valstybinis Vilniaus Gaono žydų muziejus; www.jmuseum.lt) is named after the city's most famous rabbinical scholar, the Gaon of Vilnius (1720–1797). The museum has several branches. The **Tolerance Centre** (Tolerancijos Centras, Naugarduko 10; Mon–Thu 10am–6pm, Fri and Sun 10am–4pm), has several worthwhile exhibitions about Jewish art and life in Lithuania, while the **Holocaust Exhibition** Ⓠ (Holokausto ekspozicija; Pamėnkalnio 12; Mon–Thu 9am–5pm, Fri and Sun 9am–4pm), also called the Green House, was started by Holocaust survivors and tells the history of

The Choral Synagogue's interior.

Lithuanian Jews. There are plans to set up the Memorial Museum of Holocaust in Lithuania and Vilna Ghetto at Žemaitijos gatvė 4 in the building, which had once housed the Vilna Ghetto library.

In front of the museum stands a monument to Chiune Sugihara, Japanese consul in Kaunas from 1939–40. He and his colleagues helped save 6,000 Jews by issuing them with papers to leave the country. A new branch, the **Museum of Litvak Culture and Identity** (CLCA), housed in a historic building of the former Jewish gymnasium at Pylimo 4, is intended to be a multifunctional art centre focussing on Lithuanian Jewish (called *litvaks*) works, and is due to open in the near future.

AROUND PYLIMO STREET

The western section of the Old Town is hemmed in by Pylimo gatvė, but dominated by Vokiečių gatvė (German Street), especially in summer when it is lined with outdoor cafés. The street is one of the oldest in the city.

A plan of the war-time ghettos in the former Old Town Jewish quarter.

Its name comes from the large numbers of German traders who erected most of its buildings. Most on the east side have been rebuilt since being destroyed in World War II. The wide pedestrian pavement flanked by narrow lanes of traffic going in opposite directions makes it a prime outdoor seating spot in the warmer months. At the southern end of the street at Vokiečių 2 is the modern **Contemporary Arts Centre** (Šiuolaikinio meno centras; www.cac.lt; Tue–Sun noon–8pm) with changing contemporary exhibits, except for the Fluxus room where there are nearly 100 works of the 1960s Fluxus Movement, the best known of whom is Yoko Ono.

Nearby, at Pylimo Street 17, is MO Museum (MO muziejus; https://mo; Sat–Thu 10am–8pm, Fri 10am–10pm), a new museum of Lithuanian modern and contemporary art inaugurated 2018. This private museum is housed in a new top-notch building designed by Studio Libeskind and consists of 5,000 Lithuanian works of art from the 1950s to the present day.

⊘ JEWISH EXTINCTION

A centre of Jewish culture that produced the artist Chaim Soutine and violinist Jascha Heifitz, Vilnius once had 100 or so synagogues and prayer houses stretching from Gaono to Pylimo Streets and Trakų to Rūdninkų Streets, which were, with the exception of one, destroyed during the Holocaust.

In 1941 some 50,000 Jews were herded into two ghettos. The Small Ghetto around Stiklių Street lasted from 9 June to 29 October before its 15,000 inhabitants were liquidated. The bigger ghetto, established on 6 September around Žemaitijos and Rūdninkų Streets, was liquidated two years later. Today, at Rūdninkų 18, a map showing the outlines of these two Jewish ghettos can be seen.

Most of the 50,000 Jews were killed in Paneriai (Ponar), 10km (6 miles) southeast of Vilnius off the A16/E28 on Road 106. There is also a small museum here (tel: 86 999 0384; www.jmuseum.lt; June–Sept Tue–Wed 9am–5pm, Fri and Sun 9am–4pm, Oct–May by appointment only).

The Yiddish Institute in Vilnius University is the first of its kind in post-Holocaust Eastern Europe and it organises popular Yiddish-language summer courses. The students and professors in the office welcome anybody who wants to find out more about their Jewish past in Lithuania (www.judaicvilnius.com).

ELEBRATING ART AND MUSIC

ong Vilniaus Street stands the Rad-
la family palace (known in Polish as
e Radziwiłł), all that remains of the
ty estate of a local noble family. Part
it functions as the **Radvila Palace
useum** (Radvilų rūmai; www.ldm.lt;
Je–Sat 11am–6pm, Sun noon–5pm),
here close to 200 of their family por-
aits are on display along with a small
ollection of foreign fine art. Further
ong the street, in the renovated Rad-
los Minor Palace, is the **Theatre,
usic and Film Museum** (Lietuvos
atro, muzikos ir kino muziejus; www.
mkm.lt; Tue and Thu–Fri 11am–6pm,
ed until 7pm, Sat 11am–4pm) with
e emphasis on the history of thea-
e and music in the country. There
re lovely music boxes from the early
300s, pianolas and harmoniums, the-
rical costumes and set designs, with
minimal nod to cinema. Downstairs is
so an exhibition space with the occa-
onal superb show. Entrance to both is
the back of the building.

Inside the **Teacher's House**
Mokytojų namai; Vilniaus 39; www.

kultura.lt), one of the finest multi-
functional art centres in the city, is the
Vartai Gallery (www.galerijavartai.lt;
Tue–Fri noon–6pm, Sat noon–4pm).
Founded in 1991, it never seems to
have an empty piece of wall space.
Expect thought-provoking work that
centres around the schools of Naïve
and Surrealist art. The courtyard plays
host to a large outdoor bar, Vasaros
Terasa (Summer Terrace), during the
summer, popular with the local club-
bing set.

NEW VILNIUS

New Vilnius unfolds along the central pedestrianised avenue **Gedimino
prospektas**, opposite the Cathedral.
This is where most of the administrative buildings are situated, and it
is the main shopping area in the city
centre. There are a number of striking new buildings as well as old ones
in the street, including Neringa restaurant, at No. 23 (www.restoranasner
inga.lt), once a meeting place for the
city's intellectuals and decorated
with magnificent Socialist–Realist

*Central Post Office on
Gedimino prospektas.*

murals of the coast dating from 1959. **The National Drama Theatre** (Nacionalinis dramos teatras) at No. 4 has black-robed, gold-faced muses symbolising Drama, Tragedy and Comedy on its facade. Its repertoire is principally the classics, in Lithuanian. Just round the corner at No 2/8 Totorių is the highly entertaining **Money Museum of the Bank of Lithuania** (www.pinigumuziejus.lt; Apr–Oct Tue–Fri 10am–7pm, Sat 11am–6pm, Nov–Mar Tue–Fri 9am–6pm, Sat 10am–5pm; free) with interactive exhibitions about the history of money and banking.

The former KGB and Gestapo headquarters opposite Lukiškių Square was transformed into the **Museum of Occupations and Freedom Rights** (Okupacijų ir laisvės kovų muziejus; www.genocid.lt/muziejus/en; Wed–Sat 10am–6pm, Sun 10am–5pm). This is a shrine to the victims of Soviet tyranny, where tourists may visit the former KGB prison, the place where death sentences were carried out, to see exhibitions devoted to Soviet repression and the Lithuanian fight for independence.

The 1.5km (1-mile) long avenue ends at the modern **Parliament** (Seimas) building, which was surrounded by barricades for several months after the Soviets attempted to storm the building in 1991. Some of the great concrete blocks and graffiti that regularly featured here have been preserved.

Vilnius has shed most of its blatant Soviet symbols. The statues of Stalin, Lenin and Kapsukas, a local Communist leader, are now sited with all other Lithuanian Soviet monuments in the tiny village of Grūtas near Druskininkai. However, close to Gedimino, at the far northern end of Vilniaus or the **Green Bridge** (Žaliasis tiltas) over the River Neris, stand four Soviet-era statues of sturdy peasants and factory workers dating from 1952.

Another statue to note is the bust of **Frank Zappa** (1940–93), a Kalinausko 1, hidden away behind the polyclinic building. Made in the mid-1990s, the bust is the work o

A street café on a warm summer's day.

⊘ STREET ART

Along the peaceful pedestrianised Old Town street of Literatų gatvė (a turning off Pilies gatvė), and inspired by a local poem about a melancholy young man drinking and smoking with his friends in the area, several walls towards the eastern end of the street have over the past few years been decorated with a series of prints, drawings and paintings. The artworks are dedicated to writers who all left their individual marks on the city, among them Nobel Prize-winner Polish poet Czesław Miłosz and the French novelist Romain Gary.

The sole work of local artists, the permanent outdoor gallery can be enjoyed in combination with a drink at Saint Germain (Literatų 9/32, www.saintgermain. lt), a swanky wine bar with outdoor seating found at the very end of the street.

the local sculptor Konstantinas Bogdanas, who is known for his many Soviet-era statues. Oddly enough, the deceased American rock musician had no connection whatsoever with Lithuania, and in 2010 a new cast of the statue was donated to Zappa's native Baltimore.

OUTSIDE THE OLD TOWN

The **National Art Gallery**  (Nacionalinė Dailės Galerija; Konstitucijos 22; www.ndg.lt; Tue–Wed and Fri–Sat noon–7pm, Thu until 8pm, Sun 11am–5pm; guided tours in English available), lies just over the river close to the Radisson Blu Hotel Lietuva. Its collection of 20th and 21th century Lithuanian art includes over 46 000 exhibits. It mounts a constantly changing series of superb exhibitions from home and abroad.

One church outside the Old Town worth making the effort to reach is the **Church of Sts Peter and Paul**  (Šv. Petro ir Povilo bažnyčia; Antakalnio 1; daily 6.30am–6.45pm). Commissioned in 1668 by Mykolas Kazimieras Pacas (Michał Kazimierz Pac, 1624–1682), a local military commander, it is the best example of Baroque architecture in the city. Pac's tombstone, inscribed *Hic jacet peccator* ("Here lies a sinner"), is embedded in the wall to the right of the entrance. Despite a plain facade, the Baroque interior is breathtaking, with more than 2,000 undecorated stuccoed figures crowding the vaults, representing mythological, biblical and battle scenes. The boat-shaped chandelier is also spectacular.

CEMETERIES OF THE FALLEN

Beyond this church to the northeast of the city is the **Antakalnis Cemetery** (Antakalnio kapinės; Karių apų 11), which symbolises Vilnius' complicated and bloody history. In the Soldiers' Cemetery German, Polish, Russian, Lithuanian and even Turkish soldiers lie in the same soil. In a clearing at the back four giant Soviet granite soldiers stand next to a hall of fame where the dignitaries of Soviet Lithuania are buried, while 1,700 skeletons from Napoleon's Grande Armée are in a nearby mass grave (see page 272). In the centre of the cemetery lie the graves of the seven border guards and the civilians killed beside the TV Tower during the fight for independence by the same Soviet Army.

Some 5km (3 miles) north of the centre over the Green Bridge and along Kalvarijų gatvė is **Verkiai Palace** (Verkių rūmai; Žaliųjų Ežerų 49). In this a singular neoclassical manor house is now a restaurant (www.verkiai.lt). The surrounding gardens and forest are a lovely place to relax.

The other major cemetery is to the southeast of the city. **Rasos Cemetery** (Rasų kapinės; intersection of Rasų and Sukilėlių), founded in 1801, is known as the "Pantheon of the Famous". Prominent politicians, academics (Joachim Lelewel), poets

The National Art Gallery.

(Ludwik Kondratowicz) and painters (Pranciškus Smuglevičius, 1745–1807) are among those buried here. Of particular interest are the graves of the artist and composer Mikalojus Konstantinas Čiurlionis (1875–1911), the writer Balys Sruoga (1886–1947) and author Jonas Basanavičius (1851–1927). The heart of Józef Piłsudski, the Lithuania-born Polish military general, who ensured eastern Lithuania was under Polish control from 1920 to 1939, is also buried here. The rest of his remains lie in a coffin in the crypts of Wawel Cathedral in Kraków, but as he always felt his heart was in Vilnius, his was buried along with his mother's body under a black granite slab.

PUSHKIN MUSEUM

Just out of town to the southeast, on the far side of the Markučiai district, is the **Literary Museum of A. Pushkin ⓧ** (Literatūrinis A. Puškino muziejus; Subačiaus 124; www.vilniausmuzie-jai.lt/a_puskinas; Wed–Sun 10am–5pm) in the former home of Alexander Pushkin's son, built in 1867. One room contains the poet's possessions, and you can also see the 19-hectare (47-acre) grounds where the anti-tsarist uprising of 1863 was hatched.

WEST OF THE OLD TOWN

To the west of the city, inside a crook in the meandering River Neris is **Vingis Park ⓨ** (Vingio parkas), a popular place for cyclists and skaters. The park dates back to the 16th century, when it was part of the aristocratic Radvila (Radziwiłł) estate. Tsar Alexander I was at a ball in Radvila Palace, then in Vingis, when he received the news of Napoleon's invasion in 1812 – the episode is detailed in Tolstoy's book *War and Peace*.

The first **National Song Festival** took place here in 1947, and a special stage was built in 1960 to absorb the 20,000 singers, dancers and musicians who still flock here every five years to take part in one of the country's great celebrations.

The housing districts on the far side of the river are the work of Soviet-Lithuanian architects. In 1974 the designers of the new **Lazdynai District** received the Order of Lenin for their grey prefabricated ferro-concrete housing blocks. The **Karoliniškės district** to the west of the city on the right bank of the Neris is dominated by the **Television Tower ⓩ** (Televizijos bokštas; revolving observation platform Mon–Thu and Sun 11am–9pm, Fri–Sat until 10pm), which has become infamous for the massacre on the night of 12/13 January 1991 when Soviet tanks crushed and shot 14 unarmed civilians who were defending the building. The memory of the "defenders of freedom" is preserved in a small hall of fame at the foot of the tower (daily 10am–9pm; free), as well as in the Lithuanian State Museum. The 326-metre (1,070ft) Television Tower is the tallest structure in Lithuania and has

Trakai Historical National Park.

a restaurant halfway up (Mon–Thu and Sun 11am–10pm, Fri–Sat until 11pm), from where there is a breathtaking view of the suburbs with the centre just visible on a clear day.

THE CASTLE OF TRAKAI

The former capital of the Grand Duchy of Lithuania, 27km (18 miles) to the west of Vilnius, is the most popular day trip from Vilnius. The resort village of **Trakai ❷** is surrounded by five lakes up to 48 metres (158ft) deep. In summer people swim and sail in Lake Galvė, which acts as a kind of moat around Trakai Castle's peninsula. Galvė is the Lithuanian for "head", and the story is that the lake would not unfreeze in spring unless it had been fed the heads of the Grand Duke's enemies. Lithuania's most photographed castle was the heart of the Grand Duchy until 1323, when Grand Duke Gediminas moved the capital to Vilnius. The five-storey, red-brick fortifications were constructed by Vytautas and have been undergoing reconstruction since 1952.

Trakai Castle Museum (Trakų pilies muziejus; www.trakaimuziejus.lt; May–Sept daily 10am–7pm, Mar–Apr, Oct Tue–Sun 10am–6pm, Nov–Feb Tue–Sun 9am–5pm) in the rooms around the internal courtyard offers an exhibition on prehistoric discoveries and the splendour of Lithuania's Grand Duchy, which extended from the Baltic to the Black Sea. In the outer buildings are antiques from the feudal houses of later centuries. The ruins of the town's earlier castle can be seen on the mainland nearby.

In the 14th century Grand Duke Vytautas "invited" his bodyguard of Crimean Karaite (or Karaim) to come to Trakai, where they settled around the castle. The Karaite are ethnically Turkish and practise a particular kind of Judaism, giving the royal town its distinctive touch and exotic flavour. Numbering somewhere in the region of 250, the Karaite are the smallest historically ethnic minority in Lithuania. Karaimų, the town's main street, is a good place to learn more about their culture.

At No. 22, the **S. Shapshal Karaim Ethnographic Museum** (S. Šapšalo karaimu tautos muziejaus ekspozicija; www.trakaimuziejus.lt; Wed–Sun Apr–Oct 10am–6pm, Nov–Mar 9am–5pm) has traditional costumes, jewellery and photographs of the Karaite people alongside weaponry and cooking utensils. A *kenesa*, or prayer house, of this fascinating Judaic sect who also observe elements of the New Testament and Islam, is at Karaimu 30. Their cemetery, which dates back centuries, can be found by following Karaimu north past the castle and over a small bridge. Take the next left and it's a little further along on the left hand side of the track.

There are a number of hotels in the area, and a music festival centring on the castle brings many visitors to Trakai in August.

Looking out from Karoliniškės.

KAUNAS

At the confluence of the Neris and Nemunas Rivers, Lithuania's second city is in many ways the centre of the country, with some of the best museums and a thriving commercial life.

Lithuania's second city, **Kaunas** ❸ represents the very heart of ethnic Lithuanian identity. Less than two hours from Vilnius, it can be enjoyed as a day trip, though visitors may want to stay longer. There is no shortage of places to stay. It was relatively unscathed by World War II, and large parts of the Old City remain untouched. In 2022, Kaunas will be the European Capital of Culture.

During its two decades as Lithuania's interim capital it developed from a hugely important Russian garrison town to a European city, and many of the Functionalist buildings from that period remain. It is the major commercial centre of the country, manufacturing textiles and food products, and if Vilnius now provides the country with intellectuals, Kaunas provides it with traders and businessmen.

Kaunas and Vilnius are connected by the River Neris. The point where it joins Lithuania's major river, the Nemunas, was chosen for the siting of the original castle from where the town grew. The Nemunas, once Lithuania's southern border, was on the German traders' route, and Kaunas became a Hansa town.

TOWN HALL SQUARE

The city was first mentioned in 1361, and its historical heart is by the castle in **Town Hall Square** Ⓐ (Rotušės

aikštė), surrounded by numerous 16th-century German merchant houses. In the middle of this cobblestoned open area is the **Kaunas Town Hall** (Kauno Rotušė), known as The White Swan for its elegance and 53-metre (175ft) tower. Designed in late Baroque and early classical style, it was begun in 1542 as a one-storey building. The second floor and the tower were added at the end of the 16th century. The Gothic vaulted cellar of the tower served as a prison and a warehouse, the ground floor was reserved for traders

Main attractions

Perkūnas House
Cathedral-Basilica of Sts Peter and Paul
Laisvės alėja
Mykolas Žilinskas Art Gallery
M.K. Čiurlionis National Museum of Art
Church of Christ's Resurrection
Ninth Fort
Open-Air Museum, Rumšiškės

Maps on pages 266, 298

Kaunas's Old Town in the fog.

and prison guards, and the first floor housed the magistrate's office, treasury and town archives.

Destroyed during fighting between the Russians and the Swedes, it was reconstructed in 1771 to house the local government. In 1824, under the tsarist regime, it was transformed into an Orthodox church and later it became the warehouse of the artillery. It served as the provisional residence of the tsar (1837) and as a theatre (1865–9). Under the Soviet regime it was used by the engineering department of Kaunas Polytechnic (1951–60). Renovated between 1969 and 1973, it now serves as a wedding palace, and happy couples and their entourages often line up for photographs in the square outside. The cellar of the Town Hall houses a branch of the **Kaunas City Museum** (Kauno Miesto Muziejus; www.kaunomuziejus.lt; Tue–Sat 10am–6pm, Sun 10am–4pm), displaying archaeological finds, mainly Lithuanian ceramics from a few hundred years ago – glazed tiles, jugs, jars, goblets, pans and plates.

ST FRANCIS' CHURCH

The Jesuits started to buy land and buildings in Kaunas in the early 17th century. The construction of **St Francis' Church and Jesuit Monastery** (Šv. Pranciškaus bažnyčia ir Jėzuitų vienuolynas; Rotušės aikštė 7; Mon–Sat 4–6pm, Sun 7am–1pm and 4–6pm) was finished in the middle of the 18th century. After 1812 it served as a hospital and in 1824 it became the residence of the city's archbishop. In 1924 it was returned to the Jesuits, who used it for a boys' school. The church, which has a basilica layout, fine marble altars and woodcarvings, was built in 1666 and was frequently destroyed by fires. In 1825 it became the Alexander Nevsky Orthodox Church and under the Soviets it was transformed into a vocational school. In 1990 it was returned to the Catholic church.

HUNTERS' INN

The house at Rotušės aikštė 10, which has a Renaissance facade, was once a hunters' inn and now houses a hunters' restaurant (www.medziotojai.lt) decorated with the taxidermist's art. A statue fo

Kaunas

Lithuanian poet and priest Jonas čiulis-Maironis has been erected front of No. 13, where he lived m 1910 until his death in 1932. The roque building from the late 16th ntury served as a military hospital in 12. During the 1861 uprising against ssia its cellars were used as prisons. n the northwest corner of the square the **St George Church** and **Ber- rdine Monastery** (Bernardinų vienu- rnas). With Renaissance and Gothic ments, it dates back to the late h century, when the first house was ught by nuns. The attached house of rship, the **Holy Trinity Church** (Šv. ejybės bažnyčia, 1668), was rebuilt in e Baroque style. In the 19th century possessed nine wooden altars, but ese were lost during World War I. In 78 it was given back to the Catholic minary. In 1933–4, the late-Renais- nce belfry was incorporated into the minary, which is between the church d the belfry. This building was given ck to the seminary in 1982.

The **Museum of Medicine and Phar- acy History** (Medicinos ir farmacijos istorijos muziejus; Rotušės aikštė 28; Tue–Sat 10am–5pm) is a 17th-century building that used to house a phar- macy. On display are old instruments and a reconstructed interior of a phar- macy from the early 20th century.

PERKŪNAS HOUSE

From Town Hall Square walk down Aleksoto Street towards the Nemunas. At Aleksoto Street 6 is **Perkūnas House** (Perkūno namas; www.perkunonamas.lt; Mon–Fri 10am–4.30pm or by appoint- ment). Historians cannot agree if the original purpose of this picturesque 15th-century Gothic brick building was a chapel or the Hansa office. The more romantically minded maintain it was the temple of Perkūnas, the god of thunder, since during renovation in 1818 workers found a 27cm (11in) tab- leau of a town and temples with three fishes, which came to symbolise the rivers Nemunas, Neris and the god Perkūnas. The statue has since been lost but the name stuck.

Similar to St Anne's Church in Vil- nius, Perkūnas House is one of the

Town Hall Square.

Kaunas Castle.

most original examples of late Gothic in Lithuania, and its rich architecture is a monument to the economic power of the Hansa and the German-speaking world of the time. After reconstruction in the early 19th century it served as a school, and in 1844 the first Kaunas Drama Theatre was established here. After 1863 the house fell into ruins. Renovated at the end of the 19th century it served as a religious school, and returned to the Jesuits. Now the building still houses a Jesuit gymnasium, a concert hall and the Memorial Museum of Adomas Mickevičius (Adam Mickiewicz).

On the banks of the River Nemunas stands **Vytautas Church ⓑ** (Vytauto bažnyčia), built at the beginning of the 15th century for Franciscan monks. Here foreign merchants celebrated Mass. It was built in the Gothic style, and a tower was added at the end of the same century. Napoleon's troops used it to store ammunition in 1812, and in 1915, when the German Army occupied Kaunas, it was used as a potato warehouse. In 1990 the church, with its sober white interior, was re-opened for worship. The grave of priest and writer J. Tumas Vaižgantas (1869–1933), who organised the renovation of the church in 1920, is in the outer walls on the left.

A pathway leads to the confluence of the Neris and the Nemunas Rivers. From the bank where they meet there is a good view of the Old Town spires, the Town Hall and the Jesuit and Vytautas churches. Midsummer's Eve (Joninės) on 23 June is celebrated every year on this piece of ground.

CASTLE AND CATHEDRAL

Situated on the banks of the Neris is **Kaunas Castle ⓒ** (Kauno pilis). First mentioned in the 13th century, it was the earliest stone castle in Lithuania. The surrounding walls, 2 metres (7ft) wide and 13 metres (43ft) high, could not fend off the crusaders who destroyed the castle in 1362 after a three-week siege. Six years later a stronger castle was built with walls 3.5 metres (12ft) thick and four towers. Nevertheless, over the centuries it was washed away by the Neris and the northern wall with the towers collapsed. Today, only

rt of the castle remains. Since 2011 as housed a branch of the Kaunas y Museum (Kauno Miesto Muziejus; w.kaunomuziejus.lt; June–Aug Tue–Sat am–6pm, Sun 10am–4pm, Sept–May e–Fri 10am–6pm, Sat 10am–5pm; ided tours available) with an inter- ive historical exhibition about the stle and its court.

Using Valančiaus Street, walk back Town Hall Square and turn left into niaus Street at the **Cathedral-Basil- of Sts Peter and Paul** Ⓓ (Šv. Petro Povilo arkikatedra bazilika; www. noarkikatedra.lt), which towers 42 tres (138ft) above the ground. The st church was built here in the early century but its original shape is known. The naves were added in the –16th century, and the construction s completed in 1655. Of particular erest are the Baroque high altar of 75 and the neo-Gothic chapel to the ht. It belonged to Augustine monks til 1895 when it became a cathedral. was elevated to the rank of basilica 1921. On the right, intersecting niaus Street, Zamenhofo Street

leads to the **Kaunas City Museum – Folk Music Branch** (Kauno Miesto Muziejus – tautinės muzikos skyrius; www.kaunomuziejus.lt; Zamenhofo 12; Tue–Fri 10am–6pm, Sat 10am–5pm). Inside you will find a range of Lithua- nian traditional instruments, including kanklės, usually a trapezoidal shaped piece of wood with strings attached.

FREEDOM AVENUE

Continue along Vilniaus Street going towards the city centre. In a small yard is the **Prezidentūra** (Vilniaus 33; www. istorineprezidentura.lt; Tue–Wed Fri–Sun 11am–5pm, Thu until 7pm), the resi- dence of the three Lithuanian presi- dents during the inter-war period. The single-storey building has been reno- vated and is now open to the public as a small museum.

Vilniaus Street leads into **Laisvės alėja** (Freedom Avenue), the main thoroughfare of the New Town often optimistically compared to the Champs- Elysées in Paris or Unter den Linden in Berlin. Kaunas residents love to stroll along the 1.6km (1-mile) pedestrian

Inspecting antiques at a flea market in Kaunas.

street, designed in the late 19th century. In 1982 Laisvės alėja was closed to traffic and the central tree-lined pathway was dotted with numerous benches. Restful and green in the summer, it can be quite grey and depressing in winter. Between the wars a number of administrative buildings were put up along this classy avenue now lined with shops.

At the crossing of Sapiegos Street stands the **Monument to Vytautas the Great E**. The bronze statue of "the creator of Lithuanian power" stands proudly over four defeated soldiers: a Russian, a Pole, a Tatar and a German crusader holding a broken sword, symbolising the defeat of the Teutonic Knights. A bronze plaque shows a map of medieval Lithuania extending from the Black Sea to the Baltic Sea.

In Miesto sodas, the city park facing the **Music Theatre F** (Muzikinis teatras), lies a granite monument where the name of Romas Kalanta is written into the pavement, marking the spot where the 19-year-old student protester immolated himself on 14 May 1972, sparking anti-Soviet riots.

St Michael the Archangel church.

INDEPENDENCE SQUARE

The large pedestrian mall ends in **Independence Square** (Nepriklausomybė aikštė), which is dominated by the **Church of St Michael the Archangel** (Šv. Mykolo arkangelo bažnyčia). The imposing blue neo-Byzantine building was built in 1893 by Russian architects as the Orthodox church for the army in Kaunas Castle. It was closed in 19? and transformed into a permanent exhibition of stained glass and sculpture, but after independence it reopened as a Catholic house of worship. Inside are several interesting frescoes of the Evangelists and saints, and the stained glass represents the Assumption. In autumn, which is the favourite time for weddings in Lithuania, couples queue up outside the church to be married.

On the right-hand side of the square is the modern building of the **Mykolas Žilinskas Art Gallery** (Mykolo Žilinsko dailės galerija; www.ciurlionis.lt; Tue, Wed, Fri–Sun 11am–5pm, Thu until 7pm). The austere glass-and-granite building houses 1,670 works of art donated by Lithuanian-born Žilinskas

904–92). It has Chinese, German d Dutch porcelain, Italian paintings the 16th and 18th centuries and an teresting collection of 20th-century t. In front of the museum stands a atue of a naked man created by Pets Mazūras and put up in 1991 despite me objections.

ILITARY MUSEUM

aunas has some of the country's best useums. On Donelaičio Street, north Laisvės alėja and running parallel, es Unity Square (Vienybės aikštė), here the symbols of Lithuanian stateood have been re-erected. A hall of me with the portraits of famous Lithanian politicians and writers leads om the Liberty monument to the :ernal flame, flanked by traditional ooden crosses remembering those ho died for Lithuania's independence.

The entrance to the **Military Museum f Vytautas the Great** ⓖ (Vytauto idžiojo karo muziejus; Tue–Sun 10am–m) is on Unity Square. Lithuanian milaria is shown through the ages from rehistoric times to the present day.

There is also the wreck of the *Lituanica*, the plane in which Steponas Darius and Stasys Girėnas attempted in 1933 to fly non-stop from New York. Other exhibits show the history of the Vytautas Magnus University founded in 1922, closed in 1940 and reopened in 1990.

M.K. ČIURLIONIS MUSEUM OF ART

The **M.K. Čiurlionis Museum of Art** (Nacionalinis M.K. Čiurlionio dailės muziejus; www.ciurlionis.lt; Tue–Wed and Fri–Sun 11am–5pm, Thu until 7pm) is in the building immediately behind the Military Museum and has its entrance at Putvinskio 55. Built in 1936, the gallery has some 360 works of the Lithuanian painter and composer, and it should not be missed.

The mystic and Modernist Čiurlionis (1875–1911) saw nature as an inexhaustible source of beauty. Of *Miške (In the Forest)*, Lithuania's first symphony, he wrote: "It begins with soft and wide chords, as soft and wide as the sighing of our Lithuanian pines." Čiurlionis wrote some 20 preludes, canons and

An exhibit at the Devil Museum.

Tip

Look out for concerts and choral works at the Kaunas Philharmonic (Kauno Filharmonija, Sapiegos 5, www. kaunofilharmonija.lt), which start at 5–6pm.

fugues for the organ, and harmonised around 60 folk songs. In a special listening hall, visitors can hear some of his symphonies and orchestral works. Concerts are also sometimes held in his former home, now a museum, in the spa town of Druskininkai, 124km (77 miles) south. The museum also has an exhibition featuring other Lithuanian artists.

A few houses away, at Putvinskio 64, is the **Devil Museum** (Velnių muziejus; www.ciurlionis.lt; Tue–Wed and Fri–Sun 11am–5pm, Thu until 7pm), an impressive collection of wooden devil statues amassed by the folk artist Antanas Žmuidzinavičius (1876–1966). It has grown over the years as new foreign devils have been added, and there are now more than 1,700, including Hitler and Stalin dancing over the bones of Lithuania.

ŽALIAKALNIS DISTRICT

From Putvinskio you can either take the Žaliakalnis funicular (Mon–Fri 7am–7pm, Sat–Sun from 9pm) or climb 231 steps up to the Žaliakalnis

Open-Air Museum at Rumšiškės.

district, which offers a splendid view of the city. One of the most interesting architectural monuments is the **Church of Christ's Resurrection** (Kristaus Prisikėlimo bažnyčia; www. prisikelimas.lt; observation deck Mar–Sept Mon–Fri 11.30am–6.30pm, Sat–Sun 11am–6.30pm, Oct–Feb Mon–Fri noon–6pm, Sat–Sun 11am–6pm) at Žemaičių 31b, near the funicular terminal. It was started in 1932, although with the annexation by the USSR in 1940, the 63-metre (205ft) high church did not see completion until 2004. The massive white building is fairly plain inside but is worth a visit. An observation platform on the roof can be reached via a lift for spectacular views.

THE NINTH FORT

A visit to Kaunas is not complete without a tour of the **Ninth Fort** (Devintasis Fortas; Žemaičių plentas 73; www.9fortomuziejus.lt; Apr–Oct Tue–Sun 10am–6pm, Nov–Mar Wed–Sun 10am–4pm), just off the A1 road towards Klaipėda. Built at the end of the 19th century as part of the outer town defences on the orders of Tsar Alexander II to strengthen the western border of the Russian Empire, it became infamous as a concentration camp during the Nazi occupation. In the fort you can visit the former prison cells where Jews from all over Europe were herded together awaiting execution. A silent reminder of the horror are the inscriptions preserved on the walls of the cell. *"Nous sommes 500 Français"* ("We are 500 French"), wrote Abraham Wechsler from the French town of Limoges before being killed.

The **Way of Death** (Mirties kelias) leads to the place where some 30,000 Jews were shot. The museum housed in a concrete hall near the fort describes the deportations of Lithuanians by the NKVD (the predecessor of the KGB), the Nazi and the Stalinist terror, and the resistance fighters under the Soviet occupation who fought til the early 1950s. An astonishing, -metre (105ft) reinforced-concrete onument dating from 1984 and commemorating the events at the fort is cated nearby.

ŽAISLIS MONASTERY

me 7km (4 miles) to the southeast the town centre (take trolleybus No. or 12) is Lithuania's Baroque gem, e **Pažaislis Monastery** ❶ (Pažaislio nuolynas; www.pazaislis.org; museum ne–Aug Tue–Fri 10am–6pm, Sat am–4pm, Sept–May Tue–Fri 10am– m, Sat 10am–4pm). Isolated in the untryside above a dam on the River munas, it was built in the 17th cen- y with orchards and gardens that e still cultivated. Entrance is through e Holy Gate, and the church has a fine -metre (150ft) cupola, on the inside which is a painting of the Virgin ry. The marble and oak interior is riched with frescoes restored under e aegis of the Čiurlionis Museum, ich became responsible for it in 66. Built for the obscure Camaldo- e Order, it was briefly populated by Lithuanian-American nuns in the early 20th century, and again in 1992.

The huge reservoir beside the monastery is called the **Kaunas Sea** (Kauno marios) and is popular for recreation.

OPEN-AIR MUSEUM

Some 20km (12 miles) east of the city, on the A1, is the small village of Rumšiškės, the site of the **Open-Air Museum of Lithuania** (Lietuvos liaudies buities muziejus; www.llbm.lt; May–mid-Oct daily 10am–6pm). The 176-hectare (435-acre) grounds make a good half-day out, and give time to appreciate the collections of old rural homes from all over the country. There are also re-creations of schools, pubs and a mill. It becomes quite crowded during holiday weekends, especially those related to pagan feast days. Inside the houses actors dressed as peasants work on traditional crafts. When the buildings are closed, you can still visit the site as a park (daily Apr 10am–5pm, mid-Oct–Mar 10am–4pm, May–mid-Oct after buildings close until 8pm).

> ⊘ **Tip**
>
> The children will enjoy a visit to the zoo (www.zoosodas.lt) or to the marine aquarium, the biggest in the Baltic States with sharks and fish fed on Tue, Thu, Fri at 5pm and Sat at 1pm (www.mega.lt; at the time of writing, the aquarium was under reconstruction).

Christ's Resurrection Church at Žaliakalnis.

AUKŠTAITIJA

Vilnius

This region follows the Castle Route beside the River Nemunas to the coast and heads north through agricultural land to Kernavė, one of the most important pagan sites in the country.

Map on page 266

The northern part of Lithuania between the Nemunas and Neris Rivers and the Latvian border is called Aukštaitija (literally, Highlands). The communities of Aukštaitija grew up around uniform, one-street villages, and small homesteads were created as land was divided among successive generations. The region was once known for growing flax. Primarily an agricultural area, Aukštaitija is moving towards more lucrative forms of income. In general, people from this part of the country have a reputation for being talkative, friendly and fond of songs.

Aukštaitija has two distinct regions, a rather flat western region, accessible from Kaunas, and a hilly eastern region, one of the nicest parts of the country.

THE CASTLE ROAD

The willow-lined banks beside the 141, which follows the River Nemunas for 229km (143 miles) from Kaunas to the coast, are dotted with red-brick fortified manor houses looking out over the wide valley towards Lithuania's southern neighbours. Just beyond Jurbarkas the river forms the border with Kaliningrad. Castles were built all along here when the river marked the border between the Grand Duchy and the lands of the Teutonic Order. From the 17th century, merchants and aristocrats made their castle homes here.

The first stretch of the road, from Kaunas to Jurbarkas, is a pleasant 86km (53-mile) drive. The bizarre-looking castle at **Raudondvaris** ● (Pilies takas 4; www.raudondvariodvaras.lt) on the outskirts of Kaunas was built in the 17th century and remodelled in the 19th century by the Tiškevičius (Tyszkiewicz) family, who embellished it with a picture collection and a fine library. After a large-scale renovation, it now houses a tourist centre, an art gallery, a restaurant, a concert hall and a branch of the **District Kaunas Museum**.

Aukštaitija is known for its lakes and hills.

(Wed–Sun 10am–6pm) dedicated to the history of the manor and Juozas Naujalis (1839–1934), the patriarch of Lithuanian music. The 19th-century church was built by Lorenzo Anichini, who is buried here, and the interior statuary is by Lorenzo Pompaloni. There is also a 25-metre (82ft) tower overlooking the **Nevėžis Nature Reserve**.

At **Seredžius** there is a hill fort named after a legendary hero, Duke Palemonas, who is supposed to have been descended from Roman nobility. The actor and singer Al Jolson was born Asa Yoelson in this *shtetl* in 1886, five years before his family emigrated to the United States where he starred in the pioneering 1927 "talkie" *The Jazz Singer*.

Nearby is the old Belvedere Manor (Belvederio dvaras) on a high slope, but it has been rather neglected, as has the park in which it lies. Only the park is open to the public.

Veliuona is a small and fairly unremarkable town high on the river bank with a park and two hill forts: the Castle Mountain and the Gediminas Grave (Gedimino kapas) – it is thought that Lithuania's Grand Duke died here in 1341. The town has a 17th-century Renaissance church restored at the turn of the century, and this is the burial place of Juozas Radavičius (1857–1911), a famous organ master, and Antanas and Jonas Juška, two 19th-century Lithuanian folklorist brothers whose remains were brought back here from Kazan in Russia, in 1990.

A few miles further on is **Raudonė**, a town in a similarly elevated position. Its park is full of ancient oaks. The 17th-century red-brick castle (Raudonės pilis), a mix of Renaissance and neo-Gothic, was built for a Prussian merchant, Krispin Kirschenstein. It was rebuilt in the 19th century and today it houses a school. There is a wonderful view from its tower, which is open to visitors (mid-Apr–mid-Nov Mon–Sat 10am–4pm).

The 17th-century **Panemunė Castle** (Panemunės pilis; www.panemunespi lt; May–Sept Tue–Sun 10am–6pm, Oct–Apr Tue–Sun 10am–5pm) in the village of **Vytėnai** ❺ was built by a Hungarian merchant, Janush Eperjesh, on the site of a former Teutonic fort. Set on a hill with a park, the large and somewhat tumbledown building is surrounded by cascading ponds.

JURBARKAS

Beyond Skirsnemunė (called Christmemel by the Germans) is **Jurbarkas**. It has a population of 13,000, but the Jewish cemetery – with over 300 headstones – is all that is left of the once thriving Jewish community. There is an interesting 19th-century part of the town, and the local park has a farmstead museum (Vinco Grybo memorialinis muziejus; Vydūno 31; Tue–Fri 9am–6pm, Sat 9am–5pm), devoted to the distinguished Lithuanian sculptor and Communist sympathiser Vincas Grybas, who lived here from 1926 until he was murdered by the Nazis in 1941.

KAUNAS TO KĖDAINIAI

The A8 (E67) leaves Kaunas past the Ninth Fort. After a few kilometres, the

Panemunė Castle.

144 turn-off leads up to **Kėdainiai** , an administrative centre with chemical works and a sugar industry. The recommended Old Town is comparatively large and dates back to the 15th century, when it was owned by the dukes of Radvila.

Under their patronage industry expanded, schools and publishing houses grew up, and Lutheran, Roman Catholic and Reformed churches and a synagogue, all still standing, were built. The **Kėdainiai Regional Museum** (Kėdainių krašto muziejus; Didžioji 19; www.kedaini umuziejus.lt; Wed–Fri 11am–6pm, Sat 10am–5pm, Sun 10am–3pm) tells the story of the town from ancient times to the present, with particular attention paid to the Nazi and Soviet occupations. Other branches of the museum house the Mausoleum of the Radziwiłł Dukes (Senoji 1; same hours as the museum) and a collection of wooden sculptures by Vytautas Ulevičius (J.Basanavičiaus 36; Mon–Fri 10am–2pm; free).

PANEVĖŽYS

From Kėdainiai the A8 (E67) runs to **Panevėžys**, where it becomes the A10

Autumn in Panevėžys.

(E67). Panevėžys is Lithuania's fifth-largest city, with a population of 88,600. It dates from the middle of the 16th century, when there was a community and a manor house on the River Nevėžis, where a park is laid out today. Its rapid expansion as an industrial centre has not improved its attractiveness. Since the 1960s its name has been linked with the Panevėžys Drama Theatre, which has built up an impressive reputation.

The **Ethnographic Museum** (Panevėžio kraštotyros muziejus; Vasario 16-osios 23; www.paneveziomuziejus.lt; Tue–Fri 9am–5pm, Sat 10am–4pm) is in the oldest house in the area, dating from 1614. It also has a small collection of folk art a block away (Kranto 21; tel: 59 61 81 to arrange a visit).

The karst region around **Pasvalys** , 38km (24 miles) north of Panevėžys, has underground caverns, and in the town park there are signs where some of these have caved in. The less than stable terrain is also marked by sinkholes permanently filled with water; one of the best is the Green Spring (Žalsvasis šaltinis), which is located alongside the River Lévuo and Kalno Street.

Branching off the A10, Road 125 leads up to **Biržai** . The old town of Biržai was built up around an artificial lake created in the 16th century at the confluence of the Apasčia and the Agluona. The **castle** that stood here was destroyed in the 18th century but restored in the 1980s, and there is a museum inside (Oct–Apr Tue and Sun 9am–4.30pm, Wed–Sat 9am–5.30pm; May–Sept Tue and Sun 10am–5.30pm, Wed–Sat 10am–6.30pm) presenting the history of the two and the Radvila (Radziwiłł) Family. The reconstructed area around **Radvila Palace** (www.bir zumuziejus.lt) is on the edge of a man made lake. Inside is the beautiful Baroque Church of St John the Baptist (Šv Jono bažnyčia) and a monument on the town square to a local poet and revolutionary, Julius Janonis (1896–1917), who wrote under the pseudony

Vaidila Ainis. Also beside the lake is the 19th-century neoclassical Astravas Manor (Astravo dvaras), with a palace and park now used by a linen enterprise. Try some beer while you are here. There are a number of breweries in the town, giving Biržai the reputation as the beer capital of Lithuania.

KAUNAS TO ROKIŠKIS

This route goes through the eastern edge of the Aukštaitija plains, following the River Šventoji. It leaves Kaunas on the A6 (E262), the former Warsaw to St Petersburg post-road which was paved in the early 19th century.

As the road enters **Ukmergė** ❾ there is a neoclassical post-house built in 1835 on the right. On the south side of the town at Vaitkuškis is the former country home of the Koskovskis (Kossakowski) family, arts patrons with a taste for literature who corresponded with Balzac. It's worth climbing up the old tower of the fire station to see the panorama of the town.

After Ukmergė, Road 120 heads towards Anykščiai), where wine is blended from imported grapes as well as local cherries, apples, rowan berries and redcurrants in the **Anykščiai Wine** (Anykščių vynas; www.anvynas. lt) factory. Started in a small wooden house in the town centre in 1926 by Balys Karazija, it is now the largest winery in the Baltic States. The town is also known for its literary tradition. The most famous work from the town was a lyric poem written by Antanas Baranauskas (Antoni Baranowski, 1835–1902) in response to the felling by the tsar of Anykščių Šilelis, the 2,812-sq km (700-sq mile) pine forest km (3 miles) to the south. The poem became a milestone in the idea of conservation and the countryside. In the forest is the **Puntukas Stone** (Puntuko akmuo), one of the largest in the country, weighing 265 tonnes. These big rocks, brought by glacial drift, are scattered throughout the Baltics, and

are sometimes called "presents from Scandinavia". The sculptor Bronius Pundzius turned one boulder into a monument to the transatlantic flyers Steponas Darius and Stasys Girėnas in 1943 (see page 313).

Created in 2012, the **Anykščiai Art Centre** (Anykščių menų centras; www. amenucentras.lt) has three branches: The Angel Museum and the Sacred Art Museum (Vilniaus 11; May daily 10am–5pm, June Sun–Fri 10am–5pm, Sat 10am–6pm, July–Aug Mon–Sat 10am–6pm, Sun 10am–5pm, Sept–Nov Mon–Fri 10am–5pm, Sat–Sun 10am–4pm, Dec–Apr Mon–Thu 10am–5pm, Fri–Sat 10am–4pm), and the Anykščiai chapel (Vilniaus g. 36, Mon–Fri 8am–5pm) serve as an exhibition and music hall. It's also possible to climb the tower of **Anykščiai St Matas Church** (June–Aug Fri–Sat 10am–7pm, Sun–Thu 10am–6pm, shorter hours rest of the year) ❿. The **Narrow Gauge Railway Museum** (Siauruko muziejus; Vilties 2; tel: 381 580 15; officially May–Sept Mon–Fri 9am–6pm, Sat–Sun 9am–7pm, Oct Mon–Fri 9am–5pm, Sat–Sun 9am–7pm, Nov–Apr by appointment) is

The Puntukas Stone.

interactive and fun, but is often closed. Calling the museum number usually leads to somebody rushing up the road with a set of keys. Organised excursions on an old narrow-gauge railway to a nearby lake, with food, wine and live musicians, are also on offer.

NIŪRONYS HORSE MUSEUM

In the village of **Niūronys**, just 8km (5 miles) outside of the town, the **Horse Museum** (Arklio muziejus; www.arkliomuziejus.lt; daily May–Sept 9am–6pm, Oct–Apr 9am–5pm) focuses on the role and importance of horses, which are highly regarded in Lithuania. Besides the animals, there are numerous carriages, horse-drawn buggies and agricultural machinery. There are also some areas dedicated to showing homes typical of the region. One weekend every June there is a lively horse gathering called Bėk, Bėk, Žirgeli (Run, Run, Horse), and there are races all day, from donkeys to thoroughbreds.

From **Svėdasai** beside a lake 24km (15 miles) further on, Road 118 goes northwest to **Kupiškis**, which is surrounded by manor houses, windmills and rural churches. Continuing 33km (20 miles) on Road 120 is **Rokiškis** , a regional centre with a hotel. Beside the main square is a country estate dating back to the 17th century and now housing the **Rokiškis Regional Museum** (Tyzenhauzų al. 5; www.muziejusrokiskyje.lt; Mon–Thu 8am–5pm, Fri 8am–3.45pm, lunch break at noon) with an exhibition about the history of the region, the manor house and the wooden sculptures of Lionginas Šepka. The 19th-century neo-Gothic church dedicated to St Matthew (Šv Mato bažnyčia) on the opposite side of the square is richly decorated thanks to the Tyzenhauzas family.

AUKŠTAITIJA UPLANDS

The main A2 highway runs northwest from Vilnius towards Rīga and Tallinn until it reaches **Panevėžys**. On its western side, on the banks of the Neris 32km (20 miles) from Vilnius, is the town of **Kernavė**, which can be reached by following Road 108 to Road 116. Forming a triangle with Vilnius and Trakai, this was a major trading centre in the 13th and 14th centuries. A village of just 300 or so, the site includes five hill-fort earthworks built to repel the crusaders and probably used by Mindaugas. Settlement here has been found to go back 10,000 years, and it developed into an exceptionally large defence system. It was an important feudal town until the Teutonic Order destroyed it in the late 14th century. The area is considered such a significant pagan monument that in 2004 it was designated a Unesco World Heritage Site. Its prehistoric flavour and perfect setting, with a beautiful view over the Neris Valley, make a popular gathering spot on Midsummer's Eve, when there are bonfires and all sorts of merry-making.

The **Green Lakes** (Žalieji ežerai) lie off the A14 just north from Vilnius. The area is a popular, hilly collection of summer homes, where the deep lake

Chair sculpture in Europos Park.

waters, tinted green, are a place for people from the city to cool off.

THE CENTRE OF EUROPE

After 26km (16 miles) north along the A14 there is a signpost directing you to the **Centre of Europe** ⑭. At longitude 25° 19', latitude 50° 54', members of the French National Geographic Institute "discovered" this fact in 1989, though few seem to have recognised it. More remarkable is the **Open-Air Museum at the Centre of Europe** (Europos parkas; www.europosparkas.lt; daily 10am–sunset) just south of Road 108. The area covers nearly 55 hectares (136 acres) of land, and has a growing number of sculptures by various artists from around the world who depict what Europe and its centre mean to them. The grounds also have a post office and restaurant. A speedier way to Europos parkas from Vilnius is to take Kalvarijų Street, veering right at the roundabout in Santariškės and following the Europos parkas signs; this road passes Verkių rūmai (Verkiai Palace) and the Green Lakes.

AUKŠTAITIJA NATIONAL PARK

Road 102 continues north into the **Aukštaitija National Park** (Aukštaitijos nacionalinis parkas), an area of 4,530 sq km (1,750 sq miles) of which 15 percent is lakes. Around three-quarters of the land is forested, and there is a great diversity of flora and fauna, with more than 700 species of plants, 100 species of mammals – including boar, elk, martens and beaver – and 78 species of fish. Canoeing and other water activities are popular, and there are many nature trails.

The best way to explore the park is to start in the tiny hamlet of **Palūšė** ⑮, where there is a handsome 19th-century wooden church and belfry. The park has an additional administrative centre at **Meironys**. Perhaps one of the quirkiest museums in the country is the folksy **Bee-keeper's Museum** (Bitininkystės muziejus; May–Sept Tue–Sun 10am–6pm) in the village of **Stripeikiai**. There are various hives in the shapes of pagan gods, along with woodcarvings of bee-related deities. The area surrounding the cottage is where the actual bee-keeping takes place. Honey, of course, can be

⊙ Tip

A detailed map is absolutely essential for navigating through the area, and can be obtained from the Aukštaitijos National Park Authority in Ignalina (www.anp.lt), or good bookshops.

One of the many mass grave direction markers in Lithuania.

⊙ HOLOCAUST ATLAS

The genocide of the Jewish population in Lithuania began a few days before the German invasion of the Soviet Union on 22 June 1941. In a prelude to the systematic Nazi slaughter, many ethnic Lithuanians began killing Jewish men, women and children in the countryside; their former neighbours for hundreds of years were tortured, raped, shot and buried in mass graves. An estimated 230 or so of these burial sites are believed to exist, some marked and others still not discovered or commemorated, many of them in Aukštaitija.

In 2011, "Atlas of the Holocaust in Lithuania", which aims to remember the victims and help visitors find these important historical sites was launched (www.holocaustatlas.lt).

HOLOKAUSTO AUKŲ KAPAI
HOLOCAUST MASS GRAVES

500 M

procured and boats can be hired for a better view of the surrounding lakes. **Ginučiai**, **Šuminai**, **Strazdai** and **Salos** are all pleasant villages in the vicinity.

Ignalina , the main town close to Palūšė, is a centre for the area, and the **Švenčionys Uplands** on its eastern side are an attractive hilly area. It snows more in Ignalina than anywhere else in the country and the snow stays longer, which make it popular for winter sports.

To the north is Lithuania's youngest city, **Visaginas** ⑰. Most of the almost 30,000 or so who live here are Russian-speakers brought to the town in the 1970s and 1980s to work at the nearby nuclear power plant. Its main street, Tai-kos prospektas, looks more like a boule-vard in Moscow than anything found in a small Baltic town, and is a prime example of Soviet social planning. The town is situated in a picturesque area of pine forests near a lake, in the shadow of the Ignalina Nuclear Power Plant (INPP) to the east, on the south bank of Lake Drūkšiai. Built in 1974, to the same design as the one used for disastrous Chernobyl, both INPP reactors have been decommissioned as part of the agree-ment for the country joining the EU.

ON THE BELARUSIAN BORDER

Vilnius is only 24km (15 miles) from the Belarusian border, and there are several places of interest in between. It is tempting to follow the roads into the neighbouring country, but the bor-der has become closely guarded since Lithuania joined the EU, and most visi-tors will need a visa. The A3 has been the main highway to the east since the Middle Ages, and it goes to the Belarus capital of Minsk. **Nemėžis** is the first village on the road, settled by Tatars in Vytautas' time, and they have their own chapel and cemetery here. On the oppo-site side of the valley are the remains of a 19th-century country estate and park.

The road is now in the **Medininkai Uplands**, an area of wide valleys, fewer depressions and fewer forests, formed in an earlier glacial age than other uplands in the country. At the frontier customs post are seven crosses in memory of the young Lithuanian bor-der guards killed in July 1991. Just before the border an old track goes down to the right to **Medininkai** and the Medininkai Castle (www.medininkaipilis.lt), a stone defence work from the 14th cen-tury, where Lithuania's patron saint St Casimir spent part of his childhood. The castle is now a school, cultural centre and museum with four exhibition halls displaying archaeological finds, arms (14th–18th century), silver goods and hunting trophies. The surroundings offer some spectacular walks.

Just over 3km (2 miles) to the south there is a signpost to **Juozapinė Hill** (Juozapinės kalnas), formerly the high-est point in Lithuania at a meagre 292 metres (963ft) and recently knocked into third place by more accurate measure-ments. Just over the border there are castles of ancient Lithuania at **Lyda** and at **Navagrudak** (Naugardukas in Lithua-nian and Nowogródek in Polish). The poet Adam Mickiewicz was born here in 1798.

The Lithuanian Bee-keeper's Museum in Stripeikiai village.

🔍 BASKETBALL FLYER

Basketball is Lithuania's favourite game, and one of its heroes is also remembered, with his co-pilot, for a fatal pioneering flight.

The sport at which Lithuania excels is basketball. Seven Lithuanians have Olympic gold medals. A few were even drafted into the North American National Basketball Association (NBA), including, most notably, Šarūnas Marčiulionis, who has put his money into a hotel and other businesses in Vilnius. Arvydas Sabonis, another legend, has followed suit; he owns a hotel in Palanga and has a stake in the Kaunas-based Žalgiris team.

More recently, two Lithuanian players Donatas Motiejūnas and Jonas Valančiūnas have made it to the NBA. Motiejūnas played for Houston Rockets from 2012–2016 and Valančiūnas has played for Toronto Raptors since 2012. The last big international event where Lithuania's national basketball team excelled was EuroBasket 2015 in France, where they finished second, losing in the final to Spain.

The history of the game in Lithuania begins with one of the country's great heroes, Steponas Darius. The village of Rubiškė on the coast where he was born in 1896 has since changed its name to Darius. In 1907, his family emigrated to the US and as a student he excelled at baseball and football as well as basketball. He signed up for the army in 1917 and fought in France where he was wounded and decorated. In 1920 he was a US volunteer for the Lithuanian Army and as a pilot he took part in the Klaipėda Revolt in 1923. He introduced basketball into his home country and laid down a sporting tradition that has continued to this day.

EPIC FLIGHT

Darius returned to the US in 1927 and founded a Lithuanian flying club, called Vytis. Five years later he and a colleague, Stasys Girėnas, set out to bring fame and glory to their newly independent nation by embarking on an epic flight from New York to Lithuania. They found enough money to buy an old plane they called *Lituanica*, but there was not enough for radio equipment.

The plane left New York on 15 July 1933 and flew across the Atlantic, covering 6,411km (3,984 miles) in 37 hours 11 minutes. Nobody knows why, but it never reached Lithuania and crashed at Soldin in Germany (now the town of Myślibórz in northwestern Poland). Their bodies were brought to Kaunas, where 60,000 people turned out for their funeral. The duo's portraits appeared on postage stamps, and 300 streets, 18 bridges and 8 schools were named after them. Their faces also appeared on the Lithuanian 10 Lt banknote.

MONUMENT TO THE PILOTS

The most popular monument to the heroes is near Anykščiai (between Panevėžys and Ignalina) on a huge boulder called Puntukas. In 1943 a Lithuanian sculptor, Bronius Pundzius, was in hiding from the Germans and he made himself a shelter beside the boulder. To while away his vigil, he sculpted a relief of the faces of the pilots in the stone, adding the text of their will, written before they set off.

Remnants of the aeroplane are on display in the Military Museum of Vytautas the Great in Kaunas. On the main road from Klaipėda, there is a signpost marked "S. Darius tėviškė" leading 9km (5.5 miles) to the village of Darius and a memorial museum.

Aviator Steponas Darius's significance is such that he even appears on a banknote.

S. DARIUS

Wooden church at Marcinkonys.

THE SOUTH

In the attractive south lies the spa town of Druskininkai, forever more associated with the composer and artist Mikalojus Konstantinas Čiurlionis, as well as the outrageous Grūtas Park, the world's first Soviet theme park.

The southernmost part of the country is split in two by the River Nemunas, which flows up from the Belarusian border just beyond Druskininkai to Kaunas. To the west is the region of **Suvalkija**. To the east is **Dzūkija**. Suvalkija was the land of the Sūduva and Jotvingiai tribes until it was joined to the Grand Duchy of Lithuania after the Teutonic Knights were crushed in 1410. In the following years of peace, people from Žemaitija and other neighbouring regions came to settle here, but the main villages and townships were not founded until the 17th and 18th centuries.

From 1867 to 1915 the area was part of the Russian province of Suvalkai, and although the region still bears the name, the town of Suvalkai (Suwałki) is in Poland today. After serfdom was abolished in the 19th century, peasants settled in farmsteads and a great number were able to afford to educate their own children. Since the bulk of the first group of educated people in the country came from here, their local dialect became the basis of the modern Lithuanian literary language.

People of Suvalkija have a reputation for being stingy and thrifty. They also have a reputation for hard work, summed up in the expression, "It would be better if father fell off the roof than a grain or a drop is lost."

Tranquil countryside near Lazdijai.

THE SUVALKIJA PLAIN

Marijampolė ⑱ (pop. around 36,000), the principal city of the region, is 150km (94 miles) west of Vilnius and 60km (38 miles) south of Kaunas across one of the most fertile plains in the country. It lies in a rather dull plain relieved only by the Šešupė, the region's main river. The town manufactures car parts and has one of the largest car markets in the country. The related transport and freighting businesses also generate a great deal of the city's wealth. The town takes its name from an 18th-century

Main attractions
Druskininkai
Čiurlionis Memorial
   Museum
Grūtas Park
Dzūkija National Park

Map on page 266

Marian monastery and in the 19th century it was a centre of enlightenment. The only town in Lithuania to change its name during the Soviet occupation, when it was known as Kapsukas in honour of one of the founders of the Lithuanian Communist Party, Marijampolė is on the main north–south Via Baltica, a fact that blesses it with the best hotels in the region.

Among half a dozen local museums is the **Marijampolė Local Lore Museum** (Marijampolės Kraštotyros muziejus; Vytauto 29; www.marijampolesmuziejus.lt; Tue–Sat 9am–5pm), which has an ethnographic collection of local history. At the same address is another place of interest: the Partisans and Deportation Museum (same hours as above).

Further up the River Šešupė on the A5 (E67) is **Kalvarija** ⑲. The old part is attractive with a post-house (1820) and the remains of a large jail built in 1810 to contain 1,000 prisoners. The classical-style church was built in 1840 and rebuilt in 1908, and it has some good paintings inside. A large Jewish community that settled here in the 17th

Traditional wellness at Druskininkai spa.

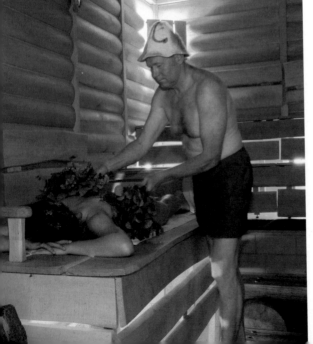

century was exterminated by the Nazis and their ethnic Lithuanian helpers.

To the west of Marijampolė, the A7 (E28) leads to the Polish border, passing through **Vilkaviškis** ⑳, a local centre that was burnt to the ground in World War II. Nearer the frontier is the **Paežeriai Manor dvaras** (Paežerių dvaras), an 18th–19th-century palace set in a park with a lake. It contains a regional museum (Vilkaviškis Area Museum; www.paezeriai.info; Apr–Sep Tue–Fri 9am–5pm, Sat 10am–6pm, Sun 11am–4pm, Oct–Mar Mon–Fri 9am–5pm, Sat–Sun by appointment) and a cultural centre. Beyond it is **Kiršai** ㉑, birthplace of the controversial poet Salomėja Nėris (1904–45).

To the south is a hilly, attractive corner of the country. In the southwest corner on Road 186 is **Vištytis**, a border town by a 180-sq km (70-sq mile) lake of the same name. Vincas Kudirka (1858–99), author of both the words and the music to the Lithuanian national anthem, was born and buried in **Kudirkos Naumiestis**, further north on Road 186. There is a memorial museum in his house in Paežerių (**Vincas Kudirka Granary Museum**, visit only by prior request, tel: 342 46 399).

SŪDUVA LAND

The southern part of Suvalkija, often called Sūduva, is a picturesque region of lakes and hills, centred on **Lazdijai** ㉒. Road 134 continues for 18km (11 miles) towards hills, forests, valleys and a lovely labyrinth of lakes around **Veisiejai**, which has a number of pleasant corners to stop for a rest. The old part of the town has a beautiful park and an early 19th-century church. Ludwik Lazar Zamenhof (1859–1917), the Białystok-born Polish physician who devised the constructed language Esperanto, lived here briefly in 1886. At J. Janokio 6 there is a well-preserved wooden synagogue built in 192

To the east of Lazdijai is **Seirijai** from where Road 181 goes throu forests and around the largest lakes in the region. The biggest of these is the 139-sq km (50-sq mile) **Lake Metelys** (Metelio ežeras), which has clear water up to 15 metres (50ft) deep and is teeming with fish. **Meteliai**, near the lake, has a 19th-century church with good interior decoration, as does the 16th-century church in nearby **Simnas**. To the north is the 100-sq km (40-sq mile) **Lake Žuvintas** (Žuvinto ežeras), surrounded by a large nature reserve, a boggy area which supports more than 600 species of plants and more than 250 species of birds.

Alytus ㉔, 24km (15 miles) east of Simnas on Road 131, lies in a deep valley of the Nemunas, surrounded by dry forests and deciduous woods on the heights above. Because the ancient town straddled the river, it developed slowly. Today it has a population of around 52,000 and up-to-date industries in building materials, machinery, textiles, food processing, and Alita, makers of the country's best champagne. It is also the cultural centre of Dzūkija. There is a local museum (Alytus Local Lore Museum; Savanorių 6; Tue–Fri 9am–6pm, Sat 10am–4pm; fee) and two 18th- and 19th-century churches. In Vidugiris, a forest in the southern part of the city, a monument has been erected to 35,000 victims of the Nazis. The bridge over the Nemunas is named after Antanas Juozapavičius, an officer killed here during the battle for independence in 1919.

DRUSKININKAI

Lithuania's best-known artist and composer, Mikalojus Konstantinas Čiurlionis (1875–1911), grew up in **Druskininkai** ㉕, the first main town on this road, 150km (96 miles) southwest of Vilnius. It is a spa town and resort of wide boulevards and old and new villas. Around 100,000 people visit each year, many of them Poles and Belarusians. The spa opened in 1832 when salty mineral water was first used

for treatment: the name Druskininkai comes from *druska*, meaning salt. Every litre of water contains 3g (0.1oz) of minerals, and it arrives at the surface, both tepid and hot, from a depth of 72 metres (235ft).

There are several parks, and treatments offered in the Health Resort Druskininkai (Druskininkų gydykla), where visitors queue up with their special cups to sample the waters in doses often prescribed by their doctors. Near the health park is a wonderful riverside walk, which traces the River Ratnyčia for 7km (4 miles) past carved seats and follies inscribed with poems and sayings. At one point the river is wide and deep enough to swim. On the riverside there is a musical fountain (May–Sept every hour 11am–11pm). It's possible to choose the song by sending a text message from a list of 115 hits by, among others, Elton John, Annie Lennox and Michael Jackson. The town also has one of the biggest Aqua Parks in Europe, an adventure park and an all-year round snow arena (see page 75).

(see page 75)

Liškiava church.

ČIURLIONIS MUSEUM

The middle of Druskininkai has a 20th-century neo-Gothic church and nearby is a memorial to Čiurlionis. His family came here when he was three, and until the age of 14 he lived in the family home in the street named after him in the south of the town. This timbered, single-storey building is now preserved as the **Čiurlionis Memorial Museum** (Čiurlionio Memorialinis Muziejus; www.ciurlionis.lt; Čiurlionio 35; Tue–Sun 11am–5pm). Famously, piano concerts are held inside during the summer, while the audience sits outside in the shade of the pretty garden. In the beautifully renovated neoclassical Villa Linksma at the lake Druskonis is the **Museum of Druskininkai Town** (Čiurlionio 59; www.druskininkumuziejus.lt; Mon–Sat 11am–5pm). At the other end of town, at Čiurlionio 102, is **Echo of the Forest** (Miško aidas; www.dmu.lt; Wed–Sun 10am–6pm), which was first was run by the Lithuanian Foresters' Union in a building that had "the forest inside of it", which basically means an oak tree coming up through the building. This is Frank Lloyd Wright's idea of architecture taken to an extreme. It has a real park gallery of wooden sculptures. Since 2004 the museum has been the education and information centre of the Druskininka Forest Company.

GRŪTAS PARK

Tucked in the woodlands around Druskininkai, which are abundant with mushrooms in autumn, there are some ancient farmsteads: at **Latežeris**, for example, just to the east. Nearby is the small village of **Grūtas** and its famous **Grūtas Park of Soviet Sculptures** (Grūto Parkas; www.grutoparkas.lt; June–Aug daily 9am–10pm, May until 9pm, Mar–Apr and Sept until 8pm, Oct until 7pm, Nov–Dec until 5pm, Jan–Feb until 6pm). A controversial and rather startling place, it has collections of former Soviet leaders and various Communist bigwigs acquired from the scrap heap of the early independence years.

DZŪKIJA NATIONAL PARK

Merkinė ㉖, 27km (17 miles) to the northeast, is at the confluence of the Rivers Nemunas and Merkys. Russia's Peter I stayed here and Władysław Waza, the King of Poland, fell ill and died here in 1648. North of Merkinė forests cover the light plains on both sides of the road from Druskininkai. The route, lined with more than 20 traditional wooden sculptures, is called the **Čiurlionis Way**, since it leads 50km (31 miles) from the family home to Varėna, the artist's birthplace. The sculptures, based on ideas from his music and paintings, were erected in 1975 on the centenary of his birth.

Merkinė also has a small, recently renovated museum of local lore located in an Orthodox church. Opposite is the visitor centre (Mon–Fri 8am–5pm, Sat 8am–3.45pm, lunch break noon) for the 560-sq km (215-sq mile) **Dzūkija National Park** (www.cepkeliai-dzukija.lt), where you can walk, ride a

Folk totem in Dzūkija National Park.

canoe on the tributaries of the Nemunas. There is another visitor centre (same hours as above) in the woodlands at **Marcinkonys** to the southeast, near the Cepkeliai Marshes. The woodland of Dzūkija is often called Dainava (from *dainuoti*, meaning to sing). The Dzūkai who live here are known for their cheerfulness and their great singing voices, as well as for an ability to scratch a living out of poor soil. They used to be said to have no saws, only axes; no bricks, only clay. One saying that still persists is, "If it weren't for the mushrooms and berries, Dzūkai girls would walk around naked." These berries and mushrooms that keep clothes on the women's backs are sold along the highways in season.

INDEPENDENT PERLOJA

Continuing east on the A4, just outside the national park in woodland beside the River Merkys, is the small town of **Perloja** ㉗, a place of independent-minded people. It declared itself the Perloja Republic (Perlojos Respublika) in 1918, a status it stubbornly maintained for five years, with a government and an armed guard of 50 men, defiant against Russians, Poles, Germans and both red and white Lithuanian factions. In the centre of the town square is a hugely patriotic statue to Vytautas, Grand Duke of Lithuania, sculpted by Petras Tarabilda (1905–1977) in 1930.

Senoji Varėna (Old Varėna) was burnt down during World War II and replaced with the new town of **Varėna** ㉘ on the River Merkys, 5km (3 miles) to the south. The town is perhaps best known locally for its annual Mushroom Festival (Grybų šventė) held each September.

Heading towards Vilnius, the road passes more hilly, sandy woodland and the resurrected village of **Pirčiupiai** ㉙, where there is a monument called *Pirčiupiai Mother (Pirčiupių motina)*, by Gediminas Jokūbonis (1927–2006). It was commissioned in remembrance of the village that was burnt to the ground, along with all 119 inhabitants, on 3 June 1944 by the Nazis. The memorial is inscribed with each of the victims' names.

Reminders of Lenin and Stalin at Grūtas Park.

⊙ "STALIN WORLD"

The Grūtas Park of Soviet Sculptures (Grūto Parkas) is the planet's first Soviet theme park. It is the audacious idea of Viliumas Malinauskas, one of Lithuania's wealthiest businessmen who made his fortune off the back of the very same Soviet system he now mocks with his park. This is a mock-up of a Soviet prison camp, surrounded by barbed wire and watchtowers and populated by bronze and granite statues of former Soviet leaders and communist bigwigs that Malinauskas has collected.

Visitors can drink shots of vodka, eat herrings and cold borscht while loudspeakers broadcast old communist hymns. There were plans to build a railway for cattle wagons from Vilnius to give modern-day Lithuanians an idea of what it would feel like to be deported. There is also a small zoo and a playground.

📷 THE BALTIC SEA

Partially enclosed and surrounded by nine countries, including Estonia, Latvia and Lithuania, the Baltic Sea is beset by a number of challenging ecological problems.

The Baltic Sea is not deep, at an average of 55 metres (180ft), but it is tideless, and nearly half of it, including the waters around Estonia, Rīga Bay and the Courland Lagoon, freeze over each winter, and ice can remain until early spring. However, as the planet warms up, algal blooms are developing – in 2010, when the water temperature at Narva Joesuu in northeast Estonia reached 26°C (79°F), a bloom the size of Germany was detected by satellite in the middle of the sea.

With only a narrow channel between Sweden and Denmark for its exit into the North Sea, the same water remains for about 30 years. It is one of the largest bodies of brackish water in the world, which means that its saltiness is somewhere between fresh water and sea water. This presents the worst possible living conditions for aquatic organisms, and the few species that survive in the waters are vulnerable to ecological change. The Baltic Sea herring has evolved as a smaller species than its Atlantic relative, while sprats seem to have benefited from the warming water. There are also cod, eel, flounder, hake, plaice, salmon, sea trout and turbot. Grey and ringed seals, once found in large numbers, are diminishing, in part because warmer winters mean seal pups are leaving their ice bases too early, and because seals are often found covered with films of oil. Harbour porpoises are all but extinct.

This does not mean that the sea around Estonia, Latvia and Lithuania is unfit for bathing: all three countries have beaches with Blue Flag status, and the waters are generally shallow and safe. The dunes that line much of the shore are susceptible to storm damage and human depredation, so grasses and trees are important in preventing erosion.

Local fishermen set out their nets and pots all arou. the coast, hauling in smelt and flounder from the shallow water.

Leisure sailing off Pirita, reconstructed for the 1980 Olympic Games. Estonia's popular harbour has berths around 300 yachts.

A World War II mine is detonated off Lithuania in Operation Open Spirit, an ongoing multinational effort to clear the sea of unexploded ordinance.

Cause for concern

Rivers and streams all around the Baltic have been dumping toxic matter into the sea for years, so that today it is one of the world's most threatened marine ecosystems. It has seven of the world's biggest marine dead zones, where oxygen depletion has been caused by an overdose of nutrients from fertilisers and sewage.

Some 90 million people live in countries around the sea, and about 2,000 vessels are out on the water every day. There are many wrecks – three British warships sunk by mines in 1919 were discovered off the Estonian island of Saaremaa only in 2010. The Baltic Sea was also the scene of fierce fighting, and there are an estimated 80,000 unexploded mines left over from World War II. In 2011, a 1,223km (750-mile) long Russian gas pipeline, operated by Nord Stream, began operating and a second one was inaugurated in 2012 to run from the Gulf of Finland to Germany. Leakage and spillage are a constant threat.

A number of initiatives have been taken by the Baltic countries since the 1990s, but pledges have proved hard to implement. All the countries around the sea are signed up to HELCOM, the Baltic Marine Environment Protection Commission (www.helcom.fi), with a rotating presidency. In has an Action Plan to "restore the good ecological status of the Baltic marine environment" by 2021.

Rising sea temperatures have had beneficial effects on stocks of sprats, which have been increasing in numbers.

such as these in Latvia are delicate ecologies and be planted to prevent erosion.

onian-registered tanker trapped in thick ice is clear by a tug in March 2010.

Neringa looks out for sailors at
Witches' Hill sculpture park.

ŽEMAITIJA AND THE COAST

The Amber Coast includes the Curonian Spit, one of the world's great sand-dune nature areas, while inland is the man-made Hill of Crosses, a place of extraordinary devotion.

he province of Žemaitija covers about quarter of Lithuania, and roughly orresponds with the Žemaitija pland. The adjacent coastal area, nown as Mažoji Lietuva or Lithuania Iinor, stretches south into the Rus-an exclave of Kaliningrad. Although e ancient tribes probably took their ames from the places they came om, the Žemaitijans (Žemaičiai) ved not in the Upland but around the nouth of the Nemunas, trading with e Aukštaitijans towards the river's ource. On this coast there is also rchaeological evidence of Romans nd Vikings, and of Bronze Age trade ith Britain and the Mediterranean.

MYSTERIOUS LAND

or 200 years the Žemaitijans had a unning battle with the German cru-aders of the Livonian Order who had stablished their Baltic base in Rīga, nd with the Teutonic Knights who har-ed them from the west. Between 1382 nd 1404 the Grand Dukes of Lithuania eded Žemaitija to the knights, but in e 15th century it became a self-gov-rning district and duchy.

To outsiders Žemaitija long seemed rather mysterious, wild and pagan nd, an image enforced by the French ramatist Prosper Mérimée's 1869 ovel *Lokis*. The Žemaitijans maintain a rong regional dialect that's a mystery

even to many Lithuanian-speakers, and they keep their links with the past.

Inhabited by men of few words, this is not a land of songs. Most of the countryside is rather severe, and the western slope of the Upland is windier, foggier and wetter than else-where. The trees are mostly firs and once-sacred oaks, and the landscape is dotted with old wooden crucifixes in roadside shrines and cemeteries. The main motorway from Vilnius to Klaipėda via Kaunas is the well-main-tained A1 (E85) dual carriageway. To

⊙ Main attractions
Oginskis Manor and Estate
Lithuania Minor Museum
Amber Museum
Curonian Spit
Nida
Nemunas Delta Regional Park
Kretinga Museum
Hill of Crosses

Map on page 266

Sand dunes at Nida.

the north and somewhat parallel to the A1 runs the A9 (E272) from Panevėžys, which becomes the A11 (E272) west of Šiauliai. The A12 (E77) runs horizontally to these roads and connects Šiauliai with Tauragė. Connecting the northerly town of Mažeikiai to southerly Tauragė (via Plungė) is the 164.

KAUNAS–KLAIPĖDA HIGHWAY

The A1(E85) motorway from Vilnius via Kaunas to the coast is a lovely 311km (193-mile) stretch. There are a number of diversions not far from the main road should you want to explore lesser-known parts of the country. The first of these that falls within the Žemaitija region is **Raseiniai ㉚**, 86km (53 miles) west of Kaunas and about 5km (3 miles) off the A1 on Route 146. This town is typical of the region and worth visiting for this reason alone. Historically significant, it was one of the focal points of the 1831 rebellion against the tsar. The 18th-century church and abbey is dedicated to the Assumption of the Holy Virgin (Švč. Mergelės Marijos Ėmimo į Dangų bažnyčia; Bažnyčios 2). Also of interest

The coast near Nida.

further into town and past the city park is the **Raseiniai Regional Histor** **Museum** (Raseinių krašto istorijos muz iejus; Muziejaus 3; www.raseiniumuzieju lt; Tue–Fri 9am–6pm, Sat 11am–4pm) a former prison building, which include photographs of prisoners from 1940–5 and exhibits about the area and the dias pora from this region. There is also a area dedicated to flax, national pattern ceramics, early 20th-century househol utensils and folk art. It's worth seein the **Pasandravys Memorial Reserv** **tion** (Bernotų ir Pasandravio villag same hours as above), the birthplace the poet Jonas Mačiulis-Maironis (1862 1932) in a picturesque, wooden house the Maironis family.

ŠILUVA

About 17km (10 miles) north of Rasein iai on Route 148 is **Šiluva ㉛**, which ha the beautiful twin-towered **Basilica** **the Birth of the Blessed Virgin** (Šv Mergelės Marijos gimimo bazilik. Jurgaičio 2), a Baroque building ded cated to the "Lourdes of Lithuania". It believed that in the mid-17th century th

Virgin Mary appeared on a rock near the site of a former church which had been seized by Calvinists, and she wept for its destruction. Moved by these tears, a passing blind man was able to remember that a former church had stood on the grounds and he was able to locate both an icon of the Virgin and the original deed to the land, and through this apparent miracle he regained his sight. The existing church was returned to the Catholics. Although this miracle was historically advantageous, many still come here to worship. Large congregations attend services on major holidays to see both the icon, which is now partially covered in gold, and the holy rock.

Tytuvėnai ㉜ is about 10km (6 miles) north on Route 148. The area surrounding the town is popular due to its lakes and forested areas. The 17th–18th-century **Church of the Holy Virgin Mary** (Švč. Mergelės Marijos bažnyčia) is one of the largest and most important religious houses in Lithuania, with a two-storey monastery, where concerts take place in summer.

VILLAGE DETOURS

Heading out of Raseiniai, Route 196 runs parallel to the significantly faster A1, or you can return to the A1 via Route 146. About 5km (3 miles) outside the tiny settlement of **Kryžkalnis** there is a small sign for **Bijotai** village. Follow the signs towards **D. Poška Hallowed Trunks** (D. Poška Baubliai, May–Oct daily 9am–6pm, lunch break at 1pm, Nov–Apr Mon–Fri 8am–5pm, lunch break at noon), the first and oldest public museum in Lithuania, in order to find Dionizas Poška's hollowed-out oak-tree trunks with pagan carvings in them.

Along the same road, heading away from the A1, is the town of **Girdiškė**. Its church, dedicated to the Virgin, has an oak altar with six main branches shooting upwards and intertwined. Continue along the road and circle round the church in the village of Pyna to return to the A1 at the town

of Prienai via Gudirvės. Stasys Girėnas, the doomed transatlantic aviator, was born into a peasant family in 1893 in **Vytogala**, a little further west. He was the youngest in a family of 16 children. There is a small memorial museum in this village (Tue–Sat 9am–5pm).

Another detour from the A1 is along Route 164 towards the town of **Rietavas**, an ancient settlement (pop. approx. 3,000) centred around an old square. The main attraction is the **Manor House and Estate of the Oginskis (Oginński) Family** housing the Culture History Museum of Rietavas Oginskiai (Rietavo Dvaras sodyba; Parko 10; www.oginskiriet.lt; Tue–Fri 9am–5pm, Sat–Sun 10am–3pm; free). From 1812 to 1909 they ruled over their own autonomous domain, with their own laws and even their own currency. In 1835 they granted civil rights to their peasants, organised agricultural exhibitions, promoted Lithuanian culture and written language, and started publishing the Lithuanian calendar. They established a music school in the town, and in 1872 mustered a famous brass

Amber for sale at Klaipėda.

band. The manor house is famous for being the first residential property in Lithuania to have electric lighting, courtesy of its own power station, in 1892, and the building is an intriguing place to spend an hour or so. In 1874 a beautiful church in the Venetian style was built on their orders by the Prussian architect Friedrich August Stüler.

The road continues through 50km (30 miles) of uninhabited forest. At Endriejavas there is a small lake and 8km (5 miles) to the north is the former village of Ablinga. On 23 July 1941 it was burnt down by the Nazis and its 42 inhabitants perished. A wooden sculpture has been erected to each of the dead.

BALTIC COAST

The coastal plain, Pajūris, is 15–20km (10–13 miles) wide and rises to around 40 metres (132ft). The landscape is diverse, consisting of fertile clay soils, dunes, sandy forests and wet bogs. In the south is the swampy Nemunas Delta and the 1,600 sq km (618 sq miles) and 4-metre (13ft) deep **Curonian Lagoon**

(Kuršių marios). The coastline has urbanised resorts, around Palanga in the north, and in Neringa along the Curonian Spit (Kuršių Nerija), which like much of the area was part of Prussia's Memelland. Neringa is not actually a town, but an administrative area with its capital at Nida, near the border with Kaliningrad at the southern end of the spit. The area has many miles of empty beaches and some nature reserves.

KLAIPĖDA

Klaipėda ㊳ is the main city on the coast, situated at the mouth of the River Danė at the far northern end of the Curonian Spit and Lagoon. It suffered colossal damage during World War II, when it was used by the Germans as a submarine base. Since the 1970s, when investment was ploughed into local industry, its population has dramatically risen and then fallen. It is currently around 149,000, making it the third-largest city in Lithuania. In 1252 the Livonian Order built a castle here, called Memelburg, and the city became known as Memel in German

Klaipėda Timepiece Museum.

...day the port city has a flourishing shipbuilding industry, a thriving expat community and ferry services to Germany and Sweden.

What is left of the Old Town is strung out along a small network of cobbled streets on the left bank of the Danė, where there are some decent bars and restaurants plus a few remaining half-timbered (Fachwerk) buildings. The area around Daržų and Bažnyčių streets is of special interest as it is peppered with craft workshops, small galleries and souvenir shops. The city also has two theatres, at one of which Hitler spoke from the balcony in March 1939 in the old town square, where the resurrected Annchen von Tarau statue now stands. The original, erected in 1912, was dedicated to the native Prussian German poet Simon Dach, and it is still a matter of debate whether it fell into the hands of the Nazis or Soviets.

Also of interest in the Old Town is the **History of Lithuania Minor Museum** (Mažosios Lietuvos istorijos muziejus; Didžioji Vandens 6; www.mlimuziejus.lt; Tue–Sat 10am–6pm), which houses all sorts of ethnic, archaeological and historical pieces related to the area and its former inhabitants. Most attention-grabbing are the eerie photographs of the city during World War II.

South of the Old Town is the **Blacksmiths' Museum** (Kalvystės muziejus; Saltkalvių 2a; www.mlimuziejus.lt; Tue–Sat 10am–6pm), which is both a museum and a working smithy, where perspiring blacksmiths forge all types of ironwork.

On the other side of the Danė, the **Klaipėda Clock and Watch Museum** (Klaipėdos laikrodžių muziejus; Liepų 12; www.ldm.lt; Tue–Sat noon–6pm, Sun noon–5pm; guided tours available in English) is another strangely satisfying museum. Centred around clocks and how they are made, it displays mechanisms from sundials to atomic clocks. In the rear courtyard is a splendid sundial.

Almost next door at Liepų 12 is the magnificent, 19th-century neo-Gothic **Post Office**. A 48-bell carillon in its tower is played to startling effect by local enthusiasts every Sunday at noon.

⊙ **Drink**

When in Klaipėda, have a glass of Švyturys beer. The brewery has been here since 1784, and its reputation in recent years has been spreading.

Klaipėda's old town.

AMBER

Amber is interwoven in Lithuanian folklore, and leaving the country without a piece or two is bordering on sin.

There is amber everywhere in the southern half of the Baltics. At any opportunity, stalls are set up to sell bracelets, necklaces, earrings, key rings and brooches. In its raw state, buffeted by tides and exposed to the elements, these are dull stones, scattered like pebbles the length of the beaches. People are always on the lookout for them, particularly after storms, though most of the amber bought today will have been dug out of the ground by excavators in Kaliningrad.

Amber is not, in fact, a stone, but fossilised resin of primeval pine trees. The amber deposit, dating back 40 million years, forms a seam 60–90cm (2–3ft) thick beneath the surface of the seabed. In spring, fishermen used to comb the beaches with large nets to pull in flotsam that might contain amber. The Curonian Lagoon was also a source of it. In the 19th century Juodkrantė was known as Amber

You can buy amber from various vendors along Nida's waterfront.

Cove: the Stantien and Becker company used to dredge up to 85 tonnes of it here every year.

UNUSUAL ATTRACTION

The stone's peculiarity is that, while it was sticky resin, insects were attracted to it, and it often solidified while they were trapped by its surface. If you hold a polished stone to the light you will see flies and mosquitoes perfectly preserved inside. The 18th-century English poet Alexander Pope wrote:

Pretty! in amber, to observe the forms
Of hairs, or straws, or dirt, or grubs or worms;
The things, we know, are neither rich nor rare,
But wonder how the devil they got there.

Amber was a commodity that the earliest tribes could easily trade: according to Tacitus, the price it fetched astonished them. It has been found in the tombs of Mycenae, and Tutankhamun's treasure included an amber necklace. The Baltic shoreline was first called the Amber Coast by the ancient Greek poet Homer, who described the brilliant "electron" on his warriors' shields. The best place to see amber is at the Amber Museum in Palanga.

A PALACE OF AMBER

A local legend tells how "Lithuanian gold" was created. There was once a Baltic queen named Jūratė who lived in a submarine palace made of amber. She was to be the bride of Patrimpas, god of water, but she fell for a mortal fisherman called Kastytis whom she visited in his hut on the banks of the Nemunas near Klaipėda at sunset every night for a year. The liaison came to the attention of Perkūnas, god of thunder, and in a rage he threw down bolts of lightning, killing Jūratė and shattering her amber palace into 10,000 pieces. Perkūnas then punished Kastytis by binding him to a rock on the seabed. It is said that when the west wind blows Kastytis can be heard moaning for his love, and when the wind dies the shore is strewn with fragments of Jūratė's palace.

Even today many people hope to find the scattered pieces of the precious palace. According to the cogniscenti, the best time to look for amber on the Baltic beaches is after a storm, early in the morning. However, it takes a lot of experience, patience and a bit of luck to find a nugget of the Baltic gold.

SCULPTURE PARK

Continuing along Liepų leads to the **M. Mažvydas Sculpture Park** (M. Mažvydo skulptūrų parkas; www.mlimuziejus.lt), which is bordered by Daukanto, Liepų and Trilapio streets. The park was the city's main cemetery until the 1970s, when it was closed. Some of the crosses were salvaged and are now housed in the Blacksmiths' Museum. The 10-hectare (25-acre) park, which contains around 180 sculptures by more than 90 artists, is a nice way to come across many and disparate styles of sculpture, most with more than a touch of whimsy. In the far northern section of the park is the wonderfully bombastic **Monument to the Port Liberators** (Paminklas postamiesčio išvaduotojams), depicting the Soviet military in all its glory and unveiled in 1980 to commemorate the liberation of the city from the Nazis on their final push to Berlin.

PALANGA

At 33km (20 miles) and 46km (29 miles) north of Klaipėda on the A13 respectively are the two resorts of Palanga and Šventoji. An old settlement of fishermen and amber-gatherers, **Palanga** ③④ became popular in the late 19th century when it developed as a spa and health resort. Considered the wildest of the resorts on the Lithuanian coast, Palanga still manages to maintain its charm even with the heavy influx of hotels, restaurants and bars that open their doors the moment the weather turns warm.

Meilės alėja (Lover's Lane), which runs parallel to the Baltic Sea, and Basanavičiaus, which leads into the pier, are the two most popular places to take a stroll, especially as the sun setting. A trip to Palanga without watching the sun set over the sea is a wasted trip indeed.

Despite the bars and cafés touting karaoke, drinking contests or just playing loud thumping music that leaves the sound of the ocean unheard, peace reigns in some parts of the resort. One of the best places to visit besides the beaches is the 110-hectare (272-acre) **Botanical Park** (www.pgm.lt), which lies alongside the Baltic Sea. In summer, concerts take place regularly throughout the park, where there are more than 500 plant species, dominated by pine trees.

AMBER MUSEUM

In the centre of the park is Count Tiškevičius's mansion, which is now home to the **Amber Museum** (Gintaro muziejus; Vytauto 17; www.pgm.lt; June–Aug Tue–Sat 10am–8pm, Sun 10am–7pm, Sept–May Tue–Sat 11am–5pm, Sun 11am–4pm). After touring the museum there will be no question left unanswered about Baltic gold. Numerous pieces of amber contain particles of animal or vegetable life, which adds to their fascination. Behind the mansion is a garden full of fragrant roses.

Also in the park is **Birutė's Hill** (Birutės kalnas), the tallest point in town and on which a small chapel now stands. The hill is considered to be a former pagan shrine, and the presence

> **⊙ Tip**
>
> To rent a boat for the lagoon or for the open sea, with or without a skipper, contact the Klaipėda Yacht Club, Smiltynės, Klaipėda (tel: 4639 1131).

Palanga waterfront.

of a large oak – sacred in local pagan tradition – at the foot of the hill supports this theory. In the middle of the park sits one of the most famous statues in the town, of the mythical Eglė. According to the legend, Eglė met an enchanted lake-living prince during a swim. The two married, had children and tried to live happily ever after in their lake. However, when Eglė brought her children to meet their grandparents, her brothers killed her husband. In despair Eglė turned herself and her children into trees.

Another worthwhile stop is the **Antanas Mončys House Museum** (Antano Mončio namai muziejus; Daukanto 16; www.antanasmoncys.com; May–mid-Sept Wed–Sun 2–7pm, mid-Sept–Apr Wed–Sun 11am–5pm). All the wooden pieces by the sculptor (1921–93) can be handled by visitors; in fact, the artist requested this in his will.

Šventoji ❸, a little further up the coast, is a quieter resort. On the mouth of the small River Šventoji, it is famous for its sand dunes, beach and bogs. Shown on Hansa maps, it became a resort at the beginning of the 20th century. A community of sma cottages and simple houses, this is th place to go if you want peace and quie

THE CURONIAN SPIT

The Curonian Spit (Kuršių Nerija) i named after the Curonians (Kuršia an ethnic group who lived in the regio from the 5th to the 16th century. It wa formed about 5,000 years ago and ge logically it is the youngest part of th country. It has no rivers, a few lagoor and along its shore lies a chain of mar made beaches and dunes. A bird's-ey view is a wonderful picture of whit sandy hills against a dark blue bacl ground, and it was the sight of thes extraordinary dunes that inspired th German naturalist Alexander von Hur boldt to write in 1809: "[the] Curonia Spit is such a peculiar place as Italy Spain. One must see it to give pleasu to one's soul." It was awarded Unesc World Heritage Site status in 2000.

Winds formed the long, narro coastal spit no more than a mile wic and 60 metres (200ft) high. It rur 98km (60 miles) from Klaipėda sout

A typical late-19th century house.

Kaliningrad; 51km (32 miles) of the it are in Lithuania. The lagoon on e inland side is formed by the mouth the Nemunas. On the tip of the spit posite Klaipėda is **Smiltynė**, reached regular ferries from the port.

The Lithuanian Sea Museum and lphinarium (Lietuvos jūrų muz- us delfinariumas; Smiltynės 3; ww.muziejus.lt; June–Aug Tue–Sun .30am–6.30pm, Apr–May and Sept ed–Sun 10.30am–5pm, Oct–Jan Fri– n 10.30am–4.30pm, Feb–Mar Fri–Sun .30am–5pm) is home to a number of als, penguins and dolphins. The Dol- inarium has 40-minute-long dolphin ows (July–Aug Tue–Sun at 11.30am, m, 3pm, 4.30pm, June Tue–Sun at on, 2pm, 4pm, Apr–May noon, 3pm, pt Wed–Sun noon, 3pm, Oct–Mar –Sun noon, 3pm), especially enjoy- le for younger visitors. Nearby is aipėda Yacht Club, one of the venues Klaipėda's annual Sea Festival.

GOON-SIDE VILLAGES

st of the peninsula, however, lies to e south, where all tourist traffic needs to pay a toll. All the little villages along here face the lagoon. Until 1992, the white sandy coast was occupied by the Soviet Army. Shifting sands have meant many of the villages have constantly been on the move. During the 18th and 19th centuries more than a dozen were affected, some of them covered over by sand. **Pervalka** and **Preila** are typical small seaside communities with signs for *žuvis* (fish) and locals quietly going about their business. **Juodkrantė** is larger and has a harbour once known as Amber Cove because of the amount of the material that was dredged up for the local industry.

WITCHES' HILL

Also of note when driving through town is **Witches' Hill** (Raganų kalnas), which was established in the 1980s by a group of local sculptors. This large wooden sculpture park filled with fabled fig- ures – such as the main pagan god, Perkūnas, and Neringa, a local girl who became a giant and helped sailors in trouble – makes a pleasant excur- sion through the pine trees. This spot

Curonian Spit, located close to Nida.

⊙ **Tip**

Look out for the signposts indicating that some beaches are for women only, some only for men, and others are for both. Men caught loitering on women-only beaches will often be chastised and herded off by a group of half-naked grannies.

is especially appreciated by children, as some of the sculptures double as slides and see-saws. Look for the sign on your right as you are heading south through town. A walk beside the lagoon path with its stone sculptures provides a pleasant contrast.

NIDA

At the southern end of the spit, just before the border with Russian Kaliningrad, is **Nida ㊱**, which has moved several times to escape the mobile sand. This is the largest of the resorts (pop. approximately 2,400, rising to more than 10,000 in summer), with the best facilities. It is the sunniest and most famous place on the Lithuanian part of the peninsula.

Nida has a distinctive landscape, created by the wind and the sea. White sand dunes stretch away like a desert to the south, and trunks of trees show where ancient forests once flourished. It is known among Lithuanians as a place where the landscape forces you to take stock of your life. The area is fantastic, and exploring the dunes is

an integral part of any visit. Becau of the fragile ecosystem, however, it forbidden just to traipse through ther Instead, visitors are asked to wa through the forest at the end of Nagl to view them or to walk alongside t beach and then climb the steps.

Those who plan on visiting t area's beaches should pay particul attention to the signposting as son are women-only, others are men-on According to local custom, howev men are allowed to cross women-or beaches if they are close to the wat and not disruptive.

To find out more about local life, the is a small recreated fisherman's hous the **Nida Fisherman's Ethnograph Homestead** (Nidos žvejo etnografi sodyba; www.neringosmuziejai.lt; Jun Aug daily 10am–6pm, Sept–May Tu Sat 10am–5pm) from the 19th century Naglių 4. For some local shopping a further information, head for the **Amb Gallery** (Gintaros galerija; Pamar 20; www.ambergallery.lt; daily June–A 9am–8pm, Apr–May and Sept 10am 7pm). Further along is the **Curoni**

An old fishing boat faces out to sea beneath the local village coats of arms.

Spit History Museum (Kuršių nerijos istorijos muziejus; Pamario 53; www.neringosmuziejai.lt; June–Aug daily 10am–6pm, Sept–May Tue-Sat 10am–5pm), which houses amber figures from the Stone Age as well as numerous exhibitions chronicling life on the spit as it used to be. The writer Thomas Mann lived in Nida for three consecutive summers between 1930 and 1933. There is a museum in the house he had specially built, the **Thomas Mann Memorial Museum** (Thomo Manno memorialinis muziejus; Skruzdynės 17; www.neringosmuziejai.lt; May daily 10am–5pm, June–Sept daily 10am–6pm, Oct–Apr Tue–Sat 10am–5pm). There is also a cultural centre that organizes Thomas Mann estival in July.

NEMUNAS DELTA

From Klaipėda, Road 141 runs southeast through Šilutė and Pagėgiai, following the north bank of the Nemunas to Kaunas. From the small town of **Priekulė**, Road 221 goes south, past the fishing village of **Kintai**, as it enters the **Nemunas Delta Regional Park** (Nemuno deltos regioninis parkas; www.nemunodelta.lt), an area of islands and waterways teaming with fish, and a main port of call for migrating birds.

Among the typical fishing villages here are **Mingė**, the "Venice of Lithuania", where the River Minija serves as its main street, and **Skirvytėlė**, whose traditional houses are made of timber and reeds and include an ethnological farm museum.

At the western edge of the park is **Ventės Ragas** 37, marked by a lighthouse built in 1863. The main reason for coming to this backwater is the wildlife. An important bird-ringing centre, which keeps track of the many coastal migrants, has been operating here since 1929. It has vast bird-catching nets. A small museum with erratic opening times has display cases of stuffed birds.

From Saugos the 141 falls down into the Nemunas Delta plain, passing through **Šilutė** 38 on the River Šyša. The town of Šilutė spent most of its time under German rule and was only integrated into Lithuania in 1923. Most of its economy centres on textiles,

Fact

Lithuania's national bird is the stork, seen in large numbers from April to September. Every spring and autumn around a million birds of many species pass over the Nemunas Delta.

Cyclists gather on Nida's waterfront.

⊘ Tip

You can hunt, fish and go horse riding in Žemaitija National Park (www.zemaitijosnp.lt/en), or rent boats and catamarans from the yacht club in Plateliai (Yacht Club: Ezero Street 40; tel: 6156 7354; http://www.plateliuose.lt).

livestock and machinery plants. The city has its own museum (Šilutės muziejus; Lietuvininkų 36; http://silutes-muziejus.lt; Tue–Fri 10am–6pm, Sat 10am–4.45pm), which displays a vast amount of ethnic costumes, weaponry, folk art and photographs.

In the village of **Macikai**, just off the 141 to the east of Šilutė, the former Stalag Luft VI prisoner-of-war camp for Allied airmen, and later a KGB prison for Lithuanian dissidents, opened to the public in 1995. There are photographs and lists of prisoners along with their journals and drawings. The eerie and harrowing museum (http://silutesmuziejus.lt; by appointment, tel: 4416 2207) is not suitable for youngsters.

ISLAND TOWN OF RUSNĖ

Just west of Šilutė in the Nemunas Delta is 45 sq km (17 sq miles) **Rusnė** ❿, Lithuania's only island town, which rises just 1.5 metres (5ft) above sea level. It has a community of around 3,000, who earn a living by fishing and breeding cattle. The main town for the Nemunas

Delta Regional Park, it has informati on hiring boats and bikes. There is a an ethnographic fisherman's farmste (Skirvytėlės 8; by appointment, tel: 44 0010), which shows an authentic far house of Lithuania Minor.

The next town of any size on the 1 is **Pagėgiai**, 38km (22 miles) sou of Šilutė. During World War II, in t forest to the west behind a tangle barbed wire, the Germans kept priso ers of war under the open sky: 10,0 of them died. The ground is very hil and prisoners tried to bury themselv to escape the cold. From Pagėgiai t A12 (E77) goes 32km (20 miles) nor east to **Tauragė**, which gave its nan to the Tauragė (Tauroggen) Conventi signed in 1812 between General Yor for Prussia and General Diebitsch Russia in Požeronys Mill: a monume records the event. The A12 joins w the Kaunas–Klaipėda (A1) highway.

NORTH ŽEMAITIJA

One of the most interesting diversio in northern Žemaitija is the region capital of **Kretinga** ❹ (pop. 17,00

An 18th-century wooden church on the shores of Lake Plateliai.

Although parts of the city are not particularly eye-catching, all is made up for by the **Kretinga Museum** (Kretingos muziejus; Vilnaus 20; www.kretingosmuziejus.lt; Wed–Sun 10am–6pm, winter garden June–Aug Mon 10am–6pm, Tue–Sun 10am–8.30pm, Sept–May Tue–Fri and Sun 10am–6pm, Sat 10am–7pm). It is housed in a former mansion of Count Tiškevičius (Tyszkiewicz, 1814–73) and has collections of numerous Žemaitijan craftwork and articles belonging to the count and his family. There are also objects found from archaeological digs displayed in the cellar. The winter garden (Kretingos Žiemos Sodas) is one of the most spectacular displays in the area; it is covered by plants, their leaves regularly dusted by women attendants. The indoor café adds to the experience. The town has an important Franciscan monastery, founded in 1602, and concerts are sometimes given in its courtyard.

On the A11 (E272) between Kretinga and the next main town of Plungė is **Kartena** ㊶, situated in the beautiful valley of the Minija. It has a 19th-century wooden church, which is dedicated to the Assumption of the Virgin (Kretingos 4).

Before reaching Plungė, an interesting diversion can be found by turning north on Route 169 towards Salantai. Here in the village of **Gargždelė** ㊷ is the **Orvidas Farmstead Museum** (www.orvidusodyba.lt; 10am–7pm June–Aug Tue–Sun, Mar–Apr and Nov Sat–Sun, May and Sept Wed–Sun, Oct Thu–Sat), a tribute to all things wacky, serious and religious. The owner's eccentric son, Vilius Orvidas (1952–92), is now considered part of the Naïve artist movement, and the area around the farmhouse features an arresting amount of carved stones, boulders, rescued crosses and other pieces of art he created during his short life.

MOSĖDIS

An even more bizarre diversion is to be found further north in the town of **Mosėdis** ㊸ at the **Vaclovas Intas Museum of Rare Stones** (Akmenų muziejus; Salantų 2; www.akmenų muziejus.lt; Apr–Oct daily 9am–7pm,

Artwork at Gargždelė.

Nov–Mar Mon–Thu 8am–5pm, Fri 8am–3.45pm, lunch break noon), which is a collection of more than 20,000 stones and rocks from around the world. The point of this rock gathering may have most people scratching their heads, but the sheer willpower inherent in this museum's existence does have a certain appeal. Interestingly, many of the rocks have not enjoyed their captivity and spilled out over the town.

Plungė **㊹** (pop. 17,000) is a little larger than Kretinga and a centre of light industry and administration, with a long tradition of folk art. It became rich after the Oginskis (Ogiński) family arrived to buy up the local manor. They enlarged and cultivated the 18th-century park that surrounds the manor, and in 1879 entrusted the architect Karl Lorens with the building of a neo-Renaissance palace imitating the 15th-century Palazzo Vecchio in Florence. In 1889 they also sponsored the education of the painter and musician M.K. Čiurlionis. Today the building is the **Žemaitija Art Museum** (Žemaičių

The striking sight of the Hill of Crosses.

dailės muziejus; Parko 1; www.zd[...] lt; May–Oct Tue–Sun 10am–7p[...] Nov–Apr Tue–Sat 10am–5pm), whi[...] houses mostly paintings execut[...] by Žemaitijan artists either living Lithuania or abroad. There is also small area dedicated to the folk art the region.

ŽEMAITIJA NATIONAL PARK

Due east of Salantai is **Plateliai**, t[...] heart of the **Žemaitija National Pa**[...] (Žemaitijos nacionalinis parkas) a[...] its main tourist information cent[...] (Didžioji 8; www.zemaitijosnp.lt). Thou[...] lying 146 metres (480ft) above s[...] level, there is a large lake beside **Lake Plateliai** (Platelių ežeras) nearly 12 sq km (5 sq miles) in s[...] and 46 metres (150ft) deep, and it h[...] seven islands. There are boating faci[...] ties on its western side near the to[...] where there is an 18th-century wood[...] church and a ruined manor.

Other attractive small towns in th[...] region, which is rich with festivals a[...] calendar customs, include Alsėdž[...] and Seda and Žemaičių Kalvarija, pretty village that has 10 days of p[...] grimage celebration every July.

Telšiai, on the A11, is an indu[...] trial town with a population of almo[...] 24,000, but before World War II it w[...] an important religious and cultur[...] centre for both Catholics and Jew[...] with a bishop's see and seminaries f[...] priests and rabbis. It still has a sch[...] of applied art and the **Alka Museu**[...] (Žemaičių muziejus Alka; Muzieja[...] 31; www.muziejusalka.lt; Mon–Thu 8am[...] 5pm, Fri 8am–3.45pm, lunch bre[...] noon), featuring the usual colle[...] tions of local interest as well as t[...] extraordinary, recently rediscover[...] photographs of the local Jewish sal[...] photographer Chaimas Kaplansk[...] (Chaim Kaplan, c.1860–1935).

On the southeast of the town is Rai[...] iai Forest (Rainių miškelis), where Lithuanian nationalists and Nazi c[...] laborators were executed by the KGB

1941; 50 years later a chapel was built in their remembrance. East from here is **Luokė**, famous for its folklore festivals, and **Lake Germantas** (Germanto ežeras), where there are holiday facilities and an airfield for pleasure flights.

ŠIAULIAI

Heading east, at the junction of the A11 and A12, **Šiauliai** ⑤ (pop. 100,000), Lithuania's fourth-largest town, is an industrial centre, of shoes, textiles and, notably, bicycles, and here is a **Bicycle Museum** (Dviračių muziejus; Vilniaus 139; www.ausros-muziejus.lt; Tue–Fri 10am–6pm, Sat 11am–5pm). There is also a **Museum of Radio and Television** (Radijo ir Televizijos muziejus; Vilniaus 174; www.ausrosmuziejus.lt; Wed 10am–7pm, Thu–Fri 10am–5pm, Sat 11am–5pm). Šiauliai's vast 17th-century cathedral was rebuilt in 1954, as, like most other buildings in the town, it was flattened in World War II. Its spire is one of the tallest in the country. To the south are picturesque hills and lakes round **Bubiai** and **Kurtuvėnai**.

HILL OF CROSSES

Šiauliai is most famous for the **Hill of Crosses** ⑥ (Kryžių kalnas, www.hillof crosses.com), which lies in the countryside about 14km (9 miles) to the northeast on the A12 (E77). Nobody is sure of its origins, but it has been a religious site since at least the end of the 19th century. People come from all over the world to add their crosses to the thousands already here. The sight is nothing short of awe-inspiring. The hill itself is only a small hump. The Soviets bulldozed it three times, the first time in 1960, destroying an estimated 5,000 crosses. Each time they reappeared and today there are thousands of crosses, rosaries, pebbles, branches and other offerings.

The large statue of Jesus at the entrance was a gift from the late Pope John Paul II during his visit in 1993. The Pope subsequently encouraged Italian Franciscans to build a monastery for Lithuanian novitiates, and this opened in 2001 on the north side of the hill. The monastery is also open to pilgrims. The annual pilgrimage to the hill takes place on the third Sunday in July.

Lake Plateliai.

A parish church near Vastseliina castle.

ESTONIA, LATVIA & LITHUANIA

TRAVEL TIPS

TRANSPORT

By air

Estonia

The discount airlines easyJet, Wizz Air and Ryanair offer direct London–Tallinn services. Other airlines such as AirBaltic and British Airways also run direct flights to Estonia's capital. Completely rebuilt in 2008, the Lennart Meri Tallinn Airport (TLL) is one of Europe's most modern as well as one of its smallest.

Taxis and buses wait just outside the arrivals area's main door. The airport is remarkably close to the centre of the capital, and a taxi ride can take as little as 10 minutes. The fare should be no more than €10. Choose clearly marked taxis (with the logo of the company on the side door and full price list displayed on the passenger's window to avoid unpleasant surprises). City bus No. 2, which will take you to the A. Laikmaa stop next to the Viru shopping mall in the centre, departs from the airport roughly every 20 minutes (from 6.15am–11.15pm) on weekdays and twice per hour on weekends. Its timetable is posted under the blue-and-white bus sign outside and can be checked online at https://transport.tallinn.ee. You can pay for your journey with a plastic smartcard which can be bought at post offices, several shop chains and kiosks (for details see www.pilet.ee) or an e-ticket, or buy a single €2 ticket directly from the driver. E-tickets cost €1.10 per hour, €3, €5, €6 for one, three and five days respectively and €23 for a 30-day pass.

Landing at one of Estonia's other airports – Tartu and Kuressaare on Saaremaa Island – may be more convenient, depending on your plans. Finnair operates flights on the Helsinki–Tartu route and Transaviabaltika connects Tallinn and Kuressaare.

Latvia

The national carrier AirBaltic (www.airbaltic.com) is owned by the Latvian government and has successfully adopted a budget-airline business model. The airline offers affordable direct flights to Rīga from London, Manchester, Glasgow, Bristol, Brussels, Berlin, Stockholm and several other cities in Europe, Central Asia and the Middle East.

Ryanair www.ryanair.com also flies direct from several destinations in the UK to Rīga. Wizz Air connects Rīga with London.

Rīga International Airport (RIX) is a shiny modern complex 13km (8 miles) outside the city centre and is easily accessed by taxi or bus. Flights arrive and depart from only three small terminals, so getting lost is impossible. In addition to AirBaltic, Wizz Air and Ryanair, Rīga is served by several other major European airlines, including Lufthansa, Finnair and Scandinavian Airlines. For more information, visit www.riga-airport.com.

Take bus No. 22 (stop opposite the terminal behind Car Park 1) which operates every 10–30 minutes and takes about half an hour to get to the city centre. Timetables and bus routes can be checked at www.rigas satiksme.lv. A ticket bought from the driver costs €2. A cheaper alternative (€1.15) will be to buy it at the airport or at the tourist information bureau. A ticket for unlimited 24-hour travel costs €5. A queue of reputable taxis ('Red Cabs' and Baltic Taxi among them) is always available outside the airport; the trip to the city centre takes roughly 20 minutes and should cost between €11–15.

Lithuania

Vilnius International Airport (VNO, Tarptautinis Vilniaus oro uostas) is 5km (3 miles) south of the capital. Ryanair and Wizz Air connect the city with several UK destinations. The cheapest way into town is bus No. 1 to the railway station or No. 2, which stops at both Gedimino and Konstitucijos avenues. Both can be picked up right outside the arrivals hall. Tickets can be bought on the bus for €1. There are two other buses: 88 and 3G (express bus) which go to the business centre and Fabijoniškės district in the north (passing through the city centre) respectively. For bus routes and timetables see http://stops.lt/vilnius/#plan//en. A special train links the airport with the Vilnius main railway station. The railway stop is just outside the airport's passenger terminal (take a covered and well-lit pedestrian walkway to get there). A train ticket costs €0.70. Minibus service is also available.

The taxis parked outside the terminal (airport's approved taxi rank is in front of the arrival hall) will happily deliver fresh arrivals to the city centre for about €10.

The country's second airport at Kaunas has become a major hub for Ryanair, which currently flies between the city and around 10 European destinations including London (Luton, Stanstead), Bristol, and Dublin. Wizz Air flies to London Luton. Kaunas Airport (KUN, Kauno Aerouostas; www.kaunas-airport.lt) is located in the small settlement of Karmėlava, 15km (9 miles) north of the city. The cheapest way to get to the city centre is by bus No 29 and 29E (night bus). A single ticket bought from the driver costs €1. Alternatively, it is possible to buy e-tickets for the bus at the convenience store Narvesen, in the arrivals hall. The bus timetable and route can be checked at www.kvt.lt. A taxi to the city centre should not cost more than €18.

From outside Europe

One of the only direct flights to the Baltic States from outside Europe is from New York to Rīga, so in most cases you must link with one of the carriers from the Baltic States or from other countries: Aeroflot, British Airways, Czech Airlines, Finnair, KLM, Lufthansa, LOT Polish Airlines or Scandinavian Airlines (SAS). Connections from the US are possible with SAS, Finnair, Uzbekistan Air, American Airlines, Delta Airlines and United Airlines, although many will require at least two stopovers.

⊘ Flight contacts

Estonia

Tallinn Airport
Tel: (+372) 6058 888
www.tallinn-airport.ee
AirBaltic
www.airbaltic.com
Tallinn International Airport
Tel: (+371) 17107 (within Estonia)
or (+371) 6700 6006 from abroad

Flights from the UK

easyJet www.easyjet.com
Ryanair www.ryanair.com

Latvia

Rīga Airport
Tel: (+371) 1187 or (+371) 2931 1817 if calling from abroad
www.riga-airport.com
AirBaltic
www.airbaltic.com
Rīga International Airport
Tel: (+371) 9000 1100 or (+371) 6700 6006 from abroad

Flights from the UK

Ryanair www.ryanair.com
Wizz Air www.wizzair.com

Lithuania

Vilnius Airport
Tel: (+370) 6124 4442
www.vilnius-airport.lt

UK Airlines

easyJet www.easyjet.com
Ryanair www.ryanair.com
British Airways, tel: 0844 493 0787
www.britishairways.com

From Australia and New Zealand it is cheapest to fly to London and connect to a budget flight.

By rail

Thoroughly revamped, Tallinn's main railway station (Balti Jaam) is conveniently located just outside the Old Town. Elron (www.elron.ee) offers local and nationwide connections including services to Tartu, Valga, Pärnu, Viljandi, Rakvere and Narva. There is an international railway link with Rīga, but passengers need to change trains at the border crossing in Valga. There are several daily services from Tallinn to Valga. Latvian Railways (www.ldz.lv) operates services between Rīga and many cities in Latvia including Liepāja, Sigulda, Skulte and Daugavpils, as well as overnight trains to Moscow and St Petersburg in Russia.

Lithuania Lietuvos Geležinkeliai, the Lithuanian rail network, connects with Poland and Germany. Train timetables and other useful information in English can be viewed on the Lithuanian rail website, www.litrail.lt. The ambitious Rail Baltica project, which envisages a high quality railway link between Tallinn and Warsaw (Poland), is due to be completed by 2024.

By car

When driving in the Baltics, be sure you carry a valid passport or ID card, driver's licence, vehicle registration and/or ownership documents and proof of valid insurance. Vehicles are required to carry a fluorescent warning triangle, fire extinguisher and first-aid kit. You must also have a national identity sticker on the rear of your vehicle. Breakdown insurance is advisable; consult your insurer before travelling.

The three countries are linked by the Via Baltica (E-67), the main highway that runs 670km (416 miles) from the Lithuanian border with Poland to Tallinn.

Because all three Baltic countries are in the Schengen visa area, there are usually no border checks between them, or on routes in from Western countries. However, border guards regularly stop vehicles along the highway to check passports. Have them at hand always to avoid problems and/or unwanted delays.

High-grade petrol is available, and garages also sell maps

(Regio produces good maps for Estonia, Jana Seta for Latvia and Lithuania), which are essential for getting around. Estonia launched the world's first national electric car fast-charging network in 2013.

There are a number of hotels and rest stops en route.

In general, the speed limit on highways is 90–110kph (55–68mph) and 50kph (30mph) in cities and towns. Most main roads in the Baltics have been upgraded and modernised in recent years so their quality is good. Unfortunately, side roads and country lanes are sometimes in much worse shape with patches and uneven surface which can damage the vehicle's suspension. Beware of reckless or drunk drivers, and pedestrians. Fines for speeding and driving after alcohol are strict and duly enforced.

Headlights must be turned on at all times. 123Baltic.travel (http://123baltic.travel) offers self-drive and tailor-made tours in the Baltic states.

See Rules of the road, page 344.

By bus

Travelling by bus can be significantly faster than travelling by train. From London, Eurolines (www.eurolines.com) offers a service from numerous destinations in Europe to the major Baltic cities and is the main means of transport between the countries. Other respectable international bus operators include Lux Express (www.luxexpress.eu) and Ecolines (http://ecolines.net/lt). These operate frequent services between the Baltic capitals and many European as well as Russian and Belarusian cities. Local buses tend to be slower as they frequently stop in the middle of nowhere. On the other hand, they provide a unique chance to interact with the locals. In most cases, tickets can be bought from the driver; however to secure a seat, it is always better to book in advance or get them at the bus station. For detailed information on bus routes and schedules in Estonia, Latvia or Lithuania go to the following websites: www.tpilet.ee; www.1188.lv/transport; www.autobusustotis.lt.

By sea

Estonia

In summer, dozens of ships make the quick, 85km (53-mile) crossing from Helsinki to Tallinn throughout the day, and larger ferries bring in passengers from other cities across the Baltic. There are several hydrofoils making regular crossings from Helsinki to Tallinn with a journey time of between one and two hours depending on the particular craft and the weather. In winter, the route is restricted to ferries, which take between two and four hours. Overnight ferries make slow but inexpensive connections from Stockholm. There are also ferries to St Petersburg in Russia.

Tallinn harbour (sadam; www.portoftallinn.com) is a 15-minute walk from the Old Town. On trams 1 or 2 coming from the Old Town or the centre, the harbour is the next stop after Mere Puiestee, or from the opposite direction, two stops after the railway station. Note that all ships operated by Tallink leave from the harbour's D-Terminal, about 500 metres/yds northwest.

Main operators:

Eckerö Line, Mannerheimintie 10, Helsinki; tel: (+358) 9 228 8544; and Passenger Port, A-Terminal, Tallinn; tel: 664 6005; www.eckeroline.ee. Inexpensive, slow ferries from Helsinki to Tallinn.

Linda Line Express, Makasiiniterminaali, Eteläsatama, Helsinki, tel: (+358) 0 600 0668 970; and Linnahall Port, Mere pst. 20E, Tallinn; tel: 6999 340; www.lindaline.ee. Helsinki–Tallinn hydrofoil service offering several 90-minute crossings a day. Subject to weather; does not operate Jan–March.

Tallink, Olympiaterminal, Eteläsatama, Helsinki; tel: (+358) 0 6001 5700; and Sadama 5/7, Tallinn; tel: 6409 808; www.tallink.com. Numerous daily express services and larger ferries from Helsinki to Tallinn; overnight services from Stockholm to Tallinn.

Viking Line, Lönnrotinkatu 2, Helsinki; tel: (+358) 0600 41577; and Hobujaama 4, Tallinn; tel: 6663 966; www.vikingline.ee. Viking Line operates ferries from Stockholm to Helsinki, and Helsinki to Tallinn.

Latvia

Tallink offers a luxurious ferry service to Rīga from Stockholm every other day (even or odd dates depending on the month). For more information visit www.tallinksilja.com. Ferries from Liepāja to Lübeck (Travemünde) in Germany depart four times a week, while from Ventspils twice a week. There is also

one weekly service from Liepāja to Nynashamn (near Stockholm), Sweden. Current timetables can be consulted at www.celotajs.lv/en/c/serv/ferry. Tallinn and Rīga are major ports of call on Baltic cruises.

The main operators are:

Tallink, Eksporta iela 3a; tel: 6709 9700; www.tallinksilja.com. Regular ferry service between Rīga and Stockholm.

Stena Line, Dārzu iela 6, Ventspils tel: 6362 2999; www.stenaline.lv. Offers regular services from Liepāja and Ventspils to Travemünde (Germany) and Nynashamn (Sweden).

Lithuania

A handful of car ferries link the Lithuanian port of Klaipėda to Kiel in Germany and Karlshamn in Sweden. For details contact DFDS Seaways, tel: (+370) 4632 3232; www.dfdsseaways.lt. The international ferry terminal is located several kilometres south of the city centre and can be reached by taxi (around €10) or bus 1a (€0.70), leaving from a stop south of the Old Market on Taikos. The journey from the city centre takes about 25 minutes.

GETTING AROUND

Public transport

Estonia

A system of **buses**, **trams** and **electric trolleybuses** makes up Tallinn's public transit system. The trams mainly service the centre of town, whereas the buses are for reaching outlying areas. Detailed maps posted on most bus stops will show you how to make your journey. (You can also buy good transport maps published by Regio.) All three modes of transit use a plastic smartcard and e-ticket system. Smartcards can be bought at post offices, R-kiosks, Maxima, Prisma and Selver shop chains, Autogrill kiosks, Stockmann shops as well as at the Tallinn City Government Info Hall (Vabaduse väljak 7). A €2 deposit has to be paid for the new smartcard, which is refundable six months after the first use. Smartcards can be topped up with e-tickets at sale points, online (www.pilet.ee) or over the phone (call 11800) and must be validated at the start of each journey (touch orange card readers). It is still possible to buy a paper ticket from the driver for €2

(no need to validate it). Holders of the Tallinn Card (www.tourism.tallinn.ee/eng/fpage/tallinncard), children under school age and adults with children under 3 are entitled to free travel.

Taxis Most of the city is walkable, but if you do need a taxi, it is best to order one by phone. Dispatchers at Linnatakso, tel: 1242/ 6442 442, and Tulika Takso, tel: 1200, usually speak some English. There is also a useful mobile phone application Taxify.eu (http://taxify.eu) providing reliable taxis. The biggest complaint among tourists in Tallinn is taxi drivers who overcharge. Before starting out, check the rates listed on the taxi's window. Typical rates are €2–3 starting fee, then about €0.50/km. If in doubt, ask a driver for an estimate before getting in.

Buses Long-distance buses are the most convenient and widely used method of getting from city to city in Estonia. In Tallinn, the modern bus station, Tallinna Bussijaam (www.bussijaam.ee) is located at Lastekodu 46; tel: 12550. A complete bus timetables in English can be checked at www.tpilet.ee. Bus tickets can be bought at the e-shop, ticket offices and from the bus driver about 15 minutes before departure (if there are seats available). Lux Express offers daily services to Kuressaare on Saaremaa and Go Bus daily connections to Kärdla on Hiiumaa.

Lux Express: Tallinn bus station; tel: 6800 909; www.luxexpress.eu.

Go Bus: Tallinn bus station; tel: 12012; www.gobus.eu.

Latvia

All public transport in Rīga, including **trams** (8 lines), **buses** (56), and **trolleybuses** (17), costs a flat fee of €1.15 for a single ticket which can be bought at Rīga Transport (Rīgas Satiksme) ticket offices and public ticket machines as well as Narvesen newsstands, post offices and Rimi supermarkets. It is also possible to buy a single ticket from the driver but it costs €2. There are many other ticket options available: one (€1.15), two (€2.30), four (€4.60), five (€5.75), 10 (€10.90) and 20 (€20.70) rides or tickets for unlimited one-day (€5), three days (€10) or five days (€15) travel. Always make sure to validate your ticket against the electronic reader as soon as you board the bus, tram or trolley. For more information in English, visit the Tram and Trolleybus Authority's excellent site, www.rigassatiksme.lv.

Minibuses called *mikroautobusi*, or *mikriņi* for short, can also be a convenient way of travelling as they will stop at any point along a given route, and are a fast way of getting around, though they are often packed.

Trams Electric trams have been in use in Rīga since 1901. Today, there are eight different tram lines, which operate from 5am to midnight. Night buses run every hour from midnight to 5am. There are also 17 trolleybus routes for which the same rules for trams apply.

Taxis Taxis in Rīga are notoriously dodgy and will often overcharge any person who doesn't speak Latvian or Russian. To avoid exorbitant prices always call a cab or ask the receptionist at your hotel to order a reputable taxi for you. Despite their dubious reputation in general, there are a few taxi companies that can be trusted. Try Smile Taxi (http://smile. taxi), tel: 2233 0330 or Red Cab Taxi (http://redcab.lv), tel: 8383. Most taxis accept credit cards.

⊙ Car hire firms

Tallinn

Avis: at the airport; tel: 6058 222; in the city at Peterburi tee 47, tel: 6671 500; www.avis.ee.
Budget: at the airport; tel: 6058 600; www.budget.ee.
Hertz: at the airport; tel: 6058 923; in the city at Tartu maantee 25; tel: 6116 333; www.hertz.ee.
R-Rent: at the airport, tel: 6058 929; www.rrent.ee.
Sir Rent: Tatari 56; tel: 5651 353; www.sirrent.ee.
Sixt: at the airport; tel: 6058 148; in the city at Maakri 19; tel: 6381 600; www.sixt.ee.

Rīga

AddCar Rental: at the airport; tel: 2658 9674; www.addcarrental.com.
Avis: at the airport; tel: 6720 7353; in the city at Jaunmoku iela 34;

tel: 6722 5876; www.avis.lv.
Car Rent Riga: tel: 2958 0448; www.carsrent.lv. Delivers cars to any location in Rīga and also offers drivers.
EgiCarRent: tel: 2570 5475; www.egi.lv. Delivers cars to any location in Rīga.
Europcar: at the airport; tel: 6720 7825; in the city at Krišjāņa Valdemāra iela 8; tel: 6722 2637; www.europcar.lv.
Sixt: at the airport; tel: 6720 71 21; www.sixt.lv.

Lithuania

Avis: at the airport; tel: 8-5 232 9316; www.avis.lt.
Budget: at the airport; tel: 8-5 230 6708; www.budget.lt.
Sixt: at the airport; tel: 8-5 239 5636; www.sixt.lt.

Lithuania

Public transport has never been the most pleasant part of a stay in Vilnius. Most systems operate from 5.30am–11pm, so late-night travel is by foot or taxi. There are no night buses, except for special occasions (New Year's Eve). Public transport is, however, inexpensive and covers most of the city, excluding the Old Town.

City buses and trolleybuses All buses and trolley buses are city-owned. Single tickets can be bought from the driver for €1 but no longer from the kiosks, where only electronic tickets (cards) are sold for €1.5. The electronic top-up system, Vilniečio Kortelė (www.vilniusticket.lt), can be a bit confusing as it offers a great variety of options. The most commonly used are those allowing for a 30-minute (€0.65) or a 60-minute (€0.90) journey. The fare is taken off when you press the electronic card against the yellow reader present on all buses and trolleys. Other possibilities include e-tickets valid from one to 365 days. Schedules can be checked online at www.vilniustransport. lt. In 2014 Vilnius authorities have also introduced a m.Ticket mobile application which allows to buy tickets using your smartphone.

Microbuses This is the fastest form of transport through the city. Microbus routes are subject to change as they are privately owned and operated. Most have signs in their front windows giving a general idea of their

trajectory. All private minibuses were scrapped by the city authorities in 2013 but the service has gradually been restored. However, not all operators have been allowed to return and the minibuses must now stop only at the public trolley or bus stops (before they could be flagged down virtually anywhere). Tickets for minibuses (around €1) are available from the driver, e-cards are also accepted. Tell the driver where you would like to be dropped off. As no one usually speaks English, it is best to have decent Lithuanian pronunciation skills or have your destination written down (see Language, page 354).

Taxis Generally, taxi drivers like to take advantage of foreigners. Most horror stories of inflated taxi prices occur when foreigners are inebriated or when the meter clicks away at a super-fast rate and goes unnoticed until the arrival at the destination. Your best bet for not getting ripped off is merely to pay attention to your surroundings. If possible, always try to call for a taxi instead of hailing one off the street as the price will be significantly cheaper. Fare per one kilometre is usually between €0.60–€0.70. Always make sure the meter is running and set to the right tariff (1 most of the time, 2 after midnight). Taxify is a practical mobile application (for Android, iPhone, iPad) which allows you to see all taxis and their fares near your location as well as users opinions which significantly reduces

the chance of being scammed. See more information at http://taxify.eu. Other reputable taxi companies include: Ekipažas (tel: 1446 or 5239 5539; www.ekipazastaksi.lt), Smart Taxi (tel: 1820 or 5200 0820; www.smart taxi.lt) and Martono Taksi (tel: 1422 or 5240 0004; www.standart-taksi.lt).

Long-distance buses Buses are more popular and expensive than trains for most domestic destinations. The bus station (*autobusų stotis*) is at Sodų 22, www.toks.lt, across from the train station. Although tickets can be bought from the driver, it is always worth booking them in advance. Main operators include Ecolines (Geležinkelio 15, tel: 5213 3300; www.ecolines.net) and Lux Express (Sodų 22, tel: 5233 6666; www.luxexpress.eu).

Trains Tickets can be purchased 24 hours a day at the railway station (*geležinkelio stotis*), www.litrail. lt, located at Geležinkelio 16 or on the train from the conductor who charges a €1.45 commission. There are numerous connections within Lithuania and abroad including services to Belarus and Russia. On overnight trains to Russia there are three different classes of tickets. The cheapest is *obschii*, which is a sitting place only. *Platzkart* is an open compartment with dormitory-style beds and *coupe* is a softer bed in a four-person compartment with a door that locks.

Women travelling alone should be aware that it is not uncommon for them to end up in a *coupe* with three men overnight, although a word in the ear of the train compartment manager once on board can sometimes result in the sleeping arrangements being changed. Czech-made modern double decker trains introduced on the Vilnius–Kaunas route have significantly cut the travelling time between these two largest Lithuanian cities and now are a faster option than long-distance buses.

Car hire

Hiring a car is generally the best way to explore the three countries, and is simple and relatively inexpensive. You must be at least 21 years of age and must possess a valid driving licence, passport and major credit card, and must have had a licence for at least two years. Most of the major international car hire agencies operate in the cities and have desks at the airports. In most cases cars can be delivered to your hotel.

Mileage is unlimited, but hirers are expected to fill the tank just before returning the car. Otherwise a top-up fee will be added to the bill, along with the price of the fuel. Prices in comparison tend to be lower than in Western Europe and the US. Pricing structures are the same as in most countries, with added fees for an additional driver, insurance, mileage and the like.

If you plan to take your hire car outside the country, you may need special documents for the border. However, many hire companies have special deals even for one-way travel within all three Baltic States.

Driving

Road conditions vary from good to poor. Estonian drivers range from the careless to the aggressive, while Latvians are not above passing on blind turns or suddenly driving in the

---

⊙ In case of a breakdown

Estonia: Falck, tel: 1888; www.falck.ee; 24-hour towing services.
Latvia: LAMB; tel: 1888; www.lamb.lv; offers a 24-hour service.
Lithuania: Falck (tel: 6610 2020; www.falck.lt); 24-hour road assistance.
All accidents, no matter how small, must be reported to the police or it will be impossible to make an insurance claim.

---

opposite lane of oncoming traffic to avoid a pothole. Your only recourse is to drive defensively.

Weather is an issue, particularly in winter when patches of ice appear on roads. If you are not experienced at driving in winter conditions, this is not the place to learn.

Also, because markings on rural routes can often be confusing, it is essential to have a good road atlas to refer to.

Parking

Parking in the centre of the three capitals can be a battle. Most street parking is paid parking, and tickets are sold in vending machines.

In **Tallinn** car parks can be found under Freedom Square (Vabaduse väljak), on Rävala 5, and at the Viru Hotel, Viru väljak 4. See www.europark.ee for a map of more options. The cost is €1.50–6/h depending on the zone.

Rīga has plenty of guarded and multi-storey car parks around town. To find the most convenient location, visit www.europark.lv.

Although you can now enter Old Rīga free of charge, you have to pay high fees for hourly parking. To make things worse, you can only pay for parking using a complicated mobile phone SMS system, which isn't very advantageous for visitors. If you would like to learn more about how to pay for parking in Old Rīga, visit www.mobilly.lv.

There are four parking zones in **Vilnius** (blue, red, yellow with subzones and green) covering large part of the city with fares ranging from €0.30 (blue, daily from 8am to midnight) to €2.50 (Mon–Sat 8am–6pm) per hour. As of May 2015, parking can only be paid over the phone by sending an SMS to the number 1332 with the code START X AAA000, where X is the parking zone (M–blue, R–red, G–yellow and Z–green) and AAA000 is the vehicle's registration number. When parking is no longer needed simply send a text message "Stop" to 1332. Some **national parks** and the Latvian seaside of Jūrmala charge drivers a small entrance fee.

Rules of the road

Traffic signs and symbols follow the European standard.
Drive on the right and overtake on the left.
Headlights must be kept on at all times, day and night, even in the city.
Passengers in both front seats must wear seatbelts at all times;

⊙ Take it easy

Latvia has one of the highest numbers of road-accident fatalities in Europe, with 70 deaths registered per one million inhabitants in 2017. In the same year, 67 people died on the Lithuanian roads and only 36 perished in Estonia.

---

back-seat passengers should wear them too if fitted.
Children under 12 are not allowed to travel in the front seat.
Winter tyres must be used from December (November in Lithuania) to March.
A first-aid kit & fire extinguisher, warning triangle and reflective jackets are compulsory aboard all motor vehicles. The use of mobile phones by drivers is prohibited without hands-free equipment.
Drivers are considered under the influence and therefore subject to arrest if they have a 0.04 percent alcohol in their blood – about a half-litre of beer – in Lithuania, 0.05 percent and only 0.02 percent in Estonia. It is best not to drink at all if you are driving. The basic speed limit outside built-up areas is 90km/h (55mph), in built-up areas 50km/h (31–37mph), and in residential areas 20km/h (13 mph). Some roads are marked with their own limits, particularly large motorways, where cars are permitted to go 110km/h (69mph) in summer. On the Vilnius–Kaunas motorway speed limits are 100km/h (62mph). On all other Lithuanian motorways the limits range from 90km/h (55mph) to 130km/h (80mph). Drivers must have a valid driving licence and car documents with them at all times.

Police are stationed at most major thoroughfares, and most drivers opt to pay their fines in cash on the spot in order to avoid having to go to a particular police station to pay the fine.

Even if you are driving by lakes and forests, remember that the town's limits extend up to the point where the sign of the town with a cross through it stands. Often police will have speed traps in these non-populated areas that are still within the town or city limits. Fines may also be imposed on drivers who fail to stop at pedestrian crossings.

If you have an accident, you are not supposed to move your vehicle until the police have arrived.

A

Accommodation

There have been a large number of three- and four-star hotels built throughout the region since the turn of the millennium, and all three capitals offer a choice of world-class hotels, with stylish rooms, in-room internet connections, free Wi-fi, business centres, top-notch restaurants and other luxury amenities, including health spas and saunas, both of which are specialities of the Baltics. Most larger hotels also have rooms or entire floors designated for non-smokers, as well as rooms equipped for disabled guests. A growing number of cosy boutique hotels, often built into refurbished Old Town buildings and rural manor houses, offer the same level of luxury in a more intimate environment. Hotels in smaller cities and in the countryside tend to be more basic, but even here, standards of quality are usually similar to Western European levels. Travellers on a tight budget should consider bed & breakfast, hostel, home stay, or tourist farm accommodation. All hotels take credit cards unless otherwise noted.

Estonia

Thanks to a tourism boom, the choice of hotels and spas in Estonia has mushroomed over the last decade. Even so, book early during the high season (May to August) to get the best deals. Tallinn offers the widest range of choice, from medieval-style boutique hotels to ultra-modern high-rises, many with spa treatment facilities. If you're travelling in a small group and spending any length of time in the capital, renting a flat is worth considering; an increasing number of firms specialise in rentals. Anyone visiting Tallinn on a tight budget should first try to find space in one the few Old Town guesthouses and hostels, then look to the outskirts for super-cheap accommodation.

Prices for rooms elsewhere in Estonia are usually drastically lower, but even here there are ways to economise.

Tourist farms (rural B&Bs) offer simple double rooms at hostel prices, though your hosts may not speak English. Many tourist farms, and even a few guesthouses in the city suburbs, will also let you pitch a tent in their garden – and use their facilities – for a small fee.

A database listing every registered accommodation facility in Estonia, with prices and links to web pages, can be found at the Tourism Board's website: www.visitestonia.com.

Campers should note that at some Estonia's official "Kämping" sites you won't even need a tent. These are typically patches of forest filled with simple little camp huts. All you need to bring with you is a sleeping bag and lots of mosquito repellent. Wild camping is tolerated.

Budget travellers should bear in mind that the term "hostel" has a much wider definition in Estonia than the familiar, friendly, backpackers' stopover, encompassing also cheap hotels and guesthouses. The latter typically offer only private rooms and lack kitchen and laundry facilities. The larger, traditional hostels offer private, bare-bones singles, doubles and triples (€20–50), as well as dorm beds (€10–16).

The Estonian Youth Hostel Association (www.balticbookings.com/eyha/#/Estonia/Tallinn), part of Hostelling International, has given its stamp of membership to 18 hostels and guesthouses in Tallinn, as well as other establishments around the country, but does not cover the most popular, recommended venues. Booking and information can be found at www.hotels.ee. You do not have to be a member of a hostelling association to stay at any of them.

Latvia

Rīga has many expensive luxury hotels, as well as many medium-range hotels, but only Old Town hotels need to be booked well in advance. When travelling throughout the country, you will find the majority of towns have at least one good hotel where facilities are usually basic but acceptable. Large towns have at least one three- or four-star hotel, and several have more.

Private bed & breakfast accommodation has flourished in Rīga and usually costs much less than a hotel room. Farmhouse and cottage accommodation can be arranged through Lauku ceļotājs (Country Traveller), Kalnciema 40, Rīga; tel: 6761 7600; www.celotajs.lv.

Lithuania

A great deal of time, effort and money has been spent to produce some swish establishments in which the visitor can rest his or her weary head. Most hotels are child-friendly, but not always pet-friendly. Rates in Vilnius, as opposed to the coastal regions, tend not to fluctuate seasonally. However, hotel prices can sometimes be lower in winter as hotels scramble to fill up their empty rooms. Breakfast is usually included in most hotels, although guests are under no obligation to eat the Soviet timewarp, squeaky omelette-style breakfasts still served in many of the cheaper places to stay.

It is always best, although not vital, to have a reservation before entering the country. Many of the newer hotels have online booking systems, making the experience hassle-free. Large hotels are hardly ever booked to capacity, but the cosier bed & breakfast or cheaper options fill up quickly in the summer. If you arrive without a reservation, there is a Vilnius Tourist Information Centre in the train station that can give you listings of accommodation in the city.

All hotels are graded by the Lithuanian Tourism Board, but the star system is based on the amount of amenities on offer, not by the level of service.

Most hotels do not have facilities for wheelchair-bound customers. It is best to ask pointed and numerous questions about the facilities if you are disabled. Those travelling with these sorts of concerns should check out newer hotels, as zoning laws tend to make them more wheelchair-friendly.

Admission charges

Museum and other attractions entry fees in the three countries vary from €2 to €15. Many museums are free to visit one day a month; some museums, galleries and churches are free of charge all the time. One- to three-day tourist cards, available at tourist offices, give discounts in the capitals (Tallinn Card, Riga Pass and Vilnius City Card).

B

Budgeting for your trip

Food, transport and entertainment are all relatively inexpensive. Lithuania is, overall, the cheapest of the three countries, Estonia the most expensive, with Latvia in between. A meal, without drinks, will typically cost from €7 to €10. In the capitals' most expensive restaurants, it will be from €20 to €50 respectively. A large beer in a local pub costs €1.80–2.00, and in a touristy café €3–5. Soft drinks are €0.80–1.

The rate for a double room in a mid-range hotel is from €50 in Latvia to €80 in Estonia, with Lithuania in between, but quite decent rooms can be found for under €35 in Lithuania and €60 in Estonia.

C

Children

Children take a central part in Baltic life and are welcomed in restaurants and other outings. Parks in the cities cater for children, but don't expect Disneyworld.

Some hotels offer child-care facilities, and children under seven travel either half-price or free on public transport.

Climate and clothing

July is by far the best time to visit. This is when the days are sunniest and it is least likely to rain. June, on the other hand, is usually rainy, especially around Midsummer's Eve in the third or fourth week of the month. In June the temperature is usually mild: the last of spring's icy spells having ended in May in Estonia and earlier in Lithuania. July is the hottest month, when temperatures can reach up to 30°C (86°F). The average for the month is a pleasant 17°C (63°F).

In winter, temperatures as low as –30°C (–22°F) have been recorded in Estonia and –20°C (–4°F) in Lithuania. In recent years, with the exception of 2009, winter temperatures have tended to be milder, seldom falling below around the –5°C (23°F) mark, and temperatures inland are generally lower than near the coast. Despite this, winters can often seem extremely cold because of the piercing coastal winds.

Snow is most prolonged in Estonia, where it can fall from January through to March.

The biggest drawback for visitors in winter is generally not the cold or the snow, but the lack of sunlight. From early November through until late March darkness never seems to lift completely, and the six or seven hours of daylight are often marred by overcast, misty conditions.

What to wear

Although people tend to dress up for concerts, the theatre and official business, the dress code in all three countries is otherwise fairly informal. When packing, bear in mind how cold the winter climate can be. From November to April minimum requirements are a heavy woollen jumper, leggings and something thick-soled and waterproof on your feet. Thermal underwear can also be welcome. From January to March it is highly advisable to wear gloves and a hat and scarf.

In summer, lightweight garments and even shorts and T-shirts are adequate. Evenings can turn chilly,

so bring a sweater and jacket to keep you warm. It is also advisable to pack waterproof clothing and an umbrella. Sensible, comfortable footwear is highly recommended as the cities' cobbled streets are uncomfortable in thin-soled shoes and treacherous in high heels.

Crime and safety

Violent crime tends to be gangland-related, and assaults on foreigners are rare and usually involve excessive alcohol use at dodgy striptease clubs in Rīga. Take the usual precautions against theft that you would when travelling anywhere – anything that you are not physically attached to is liable to walk, so be watchful. Further good advice is to remain sober; nothing could present a more appealing target than an inebriated tourist staggering through dimly lit streets.

D

Disabled travellers

The medieval Baltic capitals are a headache for anyone in a wheelchair. Pavements can be rocky, kerbs steep, and many restaurants, cafés, shops and museums can only be accessed via cramped, narrow staircases. On the positive side, traffic in the Old Towns is usually restricted, leaving the streets wide open for pedestrian explorers.

Although the situation has recently improved as all three countries are bound to meet EU regulations, visitors in wheelchairs will sometimes need to ask numerous, pointed and direct questions about a hotel's facilities in order to ensure they can be accommodated. The largest and newest hotels are fairly accessible, and almost always have rooms specially equipped for disabled guests. All new buildings and principal museums are equipped with facilities for disabled travellers.

The number of buses, trams and trolleybuses with essential equipment to aid in boarding is growing, the major taxi companies also offer cars designed for disabled passengers.

The situation gets progressively worse as you leave the capitals and go into more rural regions. However,

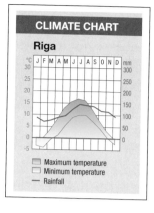

CLIMATE CHART
Riga
☐ Maximum temperature
☐ Minimum temperature
— Rainfall

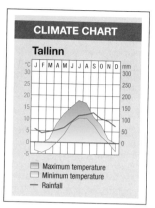

CLIMATE CHART
Tallinn
☐ Maximum temperature
☐ Minimum temperature
— Rainfall

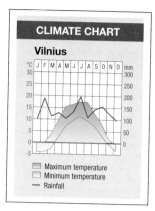

CLIMATE CHART
Vilnius
☐ Maximum temperature
☐ Minimum temperature
— Rainfall

some beaches in well-known resorts have ramps for disabled tourists.

E

Eating out

New restaurants open every month in each of the capital cities and the choice allows you to feast on French haute cuisine, sample Japanese sushi or Armenian *shashlik*, or wolf down vegetarian dishes. In the main cities, some of the bars and clubs are so stylish they would stand out in Paris, London or New York. Most waiting staff speak English – if they don't, the menu will certainly be in either English, German, French or Russian. The best hotels and restaurants have imported top international chefs, serving first-class international food.

Most restaurants accept Visa and MasterCard unless otherwise stated. In these listings, we have tried to recommend the most notable establishments, with the stress on local cuisine.

Estonia

Despite Estonia's small size, its restaurant scene is marked by sophistication and variety. Diners can find anything from medieval fare to cutting-edge fusion. Tallinn is awash with theme restaurants, and it is not uncommon to see waiters in elaborate costumes roaming the streets, handing out coupons and flyers.

One thing that is surprisingly hard to find in the city, however, is a restaurant that serves Estonian food. Even at the casual lunch cafés and pubs favoured by locals,

the choices are typically *seljanka* (a thick, Russian soup) or *schnitzel*, which are not originally Estonian. The reason for this conspicuous absence of traditional fare is that Estonian cuisine is for the most part a simple – some would say bland – affair with country roots. Favourites are *sült* (jellied meat), *mulgikapsas* (fatty sauerkraut), *rollmops* (soused herrings) and *kama* (a mixture of ground cereals taken as dessert). Estonians think of this cuisine as something they make at home, but wouldn't look for when they go out, hence its scarcity in the restaurant world. That said, visitors who know where to look can find one or two decent places to sample the local food. Not surprisingly, however, these are mainly aimed at tourists.

Out in the country it is different, and this is the place to head for if you really want to find more of the local flavour, especially locally smoked fish and meat, which you should try.

Latvia

Being a nation of farmers for so many years, Latvia's national foods are, to put it mildly, rustic in nature. *Pīrāgi* are small pastry buns traditionally, although not exclusively, filled with chopped ham and onions. A bowl of boiled grey peas fried with bacon and onions is also a favourite treat, often topped with *kefīrs*, a dairy drink similar to yoghurt.

Latvians also pride themselves on a wide variety of sausages, which, when compared to German *bratwurst* or *knockwurst*, sadly, just don't cut the mustard. However, the thin *mednieku desiņas*, or hunters' sausages, are definitely worth a try.

Although difficult to find in Rīga, *grūdenis* is a thick country stew that

uses half a pig's head as a base. The pork chop or *karbonāde* is the most prevalent national dish, usually complemented by potatoes, *sauerkraut* and a slice of delicious rye or black bread baked only with natural ingredients. Due to so many years of culinary isolation, dill and caraway seeds are often the only seasonings used by chefs at Latvian restaurants.

Rīga is a food haven with ethnic cuisines from Tex-Mex to Korean. There are excellent (and expensive) upmarket restaurants in dozens of luxurious hotels throughout the city. Hotel Bergs and Hotel Neiburgs are among the best.

Good Latvian home cooking is served in a number of Lido establishments, notably at Dzirnavas, Lido Atpūtas Centrs or Vērmanītis (further details below). These places have made country cooking their trademark, but do not accept credit cards.

Lithuania

In Lithuania's cities you can find almost all major cuisines. Top hotels often have some of the city's best restaurants and can be a safe bet for those who wish to ease themselves slowly into the local cuisine.

Lithuanian cuisine, which is mainly based on potatoes and borrows heavily from Slavic and Jewish cuisine, is rich and rather fatty. The national dish, *cepelinai*, sticky potato rolls filled with meat or cottage cheese and usually dripping in a buttery bacon sauce *(spirgučiai)*, probably made their way to the country with the Germans during World War I and are quite a mouthful in more ways than one. Although traditional Lithuanian food tends to be some combination of meat (usually pork), cabbage and potatoes, there are many pleasant exceptions to the rule. Lighter eaters will enjoy the array of salads and soups, which usually are more than just a fair sprinkling on the menu. Most menus are written in Lithuanian, Russian and English.

Electricity

The electricity in all three countries is 220 volts AC, 50Hz. Plugs are the round, two-pinned variety used in Continental Europe. In Estonia, adaptors can be found in electronic shops and in department stores such as Tallinna Kaubamaja, and are readily available in Lithuania, but you are advised to take one with you if travelling in Latvia, or the countryside.

Embassies and consulates

The embassies are all in the capital cities. When there is no local embassy, Australians, Irish, New Zealanders and South Africans should contact the UK Embassy, or their own embassy in a neighbouring country.

Tallinn
Canada (Representative office only) Toomkooli 13; tel: 6273 311.
Ireland Rahukohtu 4-II; tel: 6811 870.
UK Wismari 6; tel: 6674 700.
US Kentmanni 20; tel: 6688 100.

Rīga
Canada Baznīcas 20/22; tel: 6781 3945
Ireland Alberta 13; tel: 6703 9370
UK Alunāna 5; tel: 6777 4700
US Samnera Velsa 1; tel: 6710 7000

Vilnius
Australia (Honorary Consulate) Vilniaus 23; tel: 212 3369
Canada (Representative office only) Jogailos 4; tel: 249 0950
UK Antakalnio 2; tel: 246 2900
US Akmenų 6; tel: 266 5500

Emergencies

An all-encompassing emergency number, **112**, works in all three countries. They try to staff with English-speaking personnel at all times, though a non-English-speaker may get your call.
You can also call:
Police in Estonia, **110**. In Latvia and Lithuania, **02**.
Paramedics in Latvia and Lithuania, **03**.

Etiquette

Estonians are very polite but without being friendly; an invitation to an Estonian household is rare. But old habits are changing these days, especially with the younger generation. Latvians are fairly hospitable, too, and tend to be more relaxed. By contrast, Lithuanians are very hospitable and easily become friends. If foreigners stay a few days in Vilnius, they are likely to be invited into a Lithuanian home and introduced to family and friends.

G

Genealogy

Those wanting to track down information about their Baltic ancestry can get help from several agencies that specialise in such matters.

Estonia
Estonian Genealogical Society (Eesti Genealoogia Selts); www.genealoogia.ee. The society doesn't have an office, but its extensive website in English is an excellent starting point for research.
Estonian Biographical Centre (Eesti Isikuloo Keskus), Tiigi 10-51, Tartu; tel: 7420 882; www.isik.ee. The centre specialises in genealogical research and, for a fee, will track down relatives and create a family tree.
National Archives of Estonia (Rahvusarhiiv), Nooruse 3, Tartu; tel: 7387 521; www.eha.ee. Archivists charge an hourly rate for researching and creating a family tree, but visitors can look through the archives at no expense.

Latvia
In Latvia contact the **State History Archive** (Valsts Vēstures Arhīvs) in Rīga, at Slokas 16; tel: 2001 7505.

Lithuania
In Lithuania there are several specialist agencies to assist you with your enquiries.
Lithuanian Central State Archive (Lietuvos centrinis valstybės archyvas), Milašiaus 21; tel: 247 7811; www.archyvai.lt. A directory of people living in Lithuania during the Nazi occupation (1941–2).
Lithuanian State Historical Archive (Lietuvos valstybės istorijos

archyvas), Mindaugo 8; tel: 213 7482. A Church registry until 1940.
Vilnius County Archives, o. Milašiaus 23; tel: 247 7856. Birth, death and marriage certificates from 1940 to the present.

H

Health and medical care

No vaccinations are required. One concern, however, only applies to visitors who plan to spend time deep in the Estonian wilderness or in the wilds of the Latvian or Lithuanian countryside, in which case a vaccination against tick-borne encephalitis is recommended. People are advised to check themselves for ticks – tiny black mites in the skin – after tramping through tall brush.
There are no real problems with medical care, and most Western medicines are available in all three countries. If you feel unwell, your best first stop is a pharmacy, where you can often find most of what you might need to cure common, temporary ailments.
If over-the-counter medicines do not do the trick, it is advisable to seek help from a qualified doctor.
With the European reciprocation of treatment, UK visitors should theoretically need only to present a European Health Insurance Card (see www.ehic.org.uk, or apply for a card at a UK Post Office), for free treatment, but you are strongly advised to take out private insurance, too.
Although healthcare systems are undergoing crises due to budget cuts, foreigners with money are generally well-treated. Doctors and nurses are grossly underpaid but still try to provide an adequate service.
Hospitals are usually spartan but sanitary, and the healthcare is generally good. For an ambulance, dial 112 in all three countries.

Tallinn

Pharmacies (apteek)
Tõnismäe Apteek, Tõnismägi 5, tel: 6442 282, in central Tallinn runs an all-night pharmacy window.

Hospitals (haigla)
East Tallinn Central Hospital, Ravi 18; tel: 6661 900. Open 24 hours. The paramedic service in Tallinn runs a first-aid hotline (tel: 6971

145) that can give you advice or direct you to a hospital.

Dentists (hambaravi)
Baltic Medical Partners, Tartu mnt. 32; tel: 6010 550; www.bmp.ee.
Tallinna Hambapolikliinik, Toompuiestee 4; tel: 1920; www.hambapol.ee.

Sexually Transmitted Diseases
Aids Information and Support Centre, Kopli 32; tel: 6413 165.

Rīga

Pharmacies (aptiekas)
Benu aptieka, Aleksandra Čaka 104; tel: 6731 4211. Open 24 hours.
Mēness aptieka, Vienības gatve 49; tel: 2037 7604. Open 24 hours.

Hospitals (slimnīcas)
ARS, Skolas 5; tel: 6720 1007; www.ars-med.lv. For all emergencies.
Diplomatic Service Medical Centre, Elizabetes 57; tel: 6722 9942; www.dsmc.lv. Full English-speaking staff.

Paediatrics
Dr Tirānes, Bruņinieku 67; tel: 6731 5584. American-educated paediatrician.

Dentists (zobārsti)
Adenta, Skanstes 13; tel: 6733 9300; www.adenta.lv. Canadian and local dentists.
Diplomatic Service Medical Centre, Elizabetes 57; tel: 6722 9942; www.dsmc.lv.

Vaccinations
Veselības dienests, Brīvības gatve 195; www.vd.lv.

Vilnius

Pharmacies (vaistinė)
Eurovaistinė Ukmergės 282; tel: 230 3759. A long way from the centre and best reached by taxi. Open 24 hours.
Gedimino Pharmacy, Gedimino pr. 27; tel: 261 0135.

Hospitals
Baltic-American Clinic, Nemenčinės 54a; tel: 234 2020; www.bak.lt.
Northeast of the city in a quiet forested suburb, the clinic is open 24 hours and is by far the most recommended and best known.
Vilnius University Emergency Hospital (Vilniaus Greitosios Pagalbos

Universitetinė Ligoninė), Santariškių 2; tel: 236 5000; www.santa.lt.

Dentists (stomatologos or dantistas)
Dental care in Lithuania is of a very high quality and is considerably cheaper than in the West.
Dr Br. Sidaravičius, Klaipėdos 2/14-3; tel: 262 9760; www.dantuimplantai.lt.
Periodont, Mindaugo 1A-101; tel: 231 2952; https://periodont.ltError! Hyperlink reference not valid..
Gidenta, Vienuolio 14-3; tel: 219 7799; www.gidenta.lt.

Sexually transmitted diseases
Lithuanian Aids Centre, Vytenio 37/59; tel: 230 0125; www.ulac.lt.

L

Left luggage

Estonia
In cities, left-luggage services can be found at all major transport hubs.
In Tallinn Airport, luggage lockers can be found on the 0-floor. There two sizes of lockers, small and big, costing €2–3 per day respectively. At the railway station, the room is in the centre rear of the main hall, closest to the tracks. The passenger port's A and D terminals have both luggage rooms and lockers.
At the bus station, the left luggage office is in the basement, and there are also lockers immediately to the right of the ticket windows.

Latvia
Although many small stations in the Latvian countryside may lack left-luggage rooms or lockers, Rīga has proper facilities in each of its major transport hubs.
At the airport, store luggage for €1.50 per item per 8 hours on the second floor of the public zone, registration sector "F". The luggage room at the bus station charges between €0.60 and €1.40 per hour depending on the weight of your bag. A luggage room is also available in the basement of the railway station (4.30am–midnight).

Lithuania
Most major transport points in Lithuania have left-luggage facilities (bagažinė). In Vilnius there are 24-hour left-luggage facilities at the airport and in the railway station.

Left-luggage facilities in the Vilnius bus station (Mon–Fri 5.25am–9pm, Sat–Sun 7am–8.45pm) are also available. It costs around €1 per item.

LGBTQ Travellers

Though the situation is generally improving, especially in the cities, attitudes in the Baltic States towards homosexuality are not as liberal as those elsewhere in the West. Overt displays, such as holding hands, are not yet socially acceptable and may attract the wrong sort of attention. In 2015, Rīga hosted a successful EuroPride parade; Tallinn hosted Baltic Pride in 2014 and 2017.

Tallinn has a small but active gay nightlife scene, which encompasses a handful of bars and clubs, mostly on Tatari St. X-Baar (Tatari 1) is the most established of these. Other gay venues include Sessel Salong (on Viru 3), Ring Club (http://malesecrets.eu) and Club 69 (www.club69.ee).

In **Rīga** the hippest gay and lesbian club is Golden, (www.mygoldenclub.com).

A small male gay scene does exist in **Vilnius** with Men's Factory (www.mensfactory.lt) and Soho (www.sohoclub.lt) being the most popular clubs. The hugely controversial Gay Pride marches in 2010 and 2013 met strong opposition from conservative politicians and activists.

M

Maps

In **Estonia**, free maps of Tallinn's Old Town are readily available in passenger ferries, hotel receptions and the tourist information office. More complete city maps, as well as maps of other cities and regions, produced by Regio, can be bought at bookshops and larger magazine kiosks. For more, see www.regio.ee.

In **Latvia**, city maps are readily available at the Rīga Tourist Information Centre. A wide selection of inexpensive maps and guides of Latvia and its other cities can be purchased at the Jāņa Sēta Map Shop, Elizabetes 83/85; www.mapshop.lv.

In **Lithuania** Jāņa Sēta maps are available at tourist offices, bookshops and petrol stations. There are also maps by the Vilnius publishers Briedis. Several tourist information centres also publish free maps to their respective towns and cities.

Media

Newspapers and magazines

The Baltic Times (Rupniecibas 1-5; tel: 722 9978; www.baltictimes.com), printed in Rīga, is a weekly pan-Baltic English-language newspaper covering all three states. Formerly the standby of expats and visitors, it can still be found in some kiosks and hotels. *Rīga This Week* (www.rigathisweek.lv) is a free city guide with up to date listings and tourist information. *The Baltic Review* offers independent news stories and in-depth analyses from around the Baltics.

Tallinn In Your Pocket, *Rīga In Your Pocket* and *Vilnius In Your Pocket* are handy English-language city guides, published six times a year with an updated calendar of events, full reviews about the cities' ever-changing restaurants, cafés and bars, and a selection of tourist sites. Once or twice a year the In Your Pocket team also publishes *Pärnu In Your Pocket* and *Tartu In Your Pocket* (see also http://inyourpocket.com/estonia, http://inyourpocket.com/latvia, http://inyourpocket.com/lithuania).

The *Financial Times*, *The Times*, the *New York Times* and the *New York Times International Edition* are also on sale in the main hotels and at larger newsstands.

Television and radio

Most major hotels have rooms with radios and satellite televisions; the majority of them will come with BBC World, CNN, SkyNews, plus a clutch of other channels such as Eurosport, Discovery and Cartoon Network. Much of the entertainment programming on local channels is in English with subtitles in Estonia, but not so often the case in Latvia or Lithuania. You may also be able to pick up channels from the neighbouring countries.

Television stations

Estonia There are five channels broadcasting domestically, as well as a handful of cable-based entertainment channels. Eesti Televisioon (ETV,ETV2, ETV+), the public channels, broadcast mainly cultural and documentary programming. Kanal 2 is a commercial station whose programming leans heavily towards soap operas and reality TV. Higher-quality entertainment programmes appear on TV3 and TV6. Nearly all households and businesses use digital, cable or satellite TV systems. There are also five channels broadcasting in Russian including ETV+, NTV, TVN.

Latvia The two state-owned channels LTV1 and 7 show a variety of dated sitcoms from the US as well as local programming which is rarely of interest, even to Latvians and Russians. Privately owned LNT, TV3 and TV5 often broadcast good films, reality shows and even sporting events, but most are dubbed in Latvian with Russian subtitles.

Lithuania The local channels are LRT (the national broadcasting station) and the privately owned and more popular LNK and TV3. Foreign movies or television shows are almost always dubbed into Lithuanian.

Radio

Estonia There are over 20 radio stations on Tallinn's FM band. The state-owned Eesti Raadio airs the BBC World Service on 103.5FM every day midnight–6am, 7am–8am and 7pm–8pm. Many radio stations are streaming live on the internet (for details see www.listenlive.eu).

Latvia There are over 20 FM radio stations in the capital, notably Radio Latvia (Latvijas Radio), which has three channels including Radio Klasika, a classical radio station on 103.7FM (in Rīga). The BBC World Service can be picked up 24 hours a day on 100.5FM. Of the private music and news radios, SWH on 105.2FM. SWH Rock on 89.2FM and 101 Radio at 101FM are well worth a listen.

Lithuania You can pick up more than a dozen FM radio stations in Vilnius. For news in English tune to the BBC World Service on 95.5 FM, VOA Europe on 105.6 FM or the French Radio France Internationale on 98.3 FM.

Money

Estonians parted ways with their kroons and adopted the European single currency, the euro, at the beginning of 2011. Latvia and Lithuania followed in their neighbours' footsteps and swapped their national currencies for the euro in 2014 and 2015 respectively.

Each euro is worth about £0.70. Paper bills come in denominations of €500, €200, €100, €50, €20, €10 and €5. Coins come in €2, €1, and 50-, 20-, 10-, 5-, 2- and 1-cent varieties.

In Tallinn there are plenty of ATMs and currency exchange offices (*valuutavahetus*) but it is best to avoid the ones in the airport or port as rates tend to be less favourable than elsewhere. Big banks usually offer the best deals but they're closed at night and during weekends. When in need, use exchange offices with good reputations such as Tavid at Aia 5 or Eurex at Viru väljak 4 (Viru Centre).

In Vilnius, foreign currency may be exchanged at banks, exchange offices, the airport, and the railway station. In Rīga, some exchange booths may look questionably makeshift, but these are perfectly legitimate, and many are open all night. Rates vary and tend to be poorest on the touristy streets and in the banks. ATMs are probably the easiest and safest way (particularly at night) to acquire cash.

Credit cards In the major cities almost all upmarket or mid-range establishments such as hotels, restaurants, nightclubs, bars and shops will accept most major credit cards. However, it is always best to double-check before committing to or eating up all of your intended purchase. Outside the main towns and cities, cash remains the main currency.

ATMs are easy to find in the cities and accept all major credit and bank cards, but before leaving home check with your bank that your card will be acceptable.

Travellers' cheques Establishments accepting travellers' cheques are less frequent, but you can cash them at most banks. They cannot be used as currency.

Tipping. Service is not included in most bills. Round up the sum of the bill and add a little if service was appreciated. No more than 5–10 percent is expected.

Opening hours

With the exception of major shopping centres, which usually open seven days a week 10am–10pm, most shops open 8/10am– 6/8pm on weekdays, Sat 9/10am–3/5pm, and are closed on Sundays.

Banks and government offices are generally open weekdays 8/9am–4/5pm. Museums' opening hours tend to vary according to time of the year (they close earlier in winter) and which country you are in. In general, most museums are open 9/11am–5/6pm and many are closed on Mondays and Tuesdays.

Typical office hours are Monday–Friday 8/9am–4/5pm.

P

Postal services

There are good international postal links. Letters generally take about five to seven days to reach the rest of Europe and around ten to fourteen days to arrive in the US. Stamps can be bought at post offices or hotels, which are also the best places to post your letters.

Tallinn

Tallinn Central Post Office: Narva mnt. 1 (opposite the Viru Centre); tel: 661 6616; www.omniva.ee. Mon–Fri 10am–7pm, Sat 10am–3pm. Most services are handled in the main hall, upstairs. Packages, including those sent by EMS courier service, are sent and received in an office with an entrance around the left side of the building.

DHL Express Centre, Rävala pst. 5; tel: 6652 555; http://www.dhl.ee.

Federal Express, Kesk-Sõjamäe 10a; tel: 605 8691; www.fedex.com/ee.

TNT Express Worldwide, Kesk-Sõjamäe 10a; tel: 627 1900; www.tnt.ee.

UPS, Valukoja 22; tel: 6664 700; www.ups.com/ee.

Rīga

Rīga Central Post Office, Brīvības bulv. 32; tel: 6750 2815; www.pasts.lv. Mon–Fri 7.30am–7pm, Sat 9am–3pm.

Cargo Bus, Puškina 2-11; tel: 6722 5566; www.cargobus.eu. Express parcel service in the Baltic and Scandinavian regions.

DHL, Mārupe, Plieņciema 35; tel: 6771 5500; www.dhl.lv.

FedEx, tel: 8000 5300; www.fedex.com/lv/.

TNT Express Worldwide, Mārupe, Plieņciema 11; tel: 6766 8000; www.tnt.lv.

UPS, Ulmaņa 2; tel: 6780 5650; www.ups.com/lv.

Vilnius

Central Post Office (Centrinis Paštas), Gedimino 7; tel: 262 5468; www.post.lt. Mon–Fri 9am–7pm, Sat 9am–2pm. There's also a post office in the Akropolis shopping centre, open daily 10am–10pm.

DHL, Dariaus ir Girėno 81; tel: 236 0700; www.dhl.lt.

Express Mail Service, tel: 233 3060; www.ems.post.

FedEx, Gustaičio 1; tel: 230 6069; www.fedex.com.

TNT, Dariaus ir Girėno 44; tel: 239 7556; www.tnt.lt.

UPS, Eigulių 15; tel: 247 2222; www.ups.com/lt.

Public holidays

Public holidays are cause for great celebration in the Baltics. Each state flies the flags of the other two nations on these special days, as well as their own flag – in Latvia the national flag must, by law, be displayed prominently on facades by the front door on public holidays.

Estonia

January New Year's Day (1)
February Independence Day (24)
March/April Good Friday and Easter Sunday
May Spring Day (1)
June Victory Day (23), Midsummer (24)
August Day of Restoration of Independence (20)
December Christmas (24–25), Boxing Day (26)

Memorial Day
June First mass deportations to Siberia in 1941 (14)

Latvia

January New Year's Day (1-2)
March/April Good Friday and Easter Monday
May Labour Day (1)
May Proclamation of Independence (4)
June Līgo Day (23), Jāņi summer solstice (24)
November Independence Day (18)
December Christmas (24/25/26)
December New Year's Eve (31)

Memorial Days
March mass deportation of Balts to Siberia in 1949 (25)
May World War II Memorial Day (9)

June first mass deportation of Balts to Siberia, 1941 (14)
July Jewish Genocide Day (4)
November 1919 battle, during which invading German forces were repulsed from Rīga (11)

Lithuania

January New Year (1)
February Independence Day (1918) (16)
March Restoration of Lithuania's statehood (11)
March/April Easter
May Labour Day (1), Mothers' Day (first Sunday)
June Father's Day (first Sunday)
June St John's Day/Joninės (23–24)
July Crowning of Mindaugas, Day of Statehood (6)
August Feast of the Assumption (15)
November All Saints' Day (1)
December Christmas (24–26)

R

Religious services

Tallinn
Church of the Holy Spirit, Pühavaimu 2; www.puhavaimu.ee; mass in English Sun 1pm.
St Peter and Paul's Roman Catholic Church, Vene 18; www.katoliku.ee; English service every Sat 6pm.

Rīga
St Mary Magdalene's Catholic Church, Klostera 2; service in English Sun 2pm.
St Saviour's Anglican Church, Anglikāņu iela 2; https://anglicanriga.lv; English service Sun 11am.

Vilnius
Grace Baptist Church of Vilnius, Verkiu 22; www.church.lt; service in English every Sun 11am.
Evangelican Lutheran Church, Vokiečių 20; mass in English Sun 9.30am.
St Francis of Assisi Roman Catholic Church, Maironio 10; www.bernardinu-parapija.lt; English service every Sun 9am.

S

Shopping

Estonia

Estonia is a great place to shop. Notable local products include art, knitwear, linen and a wide selection of handicrafts. Much of the delight of casual shopping here is not the goods but rather the shops themselves, many of which, particularly those in Tallinn's Old Town, possess great character.

Latvia

Latvians are renowned for their craftsmanship, and there is a wide range of paintings, ceramics, jewellery, glassware, porcelain, textiles, amber, leather, wooden crafts and locally made clothes.

Lithuania

It is impossible to walk down Pilies or Aušros Vartų in Vilnius's Old Town without being made aware of local amber, linen goods or woodcarvings for sale. There is a small market where street vendors sell similar items usually for a bit less. In the Old Town, Žydų and Stiklių streets also have shops that are worth looking around. Gedimino is geared to those wanting to purchase Western clothing or shoes. As a rule, shops in Lithuania are not open on Sundays; however, tourist-based shops in the Old Town tend to be open every day.

T

Telephones

You can direct dial to any country on the globe from almost any phone in the Baltic States. Public phones in Latvia and Lithuania (there no longer any public phones in Estonia) are card-operated and are also Wi-Fi hotspots. Instructions are available inside the phone booths. Colourful chip-cards can be bought from post offices, kiosks, shops and hotels. Some card phones can also be used with your credit card, and all of them accept incoming calls. Near-universal mobile phone ownership has rendered public card phones increasingly rare. To call anywhere in Estonia and Latvia, just dial the full seven- or eight-digit number. In Lithuania, however, it's necessary to insert an 8 at the beginning of every number, except when calling within a city from one fixed line telephone to another, or if you're dialling from outside the country.

To call any of the countries from abroad, dial your country's international dialling code (00 in Europe) and the country code:

Estonia 372
Latvia 371
Lithuania 370

followed by the number.

To call abroad dial 00, followed by the country code and then the number. You can call abroad from any phone.

Mobile phones

Mobile phones are popular in the Baltics and you will automatically be switched over to a local service once you arrive. Check with your provider at home to see if there are partnership agreements that will make roaming cheaper. To avoid roaming charges altogether, you can get a local number by buying an inexpensive starter kit, sold in kiosks and shops, which comes with prepaid credit.

Estonian mobile numbers start with 5. To call a mobile phone, simply dial the subscriber's number. From abroad, dial Estonia's country code (372), followed by the subscriber's number.

Latvian mobile phone numbers have eight digits, starting with 2. Digital rules apply. From abroad, dial Latvia's country code (371), followed by the subscriber's mobile phone number.

Lithuanian mobile phone numbers always begin with an 6. To dial a mobile phone, dial 8, wait for the changed tone, then dial the number. When calling a Lithuanian mobile from abroad, dial the country code (370), but drop the 8 so that the number begins with 6. All cities in Lithuania have a code. When calling from abroad or from one city to another the code must be dialled. For example, when calling from Kaunas to Vilnius one must press 8, wait for the changed tone and then dial 5 (Vilnius city code) followed by the number. A prepaid SIM card can be purchased in order to use your own mobile phone in the country. Bitė (Žemaitės 15, www.bite. lt), Telia (Jasinskio 16b, www.telia.lt) and TELE2 (Vytenio 9/25, www.tele2. lt) provide such services.

For citizens of 31 European Economic Area countries, roaming charges for temporary roaming were abolished in mid-2017 yet under a fair use policy some restrictions on the free use of mobile phones are still in place. It is currently not clear how the UK's exit from the European Union in March 2019 will affect this.

Internet

Many hotels and cafés in the Baltic capitals offer free Wi-fi as standard. In city centres, free access is also widely available in pubs, shopping malls and many public parks.

Time zone

The Baltic States are in the eastern European time zone which is GMT +2 hours. An hour is added between the end of March and October for daylight savings, so during the summer local time is GMT +3 hours, known as Eastern European Summer Time or EEST for short.

Tourist Information Centres

Note that tourist office opening hours often vary from year to year.

Estonia

Tallinn
Tallinn City Tourist Office & Convention Bureau, Vabaduse Väljak 7, 15199 Tallinn; tel: 6404 411; www. visittallinn.ee; for conference organisers only.
Tallinn Tourist Information Centre, Niguliste 2/Kullaseppa 4, 10146 Tallinn; tel: 645 7777; www.visittallinn. ee.
June–Aug 9am–7pm, Sun 9am–6pm; Oct–Mar Mon–Sat 9am–5pm, Sun 10am–3pm; Apr–May and Sept Mon–Sat 9am–6pm, Sun 9am–4pm.

Elsewhere in Estonia
Hiiumaa Island, Hiiu tn 1, Kärdla; tel: 5045 393; www.hiiumaa.ee.
Kuressaare (Saaremaa Island), Tallinna 2; tel: 4533 120; www.saaremaa.ee.
Narva, Peetri plats 3; tel: 359 9137; http://tourism.narva.ee.
Pärnu, Uus 4; tel: 447 3000; www.visitparnu.eu;
Tartu, Raekoja plats (in Town Hall); tel: 7442 111; www.visittartu.com.
Võru, Jüri tänav 12; tel: 7821 881; www.visitvoru.ee.
Tourist offices are generally open Mon–Fri from 9/10am–5/6pm and 10am–3pm on weekends.

Latvia
Rīga Information Centre, Rātslaukums 6; Rīga, tel: 6703 7900; www.liveriga.com.

Elsewhere in Latvia

For a full list of Latvian information centres visit www.latvia.travel.

Balvi, Brīvības 46; tel: 6452 2597; www.turisms.balvi.lv.

Bauska, Rātslaukums 1; tel: 6392 3797; www.tourism.bauska.lv.

Cesis, Baznīcas laukums 1; tel: 2831 8318; www.tourism.cesis.lv.

Daugavpils, Rīgas 22a; tel: 6542 2818; www.visitdaugavpils.lv.

Dundaga, Dundaga Castle, Pils 14; tel: 6323 2293; http://visit.dundaga.lv.

Jelgava, Lielā 11; tel: 6300 5522; www.jelgava.lv.

Jūrmala, Lienes 5; tel: 6714 7900; www.visitjurmala.lv.

Kandava, Ūdens 2; tel: 6318 1150; www.visitkandava.lv.

Kolka Information Centre, tel: 2914 9105; www.kolkasrags.lv.

Kuldīga, Baznīcas 5; tel: 6332 2259; http://visit.kuldiga.lv.

Liepāja Regional Tourism Information Bureau, Rožu laukums 5/6; tel: 6348 0808; http://liepaja.travel.

Rēzekne, Atbrīvošanas aleja 98; tel: 6460 5005; www.rezekne.lv.

Roja, Selgas 14; tel: 2863 0590; www.roja.lv.

Sabile, Pilskalna 6; tel: 6325 2344; www.sabile.lv.

Sigulda, Ausekļa 6; tel: 6797 1335; http://tourism.sigulda.lv.

Talsi, Lielā 19/21; tel: 6322 4165; www.talsitourism.lv.

Tukums, Talsu 5; tel: 6312 4451; www.visittukums.lv.

Valmiera, Rīgas 10; tel: 6420 7177; www.visit.valmiera.lv.

Ventspils, Dārzu 6; tel: 6362 2263; www.visitventspils.com.

Most tourist offices are open daily from 8.30/9am to 6pm or even longer in summer.

Lithuania

Lithuanian State Department of Tourism, Švitrigailos 11m, Vilnius; tel: 210 8796; www.tourism.lt.

Vilnius Tourist Information Centres, Pilies g. 2; tel: 262 9660; www.vilnius-tourism.lt.
Didžioji 31 (Town Hall); tel: 262 6470; www.vilnius-tourism.lt.
Rodūnios kelias 2-1; tel: 230 6841; www.vilnius-tourism.lt.

Kaunas

Kaunas Region Tourist Information Centre, Rotušės a. 15; tel: 509 91; http://visit.kaunas.lt.

Klaipėda

Klaipėda Tourist Information Centre, Turgaus 7; tel: 412 186; www.klaipedainfo.lt.

Palanga

Tourist Information Centre, Vilniaus 2B, Kretinga; tel: 731 02; www.kretingosturizmas.info.

Nida

Nida Culture and Tourism Information Centre, Taikos 4; tel: 523 45; www.visitneringa.com.

Trakai

Tourist Information Centre, Karaimų 41; tel: 519 34; http://trakai-visit.lt.

In general, tourist offices in large cities are open daily from 9am to 6pm, sometimes with a one hour lunch break.

Tour operators and travel agents

Because of the special rates they enjoy from airlines and hotels, prices for holidays booked through tour operators should cost little or no more than those booked direct.

Baltic Holidays
Individual and group arrangements. Geliu 50, Ringaudai, Kaunas, Lithuania; tel (UK): 0845 070 5711, www.balticholidays.com.

Martin Randall Travel
A regular programme of group tours specialising in art, architecture and music festivals.
Voysey House, Barley Mow Passage, London W4 4GF; tel: 020 8742 3355; www.martinrandall.com.

Naturetrek
Specialists for bird-watching tours in the Baltics.
Mingledown Barn, Wolf's Lane, Hampshire, GU34 3HJ; tel: 01962 733 051; www.naturetrek.co.uk.

Operas Abroad
Individual arrangements to opera and musical concerts; part of Regent Holidays; tel: 020 7511 9018; www.operasabroad.com.

Regent Holidays
Specialists in the Baltic States since 1992, both with group tours and individuals. It also organises city breaks throughout the year.
6th Floor, Colston Tower, Colston Street, Bristol BS1 4XE; tel: 0203 733 2907; www.regent-holidays.co.uk.

Visas and passports

Citizens of the EU, US, Canada, Australia and New Zealand need only a valid passport. Citizens of South Africa need a visa to visit the Baltic States, but can enter Estonia if they have a valid visa for Latvia or Lithuania.

Customs and export

Individuals entering and leaving the Baltic States may carry with them most articles, personal property and other valuables in unlimited quantities. However, weapons and ammunition of any kind, drugs and psychotropic substances are not allowed. Restrictions on alcohol and cigarettes/cigars also apply. Please note that it is prohibited to bring meat and milk and any items thereof from non-EU countries to Lithuania.

Websites

The best Baltic-related internet resources are:
www.ee (search the Estonian-wide web).
www.all.lv (all Latvian links).
www.on.lt (Lithuanian links).
http://inyourpocket.com (contents of the print guides are available online free of charge; events updated every two months).
www.latvia.travel (Latvia's tourist information website).
www.visitestonia.com (Estonia's official tourist information website).
www.lietuva.lt (official gateway to Lithuania).
ww.visittallinn.ee (Tallinn city website).
www.vilnius-tourism.lt (Vilnius city website).
www.liveriga.com (Rīga city website).

Weights and measures

The metric system is used for weights and measures in all three countries.
1kg = 2lbs 7oz
1km = 0.6 miles

LANGUAGE

ESTONIAN

Estonian, the official language of the Republic of Estonia, is closely related to Finnish and Hungarian. Although it uses a Latin alphabet, and each letter represents only one sound, it is a difficult language to master. There are 14 different cases of any noun, verb conjugation is complex, and the verb's meaning may also change according to how its root is pronounced. There are, however, no articles or genders in Estonian. If you can manage to pick up a few of the words listed below, this will be appreciated by the locals.

Numbers

1 *üks*
2 *kaks*
3 *kolm*
4 *neli*
5 *viis*
6 *kuus*
7 *seitse*

☺ Estonian sounds

Vowels

a – as in car
e – as in bed
i – as in beet
o – as in phone
u – as in moon
ä – as in cat
ö – as in hurt
õ – as in girl
ü – as in shoot.
When a vowel is doubled its sound is lengthened.

Consonants

These have the same sound values as in English, except:
g – always hard, as in gate
j – as the y in yet
š – tch as in match
ž – as in pleasure

8 *kaheksa*
9 *üheksa*
10 *kümme*
11 *üksteist*
12 *kaksteist*
13 *kolmteist*
20 *kakskümmend*
21 *kakskümmend-üks*
30 *kolmkümmend*
100 *sada*
200 *kaksada*
1,000 *tuhat*

Days of the week

Sunday *pühapäev*
Monday *esmaspäev*
Tuesday *teisipäev*
Wednesday *kolmapäev*
Thursday *neljapäev*
Friday *reede*
Saturday *laupäev*

Common expressions

hello *tere*
good morning *tere hommikust*
good evening *tere õhtust*
goodbye *head aega*
see you *nägemist*
thanks *aitäh* or *tänan*
please *palun*
sorry *vabandust*
excuse me *vabandage palun*
yes/no *jah/ei*
fine *hästi*
a toast *terviseks*
bon appétit *head isu*
The general purpose negative – ei ole – is used to encompass every inconvenience from "we're sold out" to "she's not here".

Useful words

airport *lennujaam*
train station *raudteejaam* (in Tallinn the station is known as Balti jaam)
harbour *sadam*
shop *kauplus/pood*

town centre *kesklinn*
market *turg*
hairdresser *juuksur*
pharmacy *apteek*
street/road *tänav tn./maantee mnt./ puiestee pst.*
every day *iga päev*
holiday *puhkepäev*

LATVIAN

Latvian is the native language of about 60 percent of the 1.95 million people living in Latvia and one of the world's endangered languages. It is one of two surviving Baltic languages of the Indo-European language group, the other being Lithuanian. Remotely related to the Slavic languages Russian, Polish and Ukrainian, Latvian has 48 phonemes – speech sounds distinguishing one word from another – 12 vowels, 10 diphthongs and 26 consonants. Stress is placed on the first syllable.

Numbers

1 *viens*
2 *divi*
3 *trīs*
4 *četri*
5 *pieci*
6 *seši*
7 *septiņi*
8 *astoņi*
9 *deviņi*
10 *desmit*
11 *vienpadsmit*
12 *divpadsmit*
20 *divdesmit*
30 *trīsdesmit*
100 *simts*
200 *divi simti*
1,000 *tūkstotis*

Days of the week

Sunday *svētdiena*
Monday *pirmdiena*

☉ Latvian sounds

Vowels

These have the same sound values as in English, with several additions:
a – as in cat
e – as in bed
i – as in hit
o – as in floor
u – as in good
a line over a vowel lengthens it:
ā – as in car
ē – as in there
ī – as in bee (Riga = Rīga)
ū – oo as in cool

Diphthongs

au – ow as in pout
ie – e as in here
ai – I as in sight
ei – ay as in sway

Consonants

Consonants have the same sound values as in English with the following exceptions:
c – ts as in tsar
č – ch as in chin
g – always hard, as in gate
ģ – as in logical. The accent can also be a "tail" under the letter.
j – as the y in yet
ķ – tch as in hatch
ļ – as in failure
ņ – as in onion
r – always rolled as in Spanish
š – sh as in shoe
ž – as in pleasure

Tuesday otrdiena
Wednesday trešdiena
Thursday ceturtdiena
Friday piektdiena
Saturday sestdiena

Common expressions

hello, hi sveiki
good morning labrīt
good afternoon labdien
good evening labvakar
goodbye uz redzēšanos/visu labu
yes jā
no nē
Please; You're welcome lūdzu
Thank you paldies
I am sorry! Excuse me Atvainojiet!
That's all right Nekas
May I ask a question? Vai drīkstu jautāt?
May I come in? Vai drīkstu ienākt?
Where can... be found? Kur atrodas...?
How much is it? Cik tas maksā?

Would you please tell me/show me? Vai Jūs lūdzu man nepateiktu/neparādītu?
Pleased to meet you Patīkami ar Jums iepazīties
Let me introduce myself Atļaujiet stādīties priekšā
My name is... Mani sauc...
Do you speak English? Vai Jūs runājiet angliski?
I don't understand/speak Latvian Es nesaprotu/nerunāju latviski
We need an interpreter Mums ir vajadzīgs tulks

Useful words

doctor ārsts
hospital slimnīca
first aid ātrā palīdzība
hotel viesnīca
restaurant restorāns
shop veikals
airport lidosta
bus station autoosta
railway station dzelzceļa stacija
petrol station degvielas uzpildes stacija
post office pasts
street iela
square laukums
closed slēgts
open atvērts

LITHUANIAN

Lithuanian and Latvian both belong to the Baltic family of the Indo-European languages. With some resemblance to Sanskrit, Lithuanian is one of the oldest surviving languages, and it has kept its sound system and many archaic forms and sentence structures. When the written language was first formalised in the first half of the 20th century, there were a variety of distinctive dialects across the country, and Suvalkiečiai, the southern sub-dialect of Western High Lithuania, was adopted as the official dialect. Today, local dialects have been largely assimilated. There are 32 letters in the alphabet. One of Lithuanian's idiosyncrasies is the tail that appears beneath its vowels.

Numbers

1 vienas
2 du
3 trys
4 keturi
5 penki
6 šeši
7 septyni
8 aštuoni
9 devyni
10 dešimt
11 vienuolika
12 dvylika
20 dvidešimt
30 trisdešimt
100 šimtas
200 du šimtai
1,000 tūkstantis

Common expressions

hello laba diena
hello Mr... laba diena, pone...
hi labas, sveikas
please prašom
excuse me atsiprašau
sorry atsiprašau, atleisk
good morning labas rytas
good evening labas vakaras
good night labanakt
goodbye Sudie, viso gero
welcome sveiki atvykę
How are you? Kaip sekasi?
Pleased to meet you Malonu susipažinti
See you later Iki pasimatymo
yes/no taip/ne
okay gerai
when? kada?
where? kur?

☉ Lithuanian sounds

Vowels

a – as in back
e – as in peck
i – as in sit
o – as in shot
u – as in should
ė – as in make
ū – oo as in stool
y – ee as in see
ą, ę, į and ų appear in special cases and are slightly longer than the equivalent letters without a "tail".

Diphthongs

ai – as in i (sometimes as in bait)
au – as in now
ei – as in make
ie – as in yellow
uo – as in wonder

Consonants

c – ts as in rats
č – ch as in chin
j – as in yes
š – sh as in she
z – as in zoo
ž – as in vision

who? *kas?*
why? *kodėl?*
Do you understand me? *Ar mane supranti?*
I don't speak Lithuanian *Aš nekalbu lietuviškai*
I understand Lithuanian *Aš suprantu lietuviškai*
Do you speak English, German, French, Russian? *Ar kalbate angliškai, vokiškai, prancuziskai,*

rusiškai lenkiškai?
I speak English, German... *Aš kalbu angliškai, vokiškai...*
I would like... *Prašyčiau...*
What time is it? *Kiek valandų?*
How much is it? *Kiek kainuoja?*
Where is the nearest shop, hotel, restaurant, café, bar, toilet? *Kur arčiausia (s) parduotuvė, viešbutis, restoranas, kavinė, baras, tualetas?*
thank you (very much) *Ačiū (labai)*

Useful words

left *kairė*
right *dešinė*
bread *duona*
butter *sviestas*
cheese *sūris*
beer *alus*
wine *vynas*
tea *arbata*
coffee *kava*

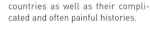

countries as well as their complicated and often painful histories.

OTHER INSIGHT GUIDES

Other Insight Guides available to northeastern Europe include recent major relaunches of *Insight Guide Poland* and *Insight Guide Russia*. Our wide breadth of European titles also includes Insight Guides to *Scandinavia*, *Sweden*, *Finland* and *Germany*.

GENERAL

Baltic Countdown, by Peggie Benton. An extraordinary account of the wife of a British diplomat caught up in Rīga at the outbreak of World War II.
The Baltic Nations and Europe, by John Hiden & Patrick Salman. A history of the 20th century in the three countries.
The Baltic Revolution, by Anatol Lieven. A fine background to the cultural, economic and political life in the region by a member of one of the foremost Baltic families, and a contributor to this book.
The Baltic States: Years of Dependence (1940–1990), by Romanuld J. Misiunas, Rein Taagepera. This is a follow up to the classic *Years of Independence (1917–1940)*, by Georg von Rauch.
The Czar's Madman, by Jaan Kross. Estonia's premier writer brilliantly evokes life in the times of the Russian occupation in the 19th century. Also by Kross: **Professor Marten's Departure**; **Treading Air**.
The Good Republic, by William Palmer. An excellent and imaginative novel about an émigré returning to the Baltic city he fled during World War II and encountering

some ghosts on his return 40 years later.
Racundra's First Cruise and Racundra's Third Cruise, by Arthur Ransome, Brian Hammett (Editor). Reprint of 1920s boating tales from the Baltic – the first around Estonia's islands, the third upriver in Latvia – from the creator of *Swallows and Amazons*.
The Singing Revolution, by Clare Thompson. Personal account of the rebirth of the Baltics by a British journalist who was there in 1989–90.
To the Baltic with Bob: An Epic Misadventure, by Griff Rhys Jones. The humourist's adventures from the Thames to St Petersburg.
Walking since Daybreak, by Modris Eksteins. An account of a Latvian family through the 20th century.
War in the Woods: Estonia's Struggle for Survival, 1944 –1956, by Mart Laar. The courageous story of the "Forest Brothers", freedom fighters who took to the woods after the second Soviet occupation.
Baltic Facades: Estonia, Latvia and Lithuania since 1945 by Aldis Purs. The author confronts the widespread myth of one Baltic identity, exploring the uniqueness of each of the three

☉ Send us your thoughts

We do our best to ensure the information in our books is as accurate and up-to-date as possible. The books are updated on a regular basis using local contacts, who painstakingly add, amend and correct as required. However, some details (such as telephone numbers and opening times) are liable to change, and we are ultimately reliant on our readers to put us in the picture.

We welcome your feedback, especially your experience of using the book "on the road". Maybe you came across a great bar or new attraction we missed.

We will acknowledge all contributions, and we'll offer an Insight Guide to the best letters received.

Please write to us at:
Insight Guides
PO Box 7910
London SE1 1WE

Or email us at:
hello@insightguides.com

CREDITS

akg-images 274
Alamy 6MR, 7ML, 51, 57, 62, 65BL, 111BR, 137, 145, 238, 248, 314, 321TR
APA/Micah Sarut 6BL, 7ML, 12/13, 14/15, 16, 17T, 17B, 18B, 18T, 19, 20, 22, 23, 29B, 60, 64/65T, 64BL, 65ML, 65BR, 68, 79, 80, 82, 83, 84, 85, 93T, 94/95, 97T, 111ML, 111TR, 114, 115, 119, 127, 133, 136, 139, 166, 170, 182/183, 184/185, 186, 187T, 187B, 200/201T, 200B, 201ML, 204, 205, 211, 213, 216, 218, 219, 221, 225, 233, 243, 247, 250, 253, 265T, 265B, 283, 292, 306, 311, 315, 316, 320/321T, 321BR, 322, 323, 324, 325, 326, 330, 332, 334, 335, 337, 338, 340, 354
APA/Mockford & Bonetti 81, 123, 128, 134, 135, 138, 148, 149, 150, 151, 173, 202/203, 207, 210, 220, 251, 284, 285, 310, 318, 319
AWL Images 235, 239
Bridgeman Art Library 44
Corbis 35, 198, 199, 241, 268, 275, 321BL
Crabapple Archive 54
Crabtree Archive 55
Devil Museum 303
Druskininkai Spa Centre 7MR
Eesti Ralva Museum 100
ESTD/Jarek Joepera 77, 97B, 146, 162,

167, 174, 177, 181
ESTD/Aivar Ruukel 67
ESTD/Andrus Teemant 71
ESTD/Jaak Nilson 140
ESTD/Kati Vaas 152
ESTD/Lembit Michelson 73, 161, 168
ESTD/Sven Zacek 66
ESTD/Toomas Olvey 90/91
ESTD/Toomas Tuul 8B, 117, 154, 175
Estonia State Tourism Dept 64BR, 163
Getty Images 1, 4, 8T, 9ML, 9TR, 21, 24, 26/27, 31, 33, 40, 41, 42, 46, 50, 52, 53, 58, 59, 72, 78, 109, 129, 143, 144, 157, 172, 178, 179, 196, 197, 208, 209, 212, 217, 223, 226, 230, 231, 232, 234, 236, 246, 249, 252, 254, 255, 260/261, 262/263, 269, 271, 273, 276/277, 278, 279, 288, 289, 290, 291, 294, 296, 299, 300, 304, 305, 312, 328, 333
iStock 6MR, 7TR, 7BR, 9BR, 36/37, 45, 48, 49, 63, 69, 74, 76, 112/113, 118, 121, 125, 155, 156, 158, 159, 160, 169, 171, 176, 180, 201BR, 201TR, 222, 228, 229, 270, 281, 297, 321ML, 327, 336, 345, 356
Jaak Nilson 141
Kobal 56
Latvia Tourist Organisation 224, 227, 244, 245, 257

Lithuania State Dept of Tourism 86/87, 88/89, 110/111T, 110B, 111BL, 331
Mary Evans Picture Library 29T, 30, 32, 101, 102, 103, 104, 105, 106, 107, 108
Parnu Spa 65TR
Photoshot 153
Public domain 28, 34, 142
Riga Museum of History and Navigation 190, 191, 192, 193, 194, 195
Shutterstock 7TL, 47, 61, 75, 93B, 120, 125, 131, 147, 165, 201BL, 214, 215, 237, 240, 242, 256, 258, 259, 264, 282, 286, 287, 293, 295, 301, 302, 307, 308, 309, 313, 317, 329
Tallinn City Tourist Office & Convention Bureau 70, 320B
TCCB/Meelia Lokk 43
TCCB/ Toomas Volmer 38, 39, 96, 122, 126, 132
TCCB/Allan Alajaan 10/11
TCCB/Kaido hagen 124
TCCB/Maret Poldveer 130
TCCB/Tavi Greep 25
Toomas Volmer/Tallinn Tourism Board 6ML
TopFoto 272

Front cover: Kuressaare Castle, Saaremaa, Estonia *Reinhard Schmid/4Corners Images*
Back cover: Latvian forest *APA/Micah Sarut*
Front flap: (from top) Kukšu Manor

House *APA/Micah Sarut*; Sculptures in Zemaitija, Lithuania *APA/Micah Sarut*; Beach football, Latvia *APA/Micah Sarut*; Šaltibarščiai *APA/Micah Sarut*
Back flap: Dunes in Lithuania *APA/Micah Sarut*

INSIGHT GUIDE CREDITS

Distribution
UK, Ireland and Europe
Apa Publications (UK) Ltd;
sales@insightguides.com
United States and Canada
Ingram Publisher Services;
ips@ingramcontent.com
Australia and New Zealand
Woodslane; info@woodslane.com.au
Southeast Asia
Apa Publications (SN) Pte;
singaporeoffice@insightguides.com
Worldwide
Apa Publications (UK) Ltd;
sales@insightguides.com
Special Sales, Content Licensing and CoPublishing
Insight Guides can be purchased in bulk quantities at discounted prices. We can create special editions, personalised jackets and corporate imprints tailored to your needs. sales@insightguides.com
www.insightguides.biz

Printed in China by CTPS

Every effort has been made to provide accurate information in this publication, but changes are inevitable. The publisher cannot be responsible for any resulting loss, inconvenience or injury. We would appreciate it if readers would call our attention to any errors or outdated information. We also welcome your suggestions; please contact us at: hello@insightguides.com

www.insightguides.com

Editor: Tom Fleming
Authors: Steve Roman, Martins Zaprauskis, Richard Schofield, Roger Williams
Head of DTP and Pre-Press: Rebeka Davies
Update Production: Apa Digital
Managing Editor: Carine Tracanelli
Picture Editor: Tom Smyth
Cartography: original cartography Stephen Ramsey, updated by Carte

First Edition 1992
Sixth Edition 2019

CONTRIBUTORS

This new edition of *Insight Guide Estonia, Latvia & Lithuania* was thoroughly updated by **Magdalena Helsztyńska-Stadnik** and copyedited by Tom Fleming. It draws on the previous work of several local experts who compiled a detailed and considered guide to these three fascinating countries: Steve Roman, who handled Estonia, Martins Zaprauskis, who managed Latvia, Richard Schofield, who tackled Lithuania, and Roger Williams, the original writer of the first edition of this title shortly after the fall of the Iron Curtain, who later contributed updated features.

ABOUT INSIGHT GUIDES

Insight Guides have more than 45 years' experience of publishing high-quality, visual travel guides. We produce 400 full-colour titles, in both print and digital form, covering more than 200 destinations across the globe, in a variety of formats to meet your different needs.

Insight Guides are written by local authors, whose expertise is evident in the extensive historical and cultural background features. Each destination is carefully researched by regional experts to ensure our guides provide the very latest information. All the reviews in **Insight Guides** are independent; we strive to maintain an impartial view. Our reviews are carefully selected to guide you to the best places to eat, go out and shop, so you can be confident that when we say a place is special, we really mean it.

Legend

City maps

Freeway/Highway/Motorway
Divided Highway
Main Roads
Minor Roads
Pedestrian Roads
Steps
Footpath
Railway
Funicular Railway
Cable Car
Tunnel
City Wall
Important Building
Built Up Area
Other Land
Transport Hub
Park
Pedestrian Area
Bus Station
Tourist Information
Main Post Office
Cathedral/Church
Mosque
Synagogue
Statue/Monument
Beach
Airport

Regional maps

Freeway/Highway/Motorway (with junction)
Freeway/Highway/Motorway (under construction)
Divided Highway
Main Road
Secondary Road
Minor Road
Track
Footpath
International Boundary
State/Province Boundary
National Park/Reserve
Marine Park
Ferry Route
Marshland/Swamp
Glacier   Salt Lake
Airport/Airfield
Ancient Site
Border Control
Cable Car
Castle/Castle Ruins
Cave
Chateau/Stately Home
Church/Church Ruins
Crater
Lighthouse
Mountain Peak
Place of Interest
Viewpoint

INDEX

INSIGHT GUIDES

OFF THE SHELF

Since 1970, INSIGHT GUIDES has provided a unique perspective on the world's best travel destinations by using specially commissioned photography and illuminating text written by local authors.

Whether you're planning a city break, a walking tour or the journey of a lifetime, our superb range of guidebooks and phrasebooks will inspire you to discover more about your chosen destination.

INSIGHT GUIDES

offer a unique combination of stunning photos, absorbing narrative and detailed maps, providing all the inspiration and information you need.

PHRASEBOOKS & DICTIONARIES

help users to feel at home, when away. Pocket-sized with a free app to download, they go where you do.

CITY GUIDES

pack hundreds of great photos into a smaller format with detailed practical information, so you can navigate the world's top cities with confidence.

EXPLORE GUIDES

feature easy-to-follow walks and itineraries in the world's most exciting destinations, with our choice of the best places to eat and drink along the way.

POCKET GUIDES

combine concise information on where to go and what to do in a handy compact format, ideal on the ground. Includes a full-colour, fold-out map.

EXPERIENCE GUIDES

feature offbeat perspectives and secret gems for experienced travellers, with a collection of over 100 ideas for a memorable stay in a city.

www.insightguides.com

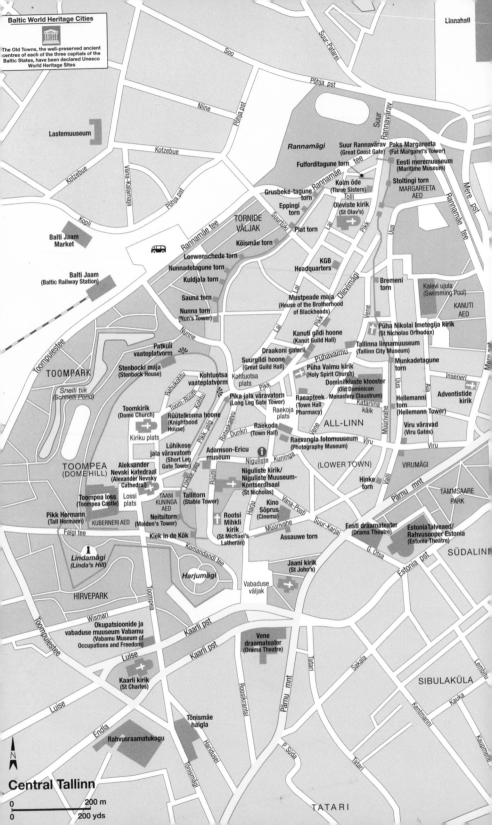